T0302139

One of the most consequential economic debates in China over the direction of reform took place in the 1980s and focused on how markets should be created. The outcome of that debate set the pattern for much of China's subsequent economic reforms. Isabella Weber, drawing on interviews of the participants and others together with many new sources of unpublished and published information, does a masterful job of explaining how this debate evolved and its ultimate impact.

DWIGHT H. PERKINS, Harvard University, Director of the
Harvard Institute for International Development, 1980–1995

This superb book presents the most compelling interpretation I have read of the sources of Chinese gradualism and its success in fostering economic growth and transformation while preserving enough social cohesion to hold the Chinese society together. It is the product of an independent, inquisitive, open mind—the only type that can hope to grasp the phenomenon that is modern China. It is also the work of a first-rate economist, in the best sense of that term.

JAMES K. GALBRAITH, The University of Texas at Austin,
former Chief Technical adviser to China's State Planning
Commission for macroeconomic reform

Isabella M. Weber's book gives an excellent historical overview of China's economic statecraft bringing the reader to the crucial period of market reforms and to the decision to avoid the full implementation of the neoliberal agenda, thus setting the stage for the fastest and longest growth in world history.

BRANKO MILANOVIĆ, LSE and CUNY, former Lead
Economist, World Bank Research Department

Isabella M. Weber succeeds in offering a powerful account of China's reform-era market creation that is of acute interest to economists and historians alike. Her book is a call to economists to ponder the relevance of political economy with its European roots in classical economics of the early modern era and with Chinese roots in a period almost two millennia earlier.

R. BIN WONG, Director of the UCLA Asia
Institute and Distinguished Professor of History

China's debates in the 1980s about reform of the non-market economy are centrally important to understanding global political economy in the 21st century. The resolution of the debates about the 'Big Bang' set China on the course of pragmatic system reform ('groping for stones to cross the river') that has remained in place ever since. Isabella M. Weber's study is unique. It uses information not only from a wide array of written documents but also from extensive interviews with participants in the debates. Her remarkable book provides a rich, balanced and scholarly analysis which illuminates the complex reality of this critically important period in modern world history.

PETER NOLAN, University of Cambridge, Founding Director
of the University's Centre of Development Studies

HOW CHINA ESCAPED SHOCK THERAPY

China has become deeply integrated into the world economy. Yet, gradual marketization has facilitated the country's rise without leading to its wholesale assimilation to global neoliberalism. This book uncovers the fierce contest about economic reforms that shaped China's path. In the first post-Mao decade, China's reformers were sharply divided. They agreed that China had to reform its economic system and move toward more marketization—but struggled over how to go about it. Should China destroy the core of the socialist system through shock therapy, or should it use the institutions of the planned economy as market creators? With hindsight, the historical record proves the high stakes behind the question: China embarked on an economic expansion commonly described as unprecedented in scope and pace, whereas Russia's economy collapsed under shock therapy. Based on extensive research, including interviews with key Chinese and international participants and World Bank officials as well as insights gleaned from unpublished documents, the book charts the debate that ultimately enabled China to follow a path to gradual reindustrialization. Beyond shedding light on the crossroads of the 1980s, it reveals the intellectual foundations of state-market relations in reform-era China through a longue durée lens. Overall, the book delivers an original perspective on China's economic model and its continuing contestations from within and from without.

Isabella M. Weber is Assistant Professor of Economics at the University of Massachusetts, Amherst.

Routledge Studies on the Chinese Economy

Series Editor
Peter Nolan
Director, Center of Development Studies;
Chong Hua Professor in Chinese Development; and
Director of the Chinese Executive Leadership Programme (CELP),
University of Cambridge

Founding Series Editors
Peter Nolan, University of Cambridge and
Dong Fureng, Beijing University

The aim of this series is to publish original, high-quality, research-level work by both new and established scholars in the West and the East, on all aspects of the Chinese economy, including studies of business and economic history.

1 Chinese Economists on Economic Reform—Collected Works of Lou Jiwei
Lou Jiwei, edited by China Development Research Foundation

2 Chinese Economists on Economic Reform—Collected Works of Ma Hong
Ma Hong, edited by China Development Research Foundation

3 Chinese Economists on Economic Reform—Collected Works of Wang Mengkui
Wang Mengkui, edited by China Development Research Foundation

4 Chinese Economists on Economic Reform—Collected Works of Yu Guangyuan
Yu Guangyuan, edited by China Development Research Foundation

5 Chinese Economists on Economic Reform—Collected Works of Zhou Xiaochuan
Zhou Xiaochuan, edited by China Development Research Foundation

6 Chinese Economists on Economic Reform—Collected Works of Li Jiange
Li Jiange, edited by China Development Research Foundation

HOW CHINA ESCAPED SHOCK THERAPY

The Market Reform Debate

Isabella M. Weber

Routledge
Taylor & Francis Group

LONDON AND NEW YORK

First published 2021
by Routledge
2 Park Square, Milton Park, Abingdon, Oxon OX14 4RN

and by Routledge
605 Third Avenue, New York, NY 10158

Routledge is an imprint of the Taylor & Francis Group, an informa business

British Library Cataloguing-in-Publication Data
A catalogue record for this book is available from the British Library

Library of Congress Cataloging-in-Publication Data
A catalog record has been requested for this book

ISBN: 978-1-138-59219-3 (hbk)
ISBN: 978-1-032-00849-3 (pbk)
ISBN: 978-0-429-49012-5 (ebk)

Typeset in Bembo
by Deanta Global Publishing Services, Chennai, India

To Fides and Lena

CONTENTS

Preface   xi
Abbreviations   xiv
List of Figures   xv
List of Illustrations   xvi

Introduction   1

PART I
MODES OF MARKET CREATION AND PRICE REGULATION   15

  1 Bureaucratic Market Participation: *Guanzi* and the *Salt and
     Iron Debate*   17

  2 From Market to War Economy and Back: American Price
     Control during the Second World War and Its Aftermath   42

  3 Re-creating the Economy: Price Stabilization and the
     Communist Revolution   69

PART II
CHINA'S MARKET REFORM DEBATE   87

  4 The Starting Point: Price Control in the Maoist Economy
     and the Urge for Reform   89

5 Rehabilitating the Market: Chinese Economists, the World
   Bank, and Eastern European Émigrés   115

6 Market Creation versus Price Liberalization: Rural Reform,
   Young Intellectuals, and the Dual-Track Price System   152

7 Debunking Shock Therapy: The Clash of Two Market
   Reform Paradigms   182

8 Escaping Shock Therapy: Causes and Consequences of the
   1988 Inflation   225

Conclusion   259

Key Chinese Reform Economists   271
Author's Interviews   291
Bibliography   294
Index   327

PREFACE

I grew up in the 1990s, in a city located about an hour's drive from what used to be the Iron Curtain. During my youth, the sense of capitalist triumphalism as well as the deep social divide between East and West Germany was a constant, subtle theme. The global socialist past was present through the stories of my relatives and friends.

In 1987, the year I was born, my grandparents traveled to China. They cruised down the Yangzi River just a few months after the famous international economics conference had taken place on a boat floating down that same river. They liked to tell the story of a young Chinese student who had accompanied them as interpreter. He told them about the ongoing cultural opening and the wide-ranging debates but also alluded to a sense of fear that all this could come to a sudden end. Some weeks after the submission of my PhD, on which this book is based, my grandmother passed away. In her house, I was amazed to find a wealth of pictures and newspaper clippings about 1980s China, including notes on some of the famous reform economists discussed in the pages of this book.

I entered my undergraduate program in Berlin during the 2008 global financial meltdown. I was one of many students shocked to find that our economics professors had little to say about the deeper reasons for the global crisis. A year later, I went to study at Peking University. Irritated with textbook economics and curious about the Chinese economy, I listened to lectures in some of China's most prestigious management and economics programs. To my astonishment, even though China's economic system was clearly different, the exact same economics was taught from the same American textbooks from which I had studied in Berlin. This observation led me to a question: How had China's economics converged with the global mainstream since the Maoist period? Back in Berlin, I worked with colleagues from the former German Democratic Republic, whose lives had drastically changed as a result of the fall of the wall. Their biographies confronted me with a second question: Why had East Germany's history taken a different course from China's? These two broad questions ultimately led to this book, which attempts to contribute toward answers.

In search of a plurality of economic theories, I entered graduate school at The New School for Social Research and was later accepted as a PhD student, advised by Peter Nolan at the University of Cambridge. Peter guided my pursuit of the central question of this book: On what intellectual grounds did China escape shock therapy in the 1980s? My research would have been entirely impossible without his relentless support and trust and without New School Economics. Thanks to Peter, I had the opportunity to interview a wide range of domestic and international participants and observers of China's fierce 1980s reform debate. Their stories are foundational to this book.

As I finalize this manuscript in 2020, the anniversary of the watershed year of 1989 has recently passed and the world is shattered by the COVID-19 pandemic. Tensions between the United States and China have increased to a level that leads many commentators to speak of a "new Cold War." I hope this history of China's escape from shock therapy in the 1980s and its reluctance to adopt the neoliberal version of capitalism in a wholesale fashion may shed some light on the present moment.

Many people have been crucial to this project. Foremost, I would like to thank all my interviewees who took the time to share their memories and perspectives on China's 1980s with me. With apologies to anyone I have forgotten, I am deeply grateful to Iwo Amelung, Bai Nanfeng, Tracy Blagden, Adrian Bradshaw, Ha-Joon Chang, Melinda Cooper, Cui Zhiyuan, Chun Xiao, Maxime Desmarais-Tremblay, Isabel Estevez, Jacob Eyferth, Nancy Folbre, Duncan Foley, Giorgos Galanis, James Galbraith, Julian Gewirtz, Benjamin Hall, Carol Heim, Lawrence King, David Kotz, János Kovács, Michael Kuczynski, Rebecca Karl, Leon Kunz, Michael Landesmann, Lei Bing, Liang Junshang, Aurelia Li, Edwin Lim, Lin Chun, Cyril Lin, Liu Hong, Liu Kang, Dic Lo, Luo Xiaopeng, Mariana Mazzucato, Maya McCollum, Branko Milanović, John Moffett, Luiza Nassif Pires, Jose Bastos Neves, Terry Peach, George Peden, Dwight Perkins, Stephen Perry, Robert Pollin, Joshua Rahtz, Carl Riskin, Eberhard Sandschneider, Leon Semieniuk, Anwar Shaikh, Fan Shitao, Bertram Schefold, Quinn Slobodian, Peter Sowden, Malcolm Thompson, Jan Toporowski, Vamsi Vakulabharanam, Vela Velupillai, Wang Xiaoqiang, Wang Xiaolu, Wei Zhong, Tom Westland, Felix Wemheuer, Adrian Wood, Bin Wong, Wu Jinglian, Zhu Ling, and Jean Zimmer.

This research has been made possible thanks to financial support by the financial support I received from the European Recovery Program, the Cambridge Trust, the Suzy Paine Fund, the Cambridge Political Economy Trust, the Universities' China Committee in London, the School of Public Management at Tsinghua University, the China Center for Economic Studies at Fudan University, the Greta Burkill Fund, the Bruckmann Fund, and the Department of Economics and the Political Economy Research Institute at the University of Massachusetts, Amherst.

The companionship and solidarity of my friends in Beijing, Berlin, Cambridge, London, New York, Nuremberg, and Amherst kept me going when my energies flagged. Conversations with my sister Anna-Magdalena Schaupp helped me regain enthusiasm when I was in despair. Gregor Semieniuk accompanied me day in and day out and critically commented on the manuscript as it evolved. And finally, without the love, trust, and support of my parents, I would never have done a PhD, let alone written this book. I extend to them all my deepest affection and gratitude.

ABBREVIATIONS

CASS   Chinese Academy of Social Sciences
CESRRI China Economic System Reform Research Institute
CPC   Communist Party of China
OPA   Office of Price Administration
PRC   People's Republic of China
RMB   Renminbi

FIGURES

0.1   China's and Russia's Shares in World GDP, 1990–2017   2

0.2   China's and Russia's Average Incomes per Adult by
Population Quantiles, 1980–2015   3

0.3   USSR and Russia (from 1990) Consumer Price Index and
Real GDP, 1980–2016   7

0.4   China CPI and Real GDP, 1980–2016.   8

0.5   Changes in the Price Determination of Retail Products,
1978–2004   8

0.6   Changes in the Price Formation of Agricultural Products,
1978–2004   9

0.7   Changes in the Price Determination of Production
Materials, 1978–2004   9

2.1   Consumer Price Inflation, 1940–1950   51

2.2   Industrial Production and Prices of Industrial Goods in
Two World Wars   53

2.3   Gross National Product of the United States, 1940–1944
(in 1940 USD Billion)   54

3.1   Price Index, December 1949 to December 1950   82

6.1   Sectoral Profit Rates in China, 1980–1989   169

6.2   Profit Rate on Investment of State-owned Enterprises, 1979   170

8.1   Inflation in China, 1986–1990   231

ILLUSTRATIONS

1 Moganshan World Bank Conference, July 11–16, 1982   137
2 Moganshan Young and Middle-Age Economists Conference,
   September 3–10, 1984   172
3 On the boat of the Bashan Conference, Yangtze, September 1985 194
4 Wang Xiaoqiang meets George Soros in Hungary, 1986   216
5 Delegation led by Premier Zhao Ziyang to study prospects for
   Coastal Development Strategy, winter 1987   237
6 Milton Friedman meets Premier Zhao Ziyang, October 1988   254

INTRODUCTION

Contemporary China is deeply integrated into global capitalism. Yet, China's dazzling growth has not led to a full-fledged institutional convergence with neoliberalism.[1] This defies the post–Cold War triumphalism that predicted the "unabashed victory of economic and political liberalism" around the globe (Fukuyama, 1989, 3). The age of revolution ended in 1989 (Wang, 2009). But this did not result in the anticipated universalization of the "Western" economic model. It turns out that gradual marketization facilitated China's economic ascent without leading to wholesale assimilation. The tension between China's rise and this partial assimilation defines our present moment, and it found its origins in China's approach to market reforms.

The literature on China's reforms is large and diverse. The economic policies that China has adopted in its transformation from state socialism are well known and researched. Vastly overlooked, however, is the fact that China's gradual and state-guided marketization was anything but a foregone conclusion or a "natural" choice predetermined by Chinese exceptionalism. In the first decade of "reform and opening up" under Deng Xiaoping (1978–1988), China's mode of marketization was carved out in a fierce debate. Economists arguing in favor of a shock therapy–style liberalization battled over the question of China's future with those who promoted gradual marketization beginning at the margins of the economic system. Twice, China had everything in place for a "big bang" in price reform. Twice, it ultimately abstained from implementing it.

What was at stake in China's market reform debate is illustrated by the contrast between China's rise and Russia's economic collapse (Nolan, 1995). Shock therapy—the quintessentially neoliberal policy prescript—had been applied in Russia, the other former giant of state socialism (Jessop, 2002, 2018). Nobel Memorial Prize laureate Joseph Stiglitz (2014, 37) attests "a causal link between Russia's policies and its poor performance." Russia's and China's positions in the world economy have been reversed since they implemented different modes of marketization. Russia's share of world GDP almost halved, from 3.7 percent in 1990 to about 2 percent in 2017, while China's share increased close to sixfold, from a mere 2.2 percent to about one-eighth of global output (see Figure 0.1). Russia underwent dramatic deindustrialization, while China became the proverbial workshop of world capitalism.[2] The average real income of 99 percent of people in Russia was lower in 2015 than it had been in 1991, whereas in China, despite rapidly rising inequality, the figure more than quadrupled in the same period, surpassing Russia's in 2013 (see Figure 0.2).[3] As a result of shock therapy, Russia experienced a rise in mortality beyond that of any previous peacetime experiences of an industrialized country (Notzon et al., 1998).[4]

Given China's low level of development compared with Russia's at the dawn of reform, shock therapy would likely have caused human suffering on an even more extraordinary scale. It would have undermined, if not destroyed, the foundation for China's economic rise. It is hard to imagine what global capitalism would look like today if China had gone down Russia's path.

Despite its momentous consequences, the key role played by economic debate in China's market reforms is largely ignored. The famous Harvard development economist Dani Rodrik represents the economics profession more broadly when he answers his own question of whether "anyone [can] name the (Western) economists or the piece of research that played an instrumental role in China's reforms" by claiming that "economic research, at least as conventionally understood" did not play "a significant role" (Rodrik, 2010, 34).

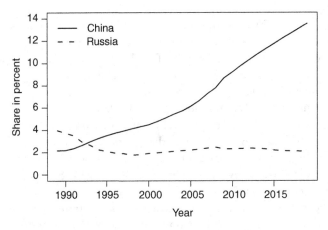

FIGURE 0.1 China's and Russia's Shares in World GDP, 1990–2017. Source: World Bank, 2019.

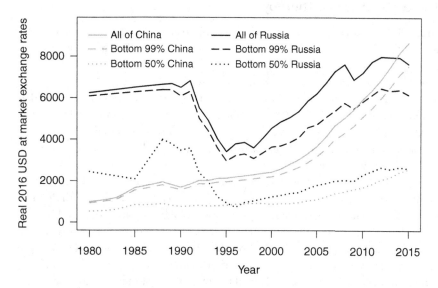

FIGURE 0.2 China's and Russia's Average Incomes per Adult by Population Quantiles, 1980–2015. Source: Alvaredo et al., 2017.

In the following chapters, I take us back to the 1980s and ask on what intellectual grounds China escaped shock therapy. Revisiting China's market reform debate uncovers the economics of China's rise and the origins of China's state-market relations.

China's deviation from the neoliberal ideal primarily lies not in the size of the Chinese state but in the nature of its economic governance. The neoliberal state is neither small nor weak, but strong (e.g., Bonefeld, 2013, 2017; Chang, 2002; Davies, 2018). Its purpose is to fortify the market. In the most basic terms, this means the protection of free prices as the core economic mechanism. In contrast, the Chinese state uses the market as a tool in the pursuit of its larger development goals. As such, it preserves a degree of economic sovereignty that buffers China's economy against the global market—as the 1997 Asian and the 2008 global financial crises forcefully demonstrated. Abolishing this form of "economic insulation" has been a long-standing goal for neoliberals, and our present global governance was designed to put an end to national protection against the global market (Slobodian, 2018, 12). China's escape from shock therapy meant that the state maintained the capacity to insulate the economy's commanding heights—the sectors most essential to economic stability and growth—as it integrated into global capitalism.

To lay the groundwork for my analysis of China's escape, I will first briefly recapitulate the logic of shock therapy.

The Logic of Shock Therapy

Shock therapy was at the heart of the "Washington consensus doctrine of transition" (Stiglitz, 1999, 132), propagated by the Bretton Woods institutions in developing countries, Eastern and Central Europe, and Russia (Amsden et al., 1998; Klein, 2007). On the surface, it was a comprehensive package of policies to be implemented in a single stroke to shock the planned economies into market economies at once (Åslund, 1992; Kornai, 1990; Sachs and Lipton, 1990; Sachs, 1992a,b). The package consisted of (1) liberalization of all prices in one big bang, (2) privatization, (3) trade liberalization, and (4) stabilization, in the form of tight monetary and fiscal policies.

The four measures of shock therapy, implemented simultaneously, should, in theory, form a comprehensive package. A closer analysis reveals that the part of this package that can be implemented in one stroke boils down to a combination of elements (1) and (4): price liberalization complemented with strict austerity.

Lipton and Sachs (1990) spoke for the proponents of shock therapy more broadly when they admitted to complications with regard to the speed of privatization, in practice. They acknowledged the magnitude of the task of privatization in an economy with primarily public ownership. Comparing the large number of state-owned enterprises in the socialist economies with the United Kingdom's privatization record, they pointed out that "Margaret Thatcher, the world's leading advocate of privatisation" (ibid., 127) had overseen the transfer of just a few dozen state enterprises to the private sector in the course of the 1980s. Hence they observed, "(t)he great conundrum is how to privatize a vast array of firms in a manner that is equitable, swift, politically viable, and likely to create an effective structure of corporate control" (ibid.). They recommended, vaguely, that "privatisation should *probably* be carried out by many means" and the "pace must be rapid, but not reckless" (ibid., 130, emphasis added). The joint report on *The Economy of the USSR* (1990, 26) likewise cautions against moving too fast with privatization "when relative prices are still unsettled." Similarly, trade liberalization in the eyes of the shock therapists requires domestic price liberalization as its precondition (ibid. 29). A big bang in price liberalization thus emerges as a condition for both privatization and trade liberalization and constitutes the "shock" in shock therapy.

What was presented as a comprehensive reform package turned out to be a policy that is extremely biased toward only one element of a market economy: the market determination of prices. This one-sidedness was not a mere result of feasibility, however. The deeper reason for the bias toward price liberalization lies in the neoclassical concept of the market as a price mechanism that abstracts from institutional realities (Chang, 2002; Stiglitz, 1994, 102, 195, 202, 249–250). In the outlook of neoliberals more broadly, the market is the only way to rationally organize the economy, and its functioning depends on free prices Weber (2018, 2022).

According to the logic of shock therapy as encapsulated, for example, by David Lipton and Jeffrey Sachs, the liberalization of all prices in "one fell swoop" would correct the distorted *relative* prices, which, as a Stalinist heritage, had been too low for heavy industry and capital goods and too high for light industry, services, and consumer goods (Lipton and Sachs, 1990, 82). Similarly, the joint report on *The Economy of the USSR* (1990, 25) by the International Monetary Fund, the World Bank, the Organization for Economic Cooperation and Development, and the European Bank for Reconstruction and Development urged,

> Nothing will be more important to the achievement of a successful transition to a market economy than the freeing of prices to guide the allocation of resources. Early and comprehensive price decontrol is essential to ending both the shortages and the macroeconomic imbalances that increasingly afflict the economy.

Such wholesale price liberalization would need to be combined with a stabilization policy to control the *general* price level (ibid., 19). As long as complementary macromeasures were put in place, price liberalization "might lead to a one-time jump in prices, but not to an on-going inflation" (Lipton and Sachs, 1990, 100), the shock therapists alleged. The true causes of persistent inflation in state socialist economies were found to be excess demand due to large budget deficits, the "soft budget constraint," easy monetary policies, and wage increases resulting from the zero-unemployment policy (Lipton and Sachs, 1990, 98). In the shock therapists' view, these problems could be alleviated by a "strong dose of macroeconomic austerity" since they were, in essence, monetary rather than structural (ibid., 89).

The "one-time jump in prices" expected to result from wholesale price liberalization was welcome since it would "absorb excess liquidity" and, as such, reinforce austerity (IMF et al., 1990, 19, 22). In other words, an increase in the overall price level would devalue the savings and thus reduce the chronic aggregate excess demand experienced in socialist economies. The cost of depriving citizens of the modest wealth they had accumulated under state socialism was considered to be a necessary pain (Reddaway and Glinski, 2001, 179). In effect, it amounted to a regressive redistribution benefiting elites who held nonmonetary assets. Redistribution from the bottom up had been a part of shock therapy since its inception in the West German postwar price and currency reform under Ludwig Erhard (Fuhrmann, 2017, 167–170; Weber, 2020b, 2021). Forcing market relations on society overnight hinged upon imposing greater inequality.

The nature and structures of the prevailing institutions that would compose the new market economy did not receive much attention from shock therapists. The package recommended by Lipton, Sachs, and many others, including economists based in the socialist world of the time, did not "create" a market economy, as the title of their influential study on Poland suggests (1990). Instead, it was hoped that destruction of the command economy would automatically give rise to a market economy (Burawoy, 1996; Hamm et al., 2012). It is a recipe for destruction, not construction. Once the planned economy had been "shocked to death," the "invisible hand" was expected to operate and, in a somewhat miraculous way, allow an effective market economy to emerge.

This is a perversion of Adam Smith's famous metaphor. Smith, a close observer of the Industrial Revolution unfolding in front of his eyes, saw the human "propensity to truck, barter and exchange one thing for another" as the "principle which gives occasion to the division of labour" (Smith, [1776] 1999, 117), but he immediately cautioned that this principle was "limited by the extent of the market" (ibid., 121). The market, according to Smith, unfolded slowly as the institutions facilitating market exchange were being built up (ibid., 121–126). In this course, the invisible hand could come into play only gradually and, with it, the price mechanism. In contrast, the logic of shock therapy makes us believe that a country can "jump to the market economy" (Sachs, 1994a).

The destruction prescribed by shock therapy does not stop at the economic system. A further condition must be fulfilled: a "revolutionary change in institutions" (Kornai, 1990, 20). Or, as Lipton and Sachs (1990, 87) put it, "(t)he collapse of communist one-party rule was the sine qua non for an effective transition to a market economy." It did, in fact, require the collapse of the Soviet state and the communist one-party rule in December 1991, before a big bang could be implemented; Russian President Boris Yeltsin eliminated almost all price controls on January 2, 1992. Under General Secretary Mikhail Gorbachev, radical price reform had been repeatedly on the agenda since 1987 but was never carried out, as Russian citizens were complaining en masse and scholars were warning of social unrest. Gorbachev attempted Chinese-style gradualism, albeit in vain (Belik, 1998; Medvedev, 1998; Miller, 2016; Yun, 1998).[5]

With the promise of long-term gain, the big bang prescribed short-term pain that immediately affected the interests of workers and enterprises as well as government departments. Radical price liberalization became politically feasible only after the Soviet state dissolved. "The collapse of communist one-party rule" turned out to be, in fact, "the sine qua non" for a big bang, but the big bang failed to achieve "an effective transition to a market economy." Instead of the predicted one-time increase in the price level, Russia entered a prolonged period of very high inflation, combined with a drop in output followed by low growth rates (see Figure 0.3).[6] Almost all of the post-socialist countries that applied some version of shock therapy experienced a deep and prolonged recession (see, e.g., Kornai, 1994; Popov, 2000, 2007; Roland and Verdier, 1999).[7] Beyond the devastation documented by economic indicators (see above), most measures of human well-being, such as access to education, absence of poverty, and public health, collapsed (European Bank for Reconstruction and Development, 1999; UNICEF, 2001).

Intellectual Foundations of China's Gradual Marketization and Escape from Shock Therapy

The macroeconomic outcome of China's market reform policies was the opposite of Russia's: inflation was low or moderate, but output growth was extremely

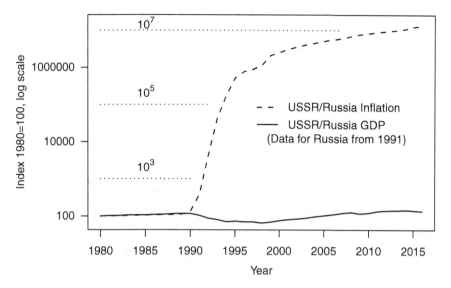

FIGURE 0.3   USSR and Russia (from 1990) Consumer Price Index and Real GDP, 1980–2016. Sources: CPI USSR, 1971–1990 (IMF et al., 1991, 100); CPI Russia, 1991 (Filatochev et al., 1992, 746), 1992 (Sachs, 1994b, 70), 1993–2016 (IMF, 2017); GDP (Alvaredo et al., 2017).

fast (see Figure 0.4). Instead of destroying the existing price and planning system in the hope that a market economy would somehow emerge "from the ruins," China pursued an experimentalist approach that used the given institutional realities to construct a new economic system. The state gradually re-created markets on the margins of the old system. As I will argue, China's reforms were gradual—not merely in the matter of pace but also in moving from the margins of the old industrial system toward its core. Unleashing a dynamic of growth and reindustrialization, gradual marketization eventually transformed the whole political economy while the state kept control over the commanding heights. The most prominent manifestation of China's reform approach is the dual-track price system, which is the opposite of shock therapy. Instead of liberalizing all prices in one big bang, the state initially continued to plan the industrial core of the economy and set the prices of essential goods while the prices of surplus output and nonessential goods were successively liberalized. As a result, prices were gradually determined by the market (see figures 0.5, 0.6, and 0.7).

The dual-track system is not simply a price policy, but rather a process of market creation and regulation through state participation. Before reform, the whole industrial economy was meant to be organized as a single factory with subordinate production units. The dual-track price system transformed the socialist production units into profit-oriented enterprises and created space

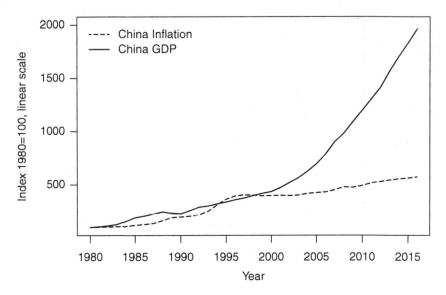

FIGURE 0.4 China CPI and Real GDP, 1980–2016. Sources: CPI (IMF, 2017); GDP (Alvaredo et al., 2017).

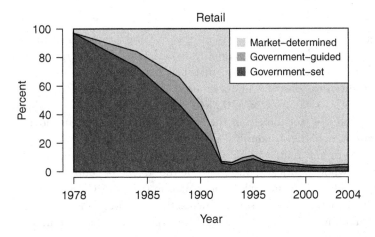

FIGURE 0.5 Changes in the Price Determination of Retail Products, 1978–2004.

for burgeoning market relations, with all their social and environmental consequences. The transformation of the economic system was steered at every step by the state. In contrast, big bang price liberalization under shock therapy caused a disorganization of existing production links without replacing them with market relations. In this void, neither the old command structures nor the

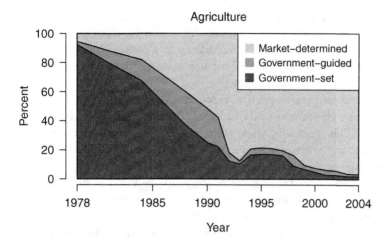

FIGURE 0.6 Changes in the Price Formation of Agricultural Products, 1978–2004.

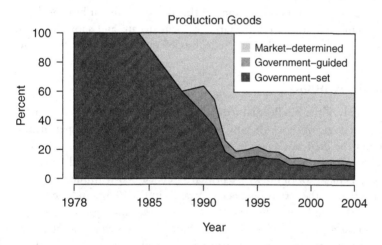

FIGURE 0.7 Changes in the Price Determination of Production Materials, 1978–2004. Source: Cheng Zhiping (2006, 163).

market operated effectively (Burawoy, 1996; Hamm et al., 2012; Roland and Verdier, 1999).

By the end of the 1970s, China had given up on the revolutionary ambitions of late Maoism. The defining question of the 1980s was not whether to reform— as the commonly invoked binary of conservatives versus reformers stresses. The question was *how* to reform: by destroying the old system or by growing the new system from the old.

To use a metaphor, if shock therapy proposed to tear down the whole house and build a new one from scratch, the Chinese reform proceeded like the game of Jenga: only those blocks were removed that could be flexibly rearranged without endangering the stability of the building as a whole. Yet, through this process, the building was fundamentally changed. As everyone who has played Jenga knows, certain blocks may not be removed lest the tower collapses.

China almost implemented such a destructive move by prematurely scrapping essential price controls in the critical first reform decade (1978–1988). But it ultimately abstained. The gradualist reform that set China on a path of catching up, reindustrializing, and reintegrating into global capitalism also implied that the institutional convergence between China and the neoliberal variety of capitalism remained incomplete. Like in the game of Jenga, the new tower was shaped by the structures of the old. As such, an escape from shock therapy was critical for both China's economic rise and its partial institutional assimilation.

Shock therapy is underpinned by neoclassical economics that constituted an intellectual bridge between mainstream economists in the West and market socialists in the East (Bockman, 2011, 2012). In contrast, we know little about the economics that provided China an escape from shock therapy—the economics of China's gradual marketization. In this book, I offer an historical and analytical account of China's 1980s market reform debate and show how the dual-track system was theorized, contested, and defended against shock therapy.

Approach of the Book

My aim is to analyze the intellectual struggle between those reform economists who pursued the logic of shock therapy and those who argued for experimental gradualism and the dual-track price system. As such, this book is complementary to Keyser's (2003) *Professionalizing Research in Post-Mao China* and Gewirtz's (2017) *Unlikely Partners*. Both books are primarily concerned with the formation of one or the other of these two intellectual strands in the 1980s, and they focus more on networks and knowledge exchanges than on an in-depth engagement with the economic arguments pronounced in China's market reform debate.[8] The study of economic discourse in China had fallen out of fashion in the English-language literature and is currently experiencing something of a revival (see, e.g., Brødsgaard and Rutten, 2017, 1; Cohn, 2017; Karl, 2017; Liu, 2010; Zhang, 2017). My work has benefited from these recent contributions as well as from earlier accounts of the history of economic reform in 1980s China (e.g., Fewsmith, 1994; Halpern, 1985, 1986, 1988; Hsu, 1991; Naughton, 1995; Shirk, 1993).

Hsu (1991) offers the most extensive review of the substance of economic theorizing in the course of China's 1980s reform. But as Halpern (1993, 267) observes, Hsu "set out to explain to himself why ... Chinese economic journals in the late 1970s and early 1980s published so many dogmatic and superficial articles." Hsu thus argues from the standpoint of the superiority of Western mainstream economics rather than trying to understand the ways in which Chinese economists theorized the problems they sought to tackle.

In contrast, I aim to analyze the different voices of reform in China on their own terms, to engage in depth with the substance, origins, and underlying logic of the economic arguments presented by competing reform economists—while also situating these arguments in their relevant context. I focus on one central issue in reform: the decisive question of price reform and market creation. Yet, in carving out the different positions on this major issue in economic reform, a broader confrontation between fundamentally opposed approaches to economic policy and doing economics becomes apparent.

This book is the perspective of an outsider looking back in history at China's market reform debate, rather than the account of a participant. This sets my work apart from firsthand accounts of the Chinese reform debate of the 1980s, such as those of Chen Yizi (2013); Dong Fureng (1986); He Weiling (2015); Hua Sheng et al. (1993); Peter Nolan and Dong Fureng (1990); Edwin Lim (2008, 2014); Lu Mai and Feng Mingliang (2012); Sun Faming (2011); Wang Xiaoqiang (1998); Wang Xiaolu (2019); Wu Jinglian (2012, 2013); Wu and Fan (2012); Wu and Ma (2016); and Zhu Jiaming (2013). All these accounts were invaluable references.

This book is based on a wide range of Chinese published and unpublished primary sources and oral history interviews with economists who participated in or witnessed China's 1980s market reform debate. (See the Bibliography for the full list of interviews.) I asked open-ended questions tailored to the interviewees' specific positions and involvement in the making of reform policies. The goal was to bring out the speakers' views on the course of reform rather than to impose a preconceived structure. I conducted most of the conversations in Chinese. The speakers provided documents and publications that form important sources. Interviewees were identified and approached based on the principle of snowballing. Beyond direct references to these interviews throughout the book, my own thinking and analysis of China's first decade of reform have been shaped by the diverse perspectives and competing interpretations presented by my interviewees. The Chinese articles from the 1980s analyzed in detail in this work were selected based on evaluations by the interviewees, who believed these publications to have set the tone of the debate and to have been considered by the Chinese leadership who pondered the question of market reform.

The interviews were the key event in my intellectual journey in trying to understand how China escaped shock therapy. To unpack the larger relevance of the insights derived from these conversations and from primary sources, Part I of the book takes a step back and situates this material in a broader context of relevant historical modes of market creation.

To conceptualize the state-market relation emerging in the dual-track system, I propose a longue durée perspective that acknowledges China's distinct institutional legacy of price regulation through state participation in the market (Chapter 1). My purpose is not to suggest any sort of monolithic continuity or even a linear development from ancient times to the crossroads of the 1980s. Instead, I use these traditional concepts of price regulation and market creation as a novel analytical perspective to shed light on China's 1980s debate. Far from essentializing China's reform as predetermined by the nature of its society or culture, I show that China's reform approach was the result of genuine intellectual struggles. This intellectual contest resonated with debates over the right handling of the market by the state that reoccurred throughout Chinese history.

I do not propose to posit China against the West, or Chinese economics against Western economics. Instead, I suggest that an approach to economics—an approach that was more inductive, institutionalist, and pragmatic than that of neoclassicism—was fiercely contested but turned out to be dominant at the critical juncture of China's first decade of reform. This kind of economics is by no means unique to China. This fact is illustrated in the book through my analysis of debates over postwar market creations in the United States, the United Kingdom, and West Germany (Chapter 2). My interviewees repeatedly made references to the postwar experiences in these countries. The transition from a planned war economy to a market economy posed challenges similar to those later encountered in the transition from socialism. American and European economists fiercely debated the question of how to deregulate prices and re-create markets after the war. The so-called "Erhard Miracle" that followed the West German wholesale price liberalization provided an important piece of anecdotal evidence in favor of shock therapy in China's reform debate (Weber, 2020b, 2021). Some prominent institutionalist economists, such as John Kenneth Galbraith in the United States and Alec Cairncross in the UK, argued for a gradual decontrol with some similarity with China's market reforms. Both Cairncross and Galbraith came to be important references for China's gradualist reformers.

In Chapter 3, I introduce an experience of market creation more immediately connected with the 1980s reform debate: the Communists' 1940s fight for price stabilization. Unlike the ancient concepts of price regulation through market participation, the 1940s experience exerted a direct and explicit influence on the ways in which Chinese economists and reformers have thought about market creation in the reform era. Many of China's most prominent reform leaders and economists of the 1980s participated in the revolutionary war. Overcoming hyperinflation and reintegrating the economy was key to the material base of the Communists' revolutionary struggle. The Communists employed a strategy of economic warfare that relied on re-creating markets through state commerce in order to re-establish the value of money. The techniques of economic warfare resembled elements of the traditional practice of price regulation and were revived in the early stages of economic reform in the 1980s as part of the efforts toward gradual marketization.

Building on my discussion of modes of market creation, the second part of the book presents an in-depth analysis of China's 1980s market reform debate. I set the stage with an overview of the Mao era development model and price system to show the challenge of introducing market mechanisms. To equip readers with an understanding of the point of departure for the debate, I examine why China turned to reform in the late 1970s. I derive how a reorientation away from the late Maoist ideal of continuous revolution to economic progress as the all-encompassing goal of reform led to the reinstatement of economics after the discipline had been banned as a bourgeois project during the Cultural Revolution (Chapter 4).

Chapter 5 dives into the early stages of China's market reform debate. It traces the intellectual origins of wholesale price liberalization, locating them in exchanges between China's established academic economists and Eastern European émigré economists, the World Bank, and other foreign visitors, including Milton Friedman. This reform approach closely resembled the logic of shock therapy and came to be called the "package reform" in the Chinese debate. As in other contexts, it was grounded in neoclassical economics, both the neoliberal and the socialist types.

Chapter 6 contrasts package reform with the outlook of young intellectuals and older officials who formed an alliance as a result of their shared concern for rural reform. This alliance played a key role in researching, theorizing, and defending the gradual marketization from the margins that emerged from on-the-ground experimentations. This approach employed an interdisciplinary, institutionalist, and inductive kind of economics that utilized methods from the social sciences.

Chapters 7 and 8 show how these two reform approaches—wholesale liberalization versus marketization from the margins—clashed when China escaped shock therapy. In 1986, Premier Zhao Ziyang was convinced by gradualist reform economists who debunked the idea of a big bang to withdraw his initiative for wholesale liberalization. In 1988, Deng Xiaoping personally called for a big bang. His plans were reversed when, in the summer of that year, China experienced the first episode of runaway inflation since the 1940s. Deng was prepared to push ahead with full-scale marketization but not at the cost of undermining the ability of the state to maintain control over society and the economy.

In 1988, China escaped shock therapy a second time. At this point, market reforms had already unleashed rapidly increasing inequalities and flourishing corruption. The "golden age of reform" of the first years, when everyone seemed to be benefitting equally, was fading. In 1988, the prospect of a further radicalization of market reforms shook the foundations of Chinese society. The 1989 social movement ended with the crackdown on Tiananmen Square. Reform came to a temporary halt. When China restarted marketization in 1992, the shock therapy agenda had by no means disappeared. On the contrary, the 1990s saw major victories for neoliberals in China. Yet the basic mode of gradual, experimentalist marketization had been set in the 1980s. Although it was renegotiated, challenged, and amended in the subsequent decades, it was not overturned.

Notes

1 See Weber (2018, 2020a) for an in-depth discussion of this point.
2 According to the Observatory of Economic Complexity (2018), 75 percent of Russia's exports were mineral products and metals in 2017, whereas China had become the world's largest export economy, mostly thanks to its competitiveness in the manufacturing sector.
3 See Novokmet, Piketty, and Zucman (2017) for a long-term analysis of inequality in Russia as well as a comparison with Eastern European countries and China.
4 For studies that link the dramatic fall in life expectancy to the social consequences of shock therapy, see, e.g., Leon and Shkolnikov (1998); Murphy et al. (2006); and Stuckler et al. (2009).
5 Other cases, such as the German 1948 price and currency reform, the 1948 Dodge Line implemented in Japan, and the numerous cases of similar reform packages applied in the developing world as part of credit conditionalities, also suggest that limited sovereignty might be a precondition for the implementation of these radical measures.
6 For a detailed analysis of the implementation and outcomes of shock therapy in Russia, see Kotz and Weir (1997, 161–199). This includes analyses of the economic impacts as well as of the collapse in many indicators of basic human well-being.
7 One case that could be considered a challenge to this verdict is Vietnam, which in 1989 imposed a big bang in price liberalization without experiencing hyperinflation or a deep recession (Wood, 1989). Given the predominant evidence from virtually all countries other than Vietnam, it is, however, not clear how China could have replicated this result. Vietnam and China are often considered as having had similar starting positions with regard to the level of GDP, industrialization, and the nature of reform up to 1989 (e.g., Popov, 2000, 2007). Two crucial factors set Vietnam and China apart; however, South Vietnam had only become part of the central command economy as recently as 1976, so it began reforming before the new economic model could have been fully institutionalized (Wood, 1989). It is also important to keep in mind that, despite a similar initial level of GDP, China's per capita growth in constant 2010 US dollars consistently outpaced that of Vietnam in the period 1990–2018, at times reaching twice the growth level (World Bank, 2019).
8 See my review of Gewirtz for a more detailed analysis (Weber, 2019a).

PART I

Modes of Market Creation and Price Regulation

1

BUREAUCRATIC MARKET PARTICIPATION

Guanzi and the Salt and Iron Debate

When things are plentiful, they will be cheap; when they are scarce, they will be expensive. ... Knowing this to be so, the prince pays attention to his country's surpluses and shortages and manages its wealth and goods. When grain is cheap, he exchanges money for food. ... He pays attention to the relative value (*qingzhong*) of things and manages them in order to maintain price stability. Therefore, the expensive and the cheap may be harmonized and the prince reaps his profits.

(Guanzi as in Rickett, 1998, 384)

One generally accepted assumption of Western economists is that, so far as ancient economic theories are concerned, only the Greeks and Romans developed anything worthy of study ... it makes Chinese history very hard to understand.

(Hu, 2009, i)

Introduction

Publications exploring ancient economic concepts increased at the dawn of China's reform, in the late 1970s and 1980s. These included articles about the *Guanzi* (管子) and the *Salt and Iron Debate* (盐铁论), two classic texts on price regulation and market management.[1] The surge in the study of such classics is clearly linked to the research undertaken on economic reform. For example, some young reform intellectuals working on questions involving rural economies in the early 1980s, such as Bai Nanfeng, engaged in what they called comparative civilization study. They believed that in order to derive practical insights on how to move forward with agricultural reform, they needed to study China's long history and intellectual traditions in comparison with the European experience (Bai, 2016; Sun, 2011, 204).

In the Chinese tradition, the study of economic issues used to be called "the study of making the country rich" (富国学) (Zhao, 2014, 68). The art of governing is commonly subsumed under the term "statecraft" (经世), but it might be better translated as "ordering the world" (Hymes and Schirokauer, 1993, 2–3; Rowe, 2001). The "right handling" of prices by the state has occupied a prominent position. In modern economics, prices are one of the purest forms of a quintessentially economic variable, belonging to the exclusive domain of the market. In contrast, the traditional Chinese discussions on prices engage in broad reflections on the relationships between the spontaneous activities of the people, the people's needs and wants, market forces, political power, and regulation by the state.

Yet, my aim in this book is *not* to search for a tangible influence whereby intellectuals, policy makers, or political campaigns of the 1980s reforms explicitly reference traditional concepts. Rather, I suggest that an engagement with traditional Chinese conceptions of markets and prices provides a useful lens of analysis for the competing logics of market creation in China's reform debate.[2]

The *Guanzi* is a core text in ancient Chinese economic thought on price stabilization. The beginning of this chapter focuses on price regulation through state commerce, in the context of the social transformation of that era. The *Guanzi*'s approach to price regulation is encapsulated in the so-called "light–heavy" (轻重, *qingzhong*) principles, where *heavy* represents "important," "essential," or "expensive," and *light* connotes "unimportant," "inessential," or "cheap." The second part of the chapter sheds light on the *Salt and Iron Debate* (Chin, 2014; Huan, 1931; Loewe, 1974) as the classic statement of two competing visions for the relation between the state and the economy. In this debate, merchant bureaucrats, articulating arguments similar to those in the *Guanzi,* compete with literati to influence the ruler on the question of whether the state should hold a monopoly over production and commerce of strategic commodities such as salt and iron. On examination of this dialogue, two alternative views on the role for state regulation and the market, as well as on the concrete question of prices, become apparent.

Throughout this book, I use my reading of the *Guanzi* and the *Salt and Iron Debate* as a lens for a fresh perspective on China's recent market reform debates and practices. By acknowledging a long standing, distinct market consciousness among Chinese imperial officials as well as indigenous theories of commercialization through the state, I avoid framing a move to the market as simply a trend imported from the West.[3] This perspective allows me to see China's 1980s market reform debates not merely as Westernization, but as a complex competition between alternative conceptions of markets and prices. To avoid suggesting the existence of some monolithic Chinese tradition of economic thought, I describe the recurrent debates over competing visions for economic governance, and I trace the confrontation between different paradigms.

It is customary to analyze China's reform path and thinking since the 1980s using concepts from contemporary economics, with its origins in the Western tradition of political economy. My attempt here is to take China's indigenous discussions of price regulation and market creation by the state as a complementary conceptual reference point. As Will and Wong (1991, 3) observe, "The emphasis on stabilizing prices represents an early Chinese awareness of the potential impact of markets and the belief that government should involve itself in supply and demand conditions." This concept of price regulation through commercial activity of the bureaucracy is distinct from the insistence on state and market as separate entities in most areas of modern economics. The latter perspective leads us to see the state as intervening in an autonomous economy or market. The approach of price regulation through state commercial activity, by comparison, suggests that the interaction between private and bureaucratic agents co-creates the market and economy. As we will see in subsequent chapters, this alternative perspective has important implications for the ways in which we understand the relationship between the plan and the market—and the renegotiation of this relationship in the 1980s reform debate.

The *Guanzi's* "Light–Heavy" Principles of Price Regulation

The Historical Context

The Spring and Autumn (772–476 BCE)[4] and Warring States (475–221 BCE) periods, widely considered "China's golden age of culture" (Hu, 2009, 19), were an "unusual age … when old orthodoxies had collapsed but new ones had not yet emerged" (Pines, 2009, 220). It was "the age of the 'Hundred Schools'" (Pines, 2018). During the Warring States Period, economic considerations became increasingly important for government theory, and economic growth emerged as a major concern in light of constant warfare (Milburn, 2007, 19).

In many ways, this period laid the foundation for Chinese philosophy and long-standing social, economic, and political practices. This is not to suggest that the period was followed by any form of stagnation or continuity. But it was a groundbreaking age for China's intellectual and institutional trajectory. Regarding economic questions, the writings collected in the so-called *Guanzi* (管子)[5] are the most important of these ancient contributions. The *Guanzi*, one of the largest of the ancient Chinese texts (Rickett, 1993, 244), is considered by some to be the "most representative … of the emerging political economy of the Warring States era" (von Glahn, 2016, 77).

Historical scholarship shows that the *Guanzi* was written by several anonymous authors, probably state planners and economic advisors (Chin, 2014, 32;

Hu, 2009, 100). Irrespective of the precise date of its creation, which is subject to scholarly debate,[6] it is important that the *Guanzi* was composed in the context of turbulent times after the collapse of the Western Zhou and before the Qin dynasty unified China into a single empire for the first time. The guiding question in the treatment of economic issues was how to govern change in the context of the transition to a new kind of economy. Most parts of the *Guanzi* were written in the form of dialogues between Duke Huan (桓公, 685–643 BCE) of the state Qi and his advisor Guan Zhong (管仲, ca. 710–645 BCE), with the latter providing answers to the pressing questions of the duke (Chin, 2014, 33; von Glahn, 2016, 77). Guan Zhong is recognized as "one of the most renowned and influential statesmen in ancient China" (Hu, 2009, 100). He was not an author of the *Guanzi*. The authors of the *Guanzi* referred to Guan Zhong to express their vision of what they imagined to be his economic policies during the rise of the state Qi to a temporary hegemon in the Spring and Autumn Period (von Glahn, 2016, 44; Hu, 2009, 100; Rickett, 1998, 341).

The years between the demise of the Western Zhou and the beginning of the Qin dynasty were "a time of rapid and drastic social change," considered by some as "without equal in Chinese history before the present [twentieth] century" (Graham, 1964, 29). The Western Zhou had been a "ritual order in which the king bestowed rank, office, and wealth according to kinship status" (von Glahn, 2016, 82). In contrast, the Spring and Autumn Period and the Warring States Period were times of chaos and war. New military and economic forces were unleashed as part of a process of "big fish eating small fish" (Li, 2013, 182). Several hundred agrarian city-states were merged into seven territorial states (von Glahn, 2016, 44, 82). This state competition spurred social and economic reform that gave rise to centralized, bureaucratic states (Li, 2013, 182). Institutions gradually developed that laid the foundation for a unified Chinese empire and shaped its future statecraft (Li, 2013, 182; von Glahn, 2016, 46). At the heart of the state were a powerful monarch and a bureaucracy operated by officials who were selected more based on merits or mercantile experience than on aristocratic descent (Li, 2013, 194–195; von Glahn, 2016, 45–46).

A deep transformation of production occurred in parallel with the emergence of a new political order from war and chaos. Previously, the nobility had controlled the land. Now, peasant families were granted proprietary rights from the state (Hu, 2009, 19; von Glahn, 2016, 46). As a result, family farms became the basic production unit (Li, 2013, 189; von Glahn, 2016, 46, 82). At the same time, the iron revolution introduced production techniques that involved the use of new metal tools (Wagner and Needham, 2008). Together, these changes brought about a drastic improvement in agricultural productivity, which in turn gave rise to increasing handicraft activities in the households and, ultimately, to an enhanced functional and regional division of labor (Hu, 2009, 19; von Glahn, 2016, 65, 82).

This transformation in production propagated a fundamental change in the organization of commerce and created the need for a new form of state-market relations. Markets in the Western Zhou Period were under strict, direct government control (Hu, 2009, 7–8). The state controlled the type of commodities allowed for sale on the market. A government official, called the price master, fixed the price at which these commodities were to be sold. Prices were allowed to fluctuate freely only on village markets (ibid., 10).

Following the breakdown of the Western Zhou institutions of control and the transformation of production, a new urge for free trading of commodities emerged (Hu, 2009, 19). The invention of coinage and the proliferation of currency by the state facilitated long-distance trade. Commerce flourished, and a new class of private merchants became prevalent (von Glahn, 2016, 46, 64). The rulers of the Warring States turned to this merchant class to assist them in establishing a new form of control over the economy (von Glahn, 2016, 46). With this historical context in mind, the authors of the *Guanzi* derived their remarkable recommendations on harnessing the newly unleashed market forces by the state. At the core of their program were price regulations based on the light–heavy (轻重) principles.

The next section introduces the basic theoretical outlook in the *Guanzi*. Following that introduction, we will turn our attention to the application in concrete policies.

The Light–Heavy Principles

In the context of the fierce interstate competition of the Spring and Autumn Period, "all ducal states had been hankering for the art of 'making the state rich and the army powerful'" (Hu, 2009, 120). The light–heavy principles were developed to meet these aims of strengthening state and army (Chin, 2014, 31). Enriching the country is the starting point: "a ruler who is good at ruling the state must first of all enrich his people, then govern them" (*Guanzi* as in Hu, 2009, 102). As Rickett (1998, 338) explains in his introduction to the *Guanzi*,

> Qing 轻 means "light" and by extension "unimportant," "inconsequential," or "cheap." As a verb, it means to accord little or no value to something. Zhong 重 means "heavy," and by extension "important," "serious," or "expensive." As a verb, it means to value something. As a compound the two characters usually mean "weight."

Based on this literary meaning, Ye's (2014, 98) translation as "Weighing and Balancing Economic Forces" is apt. From the perspective of *qingzhong*, all economic phenomena can only be understood relationally; things can be heavy or light only in relation to other things. Heavy commodities are considered essential to production or human well-being, and light commodities are seen as inessential. But precisely what commodity is defined as heavy or light is subject to constant change and reflects the season of the year, production practices, and market dynamics, among other factors. The task of economic policy is to weigh and balance, to use what is found to be heavy in order to offset what is light. Or, in the words of the *Guanzi*:

> To use the thing that is "heavy" to shoot at that which is "light," to use the cheap to level down the dear, these are the great advantages that can be drawn from the application of the "light–heavy" doctrine.
>
> *(Guanzi as in Hu, 2009, 127)*

Hence, the state should not work against the spontaneous forces inherent in the economy, society, and natural environment; it should instead use these forces to first enrich and then govern the people while generating revenue for the state. State regulation must be based on detailed knowledge of the real conditions and their changes. To this end, the *Guanzi* recommended extensive empirical surveys and the use of statistics and calculations (Chin, 2014, 42; *Guanzi* as in Rickett, 1998, 389–395; Hu, 2009, 155–157; von Glahn, 2016, 87–88). The state was to observe the movements in the market manifested in price changes as well as prevailing fundamental conditions such as population, natural resources, skills, seasonal changes, and regional peculiarities. As far as the prices of specific commodities were concerned, the ruler had to understand the following principles, determining what was "heavy," or dear, and what was "light," or cheap:

> When things are plentiful, they will be cheap; when they are scarce, they will be expensive.
>
> *(Guanzi as in Rickett, 1998, 384)*

In modern language, this principle says that the price of a commodity is determined by its scarcity. But prices were also affected by a second principle:

> Goods if concentrated will become "heavy," but will turn "light" once they are scattered about.
>
> *(Guanzi as in Hu, 2009, 124)*

This pointed to the institutional structure of suppliers as one of the determinants of prices. If the goods are in the hands of few (i.e., they are monopolized), they will be expensive. If many suppliers offer identical goods, the goods will be cheap. In other words, scarcity is not simply about the absolute quantity of goods in the market but also about the distribution of these goods across producers. If goods are concentrated in few hands, those in control of supply can generate artificial scarcity to charge higher prices. The *Guanzi* anticipated the idea of monopoly price markups.

Furthermore, the demand for goods influenced their price:

> Goods worth being hoarded will become "heavy," and conversely [if not worth hoarding] will become "light." Goods cornered will be "heavy," or otherwise will be "light."
>
> *(ibid., 124)*

This principle suggested that goods that are demanded as a store of value of some sort, rather than to satisfy some immediate need or want, will increase in price when people try to hold onto their wealth in some physical, nonmonetary form. When there is a rush on such goods and they are withdrawn from the market, they become scarce and hence expensive.

Finally, the government's taxation affected the price, according to the *Guanzi*:

> An urgent decree to collect tax in the form of certain goods will make the goods in question "heavy," but a go-slow decree will make them "light."
>
> *(ibid., 124)*

With regard to taxation, the writers of the *Guanzi* saw time as the crucial factor: if people have to pay a certain commodity as tax to the government in a rush, the price will shoot up, but when they have time to collect the required commodities, this will not be the case. In modern language, we call the underlying phenomenon a "demand shock."

All these principles build on the idea that relative value depends on supply and demand. But rather than focusing on the equilibrium between supply and demand, as economists are accustomed to doing in modern neoclassical economics, the *Guanzi* explores reasons for change. The crucial point is that all these price-determining conditions were thought to vary depending on concrete circumstances. Things are not universally "heavy" or "light"; they change their designation depending on the context, which is analyzed in ways more dynamic than a simple assessment of some given constellation of supply and demand. Therefore, the *Guanzi* suggested:

> There is no rigid art of the "light" and "heavy," but to respond to anything that is showing signs of coming and to take advantage of any tidings heard.
>
> *(Guanzi as in Hu, 2009, 127–128)*

As a result, the art of governing depended on being flexible: "The true king takes advantage of the situation, and the sage takes advantage of the principles of change" (ibid., 41).

However, it would be a mistake to conclude that the *qingzhong* principles only knew the movements in the market. *Qingzhong* economic policies aimed to use the individual pursuit of profit and self-interest to enrich the state while balancing and integrating the economy. When people valued something, it would become "heavy" or in the opposite case "light." Yet social wealth was defined not in terms of the subjective value but in terms of the fundamentals of material well-being. In a vastly agricultural society, this was essentially the ability to cultivate the land to its fullest. Labor and land were the ultimate sources of wealth, and because the subsistence of people depended on grain, it was considered the most fundamental commodity in the *Guanzi*: "A man can't eat without grain, grain can't grow without land, land can't do without man, and man can't get rich without labour" (*Guanzi* as in Hu, 2009, 104). Grain, being the centerpiece of wealth, takes the most crucial position in relation to all other commodities and is hence of utmost importance in the *qingzhong* economic policy. Grain, it is suggested, determines the price of all other commodities, including money:

> The price of commodities will rise or fall along with the value of money, and it is grain alone that will determine whether they are expensive or cheap. ... When grain is expensive, all other things are cheap, when grain is cheap, all other things are expensive.
>
> *(Guanzi as in Rickett, 1998, 367)*

This means that the value of money moves in opposite directions. The price of grain affects all people in determining the general price level. At the same time, it affects the rural and urban populations in different ways. Even before the writing of the *Guanzi*, Li Kui, the economic advisor to Duke Wen of the Wen State, noticed[7]

> If grain ... was very expensive it would injure the people (other than the farmers); while if it was very cheap it would injure the farmers. ... Consequently whether [the price was] very high or very low, the injury was one and the same.
>
> *(Han Shu as in Swann, 1950, 139–140, insertions in original)*[8]

In the *Guanzi*, this notion is further developed. The balancing of the grain price becomes the core of the "art of planned fiscal management" (*Guanzi* as in Rickett, 1998, 361), an art of government that aims to achieve stability and prosperity for the state, using the principles of *qingzhong*. This policy of balancing the grain price is the subject of the next section.

Balancing the Grain Price

Besides recognizing grain as the "people's Master of Destiny" (ibid., 384, 77), the progression of the seasons is another condition that *qingzhong* economic policies take as a starting point. We read in the *Guanzi* that "the climatic changes of the four seasons and the rotation of day and night were objective laws. They could not be decreased if they were oversupplied and could not be increased if undersupplied" (as in Hu, 2009, 105). From this, the following problem arises: *qingzhong* suggests that the price depends on whether something is oversupplied or undersupplied. Depending on the season, grain is oversupplied (harvest) or undersupplied (spring). As a result, the price fluctuates—which is bad both for peasants and for urban consumers. Thus, the ruler faced the question of how to balance the price of grain throughout the year.

According to the *Guanzi*, "states that adhere to the way of a true king act in accordance with the seasons" (ibid., 1998, 365). This suggests that, in general, the state must "make use of what is valued to acquire what is not valued and what has been acquired cheaply to ease the price of what has become too expensive" (ibid., 381–382). Furthermore, "when the prince mints coins to establish a money supply, the people all accept them as a medium of exchange" (ibid., 380). Hence, the prince can issue money. "Therefore those who are skilled in government manage mediums of exchange in order to control the Masters of Destiny" (ibid., 378). The government has a responsibility to stabilize the price of grain in order to stabilize the overall price level and the value of money.

This principle manifested as government purchase of surplus grain from the peasants in autumn, at harvest time, when it was oversupplied and its price was low—in other words, grain was "light" and money was "heavy." By demanding relatively large amounts, the government drove up the price of grain. It thereby balanced the relative quantities of money and grain in the market, prevented the downward movement of the grain price, and protected the peasants from selling their grain at overly low prices to private merchants. In each locality, the government established public granaries to store the grain. In spring, when the farmers were plowing and sowing, and in summer, when they were weeding, their grain reserves would run low. The supply of grain on the market was short, and the grain price was high. At that time, the government used parts of the grain stored away to increase the supply in the market. The government balanced the upshot in the price of grain and protected the peasants from having to buy grain at very high prices from private merchants.[9]

This scheme stabilized both the price for grain and the general price level. First, we have seen that in the *Guanzi*, the prices of all things depended on that of grain. Second, by participating in the market for grain, the state adjusted the money supply. Since the value of money, like that of all other commodities, was found to depend on its quantity, a change in the money supply would affect its value in relation to all other goods. In other words, it would change the overall price level.[10] According to the *Guanzi*, "When grain is cheap, he [the prince] exchanges money for food" (*Guanzi* as in Rickett, 1998, 377–378). In such a situation, money would be "heavy" and would buy a relatively great amount of grain, hence the price level is low. As the state bought a considerable amount of grain, the price of grain rose, but the value of money also fell, and hence a deflationary tendency was balanced. The opposite occurred in spring and summer, when grain was expensive. The state balanced the price of grain in money and the price of money in grain by balancing the quantities of money and grain in circulation. This is how the *Guanzi* envisioned the government to "manage mediums of exchange in order to control the Masters of Destiny" (*Guanzi* as in Rickett, 1998, 377–378). Beyond the immediate effects on prices, this scheme of grain price balancing had important implications for state revenues, inequality, and famine prevention through countercyclical policies.

First of all, although the state balanced the price movements, it did not aim for complete stability—"When water is perfectly level, it will not flow" (ibid., 308). The price of grain in autumn would still be higher than in spring and summer, but the price difference would be smaller than it had been without the state's participation in the market. As a result of the price difference, the state participation in the grain market generated government revenues. The state did not have to impose any direct taxes: "By taking advantage of government orders to move goods and money back and forth, there is no need to make any demands on the people in the form of special taxes and levies" (ibid., 392). The rulers of Western Zhou had fixed prices by decree and extracted surpluses from the people by direct taxation. In contrast, the new art of government was to use price fluctuations to enrich the country without undermining the enthusiasm of the peasants. Mastering this new "art of planned fiscal management" was "not something to create resentment among the people or ruin their aspirations" (ibid., 362). Instead of taking away from the people by command, the state sold grain to the people when they needed it, thereby lowering the price, and bought grain from the people when they had it to sell, thereby raising the price. Instead of being subjected to direct taxation, the people would experience the state as a benevolent government. In sum, this approach would create "stability similar to placing a square object on the ground" (ibid., 367).

Furthermore, the policy of balancing grain prices prevented the most severe forms of inequalities without making all people equal.[11] At the time, a class of private merchants was rising. In fact, the government learned the techniques of market participation from the merchants. As prices were not directly controlled by the state any longer, it became apparent that "[a]s the harvest is bad or good, grain will be expensive or cheap" (*Guanzi* as in Rickett, 1998, 379). If the government did not utilize these price movements to generate public profit, private merchants would do so: "if the prince is not able to control the situation, it will lead to large-scale traders roaming the markets and taking advantage of the people's lack of things to increase their capital a hundredfold" (ibid.).[12]

The pursuit of profits was not condemned in the *Guanzi* but was taken as a given reality: "it is the nature of men that whenever they see profit, they cannot help chasing after it" (*Guanzi* as in Rickett, 1998, 219). The task of the ruler was hence not to appeal to the morality of the people but to use the prevailing interests and "regulate the people's profits" (ibid., 379). In order to do this, the state had to "maintain control over policies affecting prices" (ibid., 366). Land reform was not enough to prevent inequalities: "Even though the land may have been divided equally, the strong will be able to gain control of it; even though wealth has been distributed equally, the clever will be able to accumulate it" (ibid., 379). If the government failed to balance the grain price, "it will only result in the people below enslaving each other." When such "great inequality exists between rich and poor," the "multitude is not well governed" (ibid., 380). Hence, "[s]hould the prince fail to maintain control over policies affecting prices ... the economic policy of the state becomes meaningless" (ibid., 366).

Finally, and most essentially, the participation in the grain market allowed the state to accumulate grain in each locality and protect people from the consequences of natural disasters. An elaborate system of famine prevention worked hand in hand with a countercyclical fiscal policy. The government's task was to protect the people from the changes of the seasons, climate, and the market and to ensure their access to daily necessities at all times. The state employed the people when the seasons did not require them to work in the field. In this way, the state prevented the source of wealth from drying up. The ruler was to practice frugality in normal times so as not to divert too much of the people's time from the fundamental occupation of agriculture. However, "prodigality should be adopted in a special situation" (Hu, 2009, 116). If the people lost the foundation of their livelihood and could not work their land because of natural disasters, the state should offer them employment. At such times, the state should also encourage the rich to create work—for example, by encouraging them to have lavish funerals (*Guanzi* as in Rickett, 1998, 319). In sum, the *Guanzi* holds that those "who are good at ruling a state simply depend upon the situation to relax or intensify their demands" (ibid., 415).[13]

The Salt and Iron Monopoly

> If you, my lord, were to issue an order stating, "I am going to impose a special tax on all adults and children," it would give rise to great yelling and screaming. But now supposing you issue orders adopting the salt plan, then even if the amount reverting to your government were a hundred times this, men would have no way to avoid it. Such would be the inevitable results.
>
> *(Guanzi as in Rickett, 1998, 374)*

The general principle in the *Guanzi* was policy activism, but as Hu (2009) comments, policy "might take different forms in accordance with the different conditions of the specific trades, no panacea being offered indiscriminately for all situations" (157). Complementary to the indirect control of grain prices by state demand and supply in the market, the *Guanzi* suggested a partial public monopoly over salt and iron.[14] When the duke asked Guan Zhong what kind of tax he should impose, he answered that any kind of special tax on an economic activity or property would result in people reducing this activity or concealing their property (*Guanzi* as in Rickett, 1998, 372–373, 382–383). The state should instead generate revenue "by managing the mountains and seas" (*Guanzi* as in Rickett, 1998, 373), that is, by bringing salt and iron under state control.

This policy recommendation was based on the insight that both salt and iron are essential commodities and as such are "heavy." As Gale (1931, xxv) observed: "Salt and iron were the two most universal necessities, after grain, in the ancient Chinese commonwealth." Every human has to consume salt. Tools for any kind of work contained iron—for example, needles, scissors, plows, and axes (*Guanzi* as in Rickett, 1998, 374–375). "Without such tools, no one in the world can be successful" (ibid.). Thus, the demands for salt and iron were inelastic. If the state controlled the selling of these two commodities, it could charge a high price and thereby collect revenue. The income from the control over the prices and trading in these commodities would be much larger than that generated by a special tax. But even if the government collected revenues from the sale of salt and iron "a hundred times this [from a special tax], men would have no way to avoid it" (ibid., 374). People would also not object to such extra charges in the way they would object to direct taxation; that would factor in maintaining political stability (Hu, 2009, 150).

In managing both salt and iron, the state had to pay attention to the characteristics of the production of the two commodities. For salt, *Guanzi* envisioned a partial monopoly in production and marketing (Hu, 2009, 157), which was to be established by "tak[ing] advantage of the season" (*Guanzi* as in Rickett, 1998, 427). At times when people were not busy with their agricultural work, the state would employ large numbers of people "for boiling salt water" (ibid.). "When agricultural work begins in the spring," the ruler would "issue orders that the people are not allowed … to hire labor to boil salt" (ibid.). This would limit the overall supply of salt and drive up the price (ibid.). The state would not monopolize all salt production and marketing. But by limiting the overall supply, the price could be manipulated, and thanks to a large market share in the production of salt, the state would reap a large profit.

While salt can be produced from salt water abundant in nature, metal ores can only be extracted from scarce, specific mountain areas. The *Guanzi* suggested strong control of these mineral resources by the state (ibid., 424). The monopoly over the extraction of these resources put the state in control of the most important input for the means of production. But, in contrast to the extraction, the *Guanzi* stipulated that iron smelting should not be under the direct control of the state. The work would be so dreadful that, if imposed on the people by the state, they would "resent their lord," which would result in being "defeated from within" (*Guanzi* as in Rickett, 1998, 469). Thus, rather than keeping direct control, the state should "let the people do it" and only take part of their profit (ibid.). Under this policy "the people [would] … rush to do their work and become captives of your government" (ibid.).

We have seen that the state occupied a crucial role in managing the newly unleashed market forces in the *Guanzi*'s vision. Thereby, the concrete policies employed by the state were highly context dependent, subject to change in circumstances, and tailored to suit the nature of the production and the essential characteristics of key commodities. For grain, peasants would work their private plots of land and sell their produce in the market. Hence, both production and circulation were private, while the state acquired grain reserves sufficiently large to balance the price and to prevent famine. For salt, both production and circulation were partially controlled by the state, while the government also controlled the overall supply and thus the price by seasonally prohibiting production. For iron, the extraction was monopolized by the state, smelting was in private hands, and the government controlled the price, both by controlling the raw material supply and by participating in the market for iron products. This points to a vision of a political economy in which consumption income was generated privately, but saving, in the form of storing grain and cash, and investment, in the form of producing means of production, was to be both in the hands of the state and private businesses.

Economic policies akin to those described in the *Guanzi* were introduced in the pre-Han Period and were revived under Emperor Wudi (141–87 BCE) until, shortly after his death, a major controversy over the right attitude of the state toward the economy broke out (Wagner, 2001, 4–21). This controversy is canonized in Huan Kuan's (first century BCE) classic account of two competing positions on the proper way for the bureaucracy to handle economic matters, the *Salt and Iron Debate* (盐铁论).

The Literati's Challenge in the *Salt and Iron Debate*

The Historical Context

When Emperor Wudi stepped onto the throne, about half a century into the reign of the Han dynasty, the country was facing a deep crisis. Both the financial and political integrity of the state were threatened (von Glahn, 2016, 113–114). Challenges from within the empire and military expansionism incurred high costs. The Han Empire faced a constant treasury deficit, and the generation of state revenue became the most pressing issue (Gale, 1931, xxv).

Wudi repudiated Wendi's (180–157 BCE) strategy of relaxing state involvement in industry and commerce (Wagner, 2001, 8). Von Glahn (2016, 114) goes as far as to call Wendi's approach a "minimalist government." Whereas Qin established a system of wide-ranging state administration of key industries in line with the policy vision of the *Guanzi*, under Wendi, "the people were permitted to cast coins, smelt iron, and boil salt" (*Salt and Iron Debate* as in Wagner and Needham, 2008, 174). This, however, resulted in powerful private monopolies challenging the state in a revolt (Wagner and Needham, 2008, 174–175). Wudi turned to a brain trust of merchants and industrialists to escape bankruptcy of the government and overcome inflation (Hu, 2009, 263). Instead of borrowing money from these business elites, Wudi appointed them as senior officials to help regain stability by reorganizing the fiscal administration (Gale, 1931, xxv; Hu, 2009, 259; von Glahn, 2016, 114).

Inspired by the *Guanzi's* economic policies,[15] Wudi again inaugurated a state monopoly on the production and sale of iron[16] and salt as well as liquor; unified and standardized the currency; and established a system to "equalize transportation" (均输),[17] in a system termed "equable marketing" (Hu, 2009, 264–273; Gale, 1931, xxv; Loewe, 1985, 259; von Glahn, 2016, 114–116, 120; Wagner and Needham, 2008, 178–179). The latter is akin to the *Guanzi's* policy of grain price balancing but encompassed a wider range of commodities and the balancing of prices across regions.

Sang Hongyang (152–80 BCE), a member of a wealthy merchant family, was instrumental both for bringing salt and iron under state monopoly and for introducing equable marketing. Sang, known for his outstanding calculating skills, was to become one of Emperor Wudi's most important economic advisors (Hu, 2009, 269–279; *Han Shu* as in Swann, 1950, 271–272; Loewe, 1985, 240; Wagner and Needham, 2008, 171). Sang later merged the system of equable marketing with that of salt and iron monopolies to institute the so-called "balanced standard" (平准) (von Glahn, 2016, 116). Public funds were now used across the whole country to buy commodities when they were cheap in one place and sell them where they were dear (ibid.). This balanced prices and generated profits for the state while creating and integrating markets.

Following the *Guanzi's* approach, the state monopolies were tailored to the concrete conditions of production. For salt, this involved public ownership of the means of production, in particular the iron salt-pan, private producers, and marketing at a state-fixed price (Hu, 2009, 265). Reflecting new production technologies that allowed much larger scales of production, the iron production[18] and all distribution, including price fixing, was under state monopoly (ibid., 266–267). The complete control over the production and marketing of iron also meant indirectly controlling the salt production, since the most important input, the salt-pan, could be produced exclusively by the state (ibid.). Finally, the wine monopoly covered only production, not marketing, which remained in the hands of private dealers (ibid., 268). The physical institutions of state monopoly were hence designed to reflect the inherent conditions of production and structures of marketing.

Sang's economic policies were successful at overcoming the fiscal deficit, stabilizing the price level, filling up the public granaries, and supplying the army (Gale, 1931, xxvi; Hu, 2009, 263–264; von Glahn, 2016, 117–118). However, many people became displeased with the high cost of salt and complained about the poor quality of the state-supplied ironware (Gale, 1931, xxv). Traditional agriculturists and philosophers criticized the policy activism from the beginning of Sang's policies onward (Wagner and Needham, 2008, 178). When, after a reign of fifty-four years,

Emperor Wudi passed away in the year 81 BCE, a "Grand Inquest" was held to debate the continuing discontent and the legacy of his policies (Gale, 1931, xxv; von Glahn, 2016, 123; Loewe, 1974, 91; Wagner and Needham, 2008, 179). The new Emperor Zhao was still a child and power was in the hands of General Huo Guang (Wagner and Needham, 2008, 179), "a political struggle [was] staged against Sang Hongyang under the guise of a survey" (Hu, 2009, 274). This set the stage for the famous *Salt and Iron Debate* (盐铁论).

On one side of the debate were the literati—"men of learning," or "classical scholars" (文学), and the "worthies" (贤良) (Chin, 2014, 49). Gale (1931, xxi) describes them as "the intellectuals not in office … pursuing certain ideas ascribed to Confucius and his successors." The literati are in places called "Confucian" in the text of the *Salt and Iron Debate* and have thus often been labeled as such by interpreters (e.g., Hu, 2009). But Gale (1931) warns that what is rendered "Confucian" in Huan Kuan's account is not consistent with the later Confucianist school, let alone with what came to be attributed to this term in modern interpretations. To avoid misunderstandings, I will therefore call the persons on this side of the debate *literati*, since their key characteristic is that they build their arguments on an exegesis of classic texts (including but not limited to Confucius) rather than on empirical investigations.

The counterpart to the literati was the "imperial counselor" (大夫). This referred to Sang Hongyang, who defended his economic policies against "the fire of a vicious attack by the men of letters" (Gale, 1931, xix). More generally, this side represents the "administrators, the responsible officials, advocating certain methods of government," with a background in commerce and industry, who during Emperor Wudi's reign had gained "the ear of their sovereign" thanks to "their effective financial resourcefulness" (ibid., xx–i).[19]

The most important source on the *Salt and Iron Debate* is Huan Kuan's (first century BCE) posthumous chronicle (Wagner and Needham, 2008, 185).[20] The account is clearly biased toward the literati. Loewe (1974) conjectures that it might have been "compiled as an exercise in political propaganda" (111). Huan Kuan's account is also described as "a work of fiction in dialogue form on a historical theme" (Guo Moruo as in Wagner, 2001, 18). Like the *Guanzi* and other early classics, Huan Kuan uses the form of a dialogue or debate. He draws on essays written in the context of the actual historical debate but enriches his account with complementary materials, importantly, unattributed quotations from the *Guanzi* (Kroll, 1978). The writer's motivation might have been to reflect on the abolition of the state monopoly—and government activism more broadly—that occurred in 44–41 BCE (Wagner and Needham, 2008, 186).[21]

Notwithstanding these limitations with regard to its historical accuracy, Huan Kuan's account presents crucial insights into competing perspectives on key issues in political economy of his time. It became a recurring reference for subsequent debates, even in modern times.[22] The *Salt and Iron Debate* articulated tensions within the political economy of imperial China that were to persist and recur for centuries to come. The next section discusses some key points of argument in the *Salt and Iron Debate* with regard to the state monopolies, price policies, and the role of economic policy-making more broadly.

The Debate: Idealism versus Realist Pragmatism

Sang Hongyang followed the basic principles underlying the *Guanzi*'s approach to policy-making. That is, "practical considerations should take priority" and "the art of government must be addressed to the needs of the prevailing situation and not to the attainment of a perfectionist state of society" (Loewe, 1974, 93–94). In Sang's pragmatic outlook, values and moral principles could be pursued only after material prosperity was achieved (ibid., 94, 106).

The literati idealists attacked Sang on the grounds that "purely material considerations" would have given way to "fundamental principles," which, in their view, were not subject to the changes of the time (ibid., 94). The encapsulation of these principles was an idealization of the ritual order of the Western Zhou and the minimalist economic policies of Emperor Wendi. The transformation toward a monetary economy and a commercial society that had occurred in the course of the previous centuries represented, for them, a form of degeneration. The goal was therefore to return to the old ways, when subsistence agriculture had been the dominant occupation and barter exchange and taxation in kind were prevalent (Hu, 2009, 278; Gale, 1931, xxviii; Loewe, 1974, 95, 100).

Sang and the bureaucrat merchants saw the deep social and economic transformation as a reality that the state had to face. To satisfy the material needs of the population and guarantee the safety of the people from invasion, the state had to participate in the economy to harness the prevailing forces, satisfy the material needs of the population, and generate profits to the benefit of the state.

The literati held against this approach, arguing that by pursuing such a commercial policy, the state would become a driving force of moral degeneration and corruption. Instead of fostering morality and prosperity, they said, the policies of equable marketing and balanced standard would divert the powers of the people away from working in the fields and into marketing and profiteering (Gale, 1931, xxvi–iii; Loewe, 1974, 94–95). In addition, government offices would become overstaffed, absorbing even more labor needed for the fundamental occupation of agriculture (Loewe, 1974, 105). Regarding inequality, the literati seemed to envision the problem as the distribution of a given amount of resources and hence of trade-offs between different uses. The primary concern of a ruler, to the minds of the literati, would "not [be] scantiness of wealth, but rather inequality in its distribution, not poverty but rather disquietude" (Huan Kuan as in Hu, 2009, 277).

Underlying the literati's vision seems to be a static outlook, which is consistent with the rejection of the social and technological change—such as the iron revolution—articulated in the debate. In their ideal of an "ancient mode of life" in which everyone is "contented with his position" (ibid.) and in which subsistence agriculture dominates, growth is likely to be low. Within this mindset, the literati's "esteeming frugality and objecting to prodigality" (Hu, 2009, 279) is almost a logical consequence. If there is no significant growth—but there are also no cycles of boom and bust—in a subsistence economy, there is no place for countercyclical government spending. But if the resources are given by the productivity of agriculture, lavish spending by the ruler will be at the cost of the peasants.

In opposition to the literati, Sang and other state officials saw the fundamental economic, social, and technological changes of their time as a given reality and as driving forces of wealth, while at the same time they also emphasized the importance of agriculture (Gale, 1931, xx). They too were opposed to inequality (Loewe, 1974, 94). They believed that a reduction of inequality should be achieved through growth and through state control over the key elements of economic progress: production of strategic commodities, commerce, and money. This would allow the state to balance prices and supply across the empire[23] and prepare for famine and other natural disasters, while generating public profits. Ultimately, inequality was reduced through the state promotion of material wealth.

Bringing wine—and, more importantly, salt and iron production—under state monopoly was part of Sang's broader policy. In an early articulation of the theory of a natural monopoly as well as a prefiguring of Galbraith (see Chapter 2), Sang argued that "natural resources were usually located in out-of-the-way places. If they were thrown open to private individuals, they would most probably be controlled by magnates, with the result that people would be excluded from their sources and their economic benefit" (Hu, 2009, 260). In other words, due to their nature, natural resources, once discovered, are controlled by a monopoly. The real question is whether the monopoly is private or public—not whether extraction of geographically concentrated resources is brought under monopoly power. Hence, Sang urges, "put a ban on the utilization of mountains and water resources by private individuals" since this would enable the state to "redress the balance between those who have more than enough and those who are in want [and] give relief to the needy" (Huan Kuan as in Hu, 2009, 261).

In the literati's perspective, the annexation of monopolies, as well as corrupt government more generally, were the result of the "breakdown of the rites and righteousness" (Hu, 2009, 276; Loewe, 1974, 98). Furthermore, the literati suggested that the implements produced by the state iron monopoly were inferior in quality, limited in variety, often not conveniently supplied to the peasants, and sold at a very high price (Hu, 2009, 267; Loewe, 1974, 102; Wagner and Needham, 2008, 187–188). Salt, too, was overpriced under the state monopoly (Loewe, 1974, 102). In sum, they said, the monopolies would be harmful to the peasant majority. Therefore, the literati called for abolishing the state monopolies and returning to "small-scale family enterprises [which] produced better implements, because of pride of workmanship and because they were closer to the users" (Wagner and Needham, 2008, 188). Sang Hongyang countered with what might be the "earliest exposition on the superiority of large-scale production over small-scale production in Chinese history" (Hu, 2009, 267). The monopolies, according to Sang, would have the advantages of "abundant capital, complete equipment … and the skill of the artisans" (Huan Kuan as in Hu, 2009, 267).

The Outcome and Legacy of the Debate and the Guanzian Logic

The outcome of the debate was in favor of Sang Hongyang's policies. The wine monopoly was to be abolished, but the more important salt and iron monopolies, as well as Sang's policies of price stabilization, were continued (Loewe, 1974, 92; Wagner and Needham, 2008, 179). Despite his victory in the debate, Sang Hongyang was executed in 80 BCE as part of a plot against General Huo Guang and subsequently treated as traitor in the official history writing of the *Han Shu* (*Han Shu* as in Swann, 1950, 321; Wagner and Needham, 2008, 179–183). Yet notwithstanding Sang's fate, his economic policies persisted (Wagner and Needham, 2008, 183). Concurrent with Huan Kuan's writing of the *Salt and Iron Debate*, the state monopolies were abolished in 44 BCE, only to be reintroduced three years later (*Han Shu* as in Swann, 1950, 321; Wagner, 2001, 15). Wagner and Needham (2008, 183) argue in this regard that a major, large-scale, technologically complex industry "cannot be privatised at a stroke without consequences for the entire economy."[24] It therefore seems likely that "serious problems became apparent within a short time, and the government found it necessary to return to former arrangements" (ibid.). Still, the monopolies began to erode at some point, not as a result of a renunciation motivated by theoretical arguments but when the effectiveness of the imperial government came into crisis (Loewe, 1974, 112).

The *Guanzi*'s principles of light and heavy and Sang Hongyang's institution building created a legacy, and the monopolies recurred over the centuries, invoking repeatedly fierce debates. One prominent example in the CE 1060s is the statesman Wang Anshi's response to a deficit crisis. When the deficit remained unresolved after the implementation of austerity measures, Wang implemented economic reforms, the so-called New Policies.[25] These included a reinstatement of state monopolies as well as grain price stabilization through "Green Sprout Loans" (Eberhard, 1977, 216–217; Vandermeersch, 1985, 8; Wagner and Needham, 2008, 171). Wang Anshi defended his policies in the famous *Memorial to the Throne in Ten Thousand Characters* (万言书, CE 1058) against Sima Guang and others who took a stance along similar lines of the literati in the *Salt and Iron Debate* (ibid.; Smith, 1993, 83; Bol, 1993). The *Memorial* was referenced in critiques of privatization measures as recently as 1996 (Wu and Ma, 2016, 93, 152–153). As Smith (1993, 83) observes in his lucid analysis of the debate between Wang and Sima and the activism initiated by the New Policy, Wang

> recognized no rightful demarcation between the public and private sectors of the economy: household, public finance, and the resources of the natural economy were interlinked, so that if any one sector was to be enriched they must all be enriched.

To create wealth, Wang Anshi argued, the institutions and techniques guiding the relation of heavy and light and the collection and disbursement of goods and money in the economy as a whole had to follow good governance (Smith, 1993, 84). To achieve this, he urged, private monopolies engrossing profits should be replaced by state monopolies staffed with entrepreneurial bureaucrats.

Agriculture remained key for Wang, as it had been for the ancient scholars. To overcome a crisis in the institution of the civilian granary system, Wang proposed a policy that would supplement public supply and demand of grain for money by providing seasonal loans. The institution, commonly called the Ever Normal Granary (常平仓), is more precisely translated as "granary [for maintaining] constant [price] stability" (Dunstan, 1996, 31). Wang's Green Sprout Loans entailed that the public grain reserves were converted into a loan fund that provided credit to the peasants in springtime, to be repaid in the subsequent autumn. Instead of direct market operations, state credits were now to balance the flow of money and grain in the market across seasonal fluctuations. This also served to drive out landlords and moneylenders from the rural economy (Smith, 1993, 93–94). The Green Sprout Loan policy amounts to a financialized incarnation of the *Guanzian* price balance through market participation by the state appropriate to the rise of fiat money at the time (Li C., 2016, 213–214). While the stabilization of the grain price continued to have an important welfare dimension, a state monopoly over certain nonessential goods such as tea was, in Wang's scheme, simply a tool to extract profit for the state (ibid., 96).

Skipping ahead to the high Qing dynasty (1644–1840), the bureaucracy's commercial activities became the subject of renewed great debates among scholar officials (Dunstan, 1996, 2006; Will and Wong, 1991, 14–15; Hymes and Schirokauer, 1993, 2; Hymes, 1993). Many of the arguments on both sides were restated (Dunstan, 1996, 19, 330–331). Our understanding of these debates of economic policy among intellectuals in China's last dynasty has recently been greatly enhanced by a number of important contributions (e.g., Dunstan, 1996, 2006; Lin, 2006; Rowe, 2001, 2018; Zanasi, 2020).

Dunstan (1996, 31, 163; 2006, 55) finds that some of the arguments in these Qing discourses were reminiscent of the *Salt and Iron Debate*, while arguments in defense of price stabilization through state commerce can be traced to the

Guanzi (Dunstan, 1996, 163; 2006, 55). This includes, for example, on the side of the activist tradition, the emphasis on the need to study concrete economic relations and to adapt policy measures in an experimental fashion; the attention to cost structures and market dynamics; the emphasis on state commercial activity; and the socially responsible stabilization of the price of grain to prevent private grain hoarding and ensure monetary stability.[26]

At the high point of the Qing dynasty, the bureaucracy achieved what Rowe (2001, 2) describes as a "nearly unprecedented success in managing the massive problems of food supply and food prices." Wemheuer (2014, 30) even suggests that "the Qing dynasty had the most elaborate [famine] relief system in world history, based on state and local granaries that were used in times of shortage to stabilize food prices and provide relief to the urban and rural poor." This success was brought about by a change in the administration style—from a focus on moral values and personal example toward a pragmatic "learn truth from facts" approach (Rowe, 2001, 3) and technocratic governance in pursuit of wealth and power.

In the 1740s, a great expansion of the state granary system invoked a debate over how the state's own building up of grain stocks could occur without incurring excessive grain price rises. This quickly developed into a discourse on the principles and practices of the Ever Normal Granaries. The stockpiling by the state was attacked by proponents of laissez-faire to the market mechanism. The state civilian granaries were labeled as the biggest antisocial hoarders that drove up prices, harmed consumers and merchants, and extracted illicit profits for bureaucrats (Dunstan, 1996, 34, 63–68; 2006, 149–306; Will and Wong, 1991, 494–495). But even when the 1740s scholarly debates reached pessimistic conclusions about policy activism and when, in the second half of the eighteenth century, the activist policy position largely vanished, the institutions of state commerce and price stabilization continued and even expanded in practice (Dunstan, 1996, 331; Will and Wong, 1991, 501).[27]

In the nineteenth century, skepticism about the usefulness of the civilian granary system and the imperialist threat contributed to its decline (Wemheuer, 2014, 30; Will and Wong, 1991, 501–502). The modernizers propagating China's "self-strengthening" in the late Qing had little interest in the granary system. They argued that the state should instead invest in modernization and mechanization to achieve military and economic progress that would overcome poverty and food shortages more sustainably (Edgerton-Tarpley, 2008, 92–99). Representatives of British commerce in China also advocated for faith in science and modernization. They blamed poverty and famine on state intervention and urged the adoption of Western laissez-faire economics (ibid., 114–130).

One of the first acts of the new government—after the 1911 revolution that overthrew China's last imperial dynasty and established the Republic of China—was to abolish the public granary system and, with it, the price–stabilizing mechanism (Mallory, 1926, 67–68). Chen (1911b, 585) trained as a Chinese scholar-official and as an economist in the United States. In his writings that date to the year before the first Chinese revolution in 1911, Chen remarks that he had found that the basic principles of government granaries, price stabilization, and famine prevention still remained.

Yet, despite the abolishment of the granary system, recent research shows that famine relief in warlord China in the 1920s relied more on traditional relief systems than previous scholarship had indicated (Fuller, 2019). Li (2016, 213) suggests that as late as the 1940s, some local governments under the Nationalists still employed the principles of the Ever Normal Granary to regulate food prices. There is room for interpretation regarding the prevalence of these traditional practices in the first half of the twentieth century. Yet, considering the millennia-long reoccurring practice, the basic logic of state participation in the market to stabilize grain prices must be considered a legacy relevant also to modern economic governance in China.

In addition to grain-price-stabilizing granaries, monopolies over salt and iron were long-lasting institutions subject to repeated debates among policy activists and proponents of a more passive form of economic governance. Wagner (1997, 7) finds that the Qing government ran a state licensing system, granting monopoly rights for iron and salt to private industrialists. This came under attack from the British imperial power, following a "firm ideology, in fact an *idée fixe*, of the British traders in Guangzhou that all state regulation and all monopolies are pernicious" (ibid.). In the first of the unequal treaties after China's defeat in the first Opium War with the British, the Chinese government was forced to ban the monopoly system (ibid.); Wagner (1997, 8) sees this as the starting point of the decline of China's iron industry.

King (1965, 9) points out that the state monopoly over salt was still an important source of fiscal revenue in the second half of the nineteenth century. Gale (1930)—an officer of the Chinese Government Salt Revenue Administration in the years 1914–1927 and the first translator of the *Salt and Iron Debate*—reported on how foreigners once more attacked the Chinese state monopolies and reorganized the salt revenue administration, as part of the conditionality on foreign loans. In Gale's eyes, they thereby came to change "practices and procedures enjoying the sanction of centuries" (ibid., 242). As late as the 1930s, salt revenue was an important source of fiscal income for the Nationalist government. For example, in the Shandong province, salt accounted for almost one-fifth of the provincial fiscal revenue (Lai, 2011, 160–161).

Conclusion

We have seen that the *Guanzi* articulated distinct principles of government balancing of prices, market creation, famine prevention, and monopoly control, which were developed in a period when "a new order emerged from great chaos" (拨乱反正). These policies aimed to protect the peasant majority from violent fluctuation, cycles, and speculation in the context of the recently unleashed market powers and to increase commercialization of society while enriching the state. Rather than working against powerful economic trends, this approach to economic policy suggested that the state should unleash and harness market forces in order to promote wealth for the state and the people.

In contrast to this realist and pragmatist outlook, the idealist approach represented by the literati in the *Salt and Iron Debate* takes a vision of an ideal state in the foregone past as its reference point. Rather than utilizing the emerging material forces, the literati aimed to convince people and government officials to return to morality and righteousness by reviving the old way of living. Under the premise of the reinstatement of a ritual order and subsistence agriculture, they promoted a government that would abstain from policy activism. Yet, it may be helpful to look beyond seeing the two approaches only in opposition to one another. Despite recurring clashes, the two opposing visions might actually have nourished one another in the course of Chinese history.

The tension between these two basic outlooks on economic governance recurred throughout the centuries of imperial China in various incarnations. It inspired many debates with similarities to the *Salt and Iron Debate* and prefigured some twentieth-century controversies in economics. One of the most authoritative studies of the late imperial civilian granary system asserts, "Much of the eighteenth-century Chinese critique of granary operations is echoed in twentieth-century Western arguments against more general government intervention in markets" (Will and Wong, 1991, 495). As I derive in my analysis of the 1980s debate (see Chapters 5 through 8), similar arguments were also invoked in the quests for radical price liberalization in this recent discourse on market reform. The subsequent chapters of this book show that some of the ancient principles of economic policy-making in general and price policies in particular can be helpful in shedding light on the Communists' approach to economic warfare during the civil war. They also help to reveal the logic of Deng Xiaoping's market reforms.

While intending to take China's traditions of economic thought into account, the intent of this book is not to create a Sinocentric narrative of China's economic reforms in which the 1980s are simply a relapse of some ancient traditions. Rather, the aim is to trace several different ways of doing economics that provided competing depositories of knowledge to the 1980s reformers. In this context, China's tradition of conceptualizing and practicing the relation between the market and the state is important. But so is the experience of planned war economies and the return to postwar market economies in the Second World War.

In the 1980s, China aimed to learn from international experiences as well as from foreign economics. For many economists—Chinese and foreign alike—the practices of price control and decontrol in the context of war were an important reference point in analyzing the challenges of China's system reform. Beyond this connection between the transition from a war to a peace economy drawn by participants in the 1980s reform debate, the debates on how to stabilize and liberalize prices in the context of the Second World War provided an insightful point of comparison. The debates over war economies and the peace transition involved some of the most influential twentieth-century economists thinking through a problem accompanied by challenges similar to those presented by market reforms.

Notes

1 A search in the China National Knowledge Infrastructure (CNKI) database, which is similar to Web of Science, shows that between 1978 and 1992, between two and seven articles were published that mention the *Salt and Iron Debate* (盐铁论), as well as one to two that mention the light–heavy principles (轻重) of the *Guanzi* (管子).
2 This is a similar approach to the recognition of the importance of "powerful cultural and intellectual legacies [e.g., the ancient *Book of Change*]" by Perry and Heilmann (2011, 15) in their analysis of "guerrilla policy style."
3 Also see Dunstan (1996, 293–294, 327–333) on this point.
4 This period was chronicled in the *Spring and Autumn Annals*, sometimes attributed to Confucius, which gives it its name. Although the authenticity of Confucius's authorship is subject to debate, his life coincides with the time of writing (Li, 2013, 161).
5 This chapter relies on the translation of the *Guanzi* by Rickett (1998) as well as on relevant secondary sources.
6 Rickett (1998), in the comments of his translation of the *Guanzi*, discusses the dating of each section in detail. See also Chin (2014, 32–33) and von Glahn (2016, 77–78).
7 Hu (2009) suggests that "Li Kui was not only a well-known statesman but also the earliest thinker to emphasize agriculture" (180).
8 See Rickett (1998, 340) for elaborations on this passage.
9 The basic principles of this policy of grain price stabilization are repeated in almost all the *qingzhong* dialogues in the *Guanzi*. This is a summary of the basic principles by the present authors. Variations on this scheme include (1) the use of loans to the peasants paid out in spring in grain and pegged to the high money price to be paid back when the price of grain is low in the fall (*Guanzi* as in Rickett, 1998, 343–344, 377–380), as well as (2) the state purchase of clothes when they are cheap because grain is expensive; they are then sold by the state when clothes become expensive in the fall, at a time when grain is cheap (*Guanzi* as in Rickett, 1998, 362, 367, 384, 391). Similar, yet less encompassing, policy proposals had previously been put forward by Fan Li (Chen, 1911b, 568; Hu, 2009, 35–41; von Glahn, 2016, 64) and Li Kui (Chen, 1911b, 568; Hu, 2009, 179–184; Li, 2013, 190; Spengler, 1964, 228; von Glahn, 2016, 55).
10 In the light of this insight, the *Guanzi* is found to be one of the earliest articulations of the quantity theory of money (Hu, 2009, 131; Nolan, 2004, 129; Rickett, 1998, 4). If we consider the suggestions for countercyclical government spending, discussed later in this section, and the elaborations on hoarding, together with the grouping of different types of money according to their liquidity, a question for further research emerges: Might we find not only the earliest articulation of the quantity theory of money in the *Guanzi* but also, thanks to its focus on transitional effects, a precursor to the breaking of a pure quantity theory as in Keynes's (1936) *General Theory*?
11 Or, as Hu (2009) puts it, "The writer of *Guanzi* asserted that this inequality between rich and poor was an objective social reality, but his solution to the problem was merely to mitigate the antagonism, not to wipe it out entirely" (111).
12 Such great inequalities are, for example, reported in the *Han Shu* to have occurred in the period 246–207 BCE. After the selling and buying of land was allowed, some individuals became very rich and brought both land and natural resources under their control. The poor had to cultivate the land of the rich and "had to give five-tenths [of the crop] for rent (*shui*)" (*Han Shu* as in Swann, 1950, 182, insertion in original). "In profligacy and dissipation they [the rich] overrode government institutions; and they overstepped extravagance in order to outdo one another" (*Han Shu* as in Swann,

1950, 181). "Consequently the poor people wore at all times [garments in quality fit only] to be covering for cattle and horses. They ate, moreover food [of a standard suitable only] for feeding dogs and swine. ... The people, brought to grief, had no means of livelihood; and they became thieves and robbers" (*Han Shu* as in Swann, 1950, 182, insertion in original).

13 This proposal for a countercyclical policy of government spending clearly antici-pates, by 2000 years, Mandeville's (1970 [1724]) *Fable of the Bees*, Malthus's letters to Ricardo (as in Keynes, 1936, 362–363), and Keynes's theory of effective demand. In light of Keynes's 1912 review of Chen Huan-Chang (1911b), which contains a treat-ment of grain price policies (568–85), the question emerges whether Keynes might in fact have been inspired by ancient Chinese economic thinking.

14 Wagner (2001, 4–8) reviews archaeological and textual evidence from the Warring States to the Han Period pointing to some forms of state involvement or monopolies in the iron and salt industries.

15 The connection between the policy suggestions in the *Guanzi* and the economic policies of Sang Hongyang under Wu becomes apparent in the many attributed and unattributed references to the *Guanzi* in the *Debate on Salt and Iron*. See, for example, Gale (1931, 85–86); Hu (2009, 225, 260, 268, 271); Kroll (1978); Loewe (1985, 253); and Wagner and Needham (2008, 185, 189).

16 Wagner and Needham (2008) date the establishment of the Han iron monopoly to 117 BCE (172). See Wagner and Needham (2008, 172–174) for a discussion on state involvement in iron production in the pre-Han Period. According to their record, several of the Warring States were involved in iron production, especially the state of Qin, which later formed the administrative base of the empire. On this point, see also Swann (1950, 63). Hu (2009) suggests that the salt industry before 117 BCE was "chiefly carried on by private individuals" (264). The government was involved but did not hold a monopoly.

17 This system required relatively complex calculations in proportional distribution, which are documented in part in the *Debate on Salt and Iron* (Wagner and Needham, 2008, 191).

18 Wagner and Needham (2008, 188) point out that prior to the state monopoly, there were most likely two production techniques, one for small-scale production in remote areas for local needs and another for large-scale production for long-distance trade.

19 This group has posthumously often been labeled "the legalist school of thought." I abstain from using this label because of the variations in the visions for eco-nomic policies across different thinkers attributed to this school. The focus here remains on the approach represented in the *Guanzi* and further developed by Sang Hongyang.

20 Huan Kuan suggests that there was an actual meeting, with a face-to-face confronta-tion between sixty or so provincial scholars and worthies and the imperial counselor, Sang Hongyang, in the presence of the emperor and Huo Guang. Sources outside the *Debate on Salt and Iron* do not describe such an encounter but rather suggest that the exchange was conducted in writing (Wagner and Needham, 2008, 186).

21 In this debate, some of those persons challenging policy activism seemed to also have questioned a dominant role of the market and technology more broadly. Wagner and Needham (2008) find that the statesman Gong Yu demanded the abolition of money and a return to a natural economy without iron production, private or public (186).

22 Gale (1931) reviews the publication of various editions of the *Discourse on Salt and Iron* from the Song, to an 1891 edition on which he primarily bases his translation. See Loewe (2001) for a review of translations and subsequent Chinese editions.

23 See Huan Kuan (as in Gale 1931, 20–21) for an elaborate discussion on benefits from interregional trade resulting from different natural endowments.

24 See also Wagner (2001, 15) on this point.

25 Zhao and Drechsler (2018) argue that these policies constitute a form of proto-Keynesianism.
26 Dunstan (1996) contains an annotated translation of documents on political economy of the Qing Period that provides insights into the ways in which these questions were discussed.
27 For a detailed study of the workings and political governance of the eighteenth-century Qing granary system, see Will's (1990) seminal work.

2

FROM MARKET TO WAR ECONOMY AND BACK

American Price Control during the Second World War and Its Aftermath

After the last war [World War I] this Nation was confronted by much the same problem. At that time we simply pulled off the few controls that had been established, and let nature take its course. The result should stand as a lesson to all of us. A dizzy upward spiral of wages and the cost of living ended in the crash of 1920—a crash that spread bankruptcy and foreclosure and unemployment throughout the Nation.

(Radio Address of the President, October 30, Truman, 1945a)

Introduction

We saw in the previous chapter that China's traditions, both of the state regulation of prices and of the literati's critique of such an activist economic policy, date back to the Warring States Period. European and American traditions of economic theorizing on price control, too, are intimately connected with war. The practices and debates over price control peaked in the context of the two world wars and their aftermath. In this context, we find a confrontation between the insights of practical "price-fixers" and theoretical economists that parallels, to some extent, the one between the merchant bureaucrats and literati in the *Salt and Iron Debate,* which we discussed in the previous chapter.

At the same time, the abrupt and far-ranging postwar price liberalization is reminiscent of the big bang policy promoted in the context of transitions from socialism. In this chapter, I introduce the American debate over price control and decontrol in the time of the world wars as an important reference point in later market reform debates in socialist countries, China in particular. Through this comparison, I illustrate that while China can look back at a tradition of price regulation dating back to ancient times, there is nothing quintessentially

Chinese, traditional, or premodern about controlling prices. Yet, the practice of price regulation through state participation in the market, is revealed to be particularly prevalent in China.

Frank William Taussig (1859–1940), "one of the foremost U.S. economists for half a century" (Samuels, 2008) and celebrated by Schumpeter (1997 [1952], 220) as the "American Marshall" summarized his experience as a member of the Price-Fixing Committee during the First World War as follows:

> Government price-fixing during the war was not uniform in its objects, and was little guided by principles or deliberate policies. In the main it was opportunist, feeling its way from case to case. ... There was no more than a gradual and tentative approach to any principle of action whatever.
>
> *(Taussig, 1919, 238–239)*

Taussig found that within the limited scope of its application, price-fixing succeeded during the First World War in dampening violent fluctuations in the prices of important commodities such as food and fuel (ibid., 240). In Taussig's view, economists would formulate "[s]upply and demand, ... monetary laws ... in exact terms, with an appearance of mathematical sharpness" (ibid.). Yet "in any concrete application," there would be "abundant room for some exercise of restraining and deliberated action" (ibid., 240–241). Pure theory would suggest that the free interplay of supply and demand alone shall determine prices. In matters of practical policy price control by the state could be "of advantage to the country." But price controls cannot be guided by any precise laws only by the discretion of the price-fixing bureaucrats (ibid.).

In sharp contrast to the practical lessons drawn by one of America's leading "price-fixers," the so-called Socialist Calculation Debate of the interwar years sought to settle whether rational price control by a central planner was possible *in principle* (Cottrell and Cockshott, 1993; Hoff, 1949; Lavoie, 1985; Levy and Peart, 2008). In the light of the war experiences, the Russian Revolution, and a general perception that socialism was on the rise, the Socialist Calculation Debate asked whether an ideal-type planned economy could, in theory, rival an ideal-type market in determining equilibrium prices.[1] This question occupied the minds of some of the most prolific economists of the 1930s. It has also been revived in the context of socialist reform attempts, such as those in Poland and China in the 1950s and 1980s, respectively.

The Socialist Calculation Debate is only of limited usefulness to solve the practical problem of price control and decontrol. Maurice Dobb (1933, 589) observes that both sides of the debate subscribed to the fashion of treating "[e]conomics as a non-normative theory of equilibrium." They understand the discipline as defined by Lionel Robbins (1945 [1932], 16) as "the science which studies human behaviour as a relationship between ends and scarce means which have alternative uses." As a result, economics would "[n]o longer [supply] a collection of precepts in advice to the Sovereign, but a formal technique ...

postulating a formal relationship between certain quantities" (ibid.). From this vantage point, economics is "unconcerned with norms and ends: it is concerned solely with constructing patterns for the appropriate adaptation of scarce means to given purposes" (Dobb, 1933, 589–590). Consequently, economics in this definition is of little value to pressing practical problems of economic policy, including that of price-fixing in times of economic emergencies such as wars.

In fact, the type of economic science envisioned by Robbins that underpins the Socialist Calculation Debate did not gain great prominence during the Second World War for practical price-fixing. In this war, all major powers, with the exception of China (see Chapter 3), implemented price and wage controls that were far more comprehensive than those of the First World War: "Controls over prices and wages were the rule; freedom from such regulation was the exception" (Galbraith, 1980, 1). Some of the greatest economists of the twentieth century were involved in stabilizing the Second World War economies. Despite the new comprehensiveness of price controls, the policies were not based on a sophisticated theoretical principle but on the approach described by Taussig (1919, 238) as "feeling its way from case to case." Galbraith (1980, 45), the most prominent American price-fixer of the Second World War, described this as an evolutionary development "in the sense that the final structure was influenced less by an effort to build to an overall design than by a series of individual decisions."

This muddling through the Second World War is my subject in this chapter and provides a novel point of comparison with China's "feeling for stones" in the 1980s. I will focus on the United States to investigate how the approach to price controls advanced throughout the war and its aftermath. I have chosen to place the United States at the center of my attention since the practical necessity of price controls in wartime becomes clearest in the country commonly perceived as most dedicated to the free market and enterprise. But the US case is also important because the sudden decontrol of prices after the war prefigured the big bang price liberalization that was envisioned as pivotal to shock therapy in the context of the 1980s and 1990s transitions from socialism.

How to Pay for the War: Pondering Price Controls

> [T]he unanimity with which his [Keynes's] proposal was approved by economists and the fact that neither serious criticism of the basic idea nor a real alternative was offered are a remarkable tribute paid to the author by his colleagues. ... so far as the main outline of Mr. Keynes's proposal is concerned, this unanimity was almost complete.
>
> *(Hayek, 1940, 321–322)*

As we can see from this excerpt of a review by Hayek, who is often described as one of Keynes's fiercest adversaries, Keynes's *How to Pay for the War* (1940) set the tone for the reflections by professional economists on war finance and economic stabilization. Keynes stated both the basic parameters of the problem and its solution.

In his considerations of the war economy, Keynes radically departed from the principle of effective demand—the concept for which he is most famous.[2] Keynes had derived the importance of effective demand for the general case of peacetime in his *General Theory* (1936). But he did not believe that it applied to the special case of war. In the context of the Great Depression, one would "have become accustomed to a level of production which has been below capacity" (Keynes, 1940, 4). Under such conditions, Keynes argued, an expansion in expenditure induced an increase in production and, ultimately, an increase in consumption supply. This, however, Keynes believed, was not to be the case during the war: "[I]n war time, the size of the cake is fixed. If we work harder, we can fight better. But we must not consume more" (ibid.). As shown in this chapter, the American experience during the Second World War actually proved the contrary. According to Keynes, the reason for this difference was that, in times of war, all expansion of production is to supply the goods needed for the war: "The war effort is to pay for the war; it cannot also supply increased consumption" (ibid., 30). Hence, during wartime, Keynes thought we were back to the world of the classical economists (1936, 3), to the "Age of Scarcity" of the "'orthodox' economists" (Hayek, 1940, 322). Under these circumstances, "all aspects of the economic problem [were] interconnected. Nothing [could] be settled in isolation. Every use of resources is at the expense of an alternative use" (Keynes, 1940, 2).

Under conditions of war, Keynes argued, the government had to expand its spending and, before full employment of labor and capacity was reached, consumption goods became scarce in the sense that demand exceeded supply. This was the case because "[e]ven if there were no increases in the rates of money-wages, the total of money-earnings [would] be considerably increased" (ibid., 8). Keynes suggested that people previously unemployed or not in paid employment were drawn into military service or civilian war production and hence received a money wage. The aggregate wage fund increased, but it encountered roughly the same amount of consumption goods that had been available before that increase. Or, to put it differently, the problem of "how to pay for the war," from Keynes's viewpoint, was the question of how as many people as possible could be employed to contribute to the war effort without receiving an immediately increased enjoyment of consumption goods in return for their work.

In principle, Keynes indicated two feasible alternatives to his own plan for solving this problem. The first was based on the assumption that peacetime economic policies and taxation were, in essence, fit to serve the war economy and needed only to be complemented with propaganda to encourage voluntary saving (ibid., 58). Keynes saw this as a very unjust solution. He found it highly unlikely that voluntary savings were sufficient to limit the purchasing power in order to match the constrained consumption supply as well as to provide the necessary finance for the war effort (1940, 9, 28, 69). This scheme would imply a repetition of the policy of the First World War, which entailed a "sufficient degree of inflation to raise the yield of taxes and voluntary savings" (ibid., 58). But this would not actually be a *voluntary* saving. It would, rather, be "a method of *compulsory* saving, converting the appropriate part of the earnings of the worker which *he* does not save voluntarily into the voluntary savings (and taxation) of the entrepreneur" (ibid., 69, emphasis in original).

Keynes warned that inflation would be fueled by a price–wage spiral. As the economy approached full employment and the wage fund increased, prices would rise. If workers were compensated for the rising prices, this would put renewed pressure on the price level (ibid., 74). As a result of accelerating inflation, workers would be left without savings and without increased consumption enjoyments. Capitalists, on the other hand, would profit from the increasing prices and would become creditors to the government. Keynes cautioned that, after the war, the state would be left with very high debt in the hands of a few powerful and rich. The workers would have paid with their labor for the war but been left with nothing.

If Keynes's first alternative was on the laissez-faire end of the spectrum of policy choices, the second alternative sat on the opposite end. It was to "control the cost of living by a combination of rationing and price-fixing" (ibid., 51). Keynes took an equally critical stance toward this approach. It might be "a valuable adjunct" to his main proposal, but it would be "a dangerous delusion to suppose that equilibrium can [could] be reached by these measures alone" (ibid., 51).

In Keynes's eyes, price controls would not serve to effectively limit the excess purchasing power that resulted from the war-driven expansion of employment. "[I]t would never be practicable to cover every conceivable article by a rationing coupon" and, by the same token, to control all prices (ibid., 52). Therefore, Keynes suggested that the purchasing power would be redirected toward commodities, which remained uncontrolled because they attracted relatively little demand. The consumer would end up receiving what is "least desirable" while an overall excess demand remained and drove up the prices of these uncontrolled commodities (ibid.).

But even "if by a miracle the method [of price controls] was substantially successful, so that consumption was completely controlled and consumers were left with a significant fraction of their incomes which they were unable to spend" (ibid.), Keynes held that a "great deal of waste" would still have occurred as the consumers were deprived of their freedom to choose (ibid.): "The abolition of consumer's choice in favour of universal rationing is a typical product of that onslaught, sometimes called bolshevism, on differences between one man and another by which existence is enriched" (ibid., 53).

In sum, for Keynes, price controls and rationing were unlikely to be effective in containing the excess purchasing power. If, against his prediction, they were to be effective, the result would be an undesirable allocation of the limited supply of consumption goods.

Keynes promoted a third alternative, "a scheme of deferred pay," which he found superior under "consideration of public psychology, social justice and administrative convenience" (ibid., 58). The excess purchasing power of the wage earners should be withdrawn during wartime by forced saving with a government-run bank. This way, they would be rewarded after the war by "a share in the claims on the future which would otherwise belong to the entrepreneurs" (ibid., 74). Keynes thought that inflation would be contained by the resulting temporary reduction in aggregate demand. The same could be achieved by taxation, but in this case, the wage earner would be left without any individual claim on future wealth.

The plan of deferred pay should be assisted by very limited price controls and rationing, which would serve "to divert consumption in as fair a way as possible from an article, the supply of which has to be restricted for special reasons," such as the interruption of foreign trade (ibid., 53). Even under these conditions, such a diversion of demand should, according to Keynes, take the form of rationing and price control only "if this article is a necessary, an exceptional rise in the price of which [was] undesirable" (ibid., 54). For all other goods, demand should be checked by "the natural method" (ibid.) of a rising price in response to a limited supply.

Keynes's plan for deferred pay was the most prominent theoretical contribution to the question of war finance, not only in the United Kingdom but also in the United States (Galbraith, 1980, 5–6). Another important contribution more tailored to the specific conditions in the United States came from Alvin Hansen, an institutionalist and one of America's leading teachers of Keynesian thought at Harvard University (Hansen, 1941; Musgrave, 2008).[3]

Hansen (1941) departed to some extent from Keynes in his vision of price controls. For Hansen, "until an approach to full employment [was] reached … the main danger of inflation [was] in the development of bottlenecks" (ibid., 6) and, hence, these bottlenecks should be the primary target of anti-inflation policy. Hansen recommended that "the weapon of specific price increases where these may help eliminate bottlenecks" should be used when "provision of adequate plant and equipment capacity and … an adequate supply of skilled mechanics" was readily forthcoming (ibid.). In the event of a lack of such capacity and labor with regard to a specific bottleneck, however, direct price control and rationing could help prevent inflation.[4] Hansen saw the most serious of these bottlenecks in steel (ibid., 1). Thus, Hansen differed from Keynes by shifting attention from price controls on necessary consumption goods to those on production goods. While Keynes's plan relied almost entirely on the relationships between homogeneously perceived aggregates, Hansen considered the great asymmetries in sectorial production capacities and demand pressures.

In response to Hansen, Galbraith (1941) lifted the analysis of such heterogeneities in the form of the parallel existence of shortages and oversupply to a new level. Galbraith, too, emphasized the pressing need to prevent inflation, which had as a result of the First World War been an "almost paranoiac concern in 1940 and 1941" (1981, 127). But neither Hansen's peacetime-inspired notion of bottlenecks occurring in some few, singular places nor Keynesian considerations of some aggregate relations would serve to capture the dramatic change in requirements resulting from war and, hence, to understand the problem of war inflation. According to Galbraith, the problem of the war economy was "progressively more difficult" than these two notions suggest, and it entailed nothing less than a reorganization of the resources in the whole economy, which would face institutional and technical resistance. Under the circumstances of such restructuring, one would "encounter a steadily increasing number of industries where the supply function [would] be inelastic." As a result of these rigidities, Galbraith argued, there would be "price advances in the interim" and "[f]ull employment will have little or no relation to the appearance of inflation" (ibid., 83).

Nevertheless, Galbraith remained optimistic that "[r]easonably full use of resources without serious inflation can [could] be achieved." But, contrary to Keynes, in Galbraith's view, it was impossible to "rely entirely, or even in major part, upon measures which reduce[d] the general volume of spending in the economy" (ibid., 84). Such a reduction in aggregate demand had to be combined with direct measures to facilitate the industrial reorganization. This, according to Galbraith, had to include two main tasks: first, it was necessary to develop capacity, skills, and domestic sources of material supply to smooth the expansion of anticipated pressure points; second, "in the areas where resistance develop[ed] … specific price controls or price-fixing" supported by a degree of rationing was needed. These controls could not "be expected to be completely effective" but they would "check inflation without … curbing the consumption of commodities or the use of services which are plentiful" (ibid.) and would thus retain "a very desirable pressure for expansion of capacity and elimination of resistances" (ibid., 83). Thus, Galbraith believed in a role for Keynes's effective demand during wartime, while Keynes himself had declared his own theory inapplicable to this special case.

Galbraith later summarized in his memoirs the nature of his plan before getting involved in practical price-fixing: his "design required many more controls … than did that of Keynes or Hansen" (1981, 129). It was, as such, "a trifle more heretical," but it still relied heavily on balancing aggregate demand and supply by means of taxation and saving with only partial and auxiliary price controls. As such, Galbraith thought his plan stayed within "the limits of the larger Keynesian orthodoxy." The manuscript by the young Galbraith, a Canadian economist trained in agricultural studies and economics, challenged Hansen, his senior colleague in Harvard. It aroused great attention in Washington.

Leon Henderson was at the time heading the newly created Office of Price Administration (OPA)[5] (ibid., 124). He was a prominent economist in the Roosevelt administration, and his approach to economic policy "had the characteristic New Deal qualities of public activism, brash experimentalism, and aggressive rationalism" (Bartels, 1983, 8). Henderson had become involved in attempts at price stabilization when the prices of raw materials and industrial goods shot up after the German invasion in Poland, which he thought would impede the recovery of the American economy still suffering from the Great

Depression (Bartels, 1983, 7–8). In December 1941, when the United States entered the Second World War, Henderson immediately pushed for far-ranging controls to stabilize prices during the war effort and to prevent a boom–bust cycle after the war (War Records Section Bureau of the Budget, 1946, 239–240). Henderson, too, had become aware of Galbraith's writing and decided to offer him what would come to be called "the most powerful civilian post in the management of the wartime economy," second only to Henderson's own position (Galbraith, 1981, 124–125). Galbraith was put in command of all prices of the United States.

Practical Attempts at Price Controls in the United States

> The best, most elegant and most applauded designs can fail. … By early spring of 1942 … the extraordinarily logical model of wartime economic management that had brought me my considerable and welcome power was proving itself a disaster. That it had invited the support of the most sophisticated economists of the time would not mitigate the disaster; it would only provide me with excellent company in the debacle.
>
> *(Galbraith, 1981, 163)*

When Galbraith joined the OPA as deputy administrator of prices and took charge of prices operationally in April 1941, he took on a leading role in "the longest and most comprehensive trial [of price controls] in America's history" (Rockoff, 1984, 85). The totalitarian powers, Italy and Germany, had already introduced comprehensive price controls in 1936 (Rockoff, 1984, 86). America began with expanding but partial controls in May 1940 (ibid.). This involved an ever more complex design of commodity-specific price schedules as more and more areas of production were coming under high demand pressures (Bartels, 1983, 9).

The American price-fixers had to defend their selective price schedules on multiple fronts. They had to debate the high-powered economists with their theoretical considerations, negotiate fiercely with the industry bosses, and fight to be granted the necessary legal power from Congress. To the surprise of the price-fixers, for those commodities for which they published specific price schedules, the ceiling prices were well observed even before penalties could be imposed (Galbraith, 1981, 136, 164). By the fall of 1941, their informal controls effectively restrained about 40 percent of wholesale prices (Bartels, 1983, 9). But the task of determining commodity-specific prices for all relevant products, while allowing for a degree of flexible price adjustments, proved impossible.

The price-fixers were challenged by the complexity of input–output relations and "began to realize for the first time what an unreasonably large number of products and prices there were in the American economy" (ibid., 164). Further, they had overlooked the importance of "wage–push inflation—wages shoving up prices" (ibid., 142) rather than the other way around. The OPA, in line with the New Deal legacy, remained committed to the cause of the poor, the workers, and the farmers and initially tried to abstain from wage controls and strict price controls for agricultural goods. A mutually reinforcing upward pressure on wages as employment was expanding and, as a result, also on agricultural and industrial prices. This proved to be a great challenge to the effort of price stabilization (Bartels, 1983, 10–12).

Yet, a policy reminiscent of the Chinese Ever Normal Granary System (see Chapter 1) contributed somewhat to stabilize agricultural prices when, due to the many dispersed producers and political pressures, regular price control proved unfeasible. Since the New Deal and under the auspices of Henry A. Wallace, the United States had established a public granary and cotton stock system to absorb and redistribute surpluses—a system that was inspired by the agelong Chinese practice (Li, 2016). Public stocks of wheat, corn, and cotton were brought to the market in early 1942 in order to stabilize agricultural prices at parity and hence contain the pressure on wages (Barkley, 1942; War Records Section Bureau of the Budget, 1946, 249). But this policy, limited to staple agricultural products, was constrained by the availability of public stocks and faced severe attacks from agricultural interest groups.

Nevertheless, it became apparent that the effort of chasing individual prices, combined with a de facto exemption of wages, did not achieve a sufficient stabilization of the price level.[6] Despite the OPA's efforts, consumer prices had risen by 11.9 percent, and wholesale prices by 17.2 percent, in the course of the first year, from April 1941 to 1942 (Rockoff, 1984, 109). The pressure of inflation was much higher in the immediate aftermath of America's entry into the war than most economists had expected (Laguerodie and Vergara, 2008, 574). And, as Galbraith (1981, 163) remembered, the "beautiful Keynesian balance between total purchasing power and the aggregate of the goods and services to be purchased was like a rainbow, seen but never approached." In this situation, the OPA and Galbraith became amenable to the ideas of Bernard Baruch.

Baruch's voice was very different from that of most of the professional economists. Born in 1870, he had become rich in his early years on Wall Street and had gained influence as a political advisor to President Woodrow Wilson. He became chairman of the War Industries Board during the First World War and, as such, was also a member of the Price-Fixing Committee. Baruch experienced the challenges of controlling inflation firsthand (Baruch, 1960; Coit, 1958, 201–203; *Encyclopædia Britannica*, 2011). He lobbied for an overall price freeze in the Second World War. Instead of selective price controls, he believed that all prices should be pegged where they stood. This became known as the Baruch Plan (War Records Section Bureau of the Budget, 1946, 237–238).

Henderson, Galbraith, and their team, joined by celebrated economists such as Irving Fisher, had initially lobbied against the Baruch Plan. But about a year into Galbraith's work at the OPA, they had to admit that their own attempt at scientific price-fixing had failed to prevent the price level from rising rapidly (Galbraith, 1981, 164; Rockoff, 1984, 89, 91; Bartels, 1983, 13). On April 28, 1942, the General Maximum Price Regulation was imposed under the lead of the

OPA (War Records Section Bureau of the Budget, 1946, 43). All "prices legally within reach" were set a ceiling that was defined as "the highest charged [price] in March by that seller for the same item" (Galbraith, 1981, 165), and wages were brought under government control (Rockoff, 1984, 92). As Galbraith avouched, this policy "was far less elegant in conception than the ideas that it replaced," but it presented a considerable improvement over selective controls (ibid.). The new policy was based on given prices observed in the market within a certain time span, rather than trying to determine abstractly what the price for each commodity should be. By first gaining a firm hold over most of the price system, the OPA could gradually and partially let prices fluctuate where concrete economic conditions in one sector urged an upward or downward adjustment.

The overall rise in consumption prices decelerated to 7.5 percent in the year after the General Maximum Price Regulation was imposed (Rockoff, 1984, 109; also see Figure 2.1). The increase in prices of consumption goods controlled by the General Maximum Price Regulation was as low as 0.5 to 1 percent in the first five months. But Congress delayed its approval to lift limitations on controlling the prices of agricultural foodstuff. As a result, the General Maximum Price Regulation did not cover prices of key consumption goods such as flour, meat, eggs, and vegetables, which continued to rise sharply: The prices of these foods increased by 15.9 percent within the first five months (Mansfield, 1947, 51). Nevertheless, polls showed that despite these shortcomings, the price freeze was popular with the public (Parker, 2005, 151; Rockoff, 1984, 92; War Records Section Bureau of the Budget, 1946, 266).

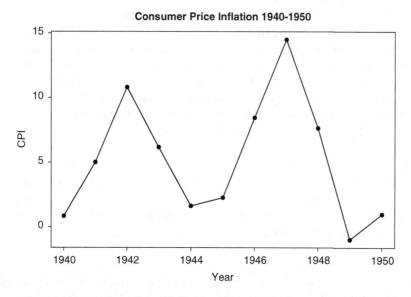

FIGURE 2.1 Consumer Price Inflation, 1940–1950. Source: *Economic Report of the President* (1958, 160); author's calculation.

Even though the General Maximum Price Regulation was more effective than selective controls, it also failed to stabilize the overall price level sustainably due to a lack of control over wages and agricultural prices. Following Henderson's initiative, Roosevelt finally received, in September 1942, backing from Congress for legislation to freeze farm prices at parity and to stabilize wages (Bartels, 1983, 15–16). This proved unpopular with both workers and farmers and caused severe losses for the Democrats in the congressional elections. As a consequence, Henderson had to resign in December 1942,[7] when, finally, the necessary legislative foundations for a coordinated stabilization effort were in place (War Records Section Bureau of the Budget, 1946, 387). On April 8, 1943, President Roosevelt issued an executive order to force an effective general price freeze. This policy was called "hold the line" and enforced that no "further increases in prices affecting the cost of living or further increases in general wage or salary rates" would be tolerated, "except where clearly necessary to correct substandard living conditions" (Roosevelt, 1943, as in Rockoff, 1984, 85).

With the executive backing of the "hold-the-line" order—and thanks to a great popularization effort to make dollar-and-cents price ceilings known to sellers and consumers—the OPA, under Henderson's successors Prentiss Brown and Chester Bowles, managed to halt inflation. The annual Bureau of Labor Statistics living cost index increased by less than 2 percent annually between spring 1943 and April 1945, or one-sixth the rate of the preceding two years. A committee under Wesley Mitchell found that some hidden factors, such as quality deterioration and black market prices, were not reflected in the official price index. But this discrepancy was marginal, and an impressive record of price stability remains (Mansfield, 1947, 56–57).

Notwithstanding this track record, consecutive price-fixers succumbed to political pressures. Despite the success and popularity of the price freeze, the OPA—and Galbraith personally—came under a severe attack by the business community, who lost great profit opportunities as prices stopped rising (Galbraith, 1981, 179–191; Parker, 2005, 150–152). Business leaders denounced Galbraith's "communist tendencies" during a congressional hearing (Parker, 2005, 152). By the end of May 1943, pressures had become so severe that Galbraith was sacked. On June 1, 1943, the front page of the *Washington Post* stated,

> Price Administrator Prentiss Brown yesterday announced the resignation of J. K. Galbraith, deputy administrator of OPA and in charge of the price section. Galbraith, a guiding star in much of OPA's policy-making to date, has been a target of bitter and continuing criticism from Congress and members of the trade group.
>
> *(Sandler, 1943)*

Galbraith was perhaps less mistaken than other famous economists who were already engaged in the theoretical debates; nevertheless, his initial plan was still not effective. Looking back on his life, Galbraith wrote: "Economics is not durable truth; it requires continuous revision and accommodation. Nearly all its error is from those who cannot change" (Galbraith, 1981, 125). Galbraith's great contribution the Second World War price stabilization lies in admitting his own mistake and forcefully implementing a pragmatic plan—one that he had earlier criticized. In parallel with Sang Hongyang's fate (see Chapter 1), Galbraith's price-control policies stayed in place after he had been forced to leave the center of economic policy-making (Harris, 1945, 10).

The Outcome of Price Controls in the United States

The benchmark for the OPA's work was to achieve greater price stability and higher output growth than occurred during the First World War. Year-by-year comparisons of the macroeconomic performance during the Second World War, relative to that of the First World War, were a common tool for evaluation as well as a public demonstration of the effectiveness of price controls (Mansfield, 1947, 82). At the end of the Second World War, the Harvard economist Seymour Harris (1945) delivered a careful empirical analysis of the detailed workings of price controls in the United States; his analysis documents the comparatively superior stabilization record. Harris suggests that "the most significant test of the success of any price-control program is its effects on production" (ibid., 11; see also Figure 2.2). As they were slowly put in place, in the later years of the war effort, the partial price controls of the First World War did help stop inflation from rising further. The experience of the First World War was one of inflation under lose price controls, while production stagnated; in the Second World War, price controls became strict, price rises were low, while the increase in output was almost beyond imagination.[8] This broad picture is in parallel to the diverging fates of Russia and China in the 1990s: wholesale price liberalization and hyperinflation on the one hand; regulation of essential prices, price stability and rapid output growth on the other (see Introduction).

Similarly, an evaluation of the effectiveness of price controls during the Second World War by the Cowles Commission for Research in Economics, based on a

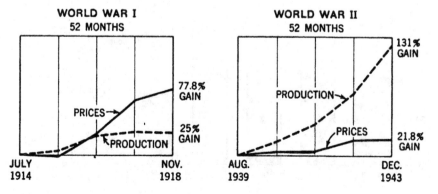

FIGURE 2.2   Industrial Production and Prices of Industrial Goods in Two World Wars. Source: Harris (1945, 34); data from Office of Price Administration.

case study of the Chicago area, concluded that price controls were effective in keeping prices down, while the author "found no support for the contention that total civilian production was lowered by price control to any substantial degree" (Katona, 1945, 225). In fact, in contrast with Keynes's assumption of a fixed "size of the cake" during wartime that necessitates the economics of scarcity (which might have been apt for Britain), the gross national product (GNP) of the United States almost doubled from 1940 to 1944: private capital formation declined but was more than compensated for by a dramatic expansion of government expenditures and a slight increase in consumer expenditures (see Figure 2.3).[9] Instead of crowding out private expenditures, government expansion drastically increased the size of the cake.

The consumption of durable goods such as automobiles and furniture declined, but personal savings rates more than tripled during the Second World War, from the prewar level of about 6 percent of GNP to more than 20 percent in the years 1942–1944 (Brunet, 2018, 33; Goldsmith, 1955, 62–65). Personal savings, which peaked at about USD 30 billion in 1945, was critical to closing the gap between the growth in purchasing power and that in the supply of consumption goods (Goldsmith, 1955, 63; Mansfield, 1947, 57). In the context of an increasing supply of consumption goods, effective rationing of scarce goods, and extremely high saving rates, black markets were by far not as pervasive as many had predicted, and quality deterioration was limited to a few products (Harris, 1945, 267; Galbraith, 1981, 171; Mansfield, 1947, 44–45). At the same time, corporate profits might not have skyrocketed in the ways some business leaders had hoped, and the profit rate fell during the war (Kalecki, 1949, 37, 40). But annual profits after taxes still more than doubled from 1939 to 1943, from USD 4 billion to USD 8.5 billion, as a result of the rapid expansion of GNP (Harris, 1945, 27).

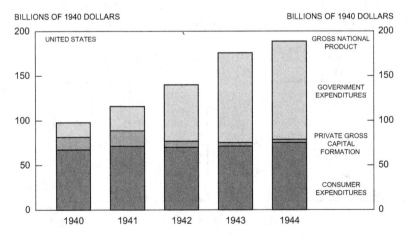

FIGURE 2.3   Gross National Product of the United States, 1940–1944 (in 1940 USD Billion). Source: War Records Section Bureau of the Budget (1946, 509).

In 1952, Galbraith wrote *A Theory of Price Control* to summarize his theoretical reflections on the workings of price controls.[10] Overall, he sticks with his "Lessons from the First Phase" (1943), where he states,

> [T]he strategy of control must involve a two-way move. Along with the controls over the growth of income from the side of taxation and savings there must be direct market controls. On this side the role of price control per se ... is strategic. No more than the economist ever supposed will it stop inflation. But it both establishes the base and gains the time for the measures that do.
>
> *(258)*

As we saw in the previous chapter, the Chinese pragmatist tradition of economic reasoning argued that economic policy had to take the prevailing conditions, rather than some ideal, as the starting point. For example, Sang Hongyang, in the *Salt and Iron Debate*, argued that it was due to the specific techniques of production that iron would be under a monopoly and, as such, subject to monopoly pricing. The question was whether iron was controlled by a private or a public monopoly—not whether or not it would be a monopoly. We find a similar line of argument in Galbraith. He suggests that price control, even without rationing, worked for many goods, partly because "it is relatively easy to fix prices that are already fixed" (Galbraith, 1980, 17). Hence, here—as in Sang Hongyang's discussion of iron production—the question is not whether prices are set by the state or determined in the free market, but whether they are fixed by government price controls or by market-dominating private producers.

According to Galbraith, the prevailing industrial structure of American capitalism at the outset of the Second World War was much further from the ideal of perfect competition than economists were able to believe: "The doubts of economists as to the technical workability of price control prior to World War II proceeded not from an error of analysis but from an error of assumption" (ibid., 25). There do exist markets with many buyers and sellers in which demand and supply functions are highly sensitive to prices, and in these markets, price controls were difficult to install and had to be backed by strict rationing. This type of market is typically in the more downstream industries, with larger product varieties. However, a large share of commodities is produced and traded under conditions of imperfect competition, with very few buyers and sellers. Under such conditions, suppliers set prices and ration goods to their customers. Hence, it is relatively easy for the price-fixer to dictate and enforce price controls and to let the supplier do the rationing (Galbraith, 1943). As a result, the OPA controlled, for example, "the prices of steel mill products with far less man power and trouble than was required for a far smaller dollar volume of steel scrap" (ibid., 17).

Following the logic set out by Keynes (1940), Galbraith (1980, 28) describes the war economy as a "disequilibrium system" in which aggregate demand exceeds supply. Under these conditions, frictional unemployment was eliminated and "approximately half of the real increase in gross national product between 1940 and 1944 has been attributed to individuals not normally in the labor market and to the increase in the average work week" (ibid., 32–33). Price controls and rationing would have contributed to limiting, not just redistributing, the demand pressure exerted by the resulting increase in individual incomes. This was the case because price controls stabilized the value of money and thus provided a critical condition for the public's willingness to save. The choice of demanding specific commodities—in particular, durables—was limited, and as a result "[i]ndividuals and firms who had no intention of saving became involuntary holders of cash or equivalents" (ibid., 36). This, however, did not induce labor or firms to withdraw their services as long as "public confidence that savings in any period will have high future value, either for the purchase of goods or for their contingency value for personal security" would be maintained (ibid., 39; Galbraith, 1981, 173). And, for this confidence, the price stability guaranteed by price controls was, in turn, crucial. As a result of such faith in their savings, people would hold money instead of hoarding goods, thus releasing the immediate pressure on demand.

In fact, as we have seen, personal savings increased dramatically during the Second World War. These savings represent the claim on civilian goods accumulated during the war (Galbraith, 1980, 52). The price-fixers at the OPA were acutely aware, from their study of the First World War, that the greatest inflationary pressure came after the war, and they were devising plans for the transition already in 1944 (Mansfield, 1947, 82). As Michał Kalecki pointed out (1947, 8–9), part of the challenge in the transition to a peace economy was figuring out how to channel the demand accumulated during the war as savings.

Galbraith argues an "economy that employs the disequilibrium system in wartime cannot make a direct transition to a peacetime free market" (ibid., 54). Time has to allow for the reorganization of the economy from its war structure toward the production of civilian goods, such that supply can slowly be adjusted to the excess demand. For this reason, Galbraith asserted, "controls, especially the price controls that inhibited spending during the war period and which accounted for the accumulation of the assets, must be continued for a period after the accumulation ceases" (ibid., 55). If controls are instead abruptly abolished and the accumulated consumption demand suddenly meets the still-limited civilian supply, the result will be inflation. It follows from Galbraith's argument that this would amount to depriving wage earners of their legitimate claim on production in return for their contribution to the war effort.

The Transition to a Peace Economy and the Lessons of the War Economy

On August 15, 1945, Japan announced its surrender. On August 18, the new President of the United States, Harry S. Truman, issued an executive order "for the orderly Modification of Wartime Controls" (Truman, 1945b). It stated the aim to "move as rapidly as possible without endangering the stability of the economy toward the removal of price, wage, production and other controls and toward the restoration of collective bargaining and the free market" (ibid.). As part of this order, direct wage controls were removed (Rockoff, 1984, 99). Truman was aware of the dangers of a hasty price increase as a result of decontrol, but he hoped to be able to relieve the direct controls *and* "hold the line" through voluntary cooperation with business leaders and trade unions (Truman, 1955, 423–424). This proved to be ineffective. Truman still reinforced his policy of decontrol in October 1945, but by December, he had come to realize that it did not work. He recalled in his memoir that at this point it had become obvious to him

> that decontrol of prices would not work, at least until the emergency was less threatening. ... The economy was certain to be plagued by warborn shortages for a considerable time and I urged further legislation to cover the period after June 1946.
>
> *(ibid., 423)*

In turning toward extending the period of compulsory price controls and a more gradual decontrol, Truman received support from the OPA (Rockoff, 1984, 100). Baruch, too, testified before Congress in favor of retaining price controls in the period of transition (Baruch, 1960, 385–386).

Fifty-four economists, including eleven former presidents of the American Economic Association and some of America's most famous economists—such as Arthur Burns, Edward Chamberlin, Irving Fisher, Alvin Hansen, Frank Knight, Simon Kuznets, Abba Lerner, Wesley Mitchell, Hans Neiser, Paul Samuelson, Henry Simons, Alan Sweezy, and Paul Sweezy—collectively published a letter in the *New York Times* on April 9, 1946. As we will see in Chapters 4 and 5, this letter foreshadows one side of the debate over price reforms in China in the 1980s:

> We urge upon Congress an extension of the Price Control Act for another year and without crippling amendments. ... Prices rise in response to an excess of demand or a deficiency of supply. Demand is likely to be unprecedented because of the excess of purchasing power. ... The supply of raw materials and consumer goods, at current demand, is inadequate to stave off serious inflation in the next year, unless price control is continued without crippling amendments. For the next six months numerous bottlenecks in raw materials, components and labor will have to be broken. And it will be a year before the flow of consumer goods in many markets reaches a peak. ... As soon as supply and demand of any important commodity are once more in balance at ceiling prices, price control should be suspended, and then removed. Ceilings on unimportant commodities should be removed as soon as there is no danger of diversion of scarce materials or manpower from important commodities.
>
> *(New York Times, 1946)*

Opinion polls showed that the general public strongly supported the plan of keeping price and wage controls (Rockoff, 1984, 101).[11] But it was to come about differently. The bill extending the price control contained so many "crippling amendments" that on June 29, Truman vetoed it, hoping for a bill that would keep price and wage controls in place more effectively (Truman, 1955, 425). In Truman's radio address on the same day, he stated:

> I wanted to sign a price control bill. I gave this bill long and careful study. I came to the conclusion that the bill which the Congress sent me was no price control bill at all. It gave you no protection against higher and higher prices.
>
> *(Truman, 1946)*

However, while the crippled bill was rejected, a more comprehensive one was never passed. So the wartime price controls were terminated (Mansfield, 1947, 100–101). Truman himself attributed this debacle to the "obstructionist tactics of special privilege groups," who would have exerted so much pressure and lobbying that the Congress was induced to let the Price Control Act expire (Truman, 1955, 424).

The sudden end to almost all price controls did, in fact, cause the inflationary rise in prices the President, the OPA staff, and the letter by economists had predicted (Kalecki, 1947, 1949; Krock, 1946; also see Figure 2.1). Some key input commodities, such as steel scrap, copper, tin, and rubber, still had their prices set by the government, and rents, sugar, and rice remained controlled (Mansfield, 1947, 101; Truman, 1955, 426). But, irrespective of this, prices rose rapidly after the failure to renew the Price Control Act. The annual overall price increase had been an average 2.3 percent per year for the period April 1943 to June 1946, the "high-tide of controls" (Rockoff, 1984, 109). In contrast, an index of twenty-eight important commodities rose by 35 percent within only the first six days of July 1946 (ibid.). Overall, commodity prices rose at a rate, within the first month without controls, that would have amounted to an annual increase of 67.4 percent. There were some aborted attempts toward recontrol in the following months, and some temporary selective controls were reintroduced, only to be abolished shortly afterward (ibid.; Mansfield, 1947, 98–102). The overall annual inflation rate remained well above 10 percent and consumer price inflation reached 14.5 percent in 1947 (Harris, 1945, 34, Figure 2.1).

Michael Kalecki (1947, 1949) analyzed postwar inflationary tendencies in the United States and other countries on behalf of the United Nations Department of Economic Affairs.[12] He showed that, in particular, the prices of essential raw materials and foodstuff, for which the respective demand by producers and consumers is inelastic, shot up (Kalecki, 1949, 38). Wage increases did not compensate for the increase in the cost of living, so price decontrols resulted in a decline in real incomes for workers. Real labor incomes had declined 8 percent by the first half of 1947, as compared with the first half of 1946 (ibid., 39). At the same time, profit margins increased, and there was a shift of gross private income from labor to capital. In the course of the war, labor had increased its share. By the first half of 1946, labor still accounted for 61.5 percent, which declined to 58.8 percent by the first half of 1947. Conversely, gross corporate profits rose from 11.6 to 14.0 percent (ibid., 40). The rapid decrease in workers' purchasing power, the redistribution of income, and the devaluation of their wartime savings unleashed the greatest wave of labor strikes of the US postwar decades (Hibbs, 1976, 160; Richter and Montgomery, 1994, 48–50). The volume of labor strikes in 1946 was about three times as high as its previous peak during the Great Depression (Hibbs, 1976, 160).[13]

The immediate postwar years saw a short, inflationary boom paired with labor unrest, followed by a sharp downturn. The United States failed to avoid the boom–bust cycle Truman had feared (Rockoff, 1984, 109; Kalecki, 1947, 1, 16–17). In November 1948, the US economy "stood at the peak of the inflationary boom" (*The Economic Report of the President*, 1950) and entered an eleven-month-long recession (NBER, 2012). The partial remobilization in the Cold War helped the US economy escape a financial crash, of which Truman and the American public were so afraid.

A brief comparison with the United Kingdom shows that the American inflation, boom–bust cycle, and social unrest were *not* without alternative. In contrast to the transition in the United States, the United Kingdom took a substantially more gradual path. As Alec Cairncross, who himself was involved in economic management in the war's immediate aftermath and contributed to the Chinese price reform debate in 1985 (see Chapter 7), summarized: "Nearly all the controls over the economy introduced in the course of the war were continued at the end of the war" (Cairncross, 1985, xiii, 333). All essential foodstuffs and scarce consumption goods, such as clothing and furniture, continued to be fully rationed (Kalecki, 1949, 29). There was agreement among the British Conservatives, Liberals, and Labour that some degree of these controls was indispensable (ibid., 300). Price controls at the end of the war had not been as comprehensive in the United Kingdom as in the United States, but also "[n]o appreciable relaxation took place until 1949–50 when some of the least effective parts of price control … were abolished" (ibid., 335). Derationing and decontrol were implemented as shortages of specific commodities were eased by increased supply (Kalecki, 1949, 31). By 1960, practically nothing remained of the controls (Cairncross, 1985, 333). They had been gradually abandoned (ibid., 343).

As Cairncross points out, this transition reflected the changing role of the government during peacetime as compared with wartime. During the war, the government directly allocated resources and planned and coordinated the production for the war effort. After the war, consumer demand would again be decisive for production decisions (ibid.). Thus, "economic planning by the government was necessarily limited to efforts to achieve specific macro-economic objectives such as stability of employment and prices, except to the extent the government chose to impose its own view of social priorities" (ibid., 344). Like

Galbraith, Cairncross suggests the following rationale for maintaining controls in the course of this transition:

> So long as supply and demand were seriously out of balance at current prices and it would have required a large increase in price to restore the balance, there was a case for maintaining control in order to reduce the risk of inflation. The case was all the stronger if there was every prospect of a gradual recovery of the supply at the going price so that the control could be relaxed progressively until it became redundant.
>
> *(ibid., 345)*

Due to the devastated state of the British economy after the war and a very large foreign deficit, inflationary pressures were arguably higher in the United Kingdom than in the United States. The United Kingdom, like the United States, faced considerable pent-up demand in the form of liquid assets, while shortages of certain essential foodstuff were acute (Kalecki, 1949, 29). Kalecki (1949, 30) argues: "In the absence of the system of controls, these factors would have resulted in open inflation." Yet, consumer price inflation never passed the 8 percent mark in the 1940s (Cairncross, 1985, 40), and labor's share in gross private income declined only slightly (Kalecki, 1949, 30). The sharp upward movement in prices following the sudden removal of price controls in the United States had been avoided in the United Kingdom, where overall inflation remained moderate. As a result, in the United Kingdom, no drastic redistribution from wages to profits occurred, and labor strikes were rare, compared with the strike waves of other countries right after the war as well as the UK's own history of labor uprisings during the Great Depression and the late 1960s (Hibbs, 1976, 160).

The case of the United Kingdom illustrates that a more gradual transition policy delivered better results in terms of price and social stability. In contrast, as I have argued elsewhere (Weber, 2020b, 2021), the case of West Germany, more specifically Ludwig Erhard's currency and price reform, is frequently invoked by neo- and ordoliberal economists as evidence for the effectiveness of overnight price liberalization of the type that resulted in a boom–bust cycle in the United States. The so-called "miracle" produced by Ludwig Erhard was cited as proof of the wonders that a big bang could achieve. It was touted by leading politicians such as Leszek Balcerowicz and Helmut Kohl as well as by prominent economists such as Milton Friedman and Jeffrey Sachs in the transition debates of Eastern Europe, Germany, Russia, and—as we will see—also of China.[14]

But recent scholarship, mainly in the German language, in particular Fuhrmann's (2017) detailed study of the immediate aftermath of price liberalization, challenges the narrative of an instantaneous success delivered by the miracles of the market. Instead, it asserts that the impact of price liberalization on the price level and social stability was similar to that in the United States. Fuhrmann's research shows that even though Erhard's overnight price liberalizations in June 1948 excluded many essential consumption and industrial goods and also rents, the price reform nevertheless caused an upshot in inflation that resulted in a general strike and ultimately in a turn from a free to a social market economy.[15]

To bring the economy back under control, the production of decontrolled essential consumption goods such as shoes and textiles, as well as of agricultural machines, was brought under the so-called "Jedermann Programm" by late 1948. This program created a centrally planned core of the economy for which inputs were allocated by the government to private enterprises and which were sold by private merchants at state-fixed prices. Beyond the production of commodities under this program, enterprises had to source their inputs at market prices and could sell to consumers at market prices (Fuhrmann, 2017, 244–252, 264–296). Essentially, the German transition policy followed a dual-track pattern with a planned core and a market-coordinated periphery.[16] This German program bears surprising similarities, even though implemented for a much shorter time and on a much smaller scale, with the dual-track system that emerged in China's reform (see Chapters 5 through 8).

The Attack on and the Recurrence of Price Controls

In the United States, as in other countries, the battle over price controls between business associations such as the National Association of Manufacturers (NAM) and price fixers was carried out not only in Congress and in backdoor meetings but also openly in the press.[17] More broadly, the postwar economic order was to be defined at this critical juncture. In this context, members of the community of businessmen who were "delighted to learn of the work of Friedrich Hayek and Ludwig von Mises, … helped to form a supportive network for the Austrian thinkers in America" and, in 1947, to found the Mont Pelerin Society, with the long-term goal of shifting the academic and public discourse in favor of the free market (Phillips-Fein, 2009, 281; Slobodian, 2018, 126–128).

Even before the war was over, Hayek (1944) had published *The Road to Serfdom*, which was to become an important reference for neoliberals across the world in the decades to come.[18] Had Hayek supported Keynes's plan for war finance, which involved a considerable degree of central planning of production and at least a limited role for price controls, none of that would, in his view, have had any role to play in a free society in peacetime.[19] Not only must central planning lead to fascism, but any concession to central guidance would lead down this dangerous path:

> The idea of complete centralisation of the direction of economic activity still appalls most people, not only because of the stupendous difficulty of the task, but even more because of the horror inspired by the idea of everything being directed from a single center. If we are nevertheless rapidly moving towards such a state this is largely because most people still believe that it must be possible to find some Middle Way between "atomistic" competition and central direction.
>
> *(Hayek, 1944, 43)*

Hence, only two ways of organizing economy and society are possible for Hayek: either central planning, which must imply totalitarianism, or a free society with free competition. There is no middle ground, only the choice between a good and a bad ideal-type. Or, as Keynes wrote in a letter to Hayek—which is, in parts, very appreciative of Hayek's latest book:

> I should guess that according to my ideas you greatly under-estimate the practicability of the *middle course*. ... [Y]ou are trying to persuade us that so soon as one moves an inch in the planned direction you are necessarily launched on the *slippery path* which will lead you in due course over the precipice.
>
> *(Keynes, 1980 [1944], 386–387, emphasis added)*

For Hayek (1944, 38), "competition as principle of social organisation" makes it

> necessary in the first instance that the parties in the market should be free to sell and buy at any price at which they can find a partner to the transaction, and that anybody should be free to produce, sell, and buy anything that may be produced or sold at all.

The price mechanism being the core of competition, state regulation of prices would obstruct the base of social organization:

> Any attempt to control prices or quantities of particular commodities deprives competition of its power of bringing about an effective coordination of individual efforts, because price changes then cease to register all the relevant changes in circumstances and no longer provide a reliable guide for the individual's actions.
>
> *(ibid.)*

Hence, price control amounts to nothing less than depriving a free society of its mechanism of economic coordination. This is the *Road to Serfdom*. According to Hayek, "[f]ew catchwords have done so much harm as the ideal of a 'stabilization' of particular prices (or wages)" (ibid., 134).

Hayek acknowledges the prevalence of monopolies. But—in contrast to Galbraith or Sang Hongyang and somewhat in agreement with the literati of the *Salt and Iron Debate*—he perceives most monopolies to be a creation of state interference limiting natural competition (ibid., 133–134). Hence, if monopoly prices are fixed, as Galbraith asserts, they are so because the state prevents the regulatory function of the price mechanism from working effectively by shielding certain firms and sectors from competition. In the few cases where "monopoly is inevitable," such as railroads, it would be still better to have "the different monopolistic industries ... in different private hands rather than combining them under the single control of the state" (ibid., 202–203).

In December 1945, Ludwig von Mises, another Austrian economist, recent émigré to the United States and initiator of the Socialist Calculation Debate, delivered his stance on the question of price controls, which is celebrated by the Mises Institute (2005) as "critically important ... during the public debate concerning whether and to what extent these controls should be reduced following the war." Von Mises (1974a [1945]) invokes an idealized vision of free competition similar to Hayek's[20] and spells out Hayek's "slippery slope" argument for any selective price control. All that government price ceilings for a particular commodity would do is limit its supply, contrary to the intentions of the consumers who had driven the price up by demanding more than that was currently available. But if "this unpleasant experience does not teach the authorities that price control is futile and that the best policy would be to refrain from any endeavors to control prices" (ibid., 74), von Mises suggests that the controls must necessarily spread until they cover the whole economy:

> The supply of those factors of production whose prices have been limited shrinks. Then again the government must expand the sphere of its price ceilings. It must fix the prices of the secondary factors of production required for the production of those primary factors. Thus the government must go farther and farther. It must fix the prices of all consumers' goods and of all factors of production, both material factors and labor.
>
> *(ibid.)*

Hence, for von Mises (1974b [1950], 22–24), just as for Hayek, a "middle-of-the-road policy leads to socialism" and government control of, for example, the milk price appears to be enough to initiate a slip into central planning and destroy free competition.

Despite such full-fledged theoretical attacks, price controls, whether effective or not, were a repeatedly used policy in the United States in the decades to come. Price controls were reintroduced during the Korean War and in the years 1971–1973 by Nixon in the context of the Vietnam War. The prices of some commodities—including milk—still remain under government control (Mihm, 2017; Mills, 1975; Rockoff, 1984). The persistence of price controls encouraged Milton Friedman's numerous attacks in a multitude of publications (e.g., Friedman, 1952, 1977; Friedman and Friedman, 1980; Friedman and Schwartz, 1963).

Hayek submitted to the need of controls for the special case of wartime. In contrast, Friedman argues that the result of direct price control from ancient times onward "has always been the same: complete failure" (ibid., 17–18). For Friedman, "[i]nflation is always and everywhere a monetary phenomenon, resulting from and accompanied by a rise in the quantity of money relative to output" (ibid., 18). Hence, the only way to stop inflation is to stop the quantity of money from increasing. Friedman believes that "people are so stubborn about the amount they hold in the form of money" (ibid., 29) that whenever the overall quantity of money increases, they simply spend this additional amount rather than increasing their money holdings. Prices will rise and inflation will occur. Under such conditions of excess money, if the government controls the price of one commodity—for example, steel—all that will happen, in Friedman's view, is that the pressure of money demand will be exerted on other commodities. The supply of steel would fall since, with the artificially low price, the producer cannot afford to produce more. Those who cannot satisfy their demand for steel, in Friedman's logic, will turn to other materials as substitutes (ibid., 20).

This line of reasoning has been challenged by Galbraith's (1980) analysis of the experience of the Second World War. As discussed, Galbraith has shown that producers in highly concentrated markets such as steel have rationed, rather than limited, their supply in light of price ceilings, in order to maintain their relation with long-term customers. At the same time, for some technologies, steel cannot be substituted with other materials in the short run. As we have seen, rather than holding a constant amount of money, individuals increased their annual savings by more than a factor of 10 in the war years. Hence, consumers chose to withhold large parts of their consumption demand instead of shifting their demand to substitutes.

Friedman invokes the analogy of a "steam-heating furnace running full blast." Let us use this to carve out the basic difference in Galbraith's and Friedman's logic. Friedman summarizes his argument against direct controls as follows:

> Controlling the heat in one room by closing the radiators in that room simply makes other rooms still more overheated. Closing all radiators lets the pressure build up in the boiler and increases the danger that it will explode. Closing or opening individual radiators is a good way to adjust the relative amount of heat in different rooms; it is not a good way to correct for overfueling the furnace.
>
> (Friedman, 1966, 20)

For Friedman, once the furnace is overheated, it is better to let it warm the whole house than to suppress the heat: "suppressed inflation is worse than open inflation" (ibid., 31). Suppressed inflation is not only ineffective but the imposition of controls—as in von Mises and Hayek—must lead to central planning. If suppressed inflation has built up as a result of price controls, there is no other way but to go through the boom–bust cycle. After the whole house has been overheated, one has to cool the whole house down: "Any effective policy to stop inflation will be painful. Once inflation gets the start it has here, there is simply no way to stop it without a slowdown in the economy and probably a recession" (Friedman, 1973, 65).

In contrast, Galbraith suggests that we should not sit and wait for the whole house to first overheat and then become an ice palace, in the course of which its inhabitants will go through great suffering. Instead, we should carefully study the flows of the heat and the structure of the house. There might be some rooms in which we can open a window. We can turn the radiator on full steam in these rooms to release pressure and turn them to a lower level in the rooms where no window can be opened. This will not fix the problem in the furnace, but it will keep the house at a livable temperature while a way can be found to fix the furnace.

Galbraith appeals to common sense. Friedman, in contrast, dismisses the capability of the layman for reasoned judgment: "To the despair of every economist, it seems almost impossible for most people other than trained economists to comprehend how a price system works" (Friedman and Friedman, 1980, 220). Friedman routinely denounced "Galbraith [as] a 'socialist' or worse"[21] (Parker, 2005, 483) and even took the trouble of writing a whole book to undermine the popularity of Galbraith's economic reasoning (Friedman, 1977). In the times of British Prime Minister Margaret Thatcher and US President Ronald Reagan, Friedman largely succeeded at convincing experts and the public that price controls could never be of any use. Subsequently, at a time when Friedmanite economics was at its zenith in the immediate aftermath of the breakdown of the Soviet Union, Galbraith reminded us of the deeply unethical underpinnings of this outlook on economics. This approach to economic policy-making, he said, would be based on the

> casual acceptance of—even commitment to—human deprivation, to unemployment, inflation, and disastrously reduced living standards. This is even seen as essential therapy: out of the experience of unemployment and hunger will come a new and revitalized work ethic, a working force eager for the discipline of free enterprise.[22]
>
> *(Galbraith, 1990)*

As we will see in the second part of this book, this is the logic of shock therapy.

Conclusion

In his research paper "Reflections on the Invisible Hand," delivered in the context of the election campaigns of Tony Benn and Margaret Thatcher, Frank Hahn (Hahn, 1981, 2) finds that both those believing in the omnipotent power of the visible and the invisible hand "take it for granted that somewhere there is a theory, that is a body of logically connected propositions based on postulates not wildly at variance with what is the case, which support their policies." The same assumption underlaid both sides in the Socialist Calculation Debate of the interwar period and the economic orthodoxy at the time. However, during the Second World War, even the self-declared pioneer of free enterprise, the United States, retreated to a pragmatic approach in its use of the visible hand and controlled, among other things, most prices and wages to finance the war while achieving low inflation. Not only had the ideal of purity of the invisible hand been given up, but, more fundamentally, it had been acknowledged that there is no such "theory, that is a body of logically connected propositions" that serves to draw up a comprehensive blueprint for economic policy. Instead, one had to apply "the wishy-wash, step by step, case by case approach," which Hahn recommended as "the only reasonable one in economic policy" (1981, 27).

As Galbraith (1980, ii) observed, this change in attitude was not to last in peacetime:

> Although the World War II experience was generally and in many ways unexpectedly successful, it did not greatly attract the attention of economists. While many from the profession were involved, when the war was over most turned back with relief not only to their colleges and universities but to the textbook economics and the uncontrolled markets that seemed the peacetime norm.

As business associations successfully lobbied for a quick end to price controls in 1946, they allied with economists who relaunched their campaign for the undisrupted invisible hand. Von Mises, Hayek, Friedman, and others insisted that any form of direct price controls would lead down the slippery slope to central planning and to the end of any freedom. It took until the 1980s for this belief in pure competition, encapsulated in the magic of the price mechanism, to gain prevalence in the public mind. But even then, certain price controls—such as in the energy sector, agricultural produce, rents, and minimum wages—were retained.

When the crisis of the socialist command economies brought up the question of how to reform in the 1980s, the proponents of the mutual exclusiveness of the visible hand and the invisible hand suggested that there was only the choice between the good ideal-type of the free market and the bad ideal-type of central planning. The latter had been proven wrong by history, they argued. Hence, this was a "choice of no choice." As had been proclaimed for decades, any concession to price controls—even if it was only for the price of milk or bread—must lead back to central planning. Thus, from this perspective, the only way was to move toward free prices in one big bang. This was the fate of the former Soviet Union and many Eastern European countries. China escaped such a big bang by reverting to harnessing of spontaneous forces by the state, which can be analyzed from the standpoint of a long tradition in Chinese statecraft. In other words, the *invisible hand was introduced under the guidance of the visible hand*. This process of market creation will be the subject of the second part of this book.

Notes

1 The initiating attack was launched by the Austrian economist Ludwig von Mises (1963 [1920]) in the interwar period, which he perceived as an "age in which we are approaching nearer and nearer to socialism" (88). Von Mises claims that a rational socialist economy is inconceivable since the price problem cannot be solved (von Mises, 1963, 104). Robbins (1934) and Hayek (1935), however, retreat to a "second line of defense" (Lange, 1936, 36) and reduce the problem to one of theoretical practicability, not of abstract possibility. For them, the price-determining system of

equations could be solved in principle, but the calculations would take too much time to be of any practical value. Finally, Lange (1936), one of the pioneers of a formal vision of market socialism, suggests "there is not the slightest reason why a trial and error procedure, similar to that in a competitive market, could not work in a socialist economy" (67). In Lange's view, there is no theoretical reason why the socialist economy with public ownership should fall short of the market economy with private ownership in determining optimal prices.

2 This contrasts with the view expressed by the ancient economic advisor Sang Hongyang, who saw a role for expansionary government spending also in the context of war (see Chapter 1).

3 But note that Hansen was not simply disseminating Keynes's thought; rather, he had independently developed some of the insights that came to be known as "Keynesian." For a systematic comparison of Hansen and Keynes, see Mehrling (1998, 130–136).

4 Hansen (1941) also challenges Keynes's plan of forced saving, stating "that probably it would not be acceptable to wage-earners." He suggests instead a state-sponsored voluntary saving scheme, complemented with consumption taxation (ibid., 6). In contrast to Keynes, Hansen sees a need for rigorous measures to withdraw purchasing power only after full employment is approached. He seems to overlook Keynes's crucial argument on the incremental increase of the wage fund.

5 This was initially called Office of Price Administration and Civil Supply (OPACS). To avoid confusion, I am using only the later and more widely known abbreviation, OPA.

6 For a detailed chronological account of the development of the OPA's efforts at price stabilization, the concrete techniques applied, and the challenges faced, see Mansfield (1947).

7 For a letter by Galbraith to Henderson at the occasion of his resignation, see Holt (2017, 38–39).

8 Harris's analysis is broadly consistent with the much more detailed descriptive statistical analysis of price and output indicators by Simon Kuznets (1945).

9 For a detailed comparative survey of assessments of the US production possibilities and the restructuring and growth of GNP during the Second World War, see Edelstein (2015).

10 Friedman (1977), in his book-length critique of Galbraith, credits Galbraith with being "the only person who has made a serious attempt to present a theoretical analysis to justify his position [on price controls], in a book called *A Theory of Price Control* he wrote not long after World War II. I happen to think that the analysis is wrong, but at least it is a serious attempt to provide a basis for a point of view" (12). Colander (1984) shows that Galbraith thought, although this was his best book, it had reached only an extremely small readership.

11 At the time, the topic of decontrol was of such great public interest that it served as a setting for a detective novel by Stout Rex (1946), *The Silent Speaker*. The novel is modeled on the conflict between the OPA and the US Chamber of Commerce and the National Association of Manufacturers. The director of the fictional price regulation bureau is killed, allegedly on behalf of the business interests.

12 I am grateful to Michael Kuczynski for bringing to my attention these two important analyses of inflation in the immediate aftermath of the war and the fact that this research was conducted by Michael Kalecki. I have consulted these reports, which are part of the Piero Sraffa papers at Trinity College, Cambridge. They contain a note that indicates Kalecki sent the reports to Sraffa. For an overview of Kalecki's contributions to the debate over the transition from a war economy—in particular, the UK, Canadian, and Polish cases—see Chapter 9 of the second volume of Toporowski's intellectual biography (2018).

13 Hibbs (1976, 156) defines strike volume as "man-days lost from strikes per thousand non-agricultural civilian employees."

14 For a detailed analysis of the role of the "Erhard Miracle" in China's reform debate, see Weber (2020, 2021).

15 See, for example, Abelshauser, 2004; Nicholls, 2000; and Zündorf, 2006a,b.

16 This dual approach to economic governance was theorized by Kromphardt (1947).

17 See, for example, Tower (1946) in the *New York Times*, February 19. Tower reports that the new director of OPA, Bowles, called the National Association of Manufacturers "an irresponsible group," while the NAM accused Bowles of discrediting "an association made up of thousands of companies from every State in the union and who turn out 85 percent of the nation's production and manufactured goods."

18 The book was first published in England and subsequently as an article in *Reader's Digest*. For a detailed account of the publication and reception history, see Burgin (2012, 87–94).

19 As Pigou summarizes in his review of Hayek, "For a State engaged in a modern war this method [central planning] is unavoidable. It is impossible to make effective war without it and, therefore, whatever the evils associated with it, they must be accepted to obviate a worse evil-military defeat. But in times of peace we are under no such compulsion" (Pigou, 1944, 218).

20 "In the free economy … coordination of the various individuals' activities, and their integration into a harmonious system for supplying the consumers with the goods and services they demand, is brought about by the market process and the price structure it generates" (von Mises, 1974a, 72).

21 Galbraith's biographer, Richard Parker (2005), suggests that this claim was "always softened for Galbraith by the fact that Friedman also deemed Social Security and the income tax 'socialist'" (483).

22 For a critique of shock therapy and an alternative transition proposal inspired in parts by Galbraith's price-fixing experience, see Galbraith (1992).

3

RE-CREATING THE ECONOMY

Price Stabilization and the Communist Revolution

New China, led by the Chinese Communist Party, successfully checked in less than one year the 12-year old rampant inflation left over from the old society. ... The situation at that time was so compelling that the bourgeoisie had no choice but to bow in submission.

(Liu and Wu, 1986, 37–38)

The government of communist China is achieving price control. ... Control of daily necessities, raw materials and fuel supply prices is maintained by buying when prices are falling and selling when prices are rising. A balanced market is maintained in this way.

(Central Intelligence Agency on China, 1952)

Introduction

Hayek's slippery slope argument holds that the imposition of price controls must lead to totalitarianism (see Chapter 1). In sharp contrast, two of the most fundamental political shifts of the twentieth century—the rise of German fascism and the victory of the Chinese Communists—were prepared by the loss of control over the price and currency system, culminating in hyperinflation.[1] In his foreword to Bresciani-Turroni (1937 [1931]), Lionel Robbins (1937, 5) wrote:

The depreciation of the mark of 1914–23 ... is one of the outstanding episodes in the history of the twentieth century. Not only by reason of its magnitude but also by reason of its effects, it looms large on our horizon. ... Hitler is the foster-child of the inflation.

In his classic study *The Chinese Inflation 1937–1949* (1963, xi), Chou Shun-Hsin observed that Robbins's comment could equally be applied to China. In Chou's analysis, as in that of most commentators, independent of political orientation, "inflation was a major cause of the downfall of the Nationalist government and the rise of Communism in mainland China" (ibid.).

As much as inflation helped the downfall of the Nationalists, the success of the Communists in enforcing price stability within a matter of months after the inauguration of the new government was an important source of their legitimacy (Fairbank, 1983, 346; Hsia, 1953, 25; Tsakok, 1979, 865; Pepper, 1999, 95–131). The Communists' rapid success in overcoming hyperinflation defeated the pessimistic predictions of the major capitalist powers, which, as the last chapter showed, were struggling to stabilize their own general price levels after the Second World War (Ling and Lei, 1959, 34).

In China's long history, dynastic cycles have frequently been in sync with cycles in monetary stability (Chang, 1958, 3; Eckstein, 1977, 160–161; Fairbank, 1983, 80–105). In imperial times, a ruler who gained control over the currency was believed to be exercising the "Mandate of Heaven"—exerting his power rightfully on behalf of divine forces while fulfilling the moral obligation to serve the people. When Chen Yun, then chairman of the government's Financial and Economic Commission and possibly the most important economic leader of the Chinese Communists, assessed the Communists' economic work at the thirtieth anniversary of the party in 1951, he singled out the stabilization of the value of money as the most important achievement (Wu, 1956, 64). No doubt, the victory against hyperinflation consolidated the Communist government's rule and was symbolically important for its power.

I argue that a key element in the Communists' success in overcoming hyperinflation in the late 1940s and early 1950s was re-creating and integrating markets through state trading agencies. Reinstating trading networks for essential goods served to revive production, reintegrate the urban and rural economy, and, ultimately, stabilize the value of money. In this process they relied on techniques of economic governance and price regulation through market participation by the state that are strikingly similar to those in the statecraft tradition discussed in Chapter 1.

I do not claim that the Communists were necessarily directly influenced in their 1940s practice by ancient texts. But there is no doubt that they were knowledgeable of the traditional techniques of economic regulation, the granary system, and the fiscal salt trade. I show that, on a conceptual level, a very similar logic underlies the 1940s "economic warfare" as that articulated for the challenges of fiscal policy and price stabilization, particularly in times of war and fiscal crisis, in the *Guanzi,* the *Salt and Iron Debate,* and later statecraft writings. This points to deep historical roots of the revolutionaries' economic warfare. Heilman and Perry (2011, 15) find "one may observe that basic features of the [Communist Party's] guerrilla policy style are congruent with a long and influential line of traditional thought which stressed fluid, dialectical, and tactical approaches to managing ubiquitous tensions and contradictions." I propose that the same holds true for the realm of economic governance.

In the late 1970s and throughout the 1980s, the question of *how* to (re-)create the economy and markets became a decisive reform question. To address this question, the experience of "economic warfare" in the Chinese Civil War and the reintegration of the national market after the revolution became key sources of knowledge for policy makers and important institutional legacies for experimentation. My argument that the experience of wartime stabilization and marketization is essential to understanding the Chinese strategy of reform is complementary to other recent contributions emphasizing the importance of the wartime experience in shaping modern China (Mitter, 2020). As the subsequent chapters show, the gradual creation of China's dual-track reform relied in parts on the experience in market creation by the old revolutionaries and local officials. After the Communist Party of China (CPC) had kept their fiscal and economic tactics during the Chinese Civil War largely secret, the 1980s saw a wave of publications on "economic warfare" (Lai, 2011, xviii). An early contribution in this regard was Xue Muqiao's (1979) *Economic Work in the Shandong Liberated Areas during the War of Anti-Japanese Resistance and Liberation*. Xue was an important architect both of "economic warfare" in the 1940s and, forty years later, of China's economic reforms. At the dawn of reform, Xue writes in the preface to his book, "A large part of the experience of our economic work during the revolutionary struggle has to be reconsidered in our present moment." The tactics of "economic warfare" shaped the economics of China's elder generation of reformers, and they inform my analysis of the 1980s market reform debate.

Hyperinflation and the Failure of Price Control

The Nationalist government's loss of control over inflation was rooted in its failure to control the national economy under conditions of war. Inflation began with the outbreak of the Sino-Japanese War in 1937 and by the mid-1940s had evolved into chronic hyperinflation. The velocity of money was accelerating as prices rose faster than the quantity of money (Campbell and Tullock, 1954, 227–228).

The basic problem of war finance, as discussed with reference to Keynes (1940) in the previous chapter, was severely aggravated in the Chinese case as the government failed to restore its revenue sources. The lack of sufficient sources of fiscal income and the high costs of war put the Nationalists into an impossible situation when the Americans demanded to balance the government budget as a condition for additional loans. As the war effort continued, the Nationalist government resorted to what Keynes had identified as the least desirable way to pay for the war: it printed money to finance its deficit (Campbell and Tullock, 1954, 226–227; Eckstein, 1977, 162; Pepper, 1986, 741–742; US Department of State, 1949, 394, 781; van de Ven, 2018, 183). The economy spiraled into ever-higher inflation, with the increase in prices outpacing the augmentation of the quantity of money (Chang, 1958, 371–375).

Hsia (1953, 23) suggested two causes of this hyperinflation. The first was "an absolute deficiency in the supply of daily necessities in the urban areas," and the second was "a continual expansion of the money income flow" (ibid.), which meant that the ever-increasing amount of money was meeting a quantity of goods that was increasingly insufficient for basic subsistence. Both factors evolved from the Japanese seizure of the most productive areas of the country, which cut off important supplies and deprived the government of crucial revenue sources, including salt (Eckstein, 1977, 161–162; Riskin, 1987, 33; Lai, 2011, 161; van de Ven, 2003, 259, 263–264).

The inadequate supply of necessities was exacerbated by three factors. The first was *the collapse of market integration*: Solomon Adler (1957, 10–11), who worked for the US Treasury Department in China from 1941 to 1947, observed "the extent of integration between the local and regional markets and between these and the national market was extremely uneven." Transportation, particularly railways, and waterways grew progressively dysfunctional as a result of Japanese blockages, war, and mismanagement (ibid., 11, 13–14; Liu and Wu, 1986, 10, 16; van de Ven, 2003, 268). The Nationalists' conscription of peasants' carts for war purposes deprived them of the means of transporting their harvest even to local markets (Myers, 1986, 269–275). The disintegration of the national market was also reflected in wide regional variations in grain prices and prices more generally (van de Ven, 2003, 270; Trescott, 2007, 288). Beyond the collapse of logistics, commerce was fundamentally hampered by the lack of a unified and stable national currency as the Nationalists, Communists, and Japanese all brought their own money into circulation (Chou, 1963, 1–7; Lai, 2011, 158).

The second factor exacerbating the supply of basic necessities was *a dramatic decrease in domestic agricultural output, combined with a breakdown of imports.* Central water conservancy and irrigation systems had not been adequately maintained, making the land vulnerable to floods and droughts. Rising urban wages and military drafts caused labor shortages in the countryside. Finding themselves cut off from transportation channels, peasants reverted increasingly to subsistence farming, switched from specialized cash crop production to basic food grains, and withdrew from the collapsing national market (Adler, 1957, 13; Liu and Wu, 1986, 10; Myers, 1986, 257–268).[2] Myers (1986, 257) argues that the breakdown of the supply and distribution system of food grains under Nationalist reign reached a scale unknown in imperial times. This caused grain prices in cities to rise to an extent that it became profitable to import grain from abroad. These newly import-dependent regions were later cut off from international trade as a result of Japanese blockages in the 1940s. They were barely able to feed themselves. Grain shortages caused panic and hoarding, which in turn aggravated the supply (van de Ven, 2003, 258–259).

The third factor was the *high profitability of speculation and hoarding, compared with industrial production.* Capitalists increasingly sought immediate profits from speculation on commodity prices, which could be realized in gold and foreign exchange and transferred abroad, rather than investing in domestic production. By 1943, China had entered an industrial depression (van de Ven, 2003, 275).

Energy and basic input prices increased as production declined. Transportation costs soared. The escalating inflation triggered large-scale strikes that the government tried to pacify by pegging wages to prices. This resulted in a price–wage spiral, further pushing up prices (Pepper, 1986, 743). Wage earners, rather than holding cash, got rid of money as quickly as possible to hoard consumption goods, aiming to ensure their livelihood (Adler, 1957, 13).

The industrial profitability crisis was exacerbated by the Nationalists' strategy for fiscal revenue collection. Before the outbreak of the war, Chiang Kai-shek had gathered some of China's leading economists at Lushan to discuss wartime finance. One prominent advisor was Ma Yinchu. Ma is mainly famous for his Malthusian economics that provided the rationale for China's one-child policy in the 1980s. He received his PhD in economics from Columbia University, where he studied New York City's finances (Trescott, 2007, 69). Upon his return to China, Ma promoted the imitation of Western institutions and practices, focusing on money, banking, and fiscal policy (Trescott, 2007, 117, 226). The policy decided at the Lushan meeting was to tax urban salaries and properties instead of the rural economy, along with issuing debt and printing money (van de Ven, 2003, 259).

The Nationalist government launched several unsuccessful efforts to stabilize the value of money. These included the introduction of new currencies and two (failed) attempts, in 1942 and 1943, to implement an American-style general price freeze, for which Leon Henderson (see Chapter 2), the former director of the US Office of Price Administration, was invited to act as advisor (Young, 1965, 145–149). Final attempts at price control combined with currency reform were launched in 1947 and 1948 (Wu, 1956, 51–52; Pepper, 1986, 743–747). However, Henderson and the Nationalist government could not replicate the United States' success in freezing prices.

The basic reasons for the failure of the Chinese price-control policy were congruent with those identified by Galbraith as underlying the same policy's success in America (see Chapter 2). Given the low degree of concentration in the largely agricultural Chinese economy, with declining industry and collapsing exchange rates, there was no self-administered rationing at stable prices by suppliers, as (Galbraith argued) was the case in the highly concentrated industrial economy of the United States. Instead, Chinese shopkeepers withdrew their regular supply and used their stocks for speculation. Even productive enterprises turned from producing new output to speculating on stocks, while disinvestment and capital flight further undermined the production capacities (Eckstein, 1977, 164; US Department of State, 1949, 569, 781).

After four years of inflation, the Chinese people had lost faith in the value of money. They were not willing to save large shares of their incomes, as the Americans had during the Second World War. On the contrary, the Chinese tried to get rid of cash as quickly as possible, thereby accelerating the velocity of money and increasing the demand pressure (Campbell and Tullock, 1954, 227–228). In contrast to the United States, which was blessed with increasing output during the Second World War, the Chinese economy failed to supply consumer goods.

Two other important reasons for the failure of price control were the high degree of regional and local price variation, resulting from market disintegration, and the uneven bureaucratic control, which was mainly concentrated in the cities. Under these conditions, traders avoided places (typically cities) where the price control was effectively policed, thereby aggravating local shortages and pressures on prices (Wu, 1956, 52; US Department of State, 1949, 278). The uneven price control across urban and rural areas also resulted in lower prices in the cities, which caused grain to be transported back to the countryside. The government failed to fulfill the rations for basic foodstuffs that it had introduced as part of the price freeze, and it relapsed into providing monetary subsidies instead. The collapse of the grain market resulted in widespread riots that undermined the price-control system (Pepper, 1986, 744).

A comprehensive state monopoly of salt, practiced in China since ancient times (see Chapter 1), was a complementary approach to a general price freeze in response to the fiscal and monetary crisis. The Nationalists considered reinstating such a monopoly, which promised to contribute to price stability while creating a source of fiscal revenue. However, while the Nationalist government had aimed to reestablish the salt monopoly in December 1940, it aborted the plan in the face of pressure from American advisors. Under the planned scheme, the government would have bought and transported the entire output of salt and sold it to merchants, who would distribute it at fixed prices (Young, 1965, 37). The arguments presented in favor of the monopoly are congruent with those put forward by Sang Hongyang in the *Salt and Iron Debate* and by proponents of a salt monopoly during the imperial period (see Chapter 1): it would eliminate tax evasion, bring the profits of middlemen into the coffers of the treasury, and prevent speculation by merchants driving up prices. Furthermore, an increase in monopoly prices would be more acceptable to the public than increased tax rates (Chang, 1958, 136–137).

When General Lockhart, the American associate director of the Salt Administration, learned about the monopoly, he "at once pointed out to Finance Minister H. H. Kung the serious objections to the scheme" (Young, 1965, 37). Arthur N. Young,[3] a Princeton University economist, former economic expert in the US State Department, and then-financial advisor to the Nationalist government and the Chinese Central Bank, joined Lockhart in his opposition to the proposal of a state monopoly over salt. Young had no high opinion of the Chinese knowledge of economic governance and found Chinese administrators to be "pretty much illiterate in economics" (Fuchs, 1974, 7).[4] He raised the standard arguments against state monopolies that are familiar in modern economics and added that the scheme violated assurances to foreign bondholders (Young, 1965, 37).

Despite this resistance by prominent American advisors, a revised version of the salt monopoly was implemented by the Nationalist government in January 1942, although it was considerably more limited than the initial plan. Notwithstanding their critical stance toward the monopoly, both Chang (1958, 137) and Young (1965, 38) had to acknowledge that revenues from salt trade and salt tax became a very important source of fiscal income, second only to the grain tax in kind. Had a comprehensive salt monopoly been implemented successfully, the Nationalist government might have opened a stream of revenue that would have ameliorated the dependence on printing money.

Finally, the relatively most successful but ultimately ineffective measure of the Nationalists to control prices (Chang, 1958, 347) was strikingly similar to the grain price stabilization by Ever Normal Granaries and to the policy of "equable" laid out in the *Salt and Iron Debate*. In late 1938, the Nationalist government inaugurated a Bureau of Purchase of Daily Necessities for Resale at Equitable Prices, which purchased certain commodities in large quantities and sold them in local markets at lower-than-market prices, thereby putting downward pressure on private sellers. This program was targeted at daily necessities such as rice, salt, edible oil, fuel, cotton, cotton yarn and cloth, paper, sugar, matches, and tobacco (Chang, 1958, 347–348; Donnithorne, 1967, 224; Hsia, 1953, 21–22). However, the government failed to acquire sufficiently large shares in the supply of these commodities, and corrupt officials used the state stocks for speculation. Thus, the effectiveness of this program remained very limited.

The failure to control the economy contributed to the downfall of the Nationalist regime. Abuse of the collection of agricultural taxes was widespread and bred fierce resentment among the peasants. Those hardest hit by inflation were urban wage earners, including intellectuals and state employees, and the inflation had detrimental effects on industrialists. As a result of the disintegration of the rural and urban economy, the most basic consumption goods became unavailable in the cities, while industrial goods found no market in the countryside. As the purchasing power of salaried bureaucrats and the food supply for the army declined, corruption became ever more pervasive. The Nationalists' base of political support was largely reduced to the class of commercial and financial capitalists and landlords who were benefitting from the spiraling inflation. The Nationalists had lost effective control over the army and bureaucracy, while intellectuals and large parts of the urban population withdrew their support (Riskin, 1987, 34; US Department of State, 1949, 567–569; Eckstein, 1977, 163–166; Pepper, 1986, 741). Adler (1957, 12) observed,

> By the end of 1948, if not earlier, the old regime was bankrupt, morally, politically and economically. In the traditional Chinese phrase, it had lost the Mandate of Heaven.

The Communists' Price Stabilization through "Economic Warfare"

> During the last five years since 1938 the public economic enterprises have made tremendous progress. This achievement is invaluable to us as well as to our nation. That is to say we have built a new model of state economy.
>
> *(Mao Zedong, 1942 as in Xue, 1960, 24)*

During the time of the Chinese War of Resistance and Liberation, the state-building project of the Communists came to rely on an economic strategy centered on techniques that were similar to the traditional practices of price stabilization and market creation through the market-balancing interventions of state trading agencies. However, this was far from an immediate or natural choice. Instead, it drew on the far-reaching debate over the nature of money and currency policy, monetary experimentation in the different revolutionary base areas, and the assessment of different policy approaches through field research in the 1920s, 1930s, and early 1940s.[5]

The development of a viable economic strategy was an essential part of the Communists' flexible, adaptable guerrilla warfare. Initially, the control and extent of markets was very limited. Like the Nationalists, the Communists tried unsuccessfully to control the value of their currency—and thereby the price level—by means of administrative price controls and by prohibitive measures such as declaring the Nationalists' banknotes, known as *fabi*, illegal. Only unification of the work on money, commerce, trade, and production as one consolidated campaign of "economic warfare" in the autumn of 1943, with the establishment of the Bureau of Industry and Commerce (*gong shang qu*), achieved a breakthrough toward a stable currency regime (Huang, 2013, 3–4; Lai, 2011, 148–160).

Chen Yun was an important protagonist in the Communists' "economic warfare." Today, Chen is best known as a key architect of China's economic reforms of the late 1970s and early 1980s. But to understand his economics of reform, we have to study his contributions as architect of the economics of guerrilla warfare. The notion of "economic warfare" suggested that a key aspect of the revolutionary struggle was to revive the economy in the liberated areas by relying on economic means. Chen was the leader of the financial committee of the Northwestern Revolutionary Base Area in the mid-1940s. At a lecture for local cadres, Chen summarized the basic premises of coordinating the economic work in the struggle for liberation. He stressed the importance of trade and commodity circulation for production and economic development. Chen warned that, without occasions for exchange, production would grind to a halt, and he argued that economic progress was the key for the revolution: "Only if we can solve the problem of food and clothing for the masses can we become leaders of the masses. Thus, a revolutionary businessman is an outright revolutionary" (Zhu et al., 2000, 387).

One of the main challenges in reviving commerce and thus production was to overcome hyperinflation by driving out the Nationalist government's legal tender *fabi* and replacing it with the revolutionary bases' own currencies.[6] In this context, at the 1944 Northwestern Financial Conference, Chen articulated the relationship between economic and political means. Rather than relying on prohibition and policing, he argued, the struggle against the *fabi* should be based on economics supplemented by politics. Chen argued that the struggle had earlier been suggested to be mainly dependent on orders and fixing prices. It should, he said, instead rely on regulating the value of the competing currencies, and for this, the trade in key commodities would be decisive. Controlling salt trade was crucial. Other important commodities included grain and cloth (Zhu et al., 2000, 392).

Xue Muqiao: Revolutionary Economist and Architect of Economic Reform

The strategy promoted by Chen Yun in 1944 had just delivered great success in the liberated areas of Shandong, and it turned the Northeastern province, largely under Japanese occupation, into a financial powerhouse for the Communist revolution. Xue Muqiao, who emerged as a leading reform economist in the 1980s, was crucial in devising the Communists' economic warfare in Shandong (Lai, 2011, 145–163; Xue, 1981, 1–6). Xue is one of China's most famous and influential economists of the twentieth century. Like many other architects of reform in the 1980s of his generation, his economic thinking was crucially shaped by the experience of devising the material foundations in the war for liberation.

Xue was the son of an educated family that belonged to a formerly wealthy clan in Jiangsu undergoing economic and social decline. While still a child, Xue lost his father, who succumbed to the family's debt burden and committed suicide (Lai, 2011, 151; Xue, 1996, 1–7). At age twenty-three, Xue joined the CPC. Imprisoned by the Nationalists, he secretly studied Marxism, economics, philosophy, and history (China Development Research Foundation, 2011). Xue first emerged as an intellectual when he joined Chen Hansheng, one of China's most prolific Marxist historians and an underground Comintern agent, in his survey work of the Chinese countryside. They aimed to settle the question of China's stage of historical development, that is, to what extent China was semifeudal and to what semicolonial. To this end, Chen and his team undertook a large-scale data collection effort.

Xue surveyed his hometown. He documented the high levels of agricultural production, long-distance trade, retail, and banking undertaken by his clan at its peak during the reign of the Jiaqing Emperor (1796–1820) and compared this with the pitiable state of opium addiction and gambling financed by excessive rent extraction at Xue's own time. In another contribution, proving the exploitative nature of China's rural economy, Xue documented that 10 percent of China's rural population owned 70 percent of the land, putting most of the rural population at the mercy of feudal landlords and rich peasants. There can be no doubt that Xue was intimately familiar with the historical evolution and the empirical reality of China's rural political economy. Xue employed this knowledge to contribute to the highly theoretical debate over the nature of China's stage of development and social relations (Lai, 2011, 151–154; Cole, 2018, 159–161).[7]

Xue joined the efforts of the CPC's economic work in Shandong early in 1943. This was some months after the first attempt to drive out the Nationalists' currency, the *fabi*, and establish an exclusive zone of the Communists' *beipiao*, its paper money, in the liberated areas. The value of the *fabi* was rapidly declining after the Japanese attack on Pearl Harbor and caused an outflow of goods from Shandong, which undermined the Communists' effort to revive the local economy. When Li Yu, the secretary of the CPC Shandong Provincial Committee, analyzed the failure of this first attempt, he stressed that it was a mistake to rely on administrative means and to set exchange rates between currencies arbitrarily. Instead, it was necessary to study market forces and use them, rather than issuing orders that went up against invisible market powers.

Months of discussion gave rise to a consensus among the Shandong CPC leadership that the currency struggle had to be connected to the CPC's grain-provisioning system, revenue collection—in particular, the salt trade—and the facilitation and regulation of trade. That meant that these three policies had to be monetized instead of being implemented in barter terms. Only by linking fiscal policy, commodity production, and circulation with the currency question could the economic struggle succeed. Promoting trade meant that the Communists' economic strategy had to reach beyond the borders of the liberated areas. Instead of "taking from the people" by taxing them or "taking from oneself" by imposing austerity, the best strategy was to "take from the enemy." This could be achieved only by undermining the enemy by economic means. Xue Muqiao became the mastermind behind the successful implementation of this strategy during five years of work in Shandong (Lai, 2011, 150–154).

In a document titled "Directives on Investigation and Research," Xue summarized his approach to working toward an effective policy. He stressed the importance of understanding the concrete conditions and on-the-ground results of policies, which could be achieved only by an in-depth study of typical cases. Understanding typical cases was necessary to move toward a comprehensive knowledge of the general situation. For Xue, research needed to be a collective effort of survey work that involved a large number of local cadres and students. Employing this research approach, Xue took the lead in working out policies to establish a stable monetary regime. The policies, critical in providing the economic base for the Communists' success in Shandong, came to serve as a role model in other revolutionary base areas and, eventually, throughout China (Fan Shitao, forthcoming).[8] Thereby—consciously or otherwise—the CPC came to replicate key practices of the ancient techniques of price regulation.

Xue's fundamental insight was in line with Li Yu and the Shandong CPC and is reminiscent of some of the basic principles articulated in the *Guanzi* discussed in Chapter 1: the political leadership should use and manipulate market forces in pursuit of its economic goals instead of risking great losses by working against these forces. From this basic principle, Xue drew concrete lessons. Against the bullionist idea that the CPC's paper money *beipiao* would have to be backed by a reserve of precious metals, Xue Muqiao held that, instead, the CPC had to control a stock of essential goods such as grain, cotton, peanut oil, and salt as backing of the currency.[9] The value of money would be ensured when people could trust that the currency could buy the most essential goods. As Xue put it, "During a period of material shortage, food and cotton are more valuable than gold and silver, which cannot fill stomachs and protect against the cold" (Xue as in Lai, 2011, 159). Therefore, the CPC had to use its trade and its grain-provisioning system to ensure the value of money by reintegrating the rural and urban economies. On the eve of the 1980s reforms,[10] Xue Muqiao reported the core of the CPC's strategy of economic warfare based on his experience in Shandong:

> During the revolutionary wars, we set up supply and marketing cooperatives throughout the rural base areas which purchased the peasants' farm produce and provided them with manufactured goods. In this way we rehabilitated agricultural production, gave much support to the war effort, and rallied the peasants around us while weakening their ties with the bourgeoisie.
>
> *(Xue, 1981, 3)*

At the same time, Xue argued, to outcompete the *fabi*, the *beipiao* had to be convertible in the market and the CPC had to use its cross-border trading to expel the *fabi* by playing the market forces. To this end, according to Xue, the CPC needed to build up reserves of the competing currencies in order to manipulate their value. The key to building up stocks of essential goods and competing currencies was the salt trade.

Shandong's salt industry had been an important source of income for China's central government for centuries. The Shandong salt revenues had also been critically important for the Nationalists, accounting for roughly 20 percent of government revenues (Lai, 2011, 160). The Japanese invasion cut the Nationalist government off this substantial stream of revenue. After taking over the salt fields, the Japanese aimed to modernize salt farming. They imposed a low price ceiling by administrative means, hoping to induce technical progress by encouraging cost cutting. In fact, they drove many salt farmers out of business and caused the price of salt to rise, creating a gateway for the Communists' economic warfare.

The CPC revived the traditional "salt channel." Similar to the institutional arrangements discussed in the *Guanzi* and the *Salt and Iron Debate* centuries earlier, under the "salt channel," the government sold the right to participate in salt farming to private businesses, who rented them to salt farmers—typically, poor peasants who could not live off agriculture. Instead of controlling the price by direct administrative means, the "salt channel" limited the salt fields for which it issued licenses. Licenses went to all salt farmers willing to collaborate with the CPC. Thereby substantial parts of the Shandong salt farming were gradual brought under Communist control. At the same time, the CPC gained took command of the salt trading routes. The salt trade was highly profitable and generated revenue for the Communists' combat. Combined with grain provisioning, it also enabled the CPC to secure the value of its *beipiao* and thus win the monetary struggle in Shandong (Lai, 2011, 159–164).

The strategy devised in Shandong under Xue's guidance became an example for the CPC in other base areas. Chen Yun, then chairman of the Financial and

Economic Commission, pointed out that putting enough grain and cotton in the hands of the central government was the major means to stabilize market forces and control prices (Liu and Wu, 1986, 27–28). Ultimately, the aim was to create an "organized socialist market" that would reintegrate the national economy and eventually outcompete the chaotic capitalist market (Ling and Lei, 1959, 38, 44).

Revolution and the Victory over Hyperinflation

Following Chiang Kai-shek's defeat in the Chinese Civil War, Mao Zedong established the People's Republic of China. On September 21, 1949, Mao Zedong (1986, 5) announced at the Chinese People's Political Consultative Conference,

> We have united and have overthrown both domestic and foreign oppressors through the People's War of Liberation and the people's great revolution, and now proclaim the establishment of the People's Republic of China.

Curbing inflation was the most pressing economic concern of the new government (Donnithorne, 1978, 2; Ling and Lei, 1959, 34). The Consultative Conference set out the overall economic policy for the newly born republic in a "Common Program" (Hsia, 1953, 25).[11] Reflecting the same approach as the Shandong monetary struggle, Article 37 stated: "State-owned trading organizations shall assume the responsibility of adjusting supply and demand, stabilizing commodity prices and assisting the people's co-operatives" (Common Program of the CPPCC, 1949). As long as the war effort continued, high military expenditures had to be shouldered, rehabilitating production and recovering state revenues were bound to be slow. The basic challenge of excess demand and a fiscal deficit could be overcome only with time. Surprisingly, as Burdekin and Wang (1999) showed, the Communist government managed to stabilize the price level before overcoming the government's budget deficit—defeating the logic of the US conditionality for loans to the Nationalists as well as the postulates by prominent neoclassical economists such as the Nobel Memorial Prize–winner Thomas Sargent (1982).

A confidential Central Intelligence Agency (CIA) (1952) report summarized the CPC's operational technique of stabilizing prices in terms strikingly similar to the traditional Chinese statecraft principles, as evidenced from the quote at the opening of this chapter. American intelligence stressed that the Communists moved from first controlling the markets for goods essential to people's livelihoods and observed that the party used private businesses and the dynamic interplay of supply and demand to stabilize prices and bring production and distribution under their control. The Communist government's strategy was to establish price leadership over essential consumption goods (Hsia, 1953, 25, 29, 33, 41). Instead of employing political pressure and policing power to curb market prices by direct means, price leadership was an indirect technique to control prices, which reanimated and channeled market forces instead of trying to suppress them. List prices[12] were applied by state-run retailers but were not immediately forced upon private sellers. List prices became dominant only once the Communist state had gained price leadership. In the meantime, a dual structure of list prices and market prices prevailed—this practice prefigured the dual-track price system of the 1980s.

The state trading agencies[13] were the army in the Communists' economic warfare. They derived their stock of commodities from the tax in kind, particularly in grain, the output of the state manufacturing enterprises, and a comprehensive salt monopoly, as well as from purchases from private firms and farmers, especially for cotton and cloth (Hsia, 1953, 34–35). Once the Communists had consolidated their control over almost all rural territories and strategic urban industries, the so-called "life lines" (*mingmai*), the state trading agencies could rapidly expand their market share in essential consumption goods and inputs.[14] The Communists rehabilitated transportation and communication and thereby reintegrated the urban and the rural economy across the People's Republic of China. Thanks to their national networks, the state trading agencies could acquire commodities wherever they were cheap and sell them where they were dear (Liu and Wu, 1986, 28)—using the same logic as Sang Hongyang's equable marketing (see Chapter 1). This remonetized the countryside that had, in vast areas, collapsed into a self-sufficient barter economy (Ling and Lei, 1959, 32, 56).

However, the reintegration of the national market also enabled speculators to coordinate large-scale purchases of the most essential commodities, such as grain, cotton yarn, and cloth (Liu and Wu, 1986, 19). The state trading agencies used such buy-ups to drive capitalists into bankruptcy. They first joined the speculative attack on a particular commodity by bulk buying, thus accelerating the price increase. When the price of the targeted commodity became very high, the state trading agencies suddenly flooded the market by releasing their stocks, causing the price of the commodity to drop drastically and the speculators to also start selling their stocks, driving prices down even further. Selling at much lower prices than they had bought, many speculators were unable to service their debt, went bankrupt, or at least realized that they could no longer expect sure gains from price hikes. The state trading agencies, on the other hand, gradually gained control over the markets and prices of the most important commodities (Ling and Lei, 1959, 52).

In parallel with their attacks against professional speculation, the state trading agencies distributed necessary consumer goods directly to the people at list prices through state-run retailers (Liu and Wu, 1986, 25). When the Chinese people realized, after years of hyperinflation, that they could acquire daily necessities at list prices with the newly issued currency, renminbi (RMB, "the people's dollar"), they gradually abstained from hoarding goods acquired from the private market at higher prices and regained trust in the value of money. As a result of the successive attacks against speculation and the satisfaction of immediate consumption demand, market prices slowly converged to list prices and the state trading agencies' list prices gained leadership (Hsia, 1953, 39–40). The dual structure of state-set list prices and black market prices gradually disappeared, and the overall price level was stabilized.

In addition to curbing price hikes in essential commodities, the CPC made efforts to bring aggregate supply and demand into balance, both by reviving production[15] and by reducing excess purchasing power. State revenues were generated by establishing an effective tax collection system and selling government bonds while expenditures in military and administration could be reduced as the war effort was phased out and the bureaucracy was streamlined (Liu and Wu, 1986, 35–37). Private saving, which had collapsed in the course of the hyperinflation, was increased by applying the basic principle found in *Guanzi* and rearticulated by Xue: the value of money in a largely agricultural economy is determined by the amount it can buy of the most essential commodities for people's livelihoods. As van der Sprenkel (1951, 37–38) observed firsthand, the "serious psychological difficulty [of] the deep distrust of all paper money" was overcome by pegging saving deposits to the newly nationalized banks and wages to the wholesale price of grain and cotton.[16] As the prices of these commodities were stabilized, so was the value of money.

The stabilization process was not smooth, and it involved a cycle from inflation to deflation (Figure 3.1; Rostow, 1954, 244–245). However, it was ultimately successful. As data reported by the CIA (1952) shows, in April 1950, hyperinflation gave way to a decrease in the general price level, followed by renewed but less severe inflation with the outbreak of the Korean War in June.[17] This general price movement closely corresponded with that of cloth and foodstuff, reflecting the CPC's price-stabilization strategy focused on essentials. The price-stabilization effort involved not only bringing down the increase in the

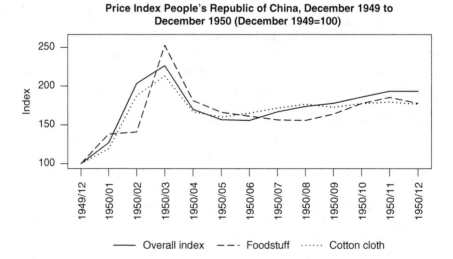

Price Index People's Republic of China, December 1949 to December 1950 (December 1949=100)

——— Overall index   – – · Foodstuff   ······ Cotton cloth

FIGURE 3.1   Price Index, December 1949 to December 1950. Source: CIA, 1952.

overall price level but also balancing *relative* prices of essential goods, thereby avoiding price-induced redistribution between the urban and rural economies. When in 1950 some regions had a bumper harvest of wheat, the state trading agencies ensured sufficient demand to prop up the wheat price by collaborating with collective and private grain merchants. They also stockpiled cloth, coal, salt, soap, matches, and other necessities—valued at hundreds of billions of RMB—to meet the peasants' demand for these industrial goods at low prices. Thus, the relative prices were stabilized by the state's deliberate efforts to channel supply and demand.

Conclusion

The Communists succeeded at reintegrating the national economy and overcoming hyperinflation after the Nationalists had failed at this task. An overall price freeze, which had been effective in the industrialized, capitalist economy of the United States during the Second World War, proved not to be applicable to the institutional realities of China's war-torn, disintegrated, and still largely agricultural economy. The Communists' attempts at administrative price controls failed too. Instead, the value of money, combined with production aimed at exchange, was reestablished using techniques reminiscent of the Chinese tradition of price stabilization through market participation by the state. Salt licensing and trade were brought under state monopolies, while the prices of essential commodities such as cotton and grain were stabilized by dual tactics: state trading agencies used speculative hikes to outplay the speculators, while at the same time the people's trust in the value of the new currency (the renminbi) was gained by guaranteeing the provision of essential goods at list prices. As a result, market prices gradually converged to list prices.

Liu and Wu (1986, 20) summarized this history from the perspective of the victorious Communists, giving a sense of the importance attached to price stabilization as the first economic breakthrough:

> leaders of some foreign countries and the Kuomintang asserted that these financial and economic difficulties were insurmountable. ... Under the leadership of the Party and the People's Government, however, the Chinese people took up the historical task of overcoming the economic difficulties and rehabilitated the national economy.

Several other commentators agree on the importance of this policy measure as part of a larger effort. Ling and Lei (1959) stressed that creating a stable currency by reviving the orderly circulation of money could not rely on purely monetary policy: price stability "could not be created by the efforts of the People's Bank alone. It was the result of the joint efforts of the financial organs, state trade, banking establishments, and all the enterprises of the socialist sector of the economy" (52). Similarly, Wu (1956) concluded that "the break in the inflationary spiral was brought about, in the first instance, largely by government open market commodity operations." Burdekin and Wang (1999), in their analysis of the "end to the big inflation in China in 1950," agreed with Wu that the actions of the state trading agencies played a critical role in stabilizing the monetary system. As we saw in Chapter 1, this logic of government participation in commodity markets with the goal of balancing prices is deeply ingrained in the Chinese tradition of economic governance. The Communists utilized these traditional policy tools in their successful struggle for revolution aimed at building a new society that would liberate China from the remnants of semifeudalism and semicolonialism.

Heilman and Perry (2011, 33) and the contributions to their volume have shown that the

> proven ability of mobile guerrilla warfare to reap unexpected gains in a highly uncertain and threatening environment left an indelible imprint on Chinese policy makers who took part in the revolution (including the age cohorts of Mao, Deng, and Hu Yaobang, who dominated Chinese politics until at least the early 1990s).

I argue that as regards the economic side of guerrilla warfare, the strategies employed by the Communist revolutionaries were at the same time rooted in traditional techniques of economic governance and provided the starting point for economic reform under Deng Xiaoping. Economic leaders such as Chen Yun, Xue Muqiao, and others who emerged as architects of China's 1980s reforms were deeply versed from their wartime experience in utilizing market forces under the most adverse conditions of economic disintegration. The Communists re-created the Chinese economy during the Chinese Civil War and the first years of the People's Republic of China by consciously exploiting market dynamics. The revolutionary generation's wartime experience in creating markets constitutes an important element of my interpretation of China's escape from shock therapy at the crossroads of the 1980s. The wartime experience provided a stepping stone to an alternative path to market reforms.

Notes

1 With regard to judgment of the scale of the German and the Chinese hyperinflation, Simkin (1978, 113) noted that it depends on the measure applied: "If one accepts Cagan's admittedly arbitrary definition of the starting point for a hyperinflation as that month in which the rate of increase of general prices first exceeds 50 percent (Cagan, 1956, 25) then the Chinese hyperinflation did not begin until January 1948. From then until April 1949, when the Communists took Shanghai, wholesale prices in that city rose by a factor of 1.80 (10^7) (Chou, 1963, 34, 264). This compares with Cagan's figures of ... 1.02 (10^{10}) for the German hyperinflation of 1922–1923. ... If, however, one prefers to think of hyperinflation as the last state of a worsening process of serious inflation, then the comparison alters. Between

December 1937, when war with Japan had begun, and April 1949, Chinese prices increased by a factor of 4.79 (10^{12}). This exceeds the factor of 1.26 (10^{12}) by which German prices rose between 1914 and 1924, and the factor of 1.71 (10^{10}) by which Russian prices rose over the same period; and the Russian hyperinflation exceeded those in Austria, Hungary, and Poland after the First World War" (Cagan, 1956, 26; Chou, 1963, 261). According to this latter measure, Chinese hyperinflation was the worst.

2   Liu and Wu (1986, 17) estimated the following decline in output at the time of the Communist takeover: "Compared with the peak year before 1937, the output value of agriculture in 1949 had dropped by more than 20 percent, with grain output down 22.1 percent ... cotton output down 48 percent ... and the number of pigs dropped 26.1 percent. ... Industrial output value plummeted 50 percent, with heavy industrial production down by 70 percent and light industrial production by 30 percent." For a discussion of the process of withdrawal from the national market and production for subsistence or local markets in the cotton sector, see Kraus (1980, 42–43).

3   Arthur N. Young resigned from his post at the US State Department in 1929 to work for the Chinese Nationalist government and central bank as a financial advisor until 1947 (Fuchs, 1974) and is described in a US Department of State report (1949, 377–378, 788) as having delivered a particularly "loyal and useful service to the Nationalist government," in comparison with other American advisors. Young was also a member of the Chinese delegation to Bretton Woods in 1944 (Fuchs, 1974).

4   Young exempts only one Harvard-educated official from this judgment.

5   For a groundbreaking survey of the monetary experiments and debates of the 1920s and 1930s, see Cole (2018).

6   For an overview of the different currencies issued, see Ling and Lei (1959, 11–12).

7   See Karl (2017, 113–140) for a theoretical analysis of this debate.

8   For a detailed survey of the evolution of the policies toward the establishment of a stable currency regime and the role of Xue Muqiao's approach in Shandong, see Huang (2013).

9   Similar ideas of a commodity standard for the value of money were articulated as a challenge against bullionism in China's 1930s debate by Xu Qingfu (Cole, 2018, 245–255).

10 The Chinese edition of Xue's *China's Socialist Economy* was published in 1979.

11 Some key elements of this program were agrarian reform, state ownership of enterprises "relating to the economic life of the country," the expansion of the cooperative economy, and ownership coexistence as a basic principle (The Common Program of the CPPCC, 1949).

12 List prices were determined based on costs plus profit calculations (Hsia, 1953, 38–39).

13 Hsia (1953) remains the best English source on the initial Communist price stabilization. He described the evolution and institutional structure of the state trading agencies in detail: "Although there were various STAs functioning prior to the founding of the CPG, the nation-wide specialized trading companies have been in existence only since March 10, 1950. On that day, the CAC of the CPG passed a directive known as 'Decisions on the Procedures Governing the Unification of State Trade,' which provided the organizational framework of state trading. The specialized state trading companies fall into two categories: those concerned with domestic trade and those concerned with foreign trade. In the first category, there are (1) the China Grain Company, (2) the China Cotton-Yarn-Cloth Company, (3) the China Salt Company, (4) the China General Goods Company, (5) the China Coal Company, (6) the China Petroleum Company, (7) the China Native Produce Company, (8) the China Industrial Equipment and Materials Company, (9) the China Construction Company ... and (10)

the China Medical Supplies Company" (Hsia, 1953, 33–34). This first category of trading agencies was most crucial for the price-stabilization effort.

14 In early 1950, the state trading agencies controlled more than 90 percent of the national supply in salt, 70 to 80 percent of the coal, 40 percent of the cotton cloth, 30 percent of the cotton yarn and rice, and 20 percent of the flour (Hsia, 1953, 35). These shares expanded rapidly in the following months. For example, the China Cotton-Yarn-Cloth Company acquired 75 percent of all cotton cloth production during the first nine months of 1950 (Hsia, 1953, 35).

15 Output had fallen far beyond the prewar levels. Ling and Lei (1959) estimated that agricultural output in 1949 stood at about 75 percent of the prewar level. For the most important industrial commodities, they estimate that pig iron had fallen to 10.9 percent, steel to 15.8 percent, coal to 44.5 percent, and cotton textiles to 72.5 percent of their prewar peaks.

16 Bodde (1951), another firsthand observer, explained how the system worked: "The bank establishes a 'unit price' which it publishes daily in the papers. Its basis is the sum total of the average market prices during the five preceding days of three key commodities: wheat and corn flour (per pound) and cotton cloth (per foot). Let us suppose that this sum, on a given day, amounts to PN$100, and that an individual opens a savings account for that amount on the day in question. By so doing he is, in effect, buying one 'savings unit' from the People's Bank. Now let us suppose that three months later, wishing to withdraw his deposit, he finds that, owing to price rises in the three basic commodities, the value of his savings unit has gone up to $150. This means that the bank now pays him, not his original $100, but the unit's new value, which is $150. At the same time the interest accruing to him is calculated proportionately" (Bodde, 1951, 138). For a third account by foreigners in China at the time, see Lapwood and Lapwood (1954, 55–59).

17 This is broadly consistent with Schran's (1977) finding: "The wholesale-price index continued to rise rapidly at first, from 47.7 in December 1949 to a peak of 108.0 in March 1950. But it fell nearly as much during the next quarter, to a low of 68.8 in June 1950. Then the Korean War renewed the inflationary pressure temporarily. The index began to climb again, reached another maximum of 106.2 in October 1951, declined moderately during 1952 to the base-year average of 100, and stabilized almost completely near parity from then on" (368).

PART II

China's Market Reform Debate

4

THE STARTING POINT

Price Control in the Maoist Economy and the Urge for Reform

It has been almost 30 years since the founding of the People's Republic of China, but there are still beggars, how can this be the case? ... If this problem [of having enough to eat] is not solved, the peasants might rise in rebellion and be led to the cities by local party leaders demanding food.

(Chen Yun to 1978 CCP Work Conference, Chen, 1999, 238)

In talking about his visit to foreign countries, [Deng Liqun] sighed with emotion that the Western countries were now prosperous, rich, civilized and polite: "There is no sign of revolution at all."

(Hua et al., 1993, 23)

Introduction

On the eve of the revolution, China was among the poorest countries in the world (Clark, 1940, 39; Cooper, 2005, 4). In 1950, China's share in world GDP had fallen from about one-third in 1820 to below 5 percent (Maddison, 2001). The Communist revolution was in pursuit of political ambitions larger than economic development; it was about the creation of a new society, freed from both feudalist oppression and capitalist exploitation. Yet, for the revolutionaries, a first task had to be to lead China out of atrocious poverty. Reporting on the celebrations on Tiananmen Square of the founding of the People's Republic, the *People's Daily* editorial proclaimed as one of the goals of the new government "to gradually change this backward agricultural country into a civilized and progressive, industrial one" (October 2, 1949).

A far cry from the revolutionaries' ambition for material improvements for the masses, ten years into the Communist reign, "the most appalling famine in the history of mankind took place" (Wemheuer, 2014, 11). By the time of Mao Zedong's death on September 9, 1976, China had long recovered from the Great Famine and had achieved remarkable progress in public health, education, efforts toward a green revolution,[1] as well as industrialization (World Bank, 1983). But China was still a very poor country.

Estimates of China's average per capita growth rates from the 1950s to 1978 vary. Maddison (2007, 100) estimates a 2.33 percent growth in GDP per capita. The first World Bank report (1983, 78) suggests a GNP growth per capita of 2.7 percent, which would have outpaced other low-income countries but was somewhat below the world average GDP growth of 2.62 percent. Johnson and Papageorgiou (2020, 140) place China among the ten worst growth performers in the 1960s, with −0.32 percent per capita growth.

Whatever the precise growth rate, it was too low to result in catching up. As a result, at the time of Mao's passing in 1976 China's share in world GDP had not increased by any considerable margin since the revolution (Maddison, 2001). Economic growth had been mainly driven by high levels of urban-industrial investment at the cost of consumption—rural consumption in particular (World Bank, 1983, 10, 81–81). One-third of the country's rural population, about 260 million people, lived in absolute poverty, according to the official Chinese poverty line (Bramall, 2004, 119), and living standards in terms of per capita grain output were stagnating on a low level (Ash, 2006, 968). In the late 1970s, the failure to overcome rural poverty created a great urge for reform.

Mao's China can claim an impressive record in an unlikely economic dimension: price stability—something typically attributed to very conservative economics. After the initial years of rehabilitation and consolidation (1950−1952)—with crucial exceptions, such as the time of the Great Leap Forward and the Great Famine (1958–1962)—price increases in China were minimal from the 1950s through the 1970s, and the People's Republic had one of the most stable fiat currencies in modern times (Burdekin, 2000, 223; Burdekin, 2008, 59; Donnithorne, 1978; National Bureau of Statistics, 2010, 21; Perkins, 1966, 227; Tsakok, 1979; Zheng and Huang, 2018, 342−343; Huang, 2013, 1). China's price stability in the first decades after the revolution also compared favorably with the sharp inflation in the young Soviet Union between 1928 and 1940 (Perkins, 1964, 360; Tsakok, 1979, 865).

It is striking that, despite the radical political shifts of the Mao era and the troubled search for a feasible development model, such price stability prevailed. Some might consider the price stability record to be a major achievement in macroeconomic management, particularly in comparison with the failure of the Nationalists just before the revolution (see Chapter 3). But price stability came at a tremendous cost, that of "squeezing the peasants" (Ash, 2006). Controlling inflation in a poor agrarian economy, aiming for rapid economic growth and industrialization was achieved, in part, by suppressing the consumption needs of China's peasant majority.

At the dawn of the reform, the famous Chinese economist Xue Muqiao[2] claimed that "China has the most stable prices in the world" (2011 [1984], 109).

But Xue also warned that, in the course of the Communist rule, "[p]rice stabilization was wrongly equated with price freezes, without understanding that
rises and falls in price are often necessary for economic development" (ibid.). He
called for a development model that would be less at the expense of the peasants.
For Xue as well as many Chinese reform-oriented economists, solving the problem of rural poverty became the starting point for reform in the late 1970s. This
required overcoming the fear of loosening control over prices.

This chapter introduces some basic principles of the Chinese price system and
its relationship with the Chinese development model during the Mao era. It is
beyond the scope of this chapter to present a comprehensive account of the complex evolution of the Mao era price system, let alone its political economy at large.
This chapter does not attempt and cannot achieve an overall evaluation of the economic development of the Mao era. Instead, I portray the origins and basic workings of the price system and the role of prices in the Mao era economy (1952–1976)
in relation to China's quest for economic development with the aim to provide
some background needed to understand the 1980s market reform debate. I do so
mostly in a conceptual rather than a detailed historical fashion, but we have to
keep in mind that Mao's China "was not a monolith" (Riskin, 1969). The next
two sections are meant to equip readers who are not familiar with the workings of
China's economy and price system during the Mao era with a basic understanding
to provide context for the subsequent chapters. In the second part of the chapter, I
move on to discuss, from the perspective of Chinese reformers, how the urge for
economic reform in the late 1970s necessarily involved price reform.

Industrialization, the Urban–Rural Divide, and Price Stability

Industrialization presented a great challenge for the newly founded People's
Republic of China (PRC), given its predominantly agricultural economy, its low
levels of real income, and its aspiration for "self-reliance." In the first years after
the revolution, the Communists could rely on reviving and controlling previously private industries (Xue, 1960, 48–54). But, in the long run, the accumulation funds were extracted from the peasants.[3] China's initial industrialization
approach was copied from the Soviet Union. It was focused on the development of heavy industry and essentially followed the Feldman-Preobrazhensky
(Stalinist) paradigm (Brødsgaard, 1983a). Despite the erratic shifts in policy paradigms throughout the Mao era, the commitment to industrialization and the
reliance on the extraction of agricultural resources remained (Ash, 2006, 968).
Or, as Eyferth (2009, 10) summarizes somewhat cynically, "The Maoist ideal
for the countryside was the self-reliant, insular collective that produced surplus
grain and other inputs for cities but required nothing from the urban sector."
This meant, in practice, that the government secured control over large shares
of agricultural output.

A few years after the revolution, the Communist government stopped
employing state commerce on open markets. In 1953, China began to follow

Stalin's example in combining collectivization with a government monopoly over-procurement and distribution of essential agricultural goods in a "unified system of purchase and sale" (统购统销). This system served to extract resources for industrialization from the countryside (Ash, 2006, 960, 969; Schran, 1977, 371). In the 1950s, China looked back at a long history of government engagement in the purchase and sale of agricultural goods (see Chapters 1 and 3). Oi (1989, 68) argues that the system of local reserves constituted a continuation of the imperial system. Yet, in the PRC, the unification and centralization reached a new scale and thereby changed its' nature. The state monopolized the procurement and sale from the countryside to the cities, as well as across regions, and for export (Oi, 1989, 68–70).[4]

The new system of grain purchase and sale was introduced in reaction to an agricultural procurement crisis in 1953 (Ash, 2006, 96; Walker, 1984, 42–44). As a result of the rehabilitation of the economy after the war, grain output had drastically increased from 1949 to 1952. But the land reform that had liberated peasants from the control by landlords also increased grain demand in the countryside. The poorest peasants, in particular, were not willing to sell to the state the surplus that they previously had had to give to landlords. Instead, they stored grain for consumption, as fodder, and for seedlings. Simultaneously, the urban population was increasing as a result of the government's industrialization push. This created a demand for more grain transfers to the city and amounted to a lasting conflict between peasants and the state. When the state could not procure sufficient crops for urban consumption, the government resorted to abolishing all private trade and establishing a state trade monopoly over all essential agricultural products. This system was to last until the 1980s reforms (Wemheuer, 2014, 89–91).

Perkins (1966, 56–60) argues that the Chinese leadership initially pursued the unified system of purchase and sale not to replace all markets but to monopolize the trade in the most essential agricultural goods. But, as it turned out, increased centralized controls quickly eliminated local exchange relations. This result was evident from a dramatic decline in small-scale "subsidiary production" for local markets,[5] and it became one of the major discussion topics at the Eighth National Congress of the Communist Party of China (CPC).[6] Prices for subsidiary products were increased following the Party Congress, but "the production of every crop whose price was raised fell" (Perkins, 1966, 71). Perkins (1966, 96) concluded that the "lack of response by cadres to price changes" showed that "in practice centralization of control in Communist China proved to be a substitute for, and not a supplement to, the market and price controls."

The introduction of the unified system of purchase and sale intensified the tension between the state and the peasants, and an initial euphoria about collectivization gave way to local protests. Peasants complained about the too-high quotas and too-low agricultural prices, which disadvantaged them in comparison with urban workers and often pushed them to the edge of subsistence. The state reacted by accusing peasants of false reporting and attacked their resistance, describing it as anti-socialist (Wemheuer, 2014, 91–92, 96–97). China's rural population—which provided food and grain for exports, as well as inputs for urban industries—had no clear prospects to reap the benefits of industrialization (Solinger, 1984, 23–24; Xue, 1982a, 29–30).

Mao reevaluated this urban industrialization–biased development strategy and acknowledged its problems in his secret speech "On the Ten Major Relationships" (Leung and Kau, 1992, 44).[7] He identified two methods for heavy industry development: "One method is to develop heavy industry by developing less light industry and agriculture; another method is to develop heavy industry by developing more light industry and agriculture." (Mao, 1992 [1956], 48) Mao concluded that the "latter method, which places the development of heavy industry on the basis of satisfying the people's daily needs and puts the development of heavy industry on a firmer foundation, will result in greater and better development of heavy industry" (ibid.). Yet, a shift to such a development strategy oriented toward light industry and agriculture was not pursued at the time (Brødsgaard, 1983a, 45–46).

The Great Leap Forward, launched in 1958, seemed to promise a different way out of the urban–rural tension. The agenda was a great push toward rural industrialization, which was to be achieved through People's Communes that organized all aspects of social welfare, including public mess halls, public work projects, and manufacturing initiatives. Instead of reallocating resources to the countryside, the communes were meant to achieve rapid local economic expansion, thanks to mass mobilization. Private plots were abolished, and all land was meant to serve the collective effort (Wemheuer, 2014, 107–111). This approach was by no means uncontested. Notably, Chen Yun, who was in charge of building up the socialist planned economy in the first years after the revolution (Vogel, 2005), had warned in 1957 that "collectivization merely created the conditions for agricultural development but could not fundamentally solve the problem [of rural development]" (Yang, 1996, 33).[8]

In the utopian mood of the Great Leap Forward, grain output projections became unrealistic. The state's net grain extraction reached deadly levels. In 1953–1957, the average net procurement out of current agricultural output was 18.3 percent; in 1959, it rose to 28 percent under the pressure of a further expansion of the urban population (Ash, 2006, 971). From 1957–1959, the number of urban workers had increased by 25.8 million (Wemheuer, 2014, 122). When the harvest was too low to fulfill the excessive state procurement quotas in 1959, the channels of communication between the state apparatus and the rural communities had already been broken by the political campaigns against peasants' underreporting of grain. With prices fixed by the state and private commerce abolished, there were, in addition, no price signals that could have indicated scarcity—as would have been the case in a market-oriented public granary system (see Chapter 1). The state was unprepared to react, and it continued to export grain. The communes had exhausted their grain storage as a result of the state's over-procurement, and the peasant households had no significant private stocks. The result was mass starvation. Death counts still vary drastically. At least 16 million, and possibly more than 40 million, peasants died of hunger (Wemheuer, 2014, 120–145; Yang, 1996, 37–39).

The disasters of the Great Leap Forward were followed by a brief period of development focused primarily on light industry and agriculture. Chen Yun was put in charge of the economy (Vogel, 2005, 755). The government temporarily reintroduced rural markets and private plots, and production was, to some extent, organized through household contracting—a policy that was to become an important stepping-stone toward market reforms in the late 1970s. Importantly, the state's net grain extraction was considerably lowered and continued to fall until the end of the Mao–era. Grain resales by the state to peasants in need became an important policy in fighting hunger and starvation (Ash, 2006, 967, 971, 981; Walker, 1984, 786). The pressure on national grain reserves was further eased through net grain imports (Ash, 2006, 982).

The temporary shift in economic model gave rise to a debate around China's development path in the 1960s. This debate harked back to a previous debate in 1956–1957, around the time of Mao's speech "On the Ten Major Relationships," and involved some of the protagonists in the reform debate of the 1980s. For example, the Soviet-trained economist and later radical market reformer Liu Guoguang argued in the late 1950s in favor of a heavy industry–focused development strategy. In contrast, Xu Dixin—who had played an important role in the price-stabilization efforts of the 1940s economic warfare in Shanghai and later came to serve as vice president of the Chinese Academy of Social Sciences in the 1980s—countered that China's development should first be grounded in the agricultural sector (Brødsgaard, 1983a, 59–67). The dominant development strategy of the Mao period remained focused on heavy industry, particularly steel.[9] China depended on extracting agricultural output to fund industrialization, while food consumption for the majority of peasants remained near subsistence levels (Ash, 2006, 983; Brødsgaard, 1983a; Donnithorne, 1967, 337; Perkins, 1966, 56–98).

Despite the draining of the rural economy, the labor mobilization strategy in the communes did achieve an impressive expansion in irrigation and multiple cropping, as well as some degree of rural industrialization. Farmland and water conservancy construction projects, as well as experiments with scientific agricultural development, were carried out on a large scale (Schmalzer, 2016). But farm output grew only slowly in the beginning and came to stagnate in the long term (Xue, 1981, 181).[10] An increase in state investment from the mid-1960s onward facilitated moderate, regionally targeted mechanization and an expansion of farm-supporting industries such as the production of chemical fertilizers (Ash, 2006, 961–965).

Yet, the clear bias toward industrial capital accumulation, at the cost of low material living standards of peasants in particular, persisted throughout the Mao years.[11] This was reflected in the relatively slower growth in light industry and agriculture, compared with that of heavy industry (Solinger, 1984, 17). The urban bias also becomes apparent in the allocation of state investment funds:

throughout the Mao period, more than 80 percent of the population lived in the countryside and more than 73 percent worked in agriculture. Only about 10 percent of the state investment fund was allocated to agriculture. Until the mid-1960s, state investment amounted to less than the taxes from the rural economy; that is, rural communities paid more to the state than they received in return in the form of investment funds (Ash, 2006, 964; Donnithorne, 1978, 10).[12] This extraction was amplified by the low price of agricultural products and the high price of industrial goods.

The Mao era price system functioned as a central mechanism to squeeze resources for urban industrialization out of the countryside. As Lardy (1984, 3) in his classic survey expressed it, "Prices in China for most of the past thirty years [1953–1983] have been set largely with a view toward determining the allocation of resources between individuals and the state, between industry and agriculture, and among different regions." The most crucial aspect of this for the industrialization project was the redistribution from the rural to the urban economy. The prices for agricultural and urban industrial goods were set so as to facilitate unequal exchange. Agricultural purchase prices were kept below their value; peasants working the same hours as urban workers achieved a lower material living standard. The communes had to pay a high price for producer goods procured from the state but received a low price for the produce that they were commanded to deliver.[13] This is the so-called "price scissors": high industrial prices and low agricultural prices diverged like the blades of a pair of open scissors.[14]

Agricultural prices rose faster than industrial prices on average from 1952 to 1975. But Lardy (1984, 8) cautions that this was mainly driven by the market-led price increases before 1953 and the adjustment of relative prices in the early 1960s to recover from the famine. For example, the prices of key agricultural goods such as rice, wheat, and corn were not adjusted from 1966 until the beginning of the Deng era in 1978. Despite recurring increases, throughout the Mao era, state purchasing prices for agricultural goods remained generally low relative to the prices of industrial goods. This unequal exchange was a key point of contest between the state and the peasants, and it resulted in underreporting on the part of the peasants, as well as black market sales (Gao, 2011, 274–278; Oi, 1989, 229).

The method of using "price scissors" to extract resources from agriculture has also been repeatedly challenged by Chinese economists. In the debate over China's economic model that followed the Great Famine, one of the most heated topics was the Marxian law of value. Chinese economists fiercely disagreed on whether the law was applicable to China's economy and whether it should be used in price determination (Lin, 1981). One crucial question was whether agricultural prices should approximate values—which were defined based on the labor theory of value—instead of being kept below value. If prices were set equal to values, the transfer of the agricultural surplus would have had to rely on a tax on peasants instead (Chen, 1966, 48–50).

Those who argued in defense of redistributive price-setting in the 1960s explicitly referred to China's long history of price regulation as a fiscal policy tool. Specifically, they held that peasants would be even less inclined to accept direct taxation. After all, redistributive pricing had long been common practice in China (see Chapter 1). Adjusting prices to reflect values would result in frequent price changes and, the skeptics warned, this would endanger price and social stability. Finally, relying on prices rather than taxes would allow the government to balance revenues and grain provision between years of bumper and poor harvests (Chen, 1966, 48–50)—as was the case under the system of the Ever Normal Granaries.

In light of the high level of tension between the peasants and the state in the early 1960s, a more direct form of extraction of resources from the countryside was ultimately deemed infeasible. China continued to rely on price differentials well beyond the 1960s debate. At the dawn of reform, the 1960s proposal to replace price differentials with taxation was revived by Sun Yefang, one of the most prominent participants of the 1960s debate and a leader of reform economics (Lardy, 1983, 218–219; Sun, 1978).

The persistence of the price scissors must be seen in the context of its contribution to price stability. Price stability served as a primary principle of price policy throughout the Mao era (Lardy, 1984, 2). In fact, the price-stabilization program of 1949–1952 was followed by a surprising record of price stability in the first three decades of the PRC (Donnithorne, 1978, 3; Schran, 1977, 368; Wang, 1980, 127).[15] Yet, the challenge of looming excess aggregate demand and thus inflationary pressures prevailed.

As discussed in Chapter 2, Keynes (1940) has shown that if, in wartime, people work to produce for the war effort rather than for consumption, aggregate demand tends to outgrow supply, causing prices to rise. The same also applies to a heavy industry–oriented development strategy in a closed economy.[16] Many investments in industrialization yield fruits only after a long time. Consider, for example, the construction of a large steel plant. The workers who built the plant receive a wage and need to be clothed, fed, and housed while their labor does not immediately add to the production that serves those needs. As a result, the wage fund tends to outgrow the provision of consumption goods, and the demand for consumption goods tends to exceed their supply.

In the Mao era, the strategy to cope with this tendency toward excess aggregate demand and inflation was to suppress peasants' cash incomes through low procurement prices for agricultural goods, often shifting the burden of producing basic goods such as clothes to female labor in peasant households (Eyferth, 2012). The portion of the population working for urban wages was small in relation to the rural population.[17] Urban wages were higher than rural incomes but were still kept on a low level. The low prices of rationed agricultural products, which constituted the largest share in urban consumption,[18] together with low rents for assigned housing, made it possible to keep urban wage levels below increases in productivity (Donnithorne, 1978, 6).[19] In addition, wages were insulated from upward pressure by the limited use of money. Many consumption items were allocated by coupon as rations or rewards and could not simply be bought with cash (ibid., 10; Solinger, 1984, 25–27). Another factor enabling low urban wages was that in China, unlike in the Soviet Union, workers were abundant. Enterprises did not compete for labor, and wages played a minimal role in labor allocation (Perkins, 1966, 137–138).

Price stability in China was built on what has been described as a "dual society" (二元社会). One part was the subsidized urban sphere; the other part, the rural sphere, provided a transfer to the urban economy and had to rely on its own resources for subsistence and development (Wemheuer, 2014, 43). To maintain this inequality, the masses of peasants were prevented from migrating permanently to the cities and were excluded from the urban wage bill by administrative means, such as the issuance of urban residence permits and local ration cards. The household registration system (户口), instituted in 1955, categorized citizens as either rural or urban. It was key to sustaining this social stratification (Wu and Treiman, 2004).

Keeping rural incomes low and monopolizing trade also came at the cost of a widespread demonetization of the countryside (Solinger, 1984, 24–25; Peebles, 1991, 86).[20] This had important implications for rural price stability. When private grain trade had been widespread, the grain purchases by state trading agencies helped to balance market prices across seasons and regions (see Chapters 1 and 3). But when the state became a monopolist purchaser under the unified purchase system, the state procurement caused a sudden injection of cash into the rural economy at harvest time. This induced speculation and black markets and destabilized prices (Lowenstein, 2019; Solinger, 1984, 23–24).

A basic problem of price stability in the rural economy was that, while the demand for consumption goods was spread over the year, cash was injected only after harvest time. To absorb the abrupt cash inflow after the harvest, credit cooperatives had been set up in the 1950s. They absorbed the excess cash into bank deposits and balanced the cash flow. Credit cooperatives also facilitated advance payments in spring for state procurement of grain; this further balanced the money flow to the rural economy (Hsiao, 1971, 178–182). The price–stabilizing effect of the credit cooperatives follows the same basic logic as the imperial Green Sprout Loans program (see Chapter 1). But in contrast to this imperial institution, the credit cooperatives were not oriented toward extracting high interest rates from the peasants.[21]

Recent research shows that another common practice to address this problem of excess cash in the rural economy was *huilong* (回笼), "to return to the cage." This term had a long tradition in China's monetary policy. Under imperial rule, paper money had at times been convertible into silver. The bank would withdraw excess paper notes from circulation by bringing them back into the bank's "cage," or *huilong* (Lowenstein, 2019, 54). One method for the state to absorb excess cash in the Mao era was to supply nonessential goods at high prices. Chen Yun alluded to this as the "pastry question" in a speech in 1961, when inflation loomed after the Great Leap (ibid., 53). Unrationed "luxury" goods, such as pastries, that traded on a free market had the critical function for the economy at large of absorbing excess liquidity and thus stabilizing prices (ibid., 53–54). Although this promoted price stability, high prices for such unrationed goods further repressed rural living standards (Solinger, 1984, 24–25; Peebles, 1991, 86).

The "pastry question" reveals a larger point about price stabilization in the Mao era. The redistributive price system was a balancing act. Designed to extract resources from the countryside for industrialization, the rate of transfer could not exceed a certain level, as the Great Famine had brutally demonstrated. High prices of nonessential goods served to balance cash flows, but if prices were set too high, demand would cease and the goal could not be achieved. The next section takes a closer look at some of the price-setting practices underpinning this balancing effort.

Basic Working of the Maoist Price-Setting System

After the revolution, the price system as a whole was not reset based on a specific price formula. Prices were instead adjusted on a case-by-case basis, guided by empirical observations and geared toward overall price stability. The Mao era price system was characterized by "diffusion of responsibility for price fixing," a "vagueness of the regulations," and an "even greater flexibility in practice" (Donnithorne, 1967, 442). As Lardy (1984, 2) put it, "The general principles of price formation are well-known but sufficiently vague to serve poorly as a guide to central pricing decisions." In what might still be the most systematic contribution available in English on the theoretical foundations of price-setting, Chen Nai-Ruenn (1966) warned that "Chinese pricing practice is not easily reducible to a single general theoretical principle" (38–39). This lack of axiomatic price-setting principles is an expression of price determination as a constant balancing act.

In addition to the transfer from the rural to the urban economy, another crucial factor for price stability was an emphasis on low and stable urban prices for essential raw materials and consumption goods (Wang, 1980, 127). This involved subsidies and rationing. In contrast, prices for nonessentials were flexibly adapted and often artificially high to absorb cash flows. We can view this through the lens of the principle derived from the *Guanzi* in Chapter 1. To use the *Guanzi*'s terms, the Communist price policy was focused on what is "heavy." The price stability of essential goods for urban consumption and production was the primary rule for price-setting. These essential goods also served to measure the purchasing power of the RMB and thus pinned down the value of money (Wang, 1980, 127–129). For all other goods, price-fixing was more situational than strictly rule based.

To be sure, in sharp contrast to the *Guanzi* and later imperial price-regulation practices (discussed in Chapter 1), the Mao era economy relied heavily on commands rather than on state market participation. The great stability of prices also reflected the relatively small role prices played as an instrument of economic regulation when the Chinese economy was developing into a command economy. Beyond their crucial role as a tool for redistribution, prices played a secondary role in production decisions of enterprises, and consumption decisions were guided by rationing.

Commodity Classification and Types of Prices

Under the system of price determination of the Mao era, commodities were divided into three tiers according to their relative importance for people's livelihoods, for industrial and agricultural production, and for foreign trade. First-category commodities were those most essential and most tightly controlled by the state, compared with second- and third-category goods. The concrete classifications of specific commodities have varied over time, but the basic logic of the regulation of prices based on this three-tier hierarchy of importance prevailed (Lardy, 1984, 4; Solinger, 1984, 28).

Commodities in the first category originally included food grains, edible oils, raw cotton, cotton yarn, and cotton cloth and, later, sugar, salt, tobacco, petroleum, and the most important export goods, such as tea (Solinger, 1984, 285). These essential consumption goods and industrial inputs were under the "unified system of purchase and sale" (Lardy, 1984, 4). The State Council directly controlled purchases and supplies of these goods by means of delivery quotas and rationing. Second-category commodities, under "designated procurement," were controlled by specialized ministries. This category, comprising more than hundred commodities, included agricultural products such as ramie, hemp, silk cocoons, eggs, pork, animal hides, tea, and some items for export.[22] For most of these commodities, prices were also set by the state (Lardy, 1984, 4; Schran, 1977, 371).[23] All remaining commodities were placed in the third category, which was generally administered by local authorities and sometimes under commodity-specific regulations.

For the first- and second-category commodities, the state commercial entities had exclusive purchasing rights. In principle, no direct trading between producers or selling from producers to consumers was allowed. The prices of these essential goods were meant to be insulated from market forces. In contrast, some third-category commodities were at times traded in rural markets, often with state regulation of prices. The prevalence of rural markets was subject to great variations across time and regions, but important first-category commodities such as cotton and grain were universally banned from such markets (Donnithorne, 1967, 284; Lardy, 1984, 5; Schran, 1977, 371).[24] Second-category goods were allowed on the market once the compulsory quota for "designated procurement" had been fulfilled. But to buy these goods, rationing coupons were required.

The most important means of production, including those of steel, iron, coal, and machinery, were outside this three-tier system. They were the backbone of the industrialization effort and under the direct auspices of the central government, which directly allocated these inputs to major producers and provincial-level authorities, circumventing state commercial organizations (Donnithorne, 1967, 285).

In the early 1950s, the Chinese government introduced the Soviet cost-plus principle, which determines prices by adding some profit or surplus to the cost of production (Chen, 1966, 39). Five types of prices were to be set by the relevant government authorities. In theory—and only in theory—the following principles for operationalizing cost-plus pricing applied:

- First, *ex-factory prices of raw materials* were fixed, based on a rough formula that added tax and policy adjustments, as well as limited corrections for quality, to the estimated cost of production.[25]
- Second, *purchasing prices of agriculture* were set to facilitate rural-to-urban transfer and were broadly based on historic prices. Relative prices of different agricultural goods were assigned with the aim of incentivizing the production of certain crops.
- Third, *wholesale prices* were based on the ex-factory and agricultural purchasing prices, with the addition of distribution costs and profits.
- Fourth, *prices paid by consumers* to retailers were determined by adding retail costs, profits, and taxes to the wholesale price.
- Fifth, state-owned producing enterprises were charged an annually *fixed allocation price* for their rationed inputs, composed of the ex-factory or agricultural purchase price plus the costs of distribution. In some cases, producers under cooperative or commune ownership were allowed to buy at the allocation price, but they generally had to pay the typically higher wholesale price (Donnithorne, 1967, 439–442).

A word of caution is needed here. This list of principles leaves the impression of rigidness and precision, but these general rules were in fact applied in a flexible manner and not based on any strict formulas. In practice, these varieties of cost-plus pricing were not applicable to a large number of cases (N. Chen, 1966, 39). Many prices were determined instead by use of empirical information of past price formations or by investigation of sample cases. Pricing was based on translating prerevolutionary practices of cost accounting into the Marxist categories of constant and variable capital or by using past relative prices between agricultural goods as reference. In particular, historical data for the years 1930–1936, which was considered a period of relatively normal economic conditions, was sometimes used as guidance for relative prices (Chen, 1966, 37–38, 40, 48).[26]

Another common empirical method of arriving at prices for specific commodities was to identify model firms that were assumed to produce under average conditions and to calculate costs based on their current production practices (N. Chen, 1966, 37–38, 40). Thereby, vast regional differences in technology and management, and hence in cost, were taken into account by identifying regionally specific model firms and allowing for interregional price variations (Chen, 1978, 93–94). The question of how to determine the surplus value—which, in Marx's price accounting, has to be added to the constant and variable capital—was subject to another important debate in the early 1960s.[27] The theoretical determination of the surplus value under socialism remained unresolved and was, in practice, handled flexibly to account for policy priorities such as the need to withdraw cash from some parts of the economy (*huilong*) and redistribution between regions, between the city and the countryside, and between the state and the people (Chen, 1966, 37–38, 40, 48).

The strictness with which general pricing principles were applied also depended on the importance of the respective goods for people's livelihoods or for industrialization. Except for the most important commodities, the central planners allowed the pricing authorities at lower levels a certain degree of flexibility within the defined principles and guidelines, accounting for seasonal conditions, variations in quality, and so on. The prices of essential goods were kept very stable, while those of nonessentials were adjusted more frequently, typically "bit by bit" (Wang, 1980, 93–94). Retail prices for goods under the first category (see above) did not change much throughout the Mao period, when these goods were rationed for urban consumers (Lardy, 1984, 6). The Chinese state exerted particularly great efforts to keep the urban grain price stable (Donnithorne, 1978, 9; Schran, 1977, 378).

Cost-plus pricing was not easy to implement because of the shortcomings of the planning system in achieving balance across sectors. Notwithstanding the unresolved question over the right calculation method of the 1950s and 1960s debate, cost-plus pricing aimed for prices to be equal to values. But we can only expect this to be the case in equilibrium. Assuming that supply meets demand in a planned economy, cost-plus pricing was not set up to reflect scarcity relations. It was therefore ill-fit to accommodate recurring shortcomings in planning and mismatches between planned inputs and outputs.

In contrast, the Chinese empirical method of price determination explicitly asked cadres to consider prevailing forces of supply and demand in their price-setting. If a consumer good was in short supply, its price should not be lowered but also not increased indiscriminately. If a good was oversupplied, its price should be lowered to prevent the building up of unnecessary stocks (Chen, 1978, 95; Chang, 1969, 148). Thus, local and product-specific forces of supply and demand were to be taken into account, but only in ways that would not result in price hikes.

Price stability remained a paramount concern of the Chinese leadership, and adjustments of specific prices also served as a tool for *huilong* by absorbing excess cash. The debate over the law of value and price determination of the early 1960s that I mentioned aimed to rationalize the whole price system, ultimately had no practical consequences. The perceived danger to price stability prevented the leadership from readjusting all prices based on an axiomatic formula (N. Chen, 1966, 51–52).

State-Owned Enterprises, Financial Targets, and Prices

The urban industrial system was broadly modeled on the Soviet example: state-owned enterprises had only very limited control over expansion or construction projects. They were production units that operated at a scale defined by the central planning authorities. State-owned enterprises received commands from the central planning authorities with targets for physical outputs and were allocated the raw materials and major equipment required as inputs in their production plans (Perkins, 1966, 100). In this system, the Planning Bureau had to balance all inputs and outputs across production units. The financial control system was built upon this system of material balancing. Financial targets served both to back up physical goals and to give broad indications for parameters that were not easily defined. For example, state-owned enterprises were set a limit on their overall wage bill rather than a specification of all positions and grades (ibid., 101).

Under this system of central command, state-owned enterprises did not control their overall funds. The scale of national investment was largely in the hands of the central planning authorities. Large portions of the revenues of state-owned enterprises from sales were channeled to the central treasury in the form of sales and profit taxes. It was up to the central planners to decide whether to reissue these funds to the state-owned enterprises. Only very small investments could be financed out of retained profits. Working capital was provided by budget allocations or in the form of loans from the People's Bank of China.[28] State-owned enterprises even had to gain approval from the bank to use their own deposits (Perkins, 1966, 101–105). Keeping tight control over the finance of state-owned enterprises was vital for the state budget, which was mostly kept in balance (Wang, 1980, 107–108). Over 90 percent of fiscal revenue came from state-owned enterprises in the form of profits, taxes, depreciation payments, and minor charges (Donnithorne, 1978, 4). The central government could abruptly and drastically cut expenditures by stopping capital construction projects if it deemed this necessary for price stability (ibid.).

As a result of the central control over state-owned enterprises' funds, prices did not affect state-owned enterprises directly. Large parts of their revenue and profits were not at their disposal, and they depended on state transfers for their operating costs (Xue, 1981, 137–138). It would be a mistake, however, to conclude from this that prices did not matter. Relative prices were used as a means of redistribution also within the urban industrial sector. Some production units operated at a planned loss; high profits on other goods subsidized these losses. For example, the prices of coal and timber, the "food of industry" (Xue, 1981, 153) that would "affect production costs of most enterprises, and ultimately people's livelihood" (Xue, 1982b, 72) were kept low. Small coal mines with high production costs were kept running due to the vital role of energy for industrialization (Donnithorne, 1967, 316; H. Chen, 1978, 94). Downstream producer goods, such as machines, were sold at relatively high prices and generated high profits. In the consumer goods sector, the prices of basic necessities (typically in the first category of commodity) were kept very low; the prices of so-called luxury goods were high relative to prices of necessities and to household incomes (Tsakok, 1979, 870).

The pricing principles of essential and nonessential consumer goods also differed. For example, cost increases of nonessentials, following rising producer goods prices, tended to be handed down to the consumers based on a cost-plus formula. Cost increases for essentials were absorbed by adjustments in taxes, subsidies, and profits of commercial entities (Schran, 1977, 378). Thus, increases in the purchase price of grain were compensated for by state subsidies to keep the sales price low. For nonessentials, too, the cost-plus formula was not applied mechanically but depended on various policy considerations and the prevailing conditions in the production and marketing of a certain commodity (Wang, 1980, 85, 127).

From the primacy of the system of physical targets and allocation, it is sometimes inferred that the People's Bank of China "played a peripheral and limited role due to the systemic subordination of finance to state plans" (Bell, 2013, 41). In contrast, Donnithorne (1978, 9) found that "[t]he bank [People's Bank of China] is the single most powerful and far reaching economic organ in China." If central planning for the whole Chinese economy was an insurmountable challenge, it was at least as demanding to keep track of all activities of state-owned enterprises in physical terms. Control over financial transactions was the only way to do this, and as such, the People's Bank of China was essential for keeping a certain degree of central control, Donnithorne argues.

The problem was, however, as Perkins (1966, 126) points out, "[f]inancial regulations were among the least obeyed of centrally issued legislation." Especially at times of mass campaigns and movements, the financial authorities had great difficulty in instituting controls (ibid., 129). It proved challenging for the central government to prevent enterprises from granting each other direct credit (ibid., 126–127; Donnithorne, 1978, 9–10). This might at times have rescued plan fulfillment, but it undermined financial control. Enterprises also often used funds for purposes other than those assigned in the plan, such as channeling circulating capital into capital construction (ibid., 127–128). Perkins (1966, 130) pointed out that, as a result of the largely ineffective financial control, factory managers tended to ignore the limited price incentives that the central government at times sought to employ.

The practical difficulties of imposing financial discipline on state-owned enterprises hampered the government's ability to exercise control over plan implementation. At the same time, the lack of financial discipline undermined attempts to use indirect means of control through price incentives. This limited effectiveness of both direct and indirect means of control meant that it proved very difficult for the central government to coordinate this large, predominantly agricultural economy and guide it toward rapid industrialization, despite the high levels of extraction from the countryside. As a result, the economy was more anarchic than the label "planned" would suggest. In the late phase of Maoism during the Cultural Revolution, the government had largely given up trying to use indirect economic means to control the economy, and it shifted to political campaigns as a means of economic mobilization. Economic incentives were condemned as bourgeois, and prices were basically frozen (Xue, 1982b, 64).

The Urge for Reform and the Role of Prices

The year 1976 was a watershed in China's modern history, marking the end of the revolutionary era. Just before the year began, the leader of the internal security apparatus, Kang Sheng, died. In the first month of 1976, Zhou Enlai, China's first premier and head of government since 1949, died. In the summer of that year, the founder of the Red Army, Zhu De, died. And finally, in September, Chairman Mao's life ended (Vogel, 2011, 157).

In my conversations with Chinese and international reform economists and officials involved with the reform process of the 1980s, I found consensus on one point: change in the late 1970s was not the result of theoretical insights or ideological battles. From their perspective, it was an economic imperative. As the economist Zhao Renwei (2016) put it, "In the years 1978 and 1979 China could not have gone on without change. Not changing was not a possibility. We had to reform. But *how* to reform? This was not clear."[29]

The first World Bank report on China (1983), which looked back to assess the development record of the Mao era, came to a positive judgment. Adrian Wood, the principal economist on the mission, recalled that the main message of the report was that "the previous 30 to 40 years of Chinese development had been remarkably successful." Wood (2016) explained,

> China had combined rapid growth and industrialization, not rapid by Chinese post-1980s standards but rapid by comparison with other developing countries. China had achieved the virtual elimination of the worst aspects of poverty. ... The other message [of the report] was that there is scope for improvement.

The Chinese reformers' assessment was drastically more critical. An example is Hu Qiaomu's famous report to the State Council in July 1978, "Act in Accordance with Economic Laws" (Hu, 1978). Hu, a member of Deng Xiaoping's Political Research Office and later the first president of the Chinese Academy of Social Sciences (CASS), pointed out that the situation of the peasants remained grave. He estimated that in more than twenty years since 1955, all that had been achieved was that grain output had kept pace with the growth in population (Fewsmith, 1994, 59–60). In fact, the picture might have been even grimmer. Lardy's (1983, 157–158) survey suggests that national consumption levels for essential goods, including grain, cotton cloth, and vegetable oil, all declined between 1957 and 1978. The burden was largely shouldered by the rural population.

Weng Yongxi (2016) was one of the "four gentlemen of reform" (改革四君子), who were among the first young intellectuals to enter into a dialogue with the top leadership in the early years of reform. He argued that change in the late 1970s was the consequence of great failure. The first generation of revolutionaries was still in charge. Weng stressed that, although they had fought great struggles to revolutionize society and ultimately improve the lives of the masses, after almost thirty years, the most basic problem of people's livelihood remained unresolved. Peasants were fleeing China to colonial Hong Kong in hopes of a better life, and they secretly divided the collectivized land of the communes among themselves to improve their basic material conditions. Tang Zongkun (2016), a prominent reform economist of the CASS, quantified the failure: for 200 million out of 800 million peasants, the problem of adequate clothing and food provision (温饱问题) was not resolved, and 10 percent of peasants were suffering from hunger.

In the economic dimension, the aspiration of the Chinese revolutionaries was not simply to eliminate the "worst aspects of poverty"—to use Wood's phrase. They aspired to overcome poverty altogether and build a wealthy, socialist society. In a 1978 speech, Deng Xiaoping recalled his reading of China's original goals: "to rid our country of poverty and backwardness," "to catch up with"—or even "surpass—the advanced countries" (Deng, 1984a, 153–154). The revival of an economic modernization agenda after years of "politics in command" during the heyday of the Cultural Revolution predated Deng Xiaoping's reforms. Mao had begun to reopen China to the West, as symbolized by US President Richard Nixon's visit in 1972. At around the same time, China rapidly increased its imports of foreign capital goods and technology.[30] This quickly resulted in a balance of payments problem (Riskin, 1987, 193). In 1975, Mao had put Deng in charge of economic modernization, mainly by means of restoring order in the bureaucracy of the planned economy after years of political mass campaigns and struggles of the Cultural Revolution (Teiwes and Sun, 2011, 6). Mao thought that Deng went too far in reversing the Cultural Revolution, and in his last year, the emerging foreign account crisis was used as the reason to remove Deng from all offices. Although Deng had been lined up to become the next leader, Mao installed Hua Guofeng as premier and his successor. But Mao did not expel Deng from the party. This left open a path for Deng's return to the center of power (Vogel, 2011, 157, 168–171).

Under Mao's designated heir, Hua Guofeng, China's opening to the capitalist world was accelerated in the first post-Mao year, 1977 (Teiwes and Sun, 2011, 11–13). This was Hua's possibly unintended, yet major, contribution to reform (Lu, 2016). Chinese delegations were sent all around the world, and exchanges with foreign countries increased rapidly. China's leaders and intellectuals realized how far they had fallen behind the Western powers and their immediate East Asian neighbors in terms of economic development (Lin, 2016; see entry quote). These travels also marked the beginning of China's new kind of opening up that was an openness to Western capitalism and a farewell to the old socialist internationalism and Third Worldism. This shift toward an opening to the Western world was consolidated with the establishment of diplomatic relations with the United States in 1979 and violently asserted when the Chinese government declared war on Vietnam the same year (Wang, 2009, 43).

The legacy of Hua Guofeng has often been reduced to his slogan of "two whatevers": to "uphold whatever policy decisions Chairman Mao made, and unswervingly follow whatever instructions Chairman Mao gave." Recent research by Teiwes and Sun (2011, 2013) has convincingly challenged such a caricature. Several of my interviewees, too, stressed the importance of Hua Guofeng in the transition from late Maoism to economic reform. Hua upheld the "whatever" slogan in the year after Mao's death. But so did Chen Yun, who jointly with Deng Xiaoping superseded Hua (Teiwes and Sun, 2011, 3). Paying tribute to Mao in the year after his passing was not unique to Hua.

Hua Guofeng's leadership marked a critical break with the Cultural Revolution in terms of China's broad ideological orientation, development strategy, and international economic relations, while constituting a revival of Deng Xiaoping's 1975 efforts. Shortly after Mao's passing, Hua attacked the Cultural Revolution approach that rejected a focus on the development of the productive forces, and he advocated for continuous revolution instead of economism. Hua redefined revolution itself as "liberation of productive forces" and elevated national economic development to the highest priority (Teiwes and Sun, 2011, 7). This was in complete agreement with Deng Xiaoping's insistence, during his short tenure in the leadership in 1975, that "The view that once revolution is grasped, production will increase naturally and without spending any effort is believed only by those who indulge in fairy tales" (Riskin, 1987, 192). By elevating economic development to the highest revolutionary principle, Hua paved the way for the Deng-era reforms. It is remarkable that such drastic changes occurred under a leader who has frequently been described as a relatively unremarkable Mao loyalist.[31] This speaks for the powerful structural forces pushing toward a change in the economic model.

Hua combined Soviet-style big push industrialization with an opening up to the capitalist world. Under Hua, the first Special Economic Zone opened in China, and major efforts to attract foreign direct investment were launched (Vogel, 2011, 185). China was meant once more to push forward, this time in a Ten-Year Plan with overoptimistic ambitions and an emphasis on heavy industry (Brødsgaard, 1983b, 258–260; Teiwes and Sun, 2011, 8–10). As Naughton (1995, 67) pointed out, the "Ten Year Plan was as close as China ever came, after the 1950s, to explicitly following Stalinist development priorities." Agricultural productivity was to be improved by investments in construction projects, large-scale mechanization, and the use of fertilizers. Synthetic substitutes—for example, for cotton—were intended to relieve pressure from the countryside for more clothing. This time, the crucial inputs for agricultural advancement and for megaprojects in heavy industry were to come from imports, not from the peasants. Those imports were hoped to be financed from petroleum exports. Petroleum was one of the few sectors that grew rapidly in the late-Mao period (Naughton, 1995, 69; Fewsmith, 1994, 57–58).

The "Petroleum Group" around Yu Qiuli, who had made their careers in the petroleum sector, were put in charge of national planning under Hua (Fewsmith,

1994, 58; Naughton, 1995, 69). When the projected oil field discoveries did not materialize, however, China faced a lack of foreign currency from anticipated petroleum exports. The planned inputs for economic development could be imported only in the context of a deteriorating foreign exchange position. The situation was aggravated because central planning organs were just recovering. Financial discipline was lax, and enterprises entered a bidding contest for ever-more foreign imports.[32] Hua was criticized for his "Western-led Leap Forward" (Vogel, 2011, 185). It constituted another vain attempt at pushing ahead in one go after the dramatic failure of the Great Leap Forward.

While the Ten-Year Plan was in crisis, a democracy movement was growing around Tiananmen Square in late 1978 (Meisner, 1999, 434). The Third Plenary Session of the 11th Central Committee of the CPC in December of that year brought a decisive change in path; it is generally recognized as the beginning of the Deng era, both in China and in Western scholarship (Resolution on Certain Questions in the History of Our Party, 1986, 610; Liu and Wu, 1986, 434; Naughton, 1995, 74). Deng Xiaoping took over effective control of the Central Committee and the Politburo, replacing Hua Guofeng (Meisner, 1999, 434–435).

Even more symbolic for the shift in economic policy was that Chen Yun became a member of the Politburo's Standing Committee (Naughton, 1995, 74; Luo, 2017). Deng Xiaoping had cooperated with the Petroleum Group during his short return to power in 1973 (Fewsmith, 1994, 57–58; Naughton, 1995, 69).[33] Chen, in contrast, had since the 1950s consistently criticized the one-sided emphasis on heavy industry represented by this group. He had lobbied for an alternative development path that dedicated more resources to agriculture and light industry, one that resembled Mao's insights in the speech "On the Ten Major Relationships." As described earlier, Chen was a veteran revolution-ary, and he led the financial and economic work during the crucial stabiliza-tion period after 1949. Chen was again put in charge of economic work when the Chinese economy was having grave difficulties in the context of the Great Famine in the early 1960s and economic policy returned to using market forces as a tool of regulation (Editorial Board of Who's Who in China, 1989, 68–69; Vogel, 2011, 719–721).[34] In the mid-1960s, the Petroleum Group took over from Chen (Fewsmith, 1994, 58). Now, Chen Yun was once more in control of the economy.

In their effort to reform the Chinese economy, the new leadership invoked the Communist success of the very early years (Deng, 1984a, 164). In order to finally achieve socialist modernization and face the great challenges of reform, Deng chose the slogan "seek truth from facts" (实事求是) as the guiding prin-ciple (Deng, 1984b, 141; Pantsov and Levine, 2015, 328). Seeking truth from facts was a key tenet of the eighteenth-century pragmatist "school of empirical research." In Chen Yun's view, the principle influenced Mao's thought dur-ing the Chinese Civil War (Schwartz, 1964, 6–7; Zhu et al., 2000, 376). The Communiqué of the Third Plenary Session (1986, 574) described the slogan "seeking truth from facts" as "proceeding from reality and … linking theory with practice." "Seeking truth from facts" was not only used as an attack on Hua Guofeng, who was increasingly reduced to the rhetoric of "two whatevers," but was initially a call to reject any form of doctrinaire approach (Deng, 1984b, 141). Deng (1984a, 153–154) warned,

> Once people's thinking becomes rigid, book worship, divorced from real-ity, becomes a grave malady. Those who suffer from it dare not say a word or take a step that isn't mentioned in books, documents or the speeches of leaders: everything has to be copied. ... When everything has to be done by the book, when thinking turns rigid and blind faith is the fashion, it is impossible for a party or a nation to make progress. Its life will cease and that nation or party will perish.

Deng called on the CPC to begin learning "through practice, from books and from the experience, both positive and negative, of others as well as our own" (Deng, 1984a, 165).

In terms of the approach to policy-making and the development strategy, the reformers reached back to the early post-liberation years. Reflecting Chen Yun's priorities, the Communiqué of the Third Plenary Session (1986, 568) elevated Mao's "On the Ten Major Relationships" to serve as the basic guideline for economic policy-making. The speech had been reprinted according to Hua's instructions (Teiwes and Sun, 2011, 5). The desired development approach was now "to develop heavy industry by developing more light industry and agricul-ture" (Mao, 1992, 48). The Communiqué (1986, 570) particularly stressed the importance of advancing agriculture, "the foundation of the national economy," which had been "seriously damaged." Rather than relying on investment in col-lective mechanization, as the Petroleum Group had attempted, the advancement of agriculture would rely on price adjustments made effective by reviving eco-nomic incentives. Egalitarianism was to be replaced by the principle of "to each according to his work," which required "work[ing] out payment in accordance with the amount and quality of work done" (ibid.).

In line with this shift in development strategy, the most important price adjustment was to overcome the "scissors gap": in order to

> reduce the disparity in prices between industrial and agricultural products, the plenary session suggests that the State Council make a decision to raise the grain purchase price by 20 percent, starting in 1979[35] ... and the price for the amount purchased above the quota by an additional 50 percent, ... [while the prices for] manufactured goods for farm use will be cut by 10 to 15 percent.
>
> *(ibid., 571)*

This indicated a crucial step away from the transfer of resources from the coun-tryside to the city through unequal exchange. Peasants were to get more for their produce and pay less for their inputs. But the Communiqué did not touch urban prices for agricultural goods. The old principle of keeping the retail price of grain low and stable for the urban population was maintained. The Communiqué stated that the "market price of all food grain will remain unchanged," implying that "appropriate subsidies will be given to the consumers" (ibid., 571). This meant the continuation of a trend that had already prevailed for a few years in 1978: the state sustained losses in grain trade, which is to say it paid considerable subsidies to urban consumers (Donnithorne, 1978, 8–9). The challenge of how to raise agricultural prices without also increasing urban retail prices prevailed throughout the 1980s and, toward the end of the first reform decade, contributed to a growing fiscal deficit.

The Communiqué also reintroduced small-scale private production by the members of the communes as a legitimate form of production under socialism: "small plots of land for private use by commune members, their domestic side-occupations, and village fairs are necessary adjuncts of the socialist economy, and must not be interfered with" (ibid., 570). The prices of such side-line products should be raised "step by step, depending on the concrete conditions" according to the Communiqué (ibid., 571). This was a small but significant first step toward decollectivization and helped pave the way toward the dismantling of the communes.

More generally, reform marked a radical departure from the approach of late Maoism, which had relied heavily on political enthusiasm, egalitarianism, collective efforts, and commands. The material interests of the people and cadres, narrowly defined, should now become the new driving force (Weber, 2020). Hu Qiaomu (1978) expressed this rupture in his pathbreaking speech "Act in Accordance with Economic Laws." According to Hu, the Gang of Four—who had been arrested and found guilty for all aberrations of the Cultural Revolution—would have tried to jump forward in history by raising the consciousness of the masses and revolutionizing the relations of production. In contrast, historical materialism taught that economic development decided historical progress. Thus China, as a backward country, had to put all its efforts into improving its forces of production.

In preparing the Third Plenary Session, Deng Xiaoping (1984a, 162) made clear what this shift in paradigm meant for the new criteria by which economic work would henceforth be judged:

> the quality of leadership … in an economic unit should be judged mainly by the unit's adoption of advanced methods of managements, by the progress of its technical innovation, and by the margins of increase of its productivity of labour, its profits, the personal income of its workers and the collective benefits it provides.

As Deng pointed out, to allow for such performance-based judgments, responsibilities would have to be defined clearly: "In theory, there [was] collective responsibility. In fact, this mean[t] that no one [was] responsible" (ibid.).

A fundamental problem with such a shift to a responsibility-based system was that the price structure was not set up to provide incentives to individual production units. Instead, the system relied on conscious redistribution between and within sectors. As we have seen, some units were meant to make high profits, others to sustain losses. To overcome this challenge, prices were now to be brought in line with the law of value (Communiqué, 1986, 569), meaning that they would somehow be determined based on the average number of hours required to produce a good—that is, the socially necessary labor time (Hu, 1978). However, basing prices on the law of value posed a great problem in itself. As we have seen, the prevailing price structure was not based on a strict application of a cost-plus principle or any other formula. It was a tremendous, if not impossible, task to determine the socially necessary labor time for the manufacture of all products. It was also unclear how such an overall price adjustment could be achieved. After all, as mentioned, prices had never been set from scratch.

Even if prices could be aligned with values, the dramatically diverging production conditions across the country suggested that the prospects for rewards in different production units would be extremely unfair. Deng Xiaoping (1984a, 164) promoted the idea that "some regions and enterprises and some workers and peasants [should] earn more and enjoy more benefits sooner than others." This constituted a drastic departure from the Maoist ideal of egalitarianism. But those benefits should, in Deng's meritocratic vision, be "in accordance with their hard work and greater contribution to society" and should not be the result of environmental conditions or historical privileges.

Another problem that prevailed throughout the 1980s reforms also arose in these early days of reform: price adjustments tended to conflict with the aim of keeping consumer and input prices stable. To prevent price increases from being passed on, adjustments to procurement prices incurred high subsidies, which placed pressure on the state budget. Xue Muqiao (1981, 146) therefore argued that price adjustments were ultimately a matter of distribution across the economy. In his view, this could only be solved "in the course of industrial and agricultural growth and should be conducted in a way that promotes the latter." How exactly this would be achieved in practical terms was to become the subject of a great debate throughout the 1980s.

Conclusion

Achieving price stability after prolonged hyperinflation was an important source of legitimacy for the revolutionary government and was maintained, with few exceptions, throughout the Mao period. But this came at a high cost: the squeezing of the peasants. China's heavy industry–focused industrialization strategy of the Mao era faced a macroeconomic challenge similar to that of a war economy. Large investments in heavy industries did not generate an increase in consumption goods in the short to medium term. Yet, workers building these industries had to be fed, clothed, and housed. This burden was carried largely by China's peasant majority. Under the state monopoly of purchase and sale, the agricultural communes had to deliver considerable shares of their output under state quotas. Prices were set to the disadvantage of the rural economy, thus extracting the inputs, food, and funds needed for industrialization from the countryside.

Prices were increasingly centrally dictated as production, both in industry and agriculture, was integrated into a command economy. Nevertheless, the degree of price control depended on the importance of the commodities for production and livelihoods. The most essential goods were controlled the most tightly, and their prices were insulated from market fluctuations. Once production was primarily regulated by political means, price signals became largely ineffective for production decisions. Yet, the price system played a key role in the Mao era economy as a tool to facilitate cross-sectorial redistribution, particularly from the peasant majority to heavy industry.

The People's Republic of China started out as one of the poorest countries in the world. While basic industrialization had been achieved by the end of the Mao era, reformers found that living standards had been stagnating or even declining, and the most basic problem of adequate nutrition remained unresolved for a considerable proportion of the peasant population. When Mao died, China was still a very poor country. Its lagging economic capacities became startlingly clear to members of Chinese delegations who began touring the Western world under Hua Guofeng. After a last push toward Soviet-style industrialization fueled by Western technology failed under Hua Guofeng, reform led by Deng Xiaoping and Chen Yun promised a way to escape a looming crisis. Instead of relying on political enthusiasm, collective organization, and central commands, the economic interests of enterprises and individuals should be utilized to unleash China's productive powers—according to the reformers' vision.

To organize such a radical shift from collectivism and egalitarianism to individual economic incentives, the Chinese leadership acknowledged in the early days of reform that a restructuring of the price system was key. The question was *how* this daunting task could be achieved. Chinese economists, in dialogue with their foreign counterparts, struggled to find a practical solution to the problem of price reform and market creation, oscillating between "book worship" and "seeking truth from facts."

Notes

1 See Schmalzer (2016) for a comprehensive account of China's green revolution and the Maoist notion of revolutionary science.
2 See Chapter 3 for the biographical background of Xue Muqiao and his role in the economic work during the Chinese Civil War.
3 The term "peasant" is not used in a pejorative sense; it also does not map to the common English use, referring to farm households working the land for their own

subsistence needs. Rather, I follow the convention in China scholarship to use the term "to denote anyone who lives in the Chinese countryside, as demarcated by the household registration system" (Yang, 1996, 8). In the Maoist period, a large share of this population was working in agriculture.

4 See Wemheuer (2014, 87–89) for a detailed description and illustration of the workings of this system.

5 Before collectivization, about 30 percent of the gross value of agricultural output was in subsidiary rural production, pursued by household members not otherwise engaged in production or between duties in the fields, and included hog- and poultry-raising, vegetable and fruit cultivation, and household manufacture of clothes and small-farm implements (Perkins, 1966, 74).

6 For speeches at this occasion by Li Xiannian, then vice premier and minister of finance, and Chen Yun, then vice premier and minister of commerce, see Chen Yun (1956, 1983a) and Li Xiannian (1956).

7 As this speech contained an "unprecedented critique of the Soviet model of development," it was not published until much later (Leung and Kau, 1992, 44).

8 Also see Chen Yun (1983b).

9 The Great Leap Forward, which had the goal of achieving industrialization within only a few years, is the most extreme case of this approach and caused China to endure "unquestionably ... in 1959–61 the worst famine of the twentieth century" (Nolan, 1993, 4). As part of the Great Leap Forward, the aim for 1958 was to double steel output from 5.35 million tons in 1957 to 10.7 million tons and almost double grain output from 390 billion jin to 700 billion jin. Although the actual outputs were only 8 million tons and 400 million jin, respectively, even more ambitious goals were set for 1959 and 1960 (Xue, 1982a, 31).

10 Perkins (1966, 81) reported that, in the initial years of centralized control over agriculture in 1956 and 1957, agricultural production increased by 4.9 percent and 3.5 percent, respectively. Nolan (1995, 51) found that the net value of per capita agricultural output grew by just 0.3 percent per annum from 1957 to 1975. Xue (1981, 180) made the same observation: "The per capita grain output in 1977 was roughly the same as in 1957 and total cotton output remained at the 1965 level." Xue (1982a, 32–33) also noted that agricultural output stagnated in 1967 and that the output of food grain dropped by 4 percent in 1968. Orders by Mao Zedong and Zhou Enlai in 1969 to stop armed conflict would have reversed the trend.

11 Nolan (1995, 51) suggested that the share of heavy industry in total state investment rose from 36 percent of total state investment in the first Five-Year Plan (FYP) to around one-half in the third and fourth FYPs. The share of light industry would have stagnated at only 5 to 6 percent. Part of this bias resulted from the need for national defense in the context of the Korean War, the Cold War more broadly, and the Sino-Russian split. As Mao put it in "On the Ten Major Relationships" (1956), "National defense is indispensable. Would it be all right for us to eliminate all our troops? No, it wouldn't be because we still have enemies who are harassing us, and we are still surrounded by them!" (Mao, 1992, 49). However, Mao also warned that the proportion of the state budget for military and administrative expenditures during the first FYP (almost one-third) was "much too high" and urged, "In the Second Five-year Plan, we should find ways to reduce this proportion so that more funds can be released for economic construction and cultural construction" (Mao, 1992, 50).

12 For a detailed discussion of prices and transfers between the urban and rural economies, see Lardy, 1983, 98–128.

13 Nevertheless, the "scissors relation," $\dfrac{\text{Index figure of retail price of industrial goods in rural areas} \times 100}{\text{Index figure of the procurement price of agricultural products}}$, with

1930–1936 as a base measure of the rural terms of trade, tended to improve at least until 1964 (Donnithorne, 1967, 448–449) and most likely stagnated as most prices were frozen during the Cultural Revolution (Xue, 2011).

14 The term "price scissors" was coined by Trotsky in the 1920s, when the Soviets pursued a market-driven industrialization strategy under the New Political Economy (Mandel, 1995, 61–64). Just as in China in the 1930s and 1940s, low agricultural prices had resulted in a withdrawal of the peasants from the market. Then the Communists' economic warfare aimed to reintegrate the countryside by means of markets and money (see Chapter 3). This involved trying to close the price scissors (Cole, 2018, 179–180).

15 Perkins (1964) and Wang Tongeng (1980, 4–10) provided a detailed discussion of Chinese price indices. While the official indices having a certain downward bias and data availability for the 1960s and 1970s is limited, there is not much doubt that price increases—at least for major commodities—were very low by international standards, particularly for a developing country.

16 The World Bank (1983, 79) suggests that all of China's domestic investments were financed by domestic savings. In contrast to other low-income countries that financed more than a quarter of their investments with foreign capital, China also exported capital in the form of aid to other developing countries.

17 Donnithorne (1978, 8) estimated that in 1964, the share of the economically active population earning wages was less than 10 percent.

18 Perkins (1964, 363) suggested that in the late 1950s, around 70 percent of the commodity outlay of the average worker was for agricultural products. In light of stagnating living standards, this share must have remained roughly constant.

19 Wages were never substantially increased from 1956 to late 1977, despite considerable increases in labor productivity (Donnithorne, 1978, 6).

20 The importance of the demonetization of the countryside was brought to my awareness in a private correspondence with Jacob Eyferth.

21 See Hsiao (1971, 51–61, 172–183) for a detailed discussion of the workings of rural credit cooperatives.

22 This second category comprised 293 commodities in 1959, whereas the first category included only 38 (Donnithorne, 1967, 285). The lists were subject to regular revisions.

23 At times, the state might have offered higher prices for above-quota deliveries and even higher negotiated prices for yet additional deliveries for goods in the first and second categories (Lardy, 1984, 5).

24 While these markets almost ceased to exist in the initial years of increasing state control over commerce, they were reopened in 1956 to counter inflationary pressures and again after the devastating famine that resulted from the Great Leap Forward (Perkins, 1966, 291–292).

25 Note that, due to the far-reaching contingencies and historical path dependencies in determining prices, it was largely impossible to know the costs of production in any terms other than the empirically given input prices (Wang, 1980, 86).

26 In a private communication, Alexander F. Day provided a revealing example involving the pricing of tea based on his archival work on a state-owned farm in the northern Guizhou county of Meitan. The archival evidence suggests that, since it was not feasible to calculate prices based on values, the historical price difference between different qualities of tea and rice was used to set tea procurement prices. When it turned out that the resulting price was too low to achieve the production targets for tea, the price was adjusted upward, in an experimental fashion, with the aim of promoting more production.

27 The competing positions are discussed in Chen Nai-Ruenn (1966). There were three schools: the first two suggested calculating the surplus value proportionately to labor costs and proportionately to the total cost of production, respectively, while the third aimed to emulate Marx's prices of production defining the surplus value based on the assumption of a constant return to capital.

28 Interest rates were charged on these loans, but they could be deducted from revenues as costs and reduced the state-owned enterprises' profits tax liability. Thus, interest rates were effectively paid by the treasury (Perkins, 1966, 105).

29 Similarly, Cheek (2016) observes, "A new ideological moment emerged for Party leaders and intellectuals alike with a new key question: how to reform China's social- ist system so that, first, the Cultural Revolution could never happen again and, second, the Party and socialism could avoid the sclerosis of state socialism in the Soviet Union and bring the prosperity and cultural richness that seemed so appar- ent in Japan, America, and Europe. It was clear that China was far behind the West. Debates focused on reform: what to reform? How to reform? How much reform was enough?" (221).

30 Trade with non-communist countries increased by 80 percent in constant dollars from 1970 to 1973 (Riskin, 1987, 193). Wen (2012, 72) estimated that between the late 1960s and the mid-1970s, machines and equipment worth USD 4.24 billion were imported. More generally, on the revival of international trade, see Teiwes and Sun (2007, 50–51).

31 See, for example, the discussion in Vogel (2011, 184–185) on contemporary observers of Hua.

32 Naughton (1995, 70–71) cited the Baoshan steel mill as a famous example of the acceleration of industrial facility imports being driven by an enterprise: "The cen- tral government originally approved in November 1977 a project to build a port and a 5 million ton iron smelting facility, to supply iron to Shanghai's existing steel mills. By September 1978, five successive design changes had expanded the project to 6 million ton capacity iron and steel mills with continuous casters, a seamless pipe mill, and hot and cold rolling mills. From an ordinary large investment, the project had been pyramided into a completely integrated state-of-the-art steel mill, with virtually all technology and equipment to be imported from Japan. Foreign exchange requirements more than tripled from about $1.8 billion in the original version, to $5.7 billion in the September 1978 version."

33 Meisner (1999, 429) suggested that "Hua's economic program was largely based on the policy documents Deng Xiaoping had drawn up for the State Council in the autumn of 1975, although the debt went unacknowledged." The Ten-Year Plan would have been a "somewhat revised version of a document drafted by the State Council in 1975 (when that body was operating under the direction of Deng Xiaoping)."

34 In the aftermath of the Great Leap Forward, Chen Yun—with support from econo- mists at the Economic Research Institute (经济研究所), including Liu Guoguang and Dong Fureng—set out to show that the Stalinist emphasis on the "constraint of the producer goods sector on economic growth was incomplete and that the growth of the consumer goods sector posed a constraint on the growth of the producer goods" (Lardy and Lieberthal, 1983, xxxiii).

35 In fact, grain prices rose by more than 20 percent in 1978 (Bramall, 2004, 124).

5

REHABILITATING THE MARKET

Chinese Economists, the World Bank, and Eastern European Émigrés

The reforms of the 1980s progressed because they were not relying on a theory. If reforms had needed to follow a theory, there would have been no progress. Zhao Ziyang was not academical. ... The old generation of Communist cadres was not concerned with settling theoretical questions.

(Li Xianglu, Zhao Ziyang's personal secretary, 2016)

Introduction

During most of the Cultural Revolution, political principles overruled scientific economic inquiry (Lin, 1981, 3). The study of issues related to forces of production such as efficiency and technical change, independent of the social relations of production, was regarded as "economism" (Riskin, 1987, 163). As part of the revival of scientific expertise, the Chinese Academy of Social Sciences (CASS) was founded in 1977 to serve national policy-making. I interviewed Tang Zongkun, one of the senior economists at the Economic Research Institute at CASS. When we met in 2016, the institute still occupied its original, simple, socialist-style building. Tang said, "During the ten years of the Cultural Revolution from 1966 to 1976, economic research was practically dead." Against this background, Deng Xiaoping's initiative to study economics in order to improve economic management marked a radical shift. The Chinese reformers launched a "reinstatement of economics" (Lin, 1981). Research institutes that had been shut reopened and new ones were created.[1] Economics as a discipline was revived at Chinese universities.

The reinstatement of economics under the reform agenda has to be understood in the context of the desperate economic situation in the late 1970s (as discussed in Chapter 4). But the institution of economics as the guiding logic of governance is more than a pragmatic response to the challenge of economic development. It accompanied a fundamental ideological shift and a revision of the basic understanding of historical progress in the Chinese leadership. The paradigm of reform turned Maoism upside down and marked a return to a more orthodox version of Soviet historical materialism. Mao had rejected Lenin's claim that the "transition from capitalism to socialism will be more difficult for a country the more backward it is." Mao stated, "Actually, the transition is less difficult the more backward an economy is" (Mao, 1977 [1967], 50).[2] Now, the doctrine of reform followed the logic of Lenin's dictum: in the words of the leading party intellectual Su Shaozhi, the "less developed the country, the more difficult the transition from capitalism to socialism" (Su, 1988, 31). According to Mao's perspective, progress could be achieved only by political means.

For the reform leadership, in contrast, progress became a function of economic development under the paradigm of reform. As Deng had proclaimed in 1975, the real enemies in his eyes were not "capitalist roaders"—Deng himself was denounced as one—but those who "still use metaphysics" and "talk only about politics but not economics; only about revolution not production" (Selden, 1979, 142). In the Deng era, catching up through reform now meant "making up missed lessons" (补课) in economics, both in Eastern European reform theories and in bourgeois economics, which had previously been condemned as "capitalist poison." But it also inspired the revival of domestic reform proposals and debates of the 1950s and 1960s, as China's economists returned to the centers of research and policy-making in Beijing.

During the Cultural Revolution, the dominant view had been that "the Law of Value led inexorably to capitalism" (Ling, 1988, 542). In sharp contrast, at the outset of reform, famous economists reinvigorated their debates of the 1950s and 1960s on the ways in which the law of value should be utilized to reform the Chinese economy—in particular, the price system (Brødsgaard and Rutten, 2017, 42–44; Fung, 1982; Garms, 1980; Xue, 1996; also see Chapters 3 and 4). Among the prominent voices were the Soviet-trained Sun Yefang, who had spent 1968–1975 in prison, and Xue Muqiao, who had been sent to the countryside in 1969 to be "reeducated by labor" (劳动改造). In the 1950s, Sun Yefang had argued that "the law of value was not the hallmark of capitalism, but rather a universal economic rule" (Brødsgaard and Rutten, 2017, 42). Encouraged by Hu Qiaomu's speech "Act in Accordance with Economic Laws," (1978) which proclaimed that "it is necessary to obey the law of value" and the "price of a commodity is based on its value,"[3] many meetings were held at the dawn of reform in the late 1970s to discuss the law of value. These events culminated in the April 1979 Wuxi Conference (Fewsmith, 1994, 62; Zhang Z., 2016).

Tang Zongkun recalled that, with more than 300 participants, the Wuxi conference was the largest economic forum since the beginning of the Cultural Revolution (Tang, 2016). Carefully prepared by bureaucratic consultation, it was a meeting of officials and established intellectuals. It involved some of China's most powerful institutions, such as ministries under the State Council and the State Price Bureau, and it was endorsed by Chen Yun in a letter to the Central Committee of the CPC (Fewsmith, 1994, 62–63). Chen set the conference's theme by noting that the planned economy was primary and the market was auxiliary. He observed, "Now, the plan is too rigid and it encompasses too much. The inevitable result is the absence of an element of spontaneous market regulation."[4]

The Wuxi Conference was notable for its open atmosphere. A wide variety of views were represented. Crucially, the participants challenged the idea that socialism required a centrally planned economy (Tang, 2016).[5] The contribution of two middle-aged economists from the Institute of Economics at CASS, Liu Guoguang and Zhao Renwei, was among the bolder ones in redefining the "Relationship Between Planning and the Market Under Socialism" (Fewsmith, 1994, 64; Hsu, 1988, 29; Liu and Zhao, 1982).[6] According to Liu and Zhao, in the past, the socialist countries had treated "economic planning and the market … as being mutually exclusive, as if there were no place for the market in a planned economy," but "such a view" had "brought a series of disasters" to China's economy (Liu and Zhao, 1982, 89). They suggested instead the promotion of free competition and the regulation of prices by supply and demand within a certain range, such that the market mechanism would become the main means in allocating manpower, materials, and funds (ibid., 94–95, 99). But at the same time, China should not "let Adam Smith's 'invisible hand' sway [the] socialist system" (ibid., 99). Guidance by planning would prevent the market from becoming anarchic.

When we discussed the 1980s in his simple apartment in Beijing (2016), Zhao Renwei was pleased to share that their article won the immediate praise of Hu Yaobang, who was at the time a member of the Central Committee and one of the political leaders of reform. Some months later, Deng Xiaoping sanctioned the theoretical breakthroughs of the Wuxi Conference, telling a foreign journalist,

> It is wrong to maintain that a market economy exists only in capitalist society and that there is only [a] "capitalist" market economy. Why can't we develop a market economy under socialism? Developing a market economy does not mean practising capitalism. While maintaining a planned economy as the mainstay of our economic system, we are also introducing a market economy. But it is a socialist market economy.
>
> *(Deng, 1984a, 173)*

Theoretical debates like the ones at the celebrated Wuxi Conference were important in consolidating the radical ideological shift away from late Maoism and breaking open the economic debate (Tang, 2016; Zhang Z., 2016; Zhao, 2016). But a divide prevailed between the immediate needs of improving economic management and the concerns of theoretical work, as vividly expressed by Deng Liqun, then head of the Policy Research Office of the Central Secretariat and vice president of CASS, in a speech to economists in June 1979[7]:

In the past, we were accustomed to going from concept to concept, from quotation to quotation; this must be changed. Before, relatively many belonged to the scholastic group [jingyuan pai] and did annotations on the classics. ... Comrades who do practical work feel that it makes no difference whether we have this kind of research work or not, or even feel that when you do it is bothersome [mafan].

(Deng Liqun in Jingjixue Dongtai, September 1979, 1,
as in Halpern, 1985, 356)

Deng Liqun went as far with his criticism of the work of academic economists as to stress that the academics had more to learn from the bureaucrats than the other way around:

If the responsible comrades [from the bureaucracy] don't personally take part, if only theoretical workers do investigation, one can investigate for a long time (ban tian) and the efficacy will still be low.

(as in Halpern, 1985, 376–377)

In January 1980, Deng Xiaoping (1984b, 230) articulated similar caution in his speech "The Present Situation and the Tasks before Us":

A good number of comrades who were shunted aside for many years and haven't been back in their original posts for very long, have lost touch with the situation; even those who stayed at their posts all through are confronted with new problems they find hard to grasp immediately.

Reinstating and reinventing academic economics took time. In the meantime, bureaucrats at all levels used the new political space to launch experiments with economic policies, including market mechanisms and more flexible ways of determining prices. In this situation, the Chinese proverb of "groping for stones to cross the river steadily" (摸着石头过河) was a "choice of no choice" (没有选择的选择) for the reformers. Chen Yun had first invoked the "river" slogan as the best approach to price stabilization after liberation in 1950, when he was Minister of Finance and Economics. At that time, Chen said,

Rising prices are not good, falling prices, too, are not good for production. It is better to be groping for stones to cross the river more steadily.

(Chen Yun to the Government Administration Council of the CPG,
April 7, 1950, as in Chen, 2000, 44)

At the Central Working Conference in 1980, when the overall approach to reform was being devised, Chen reminded the party of this popular wisdom:

We have to reform, but our steps must be steady. Because the issues in our reform are complicated, we cannot ask to be overly impatient. Admittedly reform must rely on proper theory, economic statistics and forecast, but more important is to start with experiments at selected points and to draw lessons from experience at the right times, this is to be groping for stones to cross the river. In the beginning, steps must be small, walking slowly.

(Chen Yun to the Central Work Conference, December 6,
1980, as in Chen, 1986a, 251)

Deng Xiaoping (1984c, 335) closed this Central Working Conference by proclaiming full agreement with "Comrade Chen Yun's speech." Deng concluded that Chen's insight would serve as guidance for a long time. And in fact, although this approach was repeatedly and forcefully challenged, it remained dominant throughout the first decade of reform.

As I explained in Chapter 4, a reform of the price system was a key prerequisite of Deng Xiaoping's move from egalitarianism and collectivism to relying on individual economic incentives. The first part of this chapter investigates how, in the early reform years (1978–1980), flexibility was introduced into the Maoist price system through practical experiments, while keeping the workings of the core of the economic system intact. Drawing on unique archival material, the second section of this chapter analyzes early attempts at solving the price problem theoretically. These attempts resulted from exchanges between Chinese established intellectuals and Eastern European émigré economists, with support from the World Bank. This dialogue between Chinese reform economists and their counterparts gave rise to one of the major competing approaches to market reform in China: the so-called package reform, which had radical price reform, the first step of shock therapy, at its heart.

First Steps toward Changing the Price System

The adjustments of the grain purchase price and the sale price of inputs for agriculture decided at the Third Plenum of the Eleventh Central Committee in December 1978 marked the first major step in reforming China's price structure (see Chapter 4). This was followed by Li Xiannian's announcement on behalf of the government in April 1979 that "some necessary adjustment will be made to certain prices on condition that the average price level is kept stable" (as in Hua et al., 1993, 107). Li Xiannian, a member of the Standing Committee, had overseen economic work during the Cultural Revolution. The government would also "make an overall adjustment in price structure, and improve the current situation in which many products are unreasonably priced" (ibid.). Such "an overall adjustment in the price structure" was subject to wide-ranging debates in the subsequent years. But adjustments to some prices were introduced more or less immediately by granting greater flexibility in price-setting *within* the existing system, which gradually also adjusted the overall structure.

Basic Principles of Price Reform—the Law of Value from a Guanzian Perspective

Xue Muqiao's *China's Socialist Economy* (1981 [1979]) can be described as "the most systematic and authoritative effort to articulate a theory of socialist economics to underpin the emerging Dengist reforms" (Fewsmith, 1994, 68) in the early years.[8] The law of value states that the "magnitude of value is determined by the amount of socially necessary labor time expended on a product, and commodities must be exchanged on their value." Xue (1981, 135) pointed out that this definition is incomplete. According to Xue, "[b]ecause there is often an imbalance between supply and demand, the correspondence between price and value is relative and temporary while the difference between them is absolute and frequent" (ibid., 135–136). Rather than perceiving the law of value as a static operation of adding up the socially necessary labor time, Xue countered that "The law of value regulates prices spontaneously to achieve a relative balance between supply and demand. This relative balance is made possible by a constant destruction of balance … or a constant fluctuation in balance" (ibid., 137).[9]

Xue's interpretation of this Marxian tenet as working through fluctuation leads him to describe the proper role for the state to regulate prices in ways reminiscent of the *Guanzi*'s logic: the conscious harnessing of spontaneous market forces by the state (see Chapter 1). Under socialism, Xue argued, the law of value was "often used by the state in a conscious effort to regulate production. Through its price policy the state utilizes the law of value to regulate the production and marketing of all products" (ibid.). In Xue's view, the state should employ the law of value and at the same time restrict the spontaneous operation of the law of value in order to protect people from violent price fluctuations.

Xue did not use the traditional language found in the *Guanzi*, but he consistently followed the principles of "light and heavy" (see Chapter 1) in determining the state's price policy toward certain types of commodities. The basic logic can be summarized as follows: the state must restrict the power of the law of value over things that are "heavy"—commodities that are in short supply or vital to people's livelihood and production. In contrast, the prices of things that are "light"—commodities that are oversupplied or nonessential—can be determined by spontaneous market forces, achieving balance through imbalance. Xue suggested that the state must ration and set the prices of "some vital items of consumer goods … to ensure that the people's livelihood is not affected by a rise in prices caused by the deficiency of these items" (ibid., 140).

When producers can supply more of these items than the state-rationed quota, they should be allowed to sell "at prices higher than the planned state prices" (ibid., 157). While the provision of the minimum ration is "heavy," as it immediately affects people's existential needs, the surplus production is nonessential, or "light," and can thus be subjected to market forces. This is the basic logic of what later came to be called the dual-track price system (see Chapter 6). Xue further recommended that the prices of nonessential "may be adjusted flexibly within a prescribed range by local governments and price control authorities" (ibid., 156). For agricultural production, which was dependent on weather fluctuations, Xue thought the state should enable the prices to stay within this range by a policy reminiscent of Sang Hongyang's "equable marketing" and Wang Anshi's reforms several centuries before (see Chapter 1):

> When their prices [of agricultural products] are too high, the state may stabilize them and protect consumer interests by bringing in more from other parts of the country. When the prices are too low, the state may raise the purchasing price and send the surplus supplies to other places to protect the interests of the peasants.
>
> *(ibid., 157)*

Xue Muqiao's interpretation of the law of value as regulating through deviation, achieving balance through imbalance, dated back to his contributions in the debates with his friend Sun Yefang and is to some extent original in the Chinese context. But the specific policy principles to overcome the rigidities in the Chinese price system that Xue described cannot be attributed to any single thinker. In fact, Xue's famous book *China's Socialist Economy* itself "was not the product of one person" but the result of discussions among Xue and his colleagues (Fewsmith, 1994, 68).[10] Moreover, these principles were at the heart of the Chinese bureaucratic practice of price regulation. As we have seen, they dated back to ancient times, were common in the imperial period, were used to stabilize prices after the liberation, and were an important part of the Communists' economic policies before the Cultural Revolution.

Chinese Bureaucrats Explain Price Reform to the World Bank

When the first World Bank mission arrived to investigate whether China was eligible for loans from the International Development Association, in October–November 1980, Chinese bureaucrats on the central and provincial levels presented the World Bank representatives with their views of the practice of price regulation and reform. Their assessment consistently reflected the principles outlined by Xue (1981).

The principal economist of the mission, Adrian Wood, spoke to me about the cooperation with the Chinese bureaucracy at the time. We met at his home not far from the south seacoast in England. Wood stressed,

> The Chinese were very careful to distinguish between the views of the World Bank and their own views; they always kept a clear division, this is you and this is us. ... The World Bank China relationship was a marriage made in heaven. These were two big, bureaucratic, highly professional, highly dedicated organizations, and they were perfectly suited to one another. The Chinese Communists, despite being on a different

ideological planet from the World Bank, knew exactly how to handle the relationship, which was very friendly, highly cooperative, but arm's length.

(2016)

Wood documented the meetings from the first mission in miniscule detail. They include meetings with the Central Price Bureau, the Gansu and Sichuan Price Bureaus, the Ministry of Finance, the State Planning Commission, the Commerce Department, and the State Material Supply Bureau. Wood distinguished carefully in his notes whether he was documenting the views of the Chinese counterparts or his own. An analysis of these notes in this section gives a glimpse of the stage of experimental price reform in 1980, before any wholesale price-reform program had been attempted, and the way this reform was presented to foreign experts.[11] It reveals the starting point for the dialogue on price reform between Chinese economists and foreign visitors.

At the Research Department of the State Price Bureau, the World Bank mission learned the basic Chinese perspective on the evolution of their price policy and the challenges of market reform. They were told that the Chinese price system was "inherited" from the past and that the Communists "never set all prices from scratch." The Chinese followed the Soviet example of generally low prices and profits for means of production and high prices for light industry products, in particular for inessential consumption goods such as cigarettes, wine, and watches. A basic principle throughout was price stability for daily necessities. Looking back, the State Price Bureau officials said that they used to make small adjustments to prices of nonessential goods to reflect changing labor inputs and supply demand relations. But from 1969 to 1978, the Price Bureau was shut down and prices were frozen.[12] The Price Bureau staff found that this rigidity resulted in great irrationalities in the price structure. Adjustment was inevitable, but they also cautioned that "problems accumulated in 30 years [could not] be solved overnight." Instead of aiming for such a one-stroke solution, the World Bank mission's extensive survey of institutions involved in price work shows that the hierarchy of control over commodity prices (see Chapter 4) was exploited to experimentally introduce price flexibility, beginning with the least-essential goods.

The presentations to the World Bank mission, by Chinese officials in charge of price work, demonstrated an understanding of the basic challenge of price reform and the practical approach to tackle it across a wide range of bureaucratic units, on various levels. At the core were the principles of stability, cautiousness, and using the given structure of commerce and price policy as a starting point. According to my analysis of Wood's documentation, the relative importance of commodities was not solely defined in terms of physical qualities of certain goods. Although a hierarchy reflected the physical qualities of commodities and defined them in terms of their importance for people's livelihoods and for national production, not every identical good was equally important at all times and places. Instead, it becomes clear from the conversations between the World

Bank and Chinese price-fixers that the importance of a price depended on at least four criteria:

1. *Importance was determined by whether the producer was a major producer, producing for the national plan, or a minor producer, producing only for local needs.* In the latter case, the price-setting was left to the local authorities or, depending on the importance of this good for the local economy, to the enterprise. For example, the World Bank mission learned that in Gansu province, large, central cement plants had to sell to the state at "central" prices, whereas local cement plants and other producers of building materials producing for local needs had to sell at prices set by local authorities. Sichuan was one of the most advanced provinces in enterprise reform. Representatives from Sichuan suggested that their minor consumption items produced for local needs, such as buttons, small mirrors, and pens, the prices of which had formerly been controlled by the county, could now be set freely by the enterprises. These inessential consumption goods had up to that point been highly priced, and their production could easily be expanded. Thus, the freeing of control tended to result in a downward movement of the prices of these goods. They were not only inessential in terms of their use, but also "light," in the sense that they tended to be oversupplied.

2. *The same type of commodity could be treated as more important or less important even when produced by the same enterprise, depending on whether the commodity was part of the fulfillment of the central plan.* The World Bank economists were told that a "free disposal of surplus rule" applied to all consumer goods other than the essential commodities cotton and wool cloth, which were persistently in short supply. This is to say, the above-quota production was at the discretion of the enterprise and could be sold at other prices and through other channels. The result of this rule was effectively a multi-tiered price system. With a new scheme that allowed enterprises to keep part of their profits for capital construction, technological advancement, bonuses, and workers' welfare, enterprises had high incentives to produce more than the quota—and sell it profitably.

   The pioneers of enterprise reform in Sichuan cited an illuminating example from 1979: a handkerchief factory in Chengdu had to fulfill a state plan of 840,000 pieces, but they had the capacity to produce 1 million pieces of the state type. They used their discretion to create a new type of handkerchief with a new design so that they could produce a total of 1.07 million pieces. The new design served to both lower costs and increase the market demand for their products. Yet the "free disposal of surplus rule" would have had a limited effect if the enterprises had no means for effective supply to relevant markets. Here, state commerce agencies were key. They too were granted the free disposal of their surplus commercial services. So, for a fee, the state commerce agency marketed the new handkerchief product at a price negotiated between the commerce agency and the enterprise. The enterprise also sold the new product in the streets at a market price. But the transregional market for their product that allowed the enterprise to break beyond local demand was created by state commercial agencies.

3. *The "free disposal of surplus rule" was also applied in agriculture and price stabilization through market participation.* When the World Bank mission toured China in 1980, agricultural side-line production was generally not under quota regulation anymore and could be sold in rural and urban markets. But all other goods (except for cotton) could also be sold on the market once the quota was met. These included important commodities such as edible oil, which had been rationed since 1949 (see Chapters 3 and 4). Prices in these markets were generally "free," but price stabilization through market participation by state commercial agencies was an important regulatory mechanism. Chinese officials told the World Bank economists repeatedly that state commerce agencies supplied or demanded certain commodities, reflecting the prevailing market conditions to prevent price fluctuations. At the same time, state-owned enterprises were discouraged from making large transactions at a single time on the market, to prevent large price fluctuations. The state further stabilized agricultural prices by guaranteeing demand at a certain price. Peasants could sell their above-quota production to the state at a premium above the planned price. This effectively set a floor to the market price. Whenever the market price fell below the above-quota state procurement price, the peasants could turn to the state. In Sichuan, Price Bureau officials reported that thanks to the increasing supply, the market prices had begun falling to the extent that peasants had begun to turn to the state to sell their produce.

4. *While the prices of the means of production were generally not free to be determined in the market, the prices of certain manufactured means of production in excess supply were allowed to float downward to 20 percent below the state-planned price.* Examples of these commodities were some tractors and machines and some types of glass and electrical equipment. As a result of attempts at rebalancing the economy after Hua Guofeng's overly ambitious plans, state investments were strictly reduced in 1979–1980, creating a tendency of oversupply of these means of production.[13] The Gansu Price Bureau officials pointed out to the World Bank mission that some of the prices were already hitting the lower limit of a 20 percent downward deviation from the plan price. An official at the Sichuan Price Bureau explained to the World Bank visitors that as a next step of reform, upward floating of prices for means of production in short supply was now under study. Thus far, floating had only been allowed as a downward price movement to release excess supply.

These principles of what is important, or "heavy," and what is less important, or "light" and could thus be controlled more flexibly by giving the market a role in price determination, were not applied mechanically. Rather, they were applied in experiments, one commodity and one locality or enterprise at a time, taking specific situational pressures such as local excess supply into account. State commercial agencies played a critical role by creating markets and negotiating prices as well as by stabilizing agricultural prices through market participation. In sum, five types of price determination mechanisms were applied—sometimes to the same goods: (1) *planned prices* set by the state for the most important goods, (2) *floating prices* for certain goods in excess supply, (3) *negotiated prices* settled between enterprises, between enterprise and commercial departments, or between regions, for above-quota production of goods with otherwise planned prices, (4) *free-market prices* for minor goods, and (5) *market prices stabilized through state participation* for surpluses of key agricultural products such as grain.

Against this background, the greatest challenge in price reform was how to deal with important goods in short supply, which were priced low under the pre-reform system and which were still largely supplied at those low *planned prices*. Examples included cotton, coal, and other raw materials. The case of coal illustrates this challenge. At the State Price Bureau, the World Bank officials learned that the price of coal had been adjusted upward in 1979 but was still too low—below production costs for too many mines and not reflecting the general energy scarcity. The State Price Bureau revealed that they were calculating a variety of theoretical prices based on different pricing schemes in order to adjust the prices of those raw materials.

The Price Bureau officials pointed out the basic problem of price adjustment: a potential chain reaction resulting from an increase in the price of important means of production. On the surface, they argued, price increases would affect only profits, but in reality, "ripple effects" would spread price increases across the economy. The officials pointed out that it was not an option to raise the cost of living. Inflation would already be on the rise without such a price adjustment, and any further price increases affecting the cost of living had to be absorbed by government subsidies. However, the State Planning Commission reported a budget deficit of 17.6 billion RMB in 1979, despite cuts in capital accumulation. This deficit was due in substantial part to the subsidies required to compensate for the price increases decided in 1978, in particular on grain.[14] In light of these fiscal pressures, the Chinese bureaucrats found the approach of compensating price increases with subsidies not feasible. Thus, the question of how to deal with the most important planned prices of essential goods remained unresolved.

The fear of inflation in 1980 was not limited to the rank-and-file officials who presented the state of reform to the World Bank mission. Anxiety that price increases could endanger economic and political stability occupied China's top reform leaders, many of whom, like Chen Yun, had played a key role in the price stabilization effort of the 1940s. The danger of inflation, which greatly added to the challenge of price reform, had been a looming threat since the beginning of reform. In December 1980, at the Central Work Conference, Chen Yun pointed out that "the current economic trends are as good as they have rarely been since liberation" but warned that the government had to pay attention to price rises:

> Except for those prices fixed by the state and not allowed to rise, many other prices have been rising. ... If we do not stop this, people will become very unhappy. Economic instability can lead to political instability.
>
> *(as in Xue, 1996, 363)*

As we have seen, inflation was an important economic reason for the downfall of the Nationalists (Chapter 3). The political and social danger of rising prices was thus well known to the revolutionary generation of leaders. To overcome this challenge, Chen stressed the need to reform through readjustment, overcoming imbalances between sectors and curbing investment and household expenditure (ibid., 363–364).

Zhao Ziyang (2016, 335–338) had pioneered agricultural and enterprise reforms as Sichuan's Party Secretary. He had been promoted to become a member of the Standing Committee, and he became the Prime Minister in 1980. Zhao shared Chen's concern about inflation. For example, in a meeting with cadres from the Commerce Department and the State Price Bureau in November 1981, Zhao admonished that "the basic stability of prices must be preserved." He explained that, up to that time, price reform had been "basically smooth, but it would also have caused some storms in the market, and in some places these storms were not small" (ibid., 335). In particular, the reactions to increases in the prices of cigarettes and alcohol had been underestimated (ibid., 335). Furthermore, Zhao exhorted, in response to changes in prices, "people in some places would have become so worried as to rush and buy grain, cotton cloth, sugar, wool cloth and matches for hoarding" (ibid.). Hence, the trust in the exchangeability of money had been undermined. Zhao (ibid.) repeated Chen's warning:

> We must take these problems very seriously. People are very sensitive to prices. If we do not pay attention to this, we will have a problem. Price fluctuations can breed political problems.

Exchanges with Foreign Economists: Introducing Big Bang Logic

In parallel with these ongoing changes in the price structure and gradual change in the system of price management, academic economists investigated what China could learn from international economic expertise. In particular, they were interested in the reform attempts and theories of Eastern European socialist countries. As Zhao Renwei (2016) recalled,

> The Eastern Europeans had started reforms in 1956. The language they used, the economics they studied, and their initial economic system were all very similar to ours. Thus, their experience was of great value to us.

Yet, the exchanges of Chinese economists with foreign counterparts were by the late 1970s hardly limited to foreigners who used a socialist vocabulary.[15] The first delegation of American economists in the 1970s was a group broadly associated with the Union of Radical Political Economics (URPE) in 1972, just after Nixon's visit. They were invited at least in parts due to their broadly sympathetic view of Mao's China at the time. As an irony of history, the radical economists pioneered the reengagement of Chinese economists with the American discipline. The economists visiting China became progressively less radical. The second American delegation that followed shortly after was led by the then president of the American Economics Association, John Kenneth Galbraith, joined by two distinguished predecessors and later Nobel Laureates, Wassily Leontief, and James Tobin (Weber and Semieniuk, 2019). By the beginning of reform, the Chinese economists aimed to "make up missed lessons" on the development of the economics discipline in the capitalist world, independent of ideological orientations. With regard to price reform, the disillusioned former socialist reformers Włodzimierz Brus and Ota Šik, as well as the world-famous neoliberal Milton Friedman, were among the most influential early visitors.

Reform as System Change: Brus

The first Eastern European economist to leave a deep impression on China's reform economists was Włodzimierz Brus (Liu, 2010, 280). Brus began his research career with a thesis on the law of value under socialism. Unlike some of the Chinese reform economists who became famous for their critique of Stalin's *The Economic Problems of Socialism in the USSR*, however, Brus in 1952, like Oskar Lange, hailed Stalin's book for its insistence on objective economic laws that transcend political systems (Toporowski, 2007; 2018, 204). Brus later came to support Oskar Lange against both the Stalinist position and Michael Kalecki in the late 1950s Polish reform debates. Kalecki—whose work on the post-World War II price liberalizations and inflation we have encountered in Chapter 2—challenged the applicability of marginal principles to either capitalism or socialism, and thus also the possibility of bringing the economy into equilibrium through the price mechanism alone. Kalecki stressed, instead, the importance of investment. He used the example of rolled steel to argue that adjustments to prices would have to be very slow in order to be at all suitable to reach equilibrium. In contrast, Brus built on Lange's contributions to the Socialist Calculation Debate to propose a form of market socialism in which enterprise autonomy, guided by the right set of prices, would achieve "rational economic decision-making" (Toporowski, 2018, 159, 209).

This emphasis on prices continued in Brus's more well-known writings on market socialism, such as *The Market in a Socialist Economy* (1972). In the late 1960s, Brus openly advocated democratic reforms until 1968, when he lost his prestigious chair in political economy at Warsaw University (Toporowski, 2018, 255). In 1972, Brus joined Oxford University, which "offered refuge, but remained a place of exile" (Toporowski, 2007).

In Oxford, Brus had two PhD students (Lin, 2016); one was Anders Åslund, a forceful proponent of big bang policies. Together with David Lipton and Jeffrey Sachs, Åslund would become advisor to the Russian government in the critical period of 1991–1994 (Åslund, 1989; Åslund, 1992; Åslund, 1995; Lipton and Sachs,

1992; PIIE, 2017). The other student was Cyril Lin, the brother of the first World Bank Chief of Mission Edwin Lim. Lim did fieldwork in China in 1978 in preparation for his dissertation on the "reinstatement of economics" (Lin, 1981). He found that the reform proposals of his teacher were strikingly similar to those of Sun Yefang (Lin, 2016).[16]

In contrast with Xue Muqiao, who argued that the law of value established balance through imbalance, Sun (1982, 42) understood the law to require "that prices approximate rather than deviate from values." The advantage of a socialist economy was that value would not need to be expressed in a roundabout way through exchange, which involved deviation from value, but could be directly calculated. Sun defined value, drawing on Engels, as "the relation of production costs (i.e., socially necessary labor) to utility" (ibid., 65)—a very neoclassical interpretation of this key Marxian concept. Prices, according to Sun, should be calculated in such a way that products that require the same socially necessary labor time also generate the same utility to consumers. Sun was clearly inspired by microeconomic theory and must have been familiar with the Socialist Calculation Debate and Oskar Lange's arguments on the possibility of market socialism (Trescott, 2007, 306; Weber, 2022).

For both Brus and Sun, prices were key to reform. They shared this view with the Lange–Lerner vision of market socialism (Stiglitz, 1994, 102). To rationalize the socialist economy, the central planners had to set prices equal to values. They had to let the publicly owned enterprises compete freely, in pursuit of profits within the limits of simple reproduction and under the guidance of nonbinding financial state targets. At the same time, the state would control investment decisions that went beyond the replacement of the given capital stock indirectly, through the banks' control over investment funds. Hence, expanded reproduction would be regulated by financial means. This was meant to achieve proportionate development. Taken to its logical conclusion, this implied giving up on planning in physical terms, the foundation of the material balance system. Under this old system, planning was conducted in terms of concrete, input–output relations. For example, if 100 tractors were ordered from a machine-making enterprise, the steel required to make those tractors would be ordered from a steel plant and allocated to the machine maker. Plans were drawn up to coordinate the physical production process. Under the reform approach, by comparison, enterprises would no longer be allocated their inputs centrally but would instead acquire them on the market from other enterprises. The machine maker would now buy steel under a contract drawn up directly with the steel plant instead receiving this steel as plan allocation. This necessitated a radical readjustment of prices, a resetting of all prices from scratch, which had never been done in the People's Republic before.

Dong Fureng, the deputy head of the CASS Institute of Economics, was a Soviet-trained economist who had supported Chen Yun's attack against a heavy industry–oriented development strategy in the early 1960s. He had published an article arguing for radical ownership reform. During Dong's visit to Oxford in July 1979, he invited Brus to China (Fewsmith, 1994, 67; Liu, 2009a, 2010, 280).[17] Brus took up the invitation in December 1979 to January 1980 and gave lectures to economists at CASS, evaluating the past reform experience in socialist countries and introducing his vision for reform (Liu, 2010, 280–281; Zhao, 1982).

Brus told his Chinese audience that it would be crucial to first choose the target model of reform. He explained that his model would perform best in combining the market with central planning (Zhao, 1982, 2–18). Instead of tinkering around with separate policies, he asserted, the Chinese should realize that economic reform meant transitioning from the old to a new system. Thus, reform would have to be implemented in one package (一揽子); a piecemeal approach was, in Brus's view, impossible (Liu, 2010, 283; R. Zhao, 1980). Hungary and Yugoslavia had successfully implemented their reforms in one go, whereas the Soviet Union and other Eastern European countries, which had adopted a piecemeal approach, had failed to reform (Zhao, 1980). The key to success, Brus said, was to move quickly after careful preparations, which had to include macroeconomic stability and a buyers' market (ibid.). The success or failure of economic reform would be decided by price reform, and if price reform got stuck, there would be no hope for system reform (Liu, 2011, iii). Furthermore, according to Brus, Eastern European economists had reached agreement that only a change in the political system could ensure that reform was not reversed, thus preventing a return to the old system (Liu, 2010, 283). Political change had to be part of the package.

Brus, in his lectures in China, hinted at many of the key elements of what later came to be called shock therapy (see the Introduction), but with one key difference: Brus—in line with Lange (1967) and Sun Yefang—thought it possible for the state to set rational prices. Price reform was therefore mainly a "rationalization" of the price structure. Zhao Renwei wrote a summary report on Brus's lectures (Zhao, 1980) that was circulated across the highest state and party organs.[18] Brus met with Vice Premier Bo Yibo to discuss economic reforms, but because of his status as dissident, he was not received by Premier Zhao Ziyang (Liu, 2010, 284–285).

Brus got to meet his Chinese intellectual counterpart Sun Yefang, who was hospitalized at the time because of his poor health. On this meeting, at Sun's suggestion, Brus invited Zhao Renwei to go to Oxford (Zhao, 2016j). Zhao spent four terms (1982–1984) as Brus's student, "catching up on the international scientific debates on market socialism" (ibid.). While the economic theories of Sun and Brus had some striking similarities, there was a fundamental difference between the two men. Brus had lost hope in economic reform under socialism.[19] In contrast, Sun remained a dedicated communist until his passing in February 1983 but was convinced that the socialist project should learn from capitalist economics. In April 1983, Sun wrote in a letter to Zhao,

> I believe that we have to study capitalist economics, not only for the sake of knowledge alone but also to acquire concrete research tools and methods. But I … also believe that sending middle school graduates to the economics departments of Western universities is not right, would we not breed their disciples this way, no matter whether they are Keynesians or Friedmanites?
>
> *(Zhao, 2007)*

Propagating the "Erhard Miracle" in China: Friedman[20]

It turned out that not only "middle school graduates" could become Friedmanite disciples – to use Sun's phrase. A colleague of Zhao Renwei at the Economic Research Institute, Wu Jinglian, remarked that while Milton Friedman's visit in September–October 1980 had little immediate impact on Chinese reform policies, Friedman had nevertheless shaped his own thinking on the role of prices (Wu, 2016). Wu Jinglian had a remarkable history of turnarounds. Having been a "committed" and "rigid" leftist in the early 1960s—in opposition to the reform-oriented head of the Economics Research Institute, Sun Yefang—Wu lost faith in the mid-1970s (Naughton, 2013, 107–108).[21] At the dawn of reform, Wu Jinglian's disillusionment was complete and "he needed to build a new set of skills and find a new approach to the world" (ibid., 116). He apologized to his former superior Sun and joined the ranks of reform economists (ibid., 108). The foreign visitors provided Wu with the new worldview and tools he was looking for (Wu and Ma, 2016, 142), and Wu was to become one of the foremost proponents of a big bang price liberalization in China in the mid-1980s (see Chapters 7 and 8).

Listening to Friedman's lecture at CASS, Wu became acquainted with German post–Second World War price liberalization (Friedman, 1990; Wu, 2016). Before Friedman, neoliberals of the German ordoliberal variety such as Armin Gutowski and Wolfram Engels had lectured on the West German postwar transition (Weber, 2020b; 2021). Compared with Friedman's talks, these lectures had been more focused on the actual economic history of West German price and currency reform. In Friedman's interpretation, Erhard's policies became a sort of "magic tool" for the creation of a market economy. Friedman told his Chinese audience,

> The so-called economic miracle produced by Ludwig Erhard in 1948 was a very simple thing. He abolished all price and wage controls and allowed the market to operate while at the same time keeping a strict limit on the total quantity of money issued.
>
> *(Friedman, 1990)[22]*

According to Friedman, the experiences of many countries showed that price controls only suppressed the symptoms of inflation. Sooner or later, "the bottled-up pressure has broken through, inflation has risen to even higher levels, and price and wage controls have had to be abandoned" (ibid.). Friedman ruled out the validity of cost-push inflation theories. For him, a relative change in the quantity of money was the only cause of inflation. If the quantity of money was controlled, an increase in the price of one commodity must always be compensated for by a relative decrease in other prices—and was, as such, negligible.

Such a dismissive perspective on price controls could not have been convincing to most Chinese bureaucrats at the time. They saw their success at establishing and maintaining price stability since liberation as a major achievement, and price controls had proved to be an important tool.[23] Friedman's rejection of the importance of the rise in the price of certain commodities, as opposed to a rise of the general price level, was incompatible with the great sensitivity of the Chinese leadership toward the effects of price rises of specific commodities. As we have seen, even the prices of seemingly inessential goods such as cigarettes occupied the minds of China's top reform leader Zhao Ziyang, due to the potential implications for economic and social stability. On this point, Wood scribbled a comment in his notebook during the 1980 tour, referring to the great difficulty the Chinese reformers faced in adjusting the prices of what he considered to be minor goods: "A Communist dictator who cannot even change the price of matches!"

In contrast to Friedman's interpretation of Erhard's reform as a *deus ex machina*, Erhard's price liberalization is in fact an example of the great political repercussions of price changes. It triggered very high inflation and a general strike in post-war West Germany, hence exactly the kind of political and social instability the Chinese leadership had been anxious to avoid (see Chapter 2; Weber, 2020b, 2021). Nevertheless, the "Erhard Miracle" (艾哈德奇迹) would become a frequently cited, symbolic case in the fierce struggles over price reform of the mid-1980s, repeatedly invoked by Wu and others.

Price Liberalization as Goal, Calculation as Method: Šik

Ota Šik visited China on the invitation of CASS in March–April 1981. This was Šik's first visit to a socialist country since his emigration (Wu et al., 1982, 45). The architect of the economic reforms of the Prague Spring[24] hoped China would be inspired by his model of market socialism, which had been brutally terminated in Czechoslovakia in 1968 (Kosta, 1990). Unlike some of China's elder leaders of economic reform—such as Chen Yun, who consistently criticized the Stalinist industrialization approach—Šik, like Brus, was a proponent and theoretician of Stalinist economic orthodoxy until the late 1950s, even though Šik at the same time supported *democratic* Czechoslovakian socialism (ibid., 21).

After his turn to economic reform theories, Šik envisioned a reform implemented based on a "comprehensive" plan (Bauer, 1990, 247). Following Šik's approach, the Czechoslovakian reform entailed "[c]hanges concerning all important aspects of the system [which] were introduced simultaneously and overnight" (ibid.). These included the abolishment of the system of mandatory planning and far-reaching price liberalization (ibid., 247–249; Šik, 1988, 266–278). When the Warsaw Pact troops invaded Prague in August 1968, brutally ending the reform plans, Šik happened to be on holiday in Yugoslavia. Fearing political persecution, Šik never returned to Czechoslovakia. He found exile in Switzerland, where he became a professor of economics at the University of St. Gallen (Kosta, 1990, 23–24).

Liu Guoguang, then deputy director of the CASS Institute of Economics, had been the first to suggest inviting Brus, and in 1981, he invited Šik to come to China (Liu, 2010, 280, 289). In preparation of Šik's visit, a review of Šik's *The*

Communist Power System (1981) [25] in the CASS journal *Soviet and Eastern European Issues* showed that Šik's criticism of the prevailing socialist system reached far beyond that articulated by the Chinese reformers at the time (Liu, 2010, 291): According to Šik, the Soviet Union and the Eastern European countries were "not socialist," but a system of "party bureaucracy" and "state monopoly" (Cai, 1981, 56).

Wu Jinglian had found in Brus's theories parts of the new worldview he was in search of. During our interview in his modern office in a Beijing business school, Wu explained that he was put in charge of taking care of Šik during his 1981 visit. Wu traveled with Šik to Shanghai, Suzhou, and other places (Liu, 2002, 169; Wu, 2016). After each of Šik's lectures, Wu drafted a report to Ma Hong, which Ma sent to the central government leaders. Ma was a senior economist and, at the time, founding director of the State Council's Research Center of Technology and the CASS Institute of Industrial Economics, as well as vice president of CASS (Liu, 2002, 170; Wang, 2014, xiii–xiv).

Šik's approach to reform, as presented to his Chinese audience, is documented in a little booklet that was never published, due to censorship I nevertheless managed to get hold of a copy. Šik's basic outlook in his China lectures was similar to that of Brus. Like Brus, Šik perceived reform as a system change that required a new economic and political target model and a detailed plan for simultaneous measures to transition to a new system, impose strict macroeconomic controls, and implement the reform package rapidly. But the crucial difference between Brus and Šik was that, while Brus suggested the state should use the price system as a planning tool, Šik promoted complete price liberalization as the goal. Planning as the basic system must be replaced by the market, Šik said, because central planners were able to neither solve the information problem nor resolve the contradiction between the interests of individual enterprises and society (Wu, Rong, and Ma, 1982, 54–56).[26] For Šik, there could be no socialism without the free market.

In Šik's target model, the state would guide autonomous enterprises only by macroeconomic means (ibid., 57–61). While enterprises in key industries would stay under public ownership, all minor economic activities would be in private hands. The superiority of socialism over capitalism would be achieved by establishing perfect market competition. Under capitalism, monopolies would dominate certain industries and distort the market, which would result in an opposition of private and social interests. Under socialism, by contrast, the state could smash all monopolies and ensure perfect competition (ibid., 95). Under such conditions, free-market prices would be the best tool to ensure that the self-interested decisions of enterprises would be in the best interests of society (ibid., 95–98).

In Šik's vision, investment decisions, which most proponents of market socialism suggest should be controlled centrally (Stiglitz, 1994, 102–104), would also be left to the enterprises. In Šik's target model, profit-driven exits and entries between different sectors would balance supply and demand and adjust the production structure to social needs. According to Šik, the old planning system would have to be *replaced* with a market system (Wu, Rong, and Ma, 1982,

98–115). "Some people consider whether the market could be combined with the old directive planning system," Šik told his audience, adding, "I believe, the old planning system is incompatible with the market system; therefore it is impossible to maintain directive planning while adopting market regulation" (ibid., 108). This meant reform had to entail abolishing mandatory planning, breaking up monopolies, and liberalizing prices.

Out of all the reforms, Šik, like Brus, attached the greatest importance to prices: "The first and foremost condition for the market mechanism to play its role, is to change the old price structure" (ibid.). Šik laid out a detailed plan for price reform based on the Czechoslovakian example, which was invoked in the attempt at a big bang in 1986 (see Chapter 7). Šik envisioned two major steps in price reform. First, using input–output techniques, prices for all products would be calculated so as to equalize profit rates for all products.[27] Data would be collected for all goods to allow determination of the average profit rate and all prices. The second step would be a transition to free-market prices (ibid., 151–152). The first step promised, in Šik's view, that the second step would be safe. Šik cited the Yugoslavian case to illustrate this point. According to Šik, Yugoslavia had committed a "very big mistake" when they had implemented price liberalization without previously adjusting prices by calculation (ibid., 109). Under the prevailing conditions of monopolies and a sellers' market, this had resulted in serious inflation (ibid.). Šik also hinted at the political danger involved, when he said that Yugoslavia managed to maintain the socialist system despite the long-lasting economic difficulties caused by this mistake (ibid.). As will be discussed in Chapter 7, it is, however, questionable how far Šik's approach prevents the dangers he observed in Yugoslavia. In China in 1986, economists opposed to shock therapy used the case of Yugoslavia to demonstrate the enormous risks involved in a of Šik-style reform program.

Šik's general message was that calculation-based adjustments would eliminate the dangers of radical price liberalization. Nevertheless, in light of China's reality, Šik suggested several adjustments to his basic plan. His basic plan implied higher profits for heavy industry, with a higher capital labor ratio than for the less capital-intensive light industry. This was against China's goal to balance the relation between heavy and light industry in favor of the latter. Šik thus suggested that the profit rate on fixed capital should be somewhat lower than on circulating capital. The aim was to prevent the greater share of fixed capital in heavy industry from resulting in a higher overall profit rate, compared with light industry. Šik's suggestion of adjusting all prices to equalize profit rates to the average level might have left the impression of a certain logical consistency. However, Šik entered into the terrain of rules of thumb with this amendment. He exposed his basic logical flaw of ignoring the capital labor ratio, and he could offer only some arbitrary adjustments. There is no reason to believe that adjusting prices to the values calculated based on the arbitrarily determined profit rates would prevent the catastrophic scenario Šik had just described for the case of Yugoslavia.[28]

Regarding the second step, the transition to market prices, Šik's recommendations were much more cautious than one would expect, based on the logic of his overall plan. Rather than liberalizing all prices, Šik proposed to divide all commodities into three categories of price determination: (1) state-planned prices, (2) prices fluctuating between state-set limits, and (3) free-market prices. In the beginning, the prices of basic consumer goods would remain state planned, since these prices would immediately impact the lives of the people—and if the prices were to rise, political instability would result. Basic producer goods in very short supply, such as energy and certain raw materials, would also be placed in the first category. Fluctuating prices would apply to goods subject to seasonal fluctuations. The only goods Šik explicitly recommended to be priced by the market were luxury consumption goods and certain kinds of industrial machines (ibid., 114–115).

Thus, after he had set out a complex program for demanding data collection and calculations, Šik's concrete measures fell back on rules of thumb. Moreover, Šik's recommendations on the classification of commodities were primarily based on physical characteristics of commodities. His plan was, as such, less capable of incorporating market dynamics into the state regulation of prices than was the prevalent Chinese practice at the time. In fact, since Šik admitted that a wholesale price liberalization would be too dangerous, even after the calculation-based adjustments, he was left without a consistent recommendation on how to transition from state control to market control for the commodities that he had placed in the first category—how to deal with these commodities was the most pressing concern of China's reformers.

Notwithstanding these shortcomings, the promise to have a method capable of setting all prices according to their values, which had been tested in Czechoslovakia, seemed to the Chinese government worth further exploration. After all, the aim of setting all prices equal to values had been repeatedly on the agenda of the Chinese leadership ever since the law of value debates of the 1950s and 1960s (see Chapter 4). Wu Jinglian recollected that Zhao Ziyang recommended that Šik should become the first foreign advisor to CASS and be invited to China annually. Zhao also wanted to arrange a discussion with the leading cadres in charge of economic reform. This took place on the last day of Šik's visit (Liu, 2002, 170–171, Wu, 2016). The participants included, among others, Xue Muqiao, Liao Jili, Ma Hong, and Bai Meiqing (Zhao's personal secretary in charge of economic issues). Šik presented his Czechoslovakian price-reform program. Xue Muqiao intervened in the discussion, raising the concern that it was very difficult to calculate prices: they would constantly influence each other, and would mutually be one another's cause and effect (ibid.; Lim, 2016). Šik responded that, although it was impossible to determine market prices precisely, the calculations could still approach market prices with the help of input–output techniques and modern computers. Respective adjustments would reduce the size of the shock when price liberalization was subsequently implemented (ibid.).

Using input–output techniques for planning prices was not new to Chinese researchers, and neither was the idea to apply this method to price reform. When Šik first visited China, the Research Department of the State Price Bureau was already working on calculations of theoretical prices, and these efforts could draw on theoretical and empirical input–output work dating back to the 1950s.[29] Šik's lectures on the Czechoslovakian experience further increased the leadership's interest in this line of research, and in July, the State Council decided to found a Price Research Center, under the leadership of Xue Muqiao and Ma Hong, to advise the State Council and the Central Finance and Economics Leading Group on price questions as well as to draw up reform plans (Cheng, 1998, 455; Liu, 2002, 171). The Price Research Center pursued Šik's reform approach and received advice from Jiri Skolka. Skolka had conducted input-output–based price research at the Czechoslovakian Economic Research Institute under Šik's leadership and continued his research in his Austrian exile. Šik had recommended him as an expert (Liu, 2002, 171, 2010, 294–295; Richter, 2000, 129; Skolka, 1984; Wu 2016).

Shortly after his visit, Šik himself, however, was labeled an "anti-socialist element" (反社会主义分子), future collaborations were canceled, and the publication of his lectures was stopped (Rong, 2008; Liu, 2002, 171). This drastic turn followed an interview Šik gave to the West German weekly *Wirtschaftwoche* (February 1981), which had come to the attention of the Research Office of the Central Secretariat under Deng Liqun's leadership (Liu, 2010, 294–295). In the interview, titled "Fear of Losing Power," Šik expressed the view that economic reforms without a change of the political system were doomed to fail. In the interview, Šik told the reporter,

> [The politicians in power] who understand very little or nothing about the economy and who live the old vision of the dictatorship of the proletariat, are very afraid that every liberalization and every change of the economic system towards enterprise autonomy and market orientation will undermine their position. In order to really make reform work, the party's diktat over the economy has to be put to an end.
>
> *(Šik, 1982, 56)*

Clearly, this aroused the anger of reformers such as Deng Liqun, who, in their positions as party and state officials, were pushing toward marketization. The Research Office publicly denounced Šik in an article titled "Ota Šik's Anti-Marxist Theory of Economic Reform" (Liu, 2010, 294–295). Šik never returned to China,[30] but his proposal for price reform remained an important reference for the group of Chinese economists, and it later came to be known as the Comparative Systems School of Thought.

The Moganshan World Bank Conference: Proposing the Big Bang

Several of the economists[31] at the Economic Research Institute who were involved with the visits of the Eastern European economists met with the World Bank mission on October 17, 1980, to discuss their outlook on reform. It was clear that Brus had left his mark. Wu Jinglian stood out for the boldness of his views. Wood observed, in his little notebook, that Wu held to the idea that the basic problem of reform was political, not economic. Reform, according to Wu, could succeed only if power was decentralized.[32]

Impressed with Brus and Šik, Liu Guoguang and Wu Jinglian reached out to Edwin Lim, the chief of the World Bank China mission, in 1981 and proposed a conference to learn more from Eastern European economists (Lim, 2008, 2016; Wu, 2016). During our 2016 conversation in his modernist London home, Lim described the conference. It was organized in cooperation with the newly founded Price Research Center and was held on July 11–16, 1982, at a comfortable mountain resort in Zhejiang's Moganshan. The conference was followed by a study tour in Shanghai, Hangzhou, and Chongqing (July 18–26) (Lim, 2016). The Terms of References that I found in Wood's extensive files stated, "We agree with suggestions of the World Bank staff that the discussion and investigation of the mission in China be focused on the problem of price reform." Wood explained that, reflecting a tense political atmosphere in late 1981, both sides committed to confidentiality and precluded any public reports on the meeting or the content of its discussion (Wood, 2016; Xue et al., 1982).[33] Or, as Lim (2016) put it, the conference was held "under the radar"—although, of course, the Chinese side reported in detail to the central leadership and institutions in charge of economic reform.[34]

A delegation comprising mainly Eastern European émigré economists and World Bank officials convened with Chinese economists in charge of price reform, headed by the Price Research Center's leadership: Xue Muqiao, Liu Zhuofu, and Liao Jili. Lim had recruited Brus as a consultant soon after the World Bank's mission began in China in 1980 (Lim, 2008) and put him in charge of assembling a delegation predominantly made up of exiled Eastern European reformers (Kende, 2017; Wood, 2016). Besides Lim, Wood, and Brus, the delegation members included Péter Kende,[35] a distinguished Hungarian social scientist and journalist exiled in Paris; Juliusz Strumiński, former head of the Polish Price Commission (1953–1968), who was exiled in West Germany and working as a journalist; Jirí Kosta,[36] a childhood friend of Šik's, who had worked under him on economic reform at the Czechoslovakian Economic Research Institute and was in exile as a professor in Frankfurt, Germany; and David Granick, an expert on socialist economies at the University of Wisconsin (see Illustration 1; Kornai, 2006, 9; Kosta, 1990, 20, 2004, 129–136, 155; Lim, 2008; Wood, 2016).[37]

When I met with Péter Kende in a café in Paris, he wore the same outfit he had worn in the group picture taken at the Moganshan Conference. He said it had been hot in Moganshan and that the Eastern European conference participants had been scared. All émigrés had been considered dissidents in their socialist home countries (Kende, 2017). Visiting the other side of the "iron curtain" was potentially a great personal risk. Looking back at his memorable journey to China, Kende stressed that, being considered a political enemy in Hungary, he did not feel safe until he set foot back on French soil (ibid.).[38] In Wood's notes on the conference, I found a record of a private conversation with Strumiński: the Polish reformer alerted the World Bank economist that, notwithstanding

ILLUSTRATION 1   Moganshan World Bank Conference, July 11–16, 1982. First row, left to right: Kosta, Strumiński, Xue Muqiao, Edwin Lim, Kende, Wood. Second row: Liu Zhuofu, Granick, ?, Brus, Liao Jili, Liu Moumou, Ben Chun (assistant of Xue). Courtesy of Adrian Wood.

their many differences in perspective, an important commonality among all but one of the invited experts was that they had lost faith in socialism. During the delegation's preparatory meeting in Oxford, Strumiński said, "Kende is the only member of the group [of Eastern Europeans] who still believes that reform of the socialist system is possible." Strumiński added that he would "regard the system as bankrupt, having squandered all its resources—natural and human. It is unreformable." Wood noted that other "members of the party," himself included, would "have varying degrees of scepticism." Here was a delegation of foreign experts, invited to help reform socialism, who for the most part held that socialism was unreformable.

Even beyond this question of faith in socialism, a basic problem in drawing lessons from the Eastern European experience was that the Eastern Europeans considered their own reforms to have been failures. Furthermore, as Kende put it critically when he commented on Brus's paper during their Oxford meeting, "This is excellent, but surrealistic. The actual conditions of China and Eastern Europe are so different, especially the organizational framework. These are scientific truths out of context."[39]

The Chinese side at the conference, in contrast, consistently refused to articulate any generalizable "scientific truths."[40] To the frustration of the visitors trained in formal economics, the Chinese participants focused almost exclusively on concrete issues they faced in their reform attempts.[41] More general principles emerged only implicitly from the ways in which these concrete problems were approached, as described in the previous section.

The former Director of the State Price Bureau (1979–1982) Liu Zhuofu gave the opening address. Liu was deeply versed in Chinese price regulation. He had made important contributions to price stabilization in the strategically important provinces of Shaanxi, Gansu, and Ningxia in the decisive year of the civil war and the immediate post-liberation period by applying *Guanzi*-type policies of the kind described in Chapter 3. In the most severe inflationary period of the Mao era, resulting from the disasters of the Great Leap Forward, Liu joined the State Price Regulation Commission to support Xue Muqiao in stabilizing prices, relying once more on the same approach (Cheng, 1993). In his speech, Liu summarized the existing state of China's price regulation for his international audience. Giving detailed accounts of different types of prices, he emphasized that "The price issue is very complex for each individual commodity."[42] Thus, the only basis for reform could be careful consideration of the particular situation of each good, always considering the different interests of the state, the producers, and the people, to ensure overall stability.[43]

The rise in the agricultural procurement prices was the point of departure for Liu's exposition. This adjustment was an important step for reform, but subsidies kept rising in 1980–1981, even when the price was kept constant due to the increase in agricultural output.[44] This was a great drain on state finances. Xue Muqiao explained in the subsequent discussion why retail prices could not easily be raised in order to release the pressure on state finances. He referred to the example of textiles. Synthetic fibers were still very profitable and in excessive supply, while the price for cotton was still too low and its supply was short. The State Price Bureau had suggested raising the cotton price slightly and decreasing the price for synthetic fibers by the same amount. But even this very minor change turned out to be politically infeasible, due to popular resistance against a higher cotton price. People were already dissatisfied with price increases in 1981 and were not prepared to accept further price adjustments. In theory, many relative price adjustments could be made without changing the overall price level, but Xue argued that very few could be realized, in practice, without endangering social and economic stability.

Liu also addressed the critical question of the adjustment of the prices of industrial inputs. Several of the price increases of mining and semifinished products (e.g., coal, coke, cement, and pig iron) that had been mentioned during the World Bank's 1980 visit were implemented by the time of the Moganshan Conference. At the same time, the prices of processed and final industrial goods (e.g., machinery) were lowered. But this adjustment was not sufficient to even out the profitability across sectors and production units at planned prices. Surplus sales to commercial agencies at the higher negotiated prices achieved some limited compensation, for example, for coal mines.

Xue Muqiao added that one way to improve the profitability of the production of these basic inputs (e.g., steel and coal) was to allow for direct sales. Small collective enterprises, which did not get allocations from the state plan, would purchase the above-quota production at prices even higher than the negotiated prices. This would also challenge enterprises to develop their own marketing capacities. In addition to the adjustment of plan prices, Liu discussed yet another policy that had been hinted at during the World Bank's 1980 visit. Floating prices were now allowed to move upward, and certain goods in short supply were classified as floating-price goods. Hence, floating prices were no longer only a means to reduce inventories of goods in oversupply but were also used to encourage production.

Finally, Liu estimated that in 1980, 25.3 percent of retail sales were under market regulation. Liu explained that these prices were not "free" in the sense of being unregulated by the state: state commercial agencies participated in the market by buying and selling in order to dampen price fluctuations.[45] This would allow the state to move away from a state monopoly over commerce while still being able to stabilize prices. State commerce created the market and regulated prices by commercial means in a fashion strikingly similar to the logic of *Guanzi*-type price policies. Throughout their speeches and when answering questions, Liu and the other senior economists repeatedly referenced their postliberation price policies (1949–1952) (see Chapter 3), to the point that Wood scribbled in his notebook, "Why do the Chinese answer to every question that they have to go back to the liberation period policies?"

Xue Muqiao delivered the second speech, presenting progress and difficulties of overall adjustment and reform and laying out the current macroeconomic challenges, which constituted an important background to the political tightening and the cautiousness of the reformers. Xue began by describing the great challenges the government was facing in bringing a fiscal deficit and rising prices under control. The government had failed for two years to cut down investments and thus had to impose a policy of retrenchment in 1981. After investments were finally reduced, industrial growth continued to decline for some time, which resulted in a buyers' market for certain machines as well as a rise of the output share of light industry and agriculture. In 1982, industrial output was rising again at a rate that far exceeded the target.[46] To avoid severe energy shortages, the government had to impose measures to keep heavy industry in check. China could have compensated the investment growth with higher capital imports, Xue explained, but this would have been too risky, and such a quest for instant success had to be avoided. Profit retention by enterprises[47] and wages as well as employment were rising, resulting in a wage bill increase, which outpaced the growth in the net material product.[48] At the same time, peasant[49] incomes were rising, mostly because of the unleashing of the production of cash crops and sideline production.[50] Xue concluded that these factors, taken together, were causing declining state revenues[51] and that by 1979, the money in circulation had been "slightly over-increased." Hence, inflationary pressure was imminent.

In Xue's view, before China could proceed with further reforms, several imbalances had to be corrected by administrative means. He believed that planning must continue to play a key role but that it should rely more on economic levers. For example, when administrative corrections to output had to be imposed, it showed that the price policy had failed to guide enterprises in the right direction. According to Xue, the planned management of the economy should not be weakened, but the production and prices of thousands of minor commodities should be left to the market. Liao Jili, a member of the committee of the State Planning Commission and head of the former Office of System Reform, which had been transformed into the System Reform Commission, later reemphasized that the plan had to be focused on the essential. Citing Zhao Ziyang, Liao pointed out that the plan should not be overloaded with details, and guidance and obligatory planning should be combined in a way that reflected the importance of commodities rather than aiming for universal control.

Xue closed his speech by reminding the audience that China had learned a painful lesson when it copied the Soviet model. This mistake could not be repeated. No change in abstract principles was needed, according to Xue, for the key question was how to reform in practice. China would not pursue indiscriminate or wholesale copying but would take the best from each country and find its own way.

All the foreign delegates presented papers to share their views on the reform experiences in other countries as well as their theoretical take on the price problem.[52] With regard to price reform, the contributions of Brus, Kende, Struminski, and Wood were most important. While the presentations were focused on historical lessons, the discussion was structured around pressing policy issues and brought out the radical views of some of the participants. Lim (2008) points out that the Eastern European experts, before having toured China, strongly recommended a "one package approach" that would reform all sectors at once, as quickly as possible. Effectively, they advocated the kind of big bang policies that later proved disastrous in Russia and parts of Eastern Europe.

Struminski began his presentation by saying that "in all socialist countries known [to him], the price systems are flawed." Part of the problem was that "all socialist countries have a sellers' market which would make administrative allocation necessary, but would at the same time cause the rise of parallel markets, including black markets and various forms of corruption."[53] The diversion of resources into these markets and the prospect of bribes, in turn, encouraged an intensification of controls while simultaneously making them ineffective. The result was distorted prices diverging from world market levels, which hampered international trade as well as innovation. Despite these shortcomings, there had been no qualitative change in the Soviet price system since the 1930s.

After this pessimistic introduction, Struminski launched what must have seemed to the Chinese counterparts to be an implicit attack at their reform approach. Struminski warned that the Soviets had tried to find a way out of the looming "scissors crisis" for years by introducing a three-tier price system for agricultural goods.[54] It had a quota and an above-quota procurement price, as well as a price determined in rural markets. But the results of this system were abysmal; the peasants' fulfillment of arbitrary quotas mainly depended on weather conditions, and the low quota price was essentially a tax on peasants. In the discussion, Strumiński received strong backing for his devastating judgment of multi-tiered pricing in agriculture from Brus, who pointed out that the multi-tiered price system was just an excuse for bad quota pricing.

Strumiński also addressed the problem of the divide between consumption and production prices due to the great emphasis on retail price stability that had been raised by Liu. He explained that this was also an unresolved fundamental problem in the Soviet system. Khrushchev tried to raise consumption prices in the USSR, but had to postpone the increases due to a "very unfavourable public reaction." Rather than elaborating on how this objective tension between price adjustments and social stability could be tackled, Strumiński pointed to political and ideological concerns as the reason for low prices. Low prices were used as a political means to calm dissatisfied parts of the population. But high prices for certain industrial consumption goods could not suffice to compensate for these low prices. Thus, the only way to maintain these low consumption prices was to turn to the printing press and create hidden inflation. All Communist parties had pledged to control the price level, but few Eastern European economists now thought this possible. Hence, contrary to the Chinese experience of the Mao years, Strumiński portrayed inflation as inevitable.

Even though Strumiński did not say so in public, his message—that the system was bankrupt—was clear. The socialist countries themselves were dissatisfied with their price system. They talked much about price reform, but in Strumiński's eyes, they confused the needed reform of the principles of the price system with minor adjustments. Thus, Strumiński arrived at a conclusion exactly opposite to that of Xue Muqiao, who had emphasized practicability over principles. In Strumiński's view, only simultaneous reforms of the entire system could solve the problem. The reforms should all be planned at the same time, but the first step would be to "fire most of the people in the Price Bureau and have the work done by the enterprises." The problem was that the state was never prepared for radical reforms. Reform would always be risky, but "as Clausewitz said, if you don't take risks, you cannot win." The key, according to Strumiński, was to make thorough preparations and to avoid great macro imbalances before implementing coordinated reform.

Reflecting on the course of the conference discussion, it becomes clear that Strumiński's radical recommendation failed to deliver an answer to how the Chinese government could achieve macro balance as the necessary condition for his reform program. After all, Strumiński had just laid out systemic reasons for aggregate excess demand, and Xue had just explained that the Chinese government—despite earnest efforts—had not yet succeeded at bringing the macro economy under control. Furthermore, the Soviet case invoked by Strumiński, as well as the report on the Chinese experience, suggested that already very minor price changes of individual commodities created a risk for political stability. Strumiński failed to address how the overall price reform he was proposing could avoid a major political upheaval. Given his confession that he did not believe socialism was reformable, one is left wondering whether Strumiński might have seen large-scale protests resulting from such radical price changes as a way to overcome the socialist system politically. After all, Eastern Europeans repeatedly emphasized the political conditions of reform.

Kende's contribution to the discussion on the Hungarian experience further illustrated the great political and economic risk of price reform. From Strumiński's presentation, the conference had learned that the Hungarian reform was implemented based on the logic favored by the Eastern European émigré economists: bring the economy under tight macroeconomic control, prepare a reform package, and implement it at once. Kende elaborated, in Hungary in 1968, that part of this package was a wide-ranging price liberalization, yet the prices of basic raw materials, daily necessities, and certain goods with great effects on people's daily life were generally still set by the state and not by the producers. Kende explained to the Chinese reform economists that, even though political leaders and economic experts had undertaken extensive preparations and found a consensus on the reform program after long debates, when it was implemented in 1968, it met very quickly with fierce opposition.

One important reason for this opposition, according to Kende, was the public reaction to price changes. In particular, the planned increase in rents and public transport charges aroused public anger. In the end, rents were kept stable and the hike in public transportation charges had to be compensated for by wage subsidies, adding to the inflationary pressure. Furthermore, Kende warned that, although Hungary had a comprehensive reform program, a number of ad hoc policy changes had to be introduced. One major problem was that the reformers had overestimated the enterprises' capacity to make their own production decisions. Being structured to receive orders from above, the enterprises were incapable of drawing up their own plans and reacting to the market flexibly. The only concept of competition the enterprises understood, explained Kende, was to expand by investing. Since the publicly owned enterprises faced no effective budget constraint and the credit policy was lax, this resulted in a major uptick in investments. At the same time, the unions argued that it was unfair for "prices to be Westernized, while wages were Easternized" and built-up public pressure such that the government had to give in and relax wage controls. The result, reported Kende, was high inflation, which had not been brought under control after more than ten years.[54]

In response to the presentations by the foreign guests, the Chinese conference participants stressed repeatedly that the only way was to "avoid pushing things to any extreme" and that stable prices, which had contributed to their national development since liberation, had to be preserved to maintain overall stability. In 1979, their shortcoming had been that they were too optimistic and raised agricultural prices by too large a margin. Liu Zhuofu set out once more to explain the difficulties in achieving macro-control. The best they could do at the moment, he said, was to reduce the government deficit.

Wood, who mainly argued from the standpoint of economic theory, posed a crucial question: "So why not concentrate on achieving these macro conditions and then abolish price control, close the State Price Bureau and let the market determine prices?"[55] Liu Zhuofu, a former director of the Price Bureau, hastened to answer that China needed the bureau. Control of all prices could not be the final objective of governments, but Liu Zhuofu cautioned, by pointing again to the political and economic risks, that

> Price instability distracts people from the task of readjustment and triggers reactions from workers and peasants, which has bad effects on the productions results. We perceive the irrationality of the existing prices and are in the process of making adjustments.

The real question the Chinese reformers were trying to answer was by how much they had to change these specific prices and what the effects on the overall price level would be—not whether or not to abolish their whole system of price regulation.

When the discussion moved to the topic of inflation, Brus once more tried to bring the case for radical reforms home by invoking arguments similar to those made by Friedman on suppressed inflation during his visit and drawing on Kornai's *Economics of Shortage* (1980). In Brus's eyes, there would always be suppressed inflation in socialist countries. From a macro perspective, the principle of full capacity utilization and the "output first mentality" would result in a very high investment rate and thus a large proportion of workers who consume but do not produce consumer goods, akin to the problems of a war economy. For systemic reasons, this could not be resolved, as Kornai demonstrated (1980). Under socialism, there would always be a soft budget constraint, and enterprises would always suffer from "investment hunger." Thus, aggregate shortage must always prevail, independent of the development level.

In Brus's view, administrative price controls would prevent this aggregate excess demand from driving up prices, thus suppressing inflation. If equilibrium prevailed, prices should be such that everyone could buy all the things they wanted. However, higher prices on the black market would, according to Brus, show that the state had set prices below the equilibrium level. If one would let the market determine prices, the suppressed inflation would immediately manifest itself. For Brus, as for Friedman (see Chapter 2), inflation was a necessary evil in order to obtain equilibrium. "If there is an opportune moment to release the pressure, use it, do not wait for too long," recommended Brus. He finished by invoking the Christian last judgment of God:

> When you suppress inflation, you only postpone the day of reckoning. This is sometimes advisable if the pressure is only temporary. But in general, you

are just making matters worse because at a later date much larger price rises will be needed.

The delegation returned to Beijing after visiting enterprises in various industries—a wholesale organization, a department store, local price offices, a suburban commune, and other institutions—on a study tour in Shanghai, Hangzhou, and Chongqing (July 18–26, 1982). The core team of Lim, Wood, and Brus held their first meeting with the initiators of the conference, Liu Guoguang and Wu Jinglian, on July 27. The two had opted out from participating in the conference—probably out of political opportunism (Lim, 2016). The meeting was held so the group could share observations and discuss the way forward. The men agreed that, while rural reform had made great progress, reform must now move to the cities, where the changes were "less impressive." In their eyes, the inflexibility of the price system was the chief obstacle to urban reform, while the multi-tiered price system brought more harm than good. Brus warned once more that China should not wait for suppressed inflation to become too severe.

Wood noted, on the concluding meeting with the Moganshan Conference participants as well as Wu and Liu, that the Chinese side "refused to make comments or ask questions but insisted that we [the foreign guests] go on talking."[56] Brus delivered a synthesizing presentation as head of the delegation. Showing an almost complete lack of appreciation of the ways in which the Chinese reforms were using market forces to serve reform, Brus stated,

> The attitude of those we met toward the plan and market was unsatisfactory, they would see the two as separate things which are acting on different planes: The plan operates with quotas and targets, while the market is constrained to the sphere of above-quota activity. There was no concept of using the market in implementing the plan, or using the plan to influence or regulate the market.

The delegation was impressed with the scope and success of agricultural reform but reached a devastating verdict on one of the central mechanisms of this reform, the dual-track price system:

> There is an excessive reliance on quotas for all products of all categories both with regard to output and acreage. Combined with the multi-tier pricing this leads to uncontrollable and undesirable phenomena, including screwing up planning itself. … We therefore suggest the elimination of the multi-tier pricing in favour of a uniform price.

Despite this critical assessment of the reform approach, witnessing the real changes on the ground as well as the prevailing poverty humbled the delegation members, who were acquainted mainly with failed reforms. Their conclusion was to disown their own recommendation for rapid price reforms as the first step in a comprehensive package. But since they had also urged the Chinese reformers to abolish the multi-tiered price system, which was at the heart of their prevailing reform approach, the delegation effectively failed to deliver any implementable recommendation on *how* to reform. Practically minded economists knew there was no "magic formula" and that neither the computer nor the market could instantly solve the problems they had explained to their guests without putting their party and state at risk. They must have been little impressed by the radical claims of their Eastern European colleagues, which were unsubstantiated with concrete, feasible measures. Yet, even though Brus, who had introduced the concept of "package reform," warned against its implementation in the Chinese context, some of the Chinese students of Eastern European and Western economics would come to lobby for this approach for years to come.[57]

Conclusion

We have seen that reform gave impetus to a reinstatement of economics that soon resulted in many exchanges with international visitors across the ideological spectrum. In particular, Eastern European émigré economists invited by the World Bank were influential in setting the tone for academic reform discussions. However, these reform approaches were focused on devising target models and plans to reach a desired economy that did not appear feasible to China's reform leaders in these early years. In parallel to the academic debates, experiments "on the ground" gradually exploited spaces opened up by the reform agenda and thus devised price-reform techniques through the practice of gradual market creation.

The broad agenda of the Eastern European economists was consistent with the ideas of market socialism of the Lange type. For them, the key was to get prices right, as quickly as possible, in what came to be called a big bang, in the language of shock therapy. At some points, the Eastern European reform economists did acknowledge that it was not feasible for price reform to be implemented entirely overnight and "in one go." It is, however, important to distinguish between the reform approach that prevailed in China and the form of gradualism they accepted as a necessary evil.

These two kinds of gradualism can be illustrated in light of Struminski's advice. He suggested that China should not do a "blitz price reform" but should instead institute a program, implemented in predefined steps, with a target date for eliminating rationing. This could be called *planned gradualism*. This kind of gradualism suggests crossing the river with a predefined number of steps in a set time, and as quick short as possible. Or, to quote Brus's student, "The main issue is to cross the river as fast as possible in order to reach the other shore" (Åslund, 1992, 87). In contrast, the Chinese were groping for "stones to cross the river," in Chen Yun's sense: they initiated reform with those prices that could be let free or adjusted without losing stability. They only took steps where they thought they had firm ground under their feet, and once these steps were taken, they considered the way forward anew. To find out which prices should be tackled, the specific conditions of each commodity were carefully evaluated, often using experiments. The Chinese approach can thus be labeled *experimental gradualism*.

The key difference between those two approaches is not, as is often suggested, the pace of reform. Instead, it is the basic logic of policy design. Planned gradualism defines a complete set of reform steps, derived by deductive reasoning, designed to achieve an ideal state. The type of gradualism proposed by those in favor of simultaneous package reform was to follow a planned path, strictly and swiftly. The Chinese approach was to make the path while walking. Acknowledging that they could not know what the effects of each reform step would be and what the best overall system should look like, they groped their way forward, constantly trying and reassessing. They relied on largely inductive research, first moving the least-essential parts before touching the core of the system. The clash of views between the foreign guests and the Chinese reformers at the Moganshan World Bank Moganshan Conference illustrates these two fundamentally different approaches to reform and market creation.

Notes

1 See Halpern (1985) for a detailed analysis of the institutional evolution of economic research in China from 1955 to 1983. Thanks to Barry Naughton for providing me with his copy of this unpublished PhD dissertation.
2 For a discussion of this text and Mao's critique of Soviet orthodoxy, see Meisner (1977) and Gittings (2006).
3 Translation as in Hu (1995, 178).
4 Translation as in Fewsmith (1994, 62–63), original Chen (1986b, 221).
5 Tang Zongkun participated in the Wuxi Conference.
6 Originally published in China's most prestigious economics journal at the time, *Economic Research*, May 1979 (Liu and Zhao, 1979).
7 The occasion of the speech was the establishment of the initial three groups for the study of the state of China's economy and approaches to reform coordinated by the Small Group for the Study of Economic Structural Reform (*Jingji tizhi gaige yanjiu xiaozu*), headed by Zhang Jingfu (Fewsmith, 1994, 70–71; Halpern, 1985, 356). The groups were headed by some of China's most prolific economists at the time, including Xue Muqiao, director of the Economic Research Office of the State Planning Commission (China Economic Reform Group), and Ma Hong, vice president of CASS and director of its Industrial Economics Institute (China Economic Structure Research Group). Yu Guangyuan, vice president of CASS and vice minister of the State Science and Technology Commission, later added a group on theory and method (Fewsmith, 1994, 72).
8 Fewsmith (1994) finds that Xue, in collaboration with several colleagues, began working on the study at around the time of the Third Plenum in December 1978. A first draft was finalized in August 1979, and the Chinese version of the book was published in December 1979 (68).
9 Xue's interpretation of the law of value is strikingly similar to that of the Soviet economist Isaak Illich Rubin (1886–1937). (See Weber [2019b] for a discussion of Rubin's interpretation of Marx's theories of value and money.)
10 In his preface to the English edition, Xue (1981) writes, "Thanks are due to Su Xing, He Jianzhang, Yu Xueben and Wu Kaitai who participated in the discussion and revision of the whole book and to Xu He and Wu Shuqing who took part in the discussion and writing of some chapters of a previous draft" (xii).

11 I would like to express my sincere thanks to Adrian Wood for giving me access to his personal notes and for taking time to explain to me all the relevant context. All references to meetings and activities of the World Bank in this chapter draw on these notes, unless indicated otherwise. In particular, notes on meetings (all in 1980) with the following institutions were considered in detail: Vice Minister of Finance Li Peng on October 13; Deputy Director He and other staff of the Comprehensive Planning Department of the State Planning Commission on October 14–16; Director Chang of the Planning Bureau at the Commerce Department and other staff on November 6; Deputy Director Ma of the State Material Supply Bureau on November 8; Deputy Director Guo of the Research Department at the State Price Bureau and other staff on November 10; the Gansu Price Bureau (dating not identified); and the Sichuan Price Bureau on October 29. These meetings were chosen both for their in-depth discussion of pricing policy and reform as well as to include a variety of central and provincial bureaucrats in charge of price issues.

12 See also the analysis in Chapter 4 on this point.

13 See Naughton (1995, 112–115) for a detailed discussion of marketization in the machinery industry before reform and the effects of the retrenchment policy on excess supply in certain means of production.

14 For more information about the price adjustments in 1978, see Chapter 4.

15 See, for example, Chow (1994) for a detailed account of exchanges between the American Economic Association and Chinese research institutes. Gewirtz (2017) contains information on various delegations and academic exchanges between Chinese and "Western economists."

16 The similarity between Sun's and Brus's models of market socialism was widely acknowledged by Chinese economists (Liu, 2010, 283).

17 After Dong's return to China, he published a note on his conversation with Brus. It stressed that the relation between central or local authorities and enterprises should be a market relation, guided by economic means—most importantly, prices (Dong, 1979).

18 Those included the Party Central Committee, State Council, National People's Congress, Military Commission of the Central Committee, the highest People's Court, Academy of Sciences, Chinese People's Political Consultative Conference, all regions of the People's Liberation Army, important higher education institutions, and CASS (Liu, 2010, 284).

19 Brus made public his disillusionment with socialism and with reform based on model-building in *From Marx to the Market* (Brus and Laski, 1989). In the conclusion, the authors note "This short book, unlike some of our previous works, has not been intended to investigate a normative model of an economic system which ought to emerge from the process of reforming 'real socialism.' … in our experience of past such model-building, which … in the end proved scarcely successful. We have come to share the view of those participants in the reform debates in communist countries who express doubts about the usefulness of efforts to define the ultimate model of the economic system" (150). Further, "The recourse to MS [market socialism] means that socialism should actually cease to be perceived at all as a bounded system, transcending the institutional framework developed in the past, and hence by definition postulating its total replacement by new institutional foundations, if not immediately so then in a longer perspective" (151).

20 For a more detailed account of the connection between the Erhard Miracle and the Chinese reform debate, see Weber (2020b, 2021).

21 In the context of the "Hundred Flowers Movement," Wu joined a program of economic reform design. After having been labeled a "right deviationist" in the aftermath of the movement, Wu turned around in the 1960s, "trying to distance himself from his bourgeois roots and 'remake his worldview' in line with Maoist ideals." At this time, he found himself in opposition to Sun Yefang, who was drawing up his reform program as the head of the Economic Research Institute. During the

Cultural Revolution, Wu first joined a relatively moderate left group, the "Criticism Headquarters," but later, this group fell in disgrace. Wu was designated a "counter-revolutionary" and was isolated from his colleagues to perform repetitive manual labor. Wu's final break with Maoism came when he joined a research team on the famous Dazhai Commune (Naughton, 2013, 105–115).

22 Friedman gave four lectures during his visit to China in September–October 1980. The lecture in which he introduced the "Erhard Miracle" was titled "Money and Inflation." It provided a basic introduction to Friedman's theory of inflation. A Chinese translation of this lecture was published in *Comments on International Economics* (Friedman, 1981).

23 Yang Peixin (Yang, 1980, 2–4) was at the time the deputy head of the finance research department of the People's Bank of China. He reported on a meeting with Friedman during a research tour in the United States some months before Friedman's visit to China. Friedman told the Chinese delegation that both socialism and Keynesianism had failed globally and that there was no other choice but to go back to Adam Smith's free market. The two sides got into a heated debate. Yang observed that there was no hope of convincing Friedman to believe in socialism. There was also no way the Chinese would accept Friedman's conclusion that capitalism was the only way. Yang pointed out to Friedman that the Chinese were very interested in all kinds of views, but they could not be expected to be convinced. The Chinese believed that parts of the Soviet attempts and parts of their own attempts were failures but that it was wrong to conclude that socialism itself had failed. One had to see things from two angles, they said. Capitalism would be drawn toward crisis, inflation, and unemployment. In contrast, the Chinese Communists solved these problems in the first years of their government, even though unemployment was very severe and the country was suffering from hyperinflation when they took over. Friedman acknowledged that the Chinese success in controlling inflation was impressive and exceptional in the twentieth century. (Surprisingly, Gewirtz cites Yang [1980] as if it was a reaction to Friedman's visit to China and suggests that CASS would have invited Friedman as an inflation expert, unaware of his stance on socialism before they heard his lectures: "The Chinese ... had learned the hard way about Friedman's dual persona and that his expertise on inflation could not be separated from his ideological intensity" [86–87].)

24 Šik was the director of the Economic Research Institute of the Czechoslovakian Academy of Sciences as well as the head of the Reform Commission in 1962/3 (Kosta, 1990, 22). In 1968, Šik rose to the rank of vice prime minister and minister of economics to guide the implementation of his theoretical plans (ibid., 23). The first detailed articulation of his reform vision is in Šik (1965), which was further developed and translated into several languages under the title *Plan and Market under Socialism* (Šik, 1967a). A summary of this book can be found in the Maurice Dobb Festschrift (Šik, 1967b).

25 This book was first published in German (see Šik [1976]).

26 This section relies primarily on the transcriptions of Šik's lectures in China by Wu Jinglian, Rong Jingben, Ma Wenguang, and Chai Ye for publication (Wu et al., 1982). The publication of this material was, however, stopped because of its political sensitivity.

27 The formula Šik derived for calculating prices was based on Marx's concept of production prices: $P = C + V + G$, where C is the depreciation of fixed capital plus the cost of materials, V is wages, and G is the average profit rate based on C (Šik's notation, Wu et al., 1982, 110).

28 On a more fundamental level, Šik seems to assume that by equalizing profits across products and thus setting prices equal to their values, it would be possible to calculate an equilibrium price vector. Yet, there is no reason to assume that the economy is in equilibrium. To the contrary, given the great imbalances between the different sectors, it is most likely in disequilibrium. But if this is the case, there might be no price

vector that corresponds to the given input–output relations such as to sustain them in a decentralized manner.

29 Chen Xikang, who pioneered input–output research in China in the 1960s, was a student of Qian Xuesen, "the father of Chinese rockets" (Chen, 1979, 52; Polenske, 1991, 2). Qian supported input–output research at the Chinese Academy of Sciences after he returned from the United States in 1956, and he encouraged Chen to construct plant- and province-level input–output tables (ibid.). During the Cultural Revolution, one of the very few economic research projects was the construction of the first national input–output table by specialists at the Calculation Center of the State Planning Commission, the Chinese Academy of Science Institute of Mathematics, People's University, and the Beijing Economics College during the Cultural Revolution in 1974 (Chen, 1979, 52; Halpern, 1985, 309–310). Chen (1979, 52) reported that in this context, price calculations were already considered a potential application. The first international exchanges began in 1979, when Chen was one of the first Chinese researchers to participate in the Seventh International Input–Output Conference in Innsbruck, Austria, and the exchanges continued, in collaboration with the United Nations Industrial Development Organization (UNIDO) (Chen, 1979, 46; Polenske, 1991, 1; Secretariat of UNIDO, 1984, 47).

30 Wu (2016), Liu (2002, 2010)—probably based on Wu's recollections—and Lim (2016) suggest that the intended future collaboration with Šik was never realized for political reasons. The evidence from Šik's papers cited in Gewirtz (2017, 107–108) suggests that Šik wrote several letters to different Chinese counterparts, trying to follow up on his visit. Yet in Šik's memoir, he erases any impression that he might have been ousted in China, after he had not set foot into a socialist country since having left Czechoslovakia. Regarding the Chinese invitation, Šik (1988) writes: "I had great doubts. If I really wanted to participate more with the Chinese reforms, I would have needed to consult Chinese materials to search for a tailored solution. This was not feasible in terms of time commitment" (357). Šik added that his theories would be conveyed in the translations of his books and that his wife, Lilli, who had joined the first visit in China, was unwell at the time, preventing him from traveling (ibid., 358).

31 Including, among others, Dong Fureng, Liu Guoguang, Wu Jinglian, and Zhao Renwei

32 The information about this meeting is based on Wood's personal documentation.

33 The secrecy of this exchange was demonstrated to me by the fact that many of my interview partners, who were deeply versed in the reform debates at the time but not directly involved with this conference, seemed unaware of this event. This does not diminish the importance of the conference, both for understanding the confrontation between the Chinese and Eastern European economists as well as for understanding the intellectual formation of the newly minted admirers of Brus and Šik.

34 This internal report (Xue, Liu, and Liao, 1982), titled "Symposium on Soviet and Eastern European Economic System Reform," summarized all conference presentations and discussions. The addressees of the report included the highest political level—Zhao Ziyang, Wan Li, Yao Yilin, Gu Mu, Bo Yibo, Zhang Jingfu, and others—as well as the administrative and research departments in charge of economic reform. The addressees of the report included, among others, the newly founded System Reform Commission, the State Planning Commission, the State Economic Commission, the Foreign Ministry, the Finance Ministry, the State Price Bureau, the State Price Conference, CASS, the Economic Research Center of the State Council, and the Research Center on Technology and Economics of the State Council.

35 Gewirtz (2017) inaccurately asserts that Kende was "a Hungarian official" (248).

36 Gewirtz (2017, 248) inaccurately asserts that Kosta was a "former Czech deputy prime minister."

37 A biographical commonality, at least among Brus, Kosta, and Šik, is that they were all Jewish and victims of both fascist and Stalinist anti-Semitism. These three and Kende joined the Communist movement in part as a resistance against the Nazis.

38 Pecuniary motives might have been among the driving forces for Eastern Europeans to join this risky endeavor. Kende (2017) pointed out that the World Bank's payment for the month-long engagement was the highest he ever received throughout his career.

39 This paragraph is based on Wood's personal documentation.

40 Regarding the Chinese opening speeches, Gewirtz (2017) writes, "Liu Zhuofu, Xue Muqiao, and Liao Jili delivered stiff orations to open the conference" (248). From the reports and notes available to this author, it is difficult to tell whether the "orations" were indeed "stiff." It is clear, however, that the Chinese economists delivered a very detailed account of what they saw as the concrete challenges in their attempts at price adjustment and reform, the main topic of the conference. Without taking the content of the contribution of the Chinese participants into account, it is hard to grasp just how bold the suggestions of the Eastern European economists were.

41 For example, Wood notes, on his attempt to explain to Liu Zhuofu the neoclassical concept of efficiency prices, that it would have evolved into a "long, frustrating dialogue." Zhuofu, in an attempt to give practical meaning to the concept, asks repeatedly whether concrete examples could be considered as efficiency pricing, to which Wood replies with abstract theoretical concepts unfamiliar to Liu.

42 Quoted from Wood's personal documentation.

43 The representation of the speeches of the Chinese participants is based on Wood's personal notes. The representation of the speeches and contributions to the discussion of the foreign delegates is primarily based on the internal report compiled by the Chinese delegates and complemented with information drawn from Wood's notes.

44 Liu explains later to Wood that the rise in subsidies was due to lowered procurement quotas, which increased the amount of grain sold to the state at above-quota prices, as well as to an increase in grain sales at the loss-making state-fixed retail price. Furthermore, grain would still be imported at high world market prices, and in famine-struck areas, grain would be handed out by the state without accounting for transportation costs.

45 Wood notes on this point that the activities of the state commercial agencies would be "just like capitalist speculators." Against the background of the discussion in Chapters 1 and 3, this appears to be only partly correct. It is true that the state commerce agencies use the techniques of the capitalist speculators, but their motives are quite different. The capitalist speculator can only make profits if there are price fluctuations. They thus frequently drive up prices by speculative market interventions, hoping to exit with large profits before the tide turns. The state, in contrast, aims to prevent fluctuations, counterbalancing whenever the first signs of price rises or falls appear.

46 Xue estimates that in the first half of 1982, industrial output rose by 10 percent (heavy industry by 8 percent, light industry by 12 percent); the target had been 4–5 percent.

47 Profit retention of state-owned enterprises increased, on average, from 10.7 percent of profits in 1978 to 19.3 percent in 1981, according to Xue. Since retained profits were often handed out as bonuses to the workers, this added to the wage bill.

48 According to Xue, wages increased by 25.7 percent in nominal terms and 11.9 percent in real terms in the period 1978–1981. Since employment also increased, the national wage bill increased by 44.2 percent in nominal terms and 28.4 percent in real terms in the same period. In contrast, the net material product increased only by 15.9 percent.

49 The term "peasant" is not used here in a prerogative sense, nor does it refer to the common English use referring to farm households working the land for their own subsistence needs. Rather, I follow the convention in China scholarship to use the term "to denote anyone who lives in the Chinese countryside, as demarcated by the household registration system" (Yang, 1996, 8).

50 Xue cites the following figures for peasant income in billion RMB: 134 in 1978, 160 in 1979, 191 in 1980, and 223 in 1981. Therefore, the growth of side-line production

was particularly important, accounting for 50 billion RMB out of the total increase of 89 billion RMB.

51 Xue suggests that state revenues declined from 112.1 billion RMB in 1978 to 106.4 billion RMB in 1981.

52 The papers were presented in this order: "A Comment on Recent Economic Developments in the USSR and Eastern Europe" (Brus), "Plan and Market: Controlling the Economy without Obligatory Planning" (Kende), "Decision Making Power of Industrial Enterprises in Eastern European Countries" (Granick), "The Problem of Price Formation in Socialist Economies" (Wood [this paper is not contained in the Chinese report to the leadership and the author has lost any copy, so it could not be considered here]), "Soviet and Eastern European Experience with Price Determination" (Strumiński), "Soviet and Eastern European Experience with Wages, Incentives and Income Distribution" (Kosta), and "International Perspectives on China's Issues in System Reform" (Lim) (CIR).

53 Quote from Wood's personal documentation. Wood's notes on Strumiński's speech are consistent with the Chinese report.

54 See Chapter 4 for a discussion of the "price scissors" problem.

55 This paragraph is primarily based on the Chinese internal report.

56 Quote taken from Wood's personal documentation.

57 Quote as in Wood's personal documentation; this, the following, and the previous paragraphs are based on Wood's notes.

58 Wu points out that he learned from the Eastern European economists that "any system was a totality of interrelated economic linkages, with its own logic and operational rules. Since economic structural reform was a transformation from one economic system to another economic system, piecemeal reforms would only lead to economic chaos" (Wu, 2013a, 146).

6

MARKET CREATION VERSUS PRICE LIBERALIZATION

Rural Reform, Young Intellectuals, and the Dual-Track Price System

Introduction

> Contracting production to the household (包产到户) is a creation of the peasants, dual-track pricing (双轨价格) has continuously existed in China from an early time on.
>
> *(Chen Yizi, Rural Development Group and director of the Economic System Reform Research Institute, 2013, 310)*

China's leading reform thinkers of the early days formed distinct groups that are, to some extent, defined by the generations in which they lived. Their biographies varied greatly with the different moments in China's turbulent recent history that shaped their lives, while their intellectual formation greatly depended on the specific personal and intellectual paths they took.[1] The outlook of the 1980s middle generation of established intellectuals (born 1920–1939) had been shaped by the optimism and the urge to establish a coherent political and economic system as well as a binding orthodoxy of the 1950s (Naughton, 2013, 98).[2] They were joined in the 1980s by young researchers at the Chinese Academy of Social Sciences and in Beijing's leading engineering departments, who had typically not spent the Cultural Revolution in the countryside and who shared the middle generation's belief in the powers of scientific economics.

The formative experience of the older generation (born 1900–1919), in contrast, was the revolutionary struggle in the countryside and economic warfare (see Chapter 3). Zhao Ziyang's secretary, Li Xianglu, stresses that China's veteran revolutionaries such as Zhao or Wan Li were intimately familiar with the workings of the market. Part of their success in the Chinese Civil War derived from their skills in using commerce to improve their military and economic strengths.

Furthermore, Zhao descended from a family of peasants who had attained a certain amount of wealth by skillful business practices (Li, 2016a). Many leading economists of the reform era of this generation, such as Du Runsheng and Xue Muqiao, shared this formative experience in the revolutionary struggles in the countryside. Sun Yefang emerged as a leading economist and statistician, thanks to his training in the Soviet Union during the 1920s (Garms, 1980, 8).

A cohort of young intellectuals (born 1940–1960)[3] who were "sent up to the mountains and to the countryside" (上山下乡) during the Cultural Revolution[4] emerged as influential reform economists in the course of agricultural reform. Like the veteran revolutionaries before them, their intellectual and political formation was intimately connected to the agrarian question, to China's peasant majority, and to their struggle for material well-being. These young and old intellectuals with close ties to the countryside formed an unusual alliance that proved critical for China's reform. The disruption of social order during the Cultural Revolution enabled this cross-generational cooperation (Bai, 2016; Lu, 2016; Luo, 2017).

Theoretical discussions about price reform and the ideal target system occupied the minds of middle-aged, established intellectuals who collaborated with the young scientists. Meanwhile, this alliance of the young and the old played a critical role in facilitating the breakthrough in rural reform that dramatically changed the living conditions of China's peasant majority and the basic constitution of China's political economy. As Nolan (1988, 85) summarizes: "Before 1978 most decisions on rural production and distribution were administered directly by the state or indirectly by the state's representatives in the collectives. The 1980s witnessed an explosion of independent economic decision–making by individuals and groups." Within the span of only a few years, China's agricultural economy transformed from a collective, centrally controlled economy to a market-based one with major state participation. The alliance of young and old reform intellectuals conducted on-the-ground reform experiments that aided this rapid change. Their experiences with rural reforms came to prove crucial for the more general course of China's economic system reforms.

As described in Chapter 4, China's development model in the Mao era was built on a strict urban–rural divide and the extraction of resources from the countryside for urban industrialization. Reform began with a renegotiation of this relation reflected in the increase of relative prices of agricultural products in 1978. The sharp urban–rural divide emerged with the nation-building project that followed the 1911 Republican revolution. As Honig and Zhao (2019, 8) observe: "Throughout the Republican era, urban cosmopolitanism represented the modern, in contrast to peasants, who epitomized backwardness, if not the antithesis to modernity." During the Cultural Revolution the industrialization model based on extraction from the countryside continued. But the far-reaching campaigns for reeducation of urban elites by agricultural labor replaced the sense of superiority of urban cosmopolitanism with a rhetoric of learning from the peasants. To be sure, these campaigns took a brutal form and landed many intellectuals in labor camps under most adverse conditions. Yet, as a historical irony, these Cultural Revolution campaigns also established new links between the urban and rural spheres that became instrumental for the breakthrough in the early years of reform.

The first part of this chapter shows how a group of young researchers who had spent their formative years working in agriculture in the countryside (上山下乡) moved to the heart of Chinese economic policy-making as rural reforms were successfully implemented. The second part delineates how this community of young researchers devised a theoretical justification for the prevailing dual-track price system (双轨制). Admirers of Eastern European reform economics had described the dual-track price system as inconsistent and chaotic. Theorizing the dual-track price system as a coherent reform approach helped it to become a national policy in 1985. This consolidated China's path of experimentalist reform.

Rural Reform and the Rise of the Young Intellectuals

Chen Yizi emerged as the leader of the young generation of intellectuals and played a critical role in establishing close ties with leading cadres. Chen was the son of a family with generations of influential intellectuals (Fewsmith, 1994). He spent ten years (1959–1969) at Peking University as a student of physics and Chinese literature and as a committed leader in the Communist Youth League (Chen, 2013, 71–121). After writing a letter to Mao Zedong criticizing the lack of democracy in party and state, Chen was purged as an "anti-revolutionary element" and was sent to the countryside in Henan, where he spent almost a decade (1969–1978) (ibid., 124–191). Before Chen left Beijing, he met with his closest friends, including his classmate He Weiling. He told them that, since more than 80 percent of the Chinese people lived as peasants, in order to understand China, one had to learn about real life in the countryside, and this was what he set out to do (ibid., 124).

Chen conducted deep studies of the rural living conditions, including inquiries into deaths from the Great Famine, and joined an agricultural education institute in Chumaodian prefecture. Luo Xiaopeng, who Chen knew from their time at Peking University, joined Chen later (Luo, 2017; Chen, 2013, 310). On a sunny January day in 2017, in a long interview in his modest Hong Kong apartment, Luo reflected about their joined time in Chumaodian. He stressed that Chen gained the trust of the local leaders. Generally, they were very skeptical toward urban intellectuals,[5] but they promoted Chen to join their ranks and become a local cadre (Luo, 2017). As an engineering student, Luo himself was not meant to go to the countryside, but he followed Mao's slogan "to learn from the peasants" (ibid.). Looking back, Luo points out,

> So for us this experience was to learn the heart of collectivization, the life of the peasants, the crisis of collective farming. We realised that every attempt to make collectivisation work failed, still we were true believers; we still hoped to find the right way. But the reality was hitting back at us.

The local politics turned against us after Lin Biao's death as well, so ... I went back to the city, back to normal engineering life.

(ibid.)

But Chen stayed on, and following Luo's introduction, he was joined by Deng Yingtao, the son of Deng Liqun. Deng Liqun had been the secretary to Liu Shaoqi— China's former president, who had early on insisted on the need for famine relief systems. Liu played a key role in the stabilization efforts after the Great Famine, which involved household contracting. Under household contracting, the production team drew up contracts with households, agreeing to provide land as well as access to tools and inputs in return for a fixed share of the household's harvest. Liu was the most prominent central leader branded as "capitalist roader" during the Cultural Revolution. Liu died under house arrest (Vogel, 2011, 43; Wemheuer, 2014, 84, 141–142). Deng Liqun chose to remain loyal to Liu, was purged, and, as punishment, was sent to a "May Seventh Cadre School" for reeducation by labor. Deng stayed on at the school when he was free to return to Beijing to study Marxism–Leninism (Vogel, 2011, 724). During this period, Deng Liqun became skeptical about whether collective farming was the best organizational form in China's quest for economic progress. In these years, Chen Yizi built a strong trust relationship with Deng Liqun. Deng Liqun, Deng Yingtao, and Chen Yizi openly discussed the shortcomings of the commune system and laid the foundation for their later joint efforts in economic reform (Luo, 2017). Deng Liqun knew Chen Yun from their time in the Northeast during the revolutionary struggle, and he served as a member of Deng Xiaoping's Research Office in 1975 (Vogel, 2011, 723–724). Thus, Deng had close ties with both of the key leaders of economic reforms and emerged as an important promoter of China's young reform intellectuals.

Chen Yizi also maintained a close relationship with Hu Yaobang, whom he knew from Hu's days as the secretary of the Communist Youth League (1952–1966) (Fewsmith, 1994, 33). Hu, who was born to a Hakka peasant family in Hunan, dropped out of school at age fourteen to join the Communist Party and the Red Army. He was a veteran of the Long March and a close ally of Deng Xiaoping. The two men were both twice purged and then called back to the center of power again in 1975. Hu had a record as a bold reformer in the aftermath of the Great Leap Forward (Vogel, 2011, 727–728). Luo Xiaopeng recalled that, just before the Nixon visit in 1972, he joined one of the meetings with Hu. Hu's home attracted many young people at the time. "We just came in with mutual friends, the door was open, and Hu Yaobang was open to talk about anything," said Luo. They used the opportunity to share their experiences in Henan.

It turned out that Hu was even more radical than his young friends. When they told him about their attempt to reform the agricultural school, Hu replied, "Forget about that, we now need a new approach." In retrospect, Luo says, it was clear that Hu was against collective farming (Luo, 2017). Hu was, of course, fully aware of the great sensitivity of the question and its politically charged history. In fact, when Deng Xiaoping, together with Chen Yun and others, promoted contracting production to the household in the aftermath of the Great Famine in 1962, Deng used his famous cat metaphor—which was to become the most quoted symbol of Chinese pragmatism—in a speech addressing the Communist Youth League led by Hu. Referencing their revolutionary fights, Deng said,

> When talking about fighting battles, Comrade Liu Bocheng often quotes a Sichuan proverb—"It does not matter if it is a yellow cat or a black cat, as long as it catches mice." The reason we defeated Chiang Kai-shek is that we did not always fight in the conventional way. Our sole aim is to win by taking advantage of given conditions. If we want to restore agricultural production, we must also take advantage of actual conditions. That is to say, we should not stick to a fixed mode of relations of production but adopt whatever mode can help mobilize the masses' initiative. At present, it looks as though neither industry nor agriculture can advance without first taking one step back.
>
> *(Deng, 1992)*

Mao intervened personally shortly afterward to stop the spread of household contracting. Deng learned that Mao was displeased with his speech and turned to his confidante, Hu, who had this passage removed from the transcript (Fewsmith, 1994, 26–27; Pantsov and Levine, 2015, 224).

When Deng ascended to power at the Third Plenary Session in 1978, household contracting remained illegal for the time being, but local experiments were tolerated. The most prominent example of such experiments was Anhui province under Wan Li, who was a long-term ally of Deng. Born to a poor peasant family in mountainous Shandong, Wan built his reputation for his success in organizing grain supplies for the Communist troops during the Chinese Civil War. Immediately after the revolution, Wan served as deputy head of the Southeast Ministry of Industry under Deng's leadership, where he oversaw building up manufacturing capacity and later joined Deng's 1975 push for modernization. In 1977, Hua Guofeng appointed Wan Li as first party secretary of Anhui province, which faced severe starvation (Vogel, 2011, 736–738). Wan decided to let the peasants contract production to the household in light of a major drought that hit the province in 1978 (Luo, 2017; Zhang M., 2016; Teiwes and Sun, 2015). Under the Maoist model, the harvest was produced and owned collectively by the production team with the help of inputs and machines from the brigades or communes. A share of the output was handed over to brigades (village level) and communes, generating revenue for these higher administrative levels and in fulfillment of the state-set procurement quotas. Under household contracting, the organization of production was moved from the collective to the household (Oi 1986, 1999, 19–34; Walker, 1984). Wan Li's policy prefigured national decollectivization and a move from political organization to personal incentives as a driving force. As such, Wan Li's toleration of household contracting in Anhui was a critical step toward the later dismantling of the core of the Maoist agricultural economy.

In October 1978, Hu Yaobang called Chen Yizi back to Beijing to join the efforts in agricultural reform. Hu arranged a post for Chen as researcher at the Agricultural Institute of CASS (Chen, 2013, 193–195; Fewsmith, 1994, 32–33). A year earlier, Deng Xiaoping had reinstated the university entrance exam, which allowed many of those who had spent their youth sent down in the countryside to return to Beijing and other cities and pursue higher education.

At the height of the Cultural Revolution, Mao had called for reeducation of urban youth by the peasant majority. This started a movement that would send 17 million urban youth in the years 1968–1980 to live in "a world of rural poverty they would otherwise never have known" (Honig and Zhao, 2019, 1). Some went voluntarily, with enthusiasm; others were basically forced to leave their families behind to go to a remote village. The arrival of these privileged urban teenagers in China's villages created severe challenges, both on the part of the youngsters as well as on the rural communities and cadres. As I argued in Chapter 4, China's development model rested on a deep divide between the urban and rural societies. The sent-down youth were at the frontier of this divide. Their presence was ridden with difficulties, but it also created new personal and bureaucratic connections between the villages and the cities.

The experience of rural poverty was the starting point for a movement of young intellectuals who were dedicated to rural reform after their return to the urban centers. Some of these returnees emerged as influential researchers who shaped the course of reform in the 1980s. They included, for example, Deng Yingtao and Wang Xiaoqiang, who returned from Henan; Wang Qishan, from Shaanxi; Bai Nanfeng, Lin Chun, and Wang Xiaolu, from Shanxi; Bai Nansheng, Zhang Musheng, and Weng Yongxi, from Inner Mongolia; and Chen Xiwen, Zhou Qiren, and Zhu Jiaming, from the Northeast (Liu, 2010, 410–411). Chen Yizi was one of the leaders of this group of young intellectuals.

In our interview (2016), Bai Nanfeng reflected on the motivations and positions of the returnees from remote rural life. It was clear, he said, that those who had spent many years in a poor village, often from their teenage years until their mid-twenties, had become accustomed to living among the peasants, and they were different from their younger classmates or those who had remained in the cities. The returnees' primary concern was the agrarian question. In the countryside, confronted with the hunger and poverty of the peasants, they used their time to read widely and deeply in search of a new path for Chinese socialism.

Zhang Musheng thought that for this group of young urban intellectuals, despite all the challenges of life in the countryside, "there was never again a time for such good reading as during the Cultural Revolution" (Zhang, 2009). Thanks to their family connections, they had good access to officially published and unpublished books and took as much as they could carry to their villages, where they read carefully and reflected collectively (Bai, 2016; Wang, X. L., 2016; Zhang M., 2016).[6] Zhang stressed that he was among those who went to the countryside on their own initiative in 1965, even before the Cultural Revolution and the official sent-down youth movement began (Zhang M.,

2016).[7] In 1968, he wrote a pamphlet titled "A Study of the Peasant Question in China" (中国农民问题学习). Zhang's pamphlet was circulated as a Party internal publication and was widely read. Zhang found great support from other sent-down urban youth, as well as from Hu Yaobang (Yang, 1996, 117; Zhang M., 2009, 2016). A close reading of Bukharin's debate with Stalin in the 1920s,[8] Trotsky's refutation of Stalin, and the change in Lenin's and Mao's thoughts over different periods led Zhang to conclude that the only way for China to increase agricultural production was to return to contracting production to the household (包产到户) (ibid.). Zhang's pamphlet landed him in prison in 1972 (Yang, 1996, 117).

In the late 1970s, back in Beijing, Zhang and other urban youth who had read their way to become independent thinkers in the countryside found their first opportunities to officially publish their insights. Lin Chun, for instance (the daughter of the famous economist Lin Zili), who would join the Research Office of the State Council shortly thereafter, published a paper "On the Role of the Forces of Production in Historical Development" (1977). It formed part of the larger ideological attack against the radical faction of Cultural Revolution leaders, who were labeled the "Gang of Four" by the reformers.[9] Lin used classic writings of Marx, Engels, Mao, Lenin, and Stalin to show that a correct interpretation of historical materialism must take material development as the decisive determining force in history.

In a coffee room at the London School of Economics in 2015, Lin spoke with me about her experience of the dawn of reform. She cautioned that this line of reasoning ultimately led to an extreme form of economic determinism that came to pave the way for China's gradual return to capitalism (Lin, 2015). At the time, her argument was part of the urgent quest for economic progress. In hindsight, the new emphasis on a primacy of the development of the forces of production constituted a deep ideological shift underpinning the reform agenda. This basic notion was canonized in Su Shaozhi and Feng Lanrui's conception of the "primary stage of socialism," which was at the time heavily criticized but was in 1987 sanctioned as state doctrine (Sun, 1995, 186–187; Weber, 2020 also see Chapter 8). The argument that China was in a primary state of socialism and had to focus on the development of its forces of production became a kind of "anything goes" paradigm, wherein the most capitalist reforms could be legitimized as serving socialism.

Wang Xiaoqiang had been a sent-down youth in Yan'an before joining a school for "workers, peasants, and soldiers" (工农兵) in Luoyang. He was to become an important reform intellectual and close collaborator of Chen Yizi. In the late 1970s, Wang worked as a fitter in Beijing in a neighborhood factory. He used every free minute for reading (Chen, 2013, 219; Zhang M., 2016). Wang articulated his thoughts in an essay titled "Critique of Agrarian Socialism" (1979). He challenged the Cultural Revolution model of agricultural organization from a long-term historical perspective and based his arguments on a close reading of Marxist classics. His key point was that Chinese socialism was agrarian and built on feudal relations. The essay found great appraisal and circulated quickly among

Beijing's intellectuals. It came to the attention of Lin Wei, who organized a writing group at CASS aimed at debunking the "Gang of Four" theoretically. The group edited a journal produced for internal circulation among party leaders, called "Unfinished Manuscripts" (未定稿). The journal printed Wang's paper, and with the support of Deng Liqun, Wang was invited to join the editorial team at the Chinese Academy of Social Sciences (CASS) (Chen, 2013, 218–219). Wang Xiaoqiang thus entered the circle of influential reform intellectuals.

Chen Yizi was impressed with Wang's daring analysis and passed his paper on to Wang Gengjin, the deputy director of the Agricultural Institute at CASS, who had been the first director of the agricultural department of the Central Planning Commission in the early 1950s. Wang Gengjin was one of the senior Communists who at the time reflected about past mistakes and came to support the young generation vigorously (Liu 2010, 414; Luo, 2017). Wang Gengjin arranged for Wang Xiaoqiang's paper to be officially published in *Issues in Agricultural Economics* (1980).

Middle-aged and young researchers and students such as Chen Yizi, Wang Xiaoqiang, Bai Nanfeng, Luo Xiaopeng, and Lin Chun formed a quickly growing circle of friends and collaborators. They met on weekends in an empty office, in parks, and as the number of people grew, in lecture halls of one of Beijing's universities (Bai, 2016; Lu L., 2016; Wang, 2016). At one of these gatherings, Chen met Wang Xiaoqiang. Chen was galvanized by Wang's "original views and unique perspectives" (Chen, 2013, 219). The two came to form the core of two influential reform research institutions: first the Chinese Rural Development Issues Research Group (中国农村发展问题研究组, hereafter the Rural Development Group based on the Chinese abbreviation 农发组), and later the China Economic System Reform Research Institute (中国经济体制改革研究所, hereafter the System Reform Institute based on the Chinese abbreviation 体改所). These institutions were unique as they had emerged from outside of the official party and state hierarchy and yet came to advise the highest government levels. The System Reform Institute has therefore been described to me by several interviewees as the first independent think tank in the socialist world. These young intellectuals rose to their positions of influence thanks to their contribution to the breakthrough in rural reform.

In 1979, low grain production was still a severe problem, and the high costs of grain subsidies that resulted from raised procurement prices and low sales prices were already becoming apparent. Chen Yun warned in March,

> Our country has more than 900 million people, 80% are peasants. The revolution has been won for 30 years and the people are demanding improvements in their lives. Have there been improvements? Yes. But many places still do not have enough to eat, this is a big problem. … If we keep this problem unresolved, the local cadres will start guiding people to the cities to demand food.
>
> *(Chen, 1986, 226)*

Only a few months later, Guo Chongyi, a member of the Anhui provincial Chinese People's Political Consultative Conference, came to Beijing with a report showing that Feixi county, which was one of the counties that I pioneered the contracting of production to the household, had increased their summer grain harvest by 150 percent, despite the severe drought (Fewsmith, 1994, 32).[10] Chen Yizi received a copy of the report and showed it immediately to Deng Liqun and Hu Yaobang. Hu promptly expressed his support for Feixi county (ibid., 33). Chen Yizi was so excited at this news that he arranged his own three-month study in Anhui province (April–July 1980) to survey the results of the experiments, using various forms of contracting production to lower units, including the production teams and households, as well as some unreformed collective producers for comparison (Liu, 2010, 413). Chen Yizi's report demonstrated the success of the new production arrangement in an unprecedentedly systematic fashion.

Chen Yizi and the other young researchers managed to officially establish the Rural Development Group as a subunit of the Agricultural Economics Institute at CASS with the critical support of Wang Gengjin, Deng Liqun, and Du Runsheng. The latter was the deputy director of the State Agricultural Commission (Gottschang, 1995, 2; Wang, 2014, xiv) and a revolutionary veteran who had supported Deng Xiaoping's troops in the war for liberation by leading peasant movements to implement land reform, had been a former president of the Chinese Academy of Science, described himself as an "intellectual who came from the countryside" (Du, 2014, xvii), and is called the "father of China's rural reform" (Zhang M., 2016). The Rural Development Group had a considerable budget at its disposal, arranged for by Deng Liqun (Bai, 2016; Deng, 2005, 321). Its members were independent in organizing their research; many were not party members, and they had no formal superior within CASS but reported directly to Deng Liqun and Du Runsheng (ibid.; Wang, 2017). Chen Yizi became the head, and Wang Xiaoqiang and Chen's old friend He Weiling became his deputies (Fewsmith, 1994, 38; Wang, 2017). At the official founding meeting in February 1981, Deng Liqun told the group,

> After returning to the city you are still thinking of the countryside .... You have been peasants, now you want to contribute your knowledge and abilities to develop the countryside; to use your own words, you want to dedicate your lives to this cause. ... If we solve the problem of 800 million peasants this would be a great step in the history of China and the world.
>
> *(Deng, 1981)*

Du Runsheng followed with his speech expressing his full support for the group. Du pointed out,

> We currently face many questions in the countryside, but our research specialists in the field are old, where are the suitable successors! ... We need not only to train people in a planned way, but we also have to create an

environment in which talents can develop independently and come to the fore, so that our socialist cause can advance even better.

(Du, 1981)

In fact, Du himself played a critical role in creating such an environment and encouraging young researchers to develop their skills (Zhou, 2016). Zhang M. (2016), one of the founding members of the Rural Development Group, remembers Du's great intellectual openness. Du would consider all sorts of views, clearly distinguishing his own stance from that of others, while being ready to listen even to those opposed to his socialist cause. He lived the principle of "letting one hundred flowers bloom" (ibid.). But the most important of his principles, according to Zhang, was to use an inductive instead of a deductive method whenever possible. The task of the researcher seeking solutions for social problems is to investigate the practices and demands already emerging among the masses and to derive from these observations theoretical principles and policies. In this process, the key question in Du's view was not whether something belongs to socialism or capitalism but how to nourish good creations by the people. To this end, he encouraged the young researchers to study all sorts of foreign methods and theories, which they could use in their on-the-ground investigations (ibid.).

The work of the Rural Development Group was fully in Du's spirit. In study groups and self-organized lectures, they taught one another to catch up with the most recent debates in the social sciences, philosophy, history, and economics, as well as to acquire tools from mathematics and computer sciences (Bai, 2016). In a collectively written essay on strategy research, they articulated their view on the right approach to system reform. Building on Chen Yun's famous saying, they stated,

> On the one hand, we have to grope for stones to cross the river, through practice ceaselessly and step by step clarify the situation; at the same time we have to immediately research in a systematic manner the structure, functions and operation of the future system as well as the characteristics of each stage of the transition.
>
> *(China Rural Development Issues Research Group et al.,*
> *1981, 394)*

The most important and most influential of the group's work followed up on Chen Yizi's pioneering studies of first attempts at agricultural reform. They organized systematic surveys of the results of the agricultural household contracting. The newly founded group used the summer vacation of 1981 to conduct extensive research in Anhui province, followed by surveys in other provinces documenting not only the economic, but also the social consequences of contracting production to lower levels. They used quantitative methods to produce simple statistics derived from data they collected with questionnaires. At the same time, their intimate familiarity with the peasants' lives, as well as the experience of some of their group members as local cadres, allowed them to conduct qualitative interviews effectively and to speak openly with the locals (Bai, 2016; Luo, 2017).

If the Third Plenum in 1978 was the turning point toward reform, the year 1980 marked the arrival of key reformers at the center of power. Hu Yaobang was elected chairman of the Communist Party (a title later replaced by that of General Secretary). Hu and Zhao Ziyang became members of the Politburo Standing Committee. Zhao was first elected vice premier and then premier. Wan Li became a member of the Central Committee and a vice premier (Editorial Board of Who's Who in China, 1989b,c,e; Vogel, 2011, 728–729). These three were all allies of Deng Xiaoping and driving forces behind legalizing the contracting of production to lower levels—in particular, to the household. In the beginning, this was only allowed as an exception to remote and poor areas, which had long been struggling for subsistence. The greatest political struggle arose about whether household contracting should be allowed in those places where collective farming worked relatively well. Those who thought that this was a step back on ideological grounds were opposed, as were provincial leaders who were afraid that this would destroy the strength of their mechanized agricultural production (Luo, 2017).

So, a breakthrough in rural reform could only be achieved by winning these opponents over. The surveys conducted by the Rural Development Group provided important factual evidence of the outcomes of contracting. The Rural Development Group was not alone in researching the experiments, but their observations carried special weight because they were seen as a relatively neutral entity outside of the usual party and state structures. This important advantage won the group the strong support and trust of Hu, Zhao, and Wan (Deng, 2005, 323). For these leaders, "seeking truth from facts" (实事求是) was not a mere epistemological principle but an art of government, remembers Zhao's young secretary Li Xianglu (2016b). They avoided engaging in debates about big ideological questions of capitalism and socialism with their opponents but "waited to let the facts speak" (ibid.). Thus, Zhao Ziyang went to tour Hubei, Henan, Shandong, and Heilongjiang in 1981 to investigate the changes in agricultural production himself (ibid.).

The household contracting won its "total victory" (Luo, 2017) in 1983 when the resistance of provinces such as Heilongjiang was broken with the help of on-the-ground studies conducted by the Rural Development Group.[11] These surveys showed that the peasants, against the will of their provincial leadership, were strongly in favor of being responsible for their own production.[12] This provided the critical backing for Zhao's approach, "letting the masses decide for themselves in which way they want to organize the production" (Li, 2016a). The Rural Development Group, with decisive input from Wang Xiaoqiang, gave this new policy a name that was to become famous: the Household Production Contracting Responsibility System (家庭联产承包责任制, hereafter household responsibility system) (Bai, 2016).

The household responsibility system maintained the public ownership of land and certain important means of production, but the production became the responsibility of the households. They had to contribute their share to the state quota but were free to make their own decisions on what to plant on the land they contracted and where to market it beyond the quota.[13] A multi-tiereds price system was the correlate to this system of production, with the lower price for the state quota, a higher price for the above-quota procurement to the state, and a market price for those crops allowed to be sold in fairs. Taken together, this constituted a fundamental transformation of China's agricultural political economy, replacing collectivism with individual and family incentives.

After an overwhelming success in inducing output growth in agriculture, the Rural Development Group was looking into new pressing issues in reform in 1984. One of them was price reform. Song Guoqing, a peasant's son, was a brigade leader before entering Peking University as a student in geometry, and he had combined his mathematical skills with his interest in political economy to study modern microeconomics. Song had recently joined the group, and he suggested an experiment to test the effects of two kinds of price reforms (Luo, 2017). At the time, Du Runsheng had been promoted to be the head of the Rural Development Research Center under the State Council. He supported the idea and contacted Gao Yang, an economist and revolutionary veteran who was at the time party secretary of Hebei Province (ibid.; Chen, 2013, 311; Editorial Board of Who's Who in China, 1989a). Gao agreed to provide the young researchers with whatever they needed to carry out the experiment (Luo, 2017).

The experiment was designed to apply a more cautious price reform policy to one county and a more radical one to another. Song's logic was based on the observation that the state-quota price for grain was lower than the market price. Song argued that, from the peasant's perspective, delivering the quota to the state at the lower planned price amounted to paying a tax. Reminiscent of a similar proposal of the 1960s and Sun Yefang's ideas (see Chapters 4 and 5), Song suggested that instead of delivering the quota, the peasants could pay a monetary tax that equaled the revenue loss they would otherwise face from selling their quota at a lower price.[14] The state could then use the tax revenue to buy grain in the market. This policy was tested in Gaocheng county, which was at the time under the leadership of Gao Xiaomeng. The more radical policy was implemented in Ningjin county under the oversight of Luo Xiaopeng.

Luo explained in our interview that, in addition to the first policy, inputs—most importantly, chemical fertilizers and diesel—were also no longer allocated at state-set prices but had to be acquired by the peasants from the market. With the support of what Luo, looking back, described as unusually capable leadership, they issued a new local currency to avoid any cross-regional income effects and drew up budgets for all involved parties. Both experiments failed because of the success of the household responsibility system and the adjustment in grain procurement prices in raising agricultural output.

In his memoir, Zhao Ziyang noted on the unanticipated expansion of agricultural:

> The rural energy that was unleashed in those years was magical, beyond what anyone could have imagined. A problem thought to be unsolvable had worked itself out in just a few years' time. The food situation that was once so grave had turned into a situation where, by 1984, farmers actually had more grain than they could sell. The state grain storehouses were stacked full from the annual procurement program.
>
> *(2009, 97–98)*

The supply of grain had increased by 1984 to an extent that, for the first time, the planned price and the above-quota state procurement price were higher than the market price (Luo, 2017, 2008).[15] Hence, selling the quota at the planned price was no longer a tax but a subsidy for the peasants, and selling the surplus above the quota to the state protected the peasants from bearing the whole burden of the falling market prices. This revealed a basic difference between Song's taxation scheme based on microeconomic reasoning and the state procurement of grain.

The underlying Guanzian logic[16] of the multi-tiered price system became apparent at this moment of great success of the new household responsibility system. The multi-tiered pricing initially had the effect of encouraging the peasants, who now harvested the fruits of their labor for their individual benefit, to produce more. But as the grain supply boomed and incurred a rapid fall in prices, the state procurement component of the household responsibility system protected the peasants from the consequences of violent price fluctuations. A direct tax is static. It would have been based on calculating the monetary cost of delivering a quote to the state at a price lower than the market price for some given price differential and quota. But as the grain output changed rapidly, so did the market price for crops. The household responsibility system adjusts automatically to price fluctuations. When the market price is high, the cost of having to deliver part of the harvest at a lower state-set price is high. But, thanks to the same high market prices, revenues for farmers are also high, and hence the harm from having to deliver part of the harvest at the lower state price is not too severe. When the market price is below the state-set price in times of bumper harvests, the state procurement quota changes from incurring a cost for the farmers to securing them against market price fluctuations. It turns out the state procurement under the household responsibility system dampened price fluctuations—just as the practice of the Ever Normal Granaries had done for centuries.

This price-stabilization effect of the responsibility system was not by accident, but by design. In our interview, Luo Xiaopeng stressed that Wan Li, who is generally recognized as the pioneer of agricultural reform, was keenly aware of this stabilizing function of the household responsibility system and multi-tiered pricing. When some members of the Rural Development Group had previously suggested a similar experiment to him, Wan had vigorously opposed the idea of replacing the state's participation in the grain market with taxes. In 1984, he again lobbied for maintaining the state grain procurement, despite the favorable conditions for abolishing it (Luo, 2017).

From the failed experiment, those within the Rural Development Group who might have believed in a quick and radical price reform had learned their lesson. Even when the situation appeared favorable, as it did in light of the output explosion in agriculture, a cautious approach was superior to the risk of a policy-induced shock liberalization. Furthermore, the failed experiment had demonstrated to the Rural Development Group the important function of state procurement not only in generating fiscal income and circulating commodities across regions, but also in stabilizing prices and thereby protecting both consumers and producers from violent cycles. The experiment had shown that, in contrast to the neoclassical interpretation,[17] the dual-track price system was not simply a high tax on an initial amount of output, but a regulated agricultural production through state participation in the market.

Turning Practice into Policy: The Moganshan Youth Conference and the Dual-Track Price System

> The current conditions in our country are totally different from those of the past. In the past we worried about food, about clothing; today we worry about overstocking of grain and cotton cloth in our warehouses. There is enough stock in our warehouses of other consumer goods as well, and we have no need to fear a buying frenzy.
>
> *(Xue, 1985)*[18]

Thanks to the success of the rural reform as well as the narrowing of the "scissors gap" between agricultural and industrial prices, the problem of sufficient food provision was essentially solved by 1984. At the same time, a one-time price adjustment brought a major breakthrough for the availability of clothing. If the initial push for reform had been driven by a crisis reflected in stagnating living standards and poverty, by 1984, two of the most basic challenges in people's material well-being were overcome. This created a momentum for more decisive reform in the urban industrial core of the economy. At the Moganshan World Bank Conference, Xue Muqiao had still cautioned that the people were not prepared to accept even a minor increase in the price of cotton (see Chapter 5). Some months later, in October 1983, Zhao Ziyang, who had previously warned about the reactions of the masses to price changes of daily necessities, now praised a plan presented by the State Price Bureau that recommended a decrease in the retail price of synthetic textiles and an increase in that of cotton cloth, after the prices of both had been kept stable for thirty years (Cheng, 2006, 54–59; Zhao, 2016j).[19] Zhao wrote a letter to Hu Yaobang stating that this measure would greatly relieve pressure on the state budget[20] as well as encourage people to substitute abundant synthetics for scarce cotton. Zhao was now ready to take the risk:

This decision will be of wide-ranging consequence, and could evoke a considerable shock, but it would be of great advantage to the whole economy and would constitute a breakthrough for the rationalisation of prices.

(Zhao, 2016h)

The plan became state policy in January 1983, and by the end of the year, the problem of the overstocking of synthetic clothes and the shortage of cotton clothes was overcome. The rationing of cotton, which had prevailed since the revolution, was abolished (Cheng, 2006, 56–59). There was a temporary run on cotton when the end of rationing was announced, but as supply was sufficient and prices were not rising, this did not have any political or economic consequences.[21]

In light of the great success in solving the long-standing problem of the relative price adjustments of textiles, great enthusiasm for further price adjustments was aroused in 1984. Chen Yun wrote in a letter dated September 13, 1984, to the Third Plenum of the 12th Party Congress,

Now is an opportune moment for price reform, we should progress with steady steps. The price decrease for synthetic and increase for cotton cloth has not resulted in a shock for society, this is an example of success on which we can draw.

(Cheng, 2006, 59)

This new momentum for urban reform created opportunities for young researchers to contribute their views. Under the editorship of Tang Zongkun, the direction of China's leading economics journal *Economic Research* (经济研究) was changed and young authors were encouraged to publish (Tang, 2016). One of the earliest articles by graduate students was Lou Jiwei's and Zhou Xiaochuan's "On the Direction of Reform in the Price System and Related Modeling Methods" (1984) (ibid.).[22]

Zhou Xiaochuan was the governor of the People's Bank of China since 2002, when he was appointed under Premier Zhu Rongji, until 2018. Zhou took the lead for interest and exchange rate liberalizations and was widely considered a candidate for Vice Prime Minister in the early 2000s (McGregor, 2006). When he was writing their article on price reform, Zhou was a doctoral student in applied computation at the Automation Research Institute of Tsinghua. Unlike the young intellectuals involved in rural reform, Zhou had begun his university studies at the Beijing Chemical Engineering Institute during the Cultural Revolution in 1972. He subsequently worked at the Institute of Automation (Government of the PRoC, 2017).

Lou Jiwei was the finance minister from 2013 until 2016 and is now the chair of the National Council for Social Security Fund. Lou was, at the time of the publication of the joint paper with Zhou, a master's student in the Technical Economics Department of CASS. He had spent the Cultural Revolution as a soldier in the navy and as a worker at the Beijing Institute of Automation before entering Tsinghua University for undergraduate studies in computer science (China Vitae, 2017).

Reflecting their focus of study, Lou and Zhou sought for a solution to price adjustments by employing a combination of input–output analysis, dynamic linear programming, and computable general equilibrium models. The basic logic of their recommendation was to calculate equilibrium prices based on their hybrid model and then to adjust prices toward these equilibrium prices in small steps, beginning with the most important—and hence, under the old system, underpriced—commodities such as raw materials. This measure was to be complemented by tax, foreign exchange, and income policy adjustments. For Lou and Zhou—as for Lange, Brus, Šik, and other neoclassical economists, including market socialists (Stiglitz, 1994, 195, 202, 249–50)—getting the prices right was most important for attaining equilibrium. They concluded, full of optimism, that this would be possible, thanks to the advancement in computational techniques:

> [E]ven though this appears a bit complicated, but with the macroeconomic modelling techniques and the techniques from system engineering now available, we can provide a suitable program [for price adjustments]. This only requires thorough study as well as time and energy for the implementation. There are no technical obstacles involved which could not be overcome.
>
> *(Lou and Zhou, 1984, 20)*

Following the crucial contribution of the Rural Development Group to agricultural reform, Zhao Ziyang came to support a proposal of An Zhiwen, a deputy director of the recently founded National Economic System Reform Commission (国家经济体制改革委员会， hereafter System Reform Commission based on the Chinese abbreviation 体改委), to set up a research institute staffed with young intellectuals (Deng, 2005, 322; Li, 2016a; Zhang, 2017, 501).[23] Zhao's youngest secretary, Li Xianglu, who was a frequent participant in the discussion salons held by the young intellectuals returning from the countryside and in close exchange with the Rural Development Group, recommended Chen Yizi and Wang Xiaoqiang to become the leaders of this System Reform Institute (Li, 2016a). Wang Xiaoqiang was not yet a party member at the time and held no formal position other than within the Rural Development Group (Wang, 2017). To be vetted for his suitability to lead China's first system reform think tank, Wang was invited to join premier Zhao Ziyang's investigation tour in Anhui province in September 1984 (Li, 2016a, b; Wang, 2017). When Wang approached Li Xianglu to ask for his advice on how to prepare, Li told him that price reform was the most pressing issue at the time and recommended that he read Lou and Zhou (1984) (ibid.).

In Anhui, Zhao did in fact ask Wang for his perspective on price reform (Wang, 2017). More than thirty years later, during our meeting in Hong Kong in Wang's sunny office in the research department of a bank, Wang pulled out a piece of paper to draw a graph—the same graph he had drawn for Zhao Ziyang and that he later published in his book (see Figure 6.1). The graph shows that there were essentially three groups of goods: those with a profit rate above the average, those with around-average profit rates, and those with profit rates below the average (Wang, 2017).[24] Wang explained that the products in the first group had too-high prices and attracted new entries of township and village enterprises as well as production beyond the state quota by state-owned enterprises, who were allowed to retain parts of their profits. Thus, the rural reforms and the increased enterprise autonomy had already created oversupply in these sectors, while the pressure of competition would bring down prices. The enterprises had such high stocks that they began to reduce the price by making offers such as "buy one get one free" or by selling the products through salesperson in the streets at a lower price. Typical examples were consumer durables such as wristwatches, sewing machines, bicycles, radios, and black-and-white TVs, as well as industrial machinery, which faced low demand after the state cut back on investments.[25] Wang stressed that prices for products in this category could be liberalized and determined by the enterprises. This would essentially mean turning practice into policy. As a result, prices would fall, which would induce a reduction of the overstocks and an increase of the living standard of the people (Figure 6.2).

For the second group, commodities with average profit rates, no price adjustments were needed.[26] The greatest challenge was the third category, according to Wang. Most of these goods were essential raw materials and producer goods. Prices could not be raised without potential chain reactions and, possibly, a general price rise. One approach would be that suggested by Lou and Zhou (1984), which Wang summarized at the time as "taking small steps quickly" (小步快走). As long as the adjustment of the prices would be small, the situation could be kept under control and enterprises had time to adjust to the new input and procurement prices (ibid.).

Despite the new enthusiasm among China's leaders aroused by the textile price example, which showed that people were prepared to accept price increases for some goods as long as the prices of close substitutes were falling, Wang warned that "in order to make reform safer, it should be avoided to make everybody feel the price reform." (ibid.) For example, match producers had been recording losses for a long time. But everybody had to use matches every day for heating and cooking. Thus, even though matches appeared to be a small commodity, their price could not be raised without making people angry. Ma Hong, at the above-cited dinner, told Wood that people had grumbled when the price of high-quality matches was increased by 2 or 3 cents. Wood scribbled in his notebook: "A communist dictatorship that cannot raise the price of matches by 2 cents." The situation was different for products such as color TV sets. With these, one could have a sudden price liberalization, even at the risk of rising prices, without any larger consequence (ibid.).

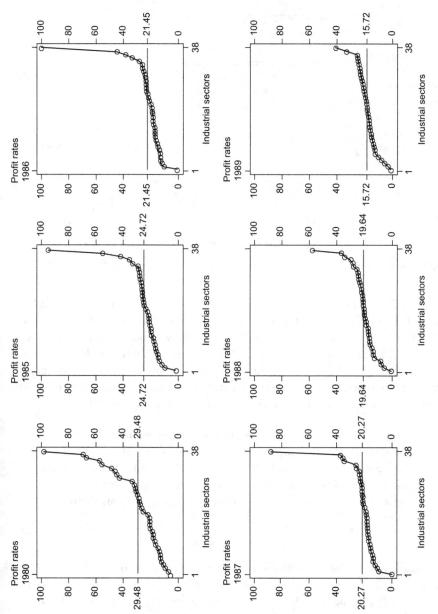

FIGURE 6.1 Sectoral Profit Rates in China, 1980–1989. Source: Wang (1998, 11).

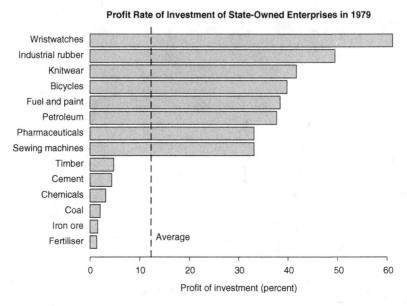

FIGURE 6.2 Profit Rate on Investment of State-owned Enterprises, 1979.

Zhao Ziyang greatly appreciated Wang Xiaoqiang (Li, 2016a,b; Zhang M., 2016). Zhao invited Wang to join the Price Reform Group under the State Council, and shortly after their tour, the System Reform Institute was formally founded, headed by Chen Yizi and Wang Xiaoqiang (Li, 2016a; Wang, 2017). Reynolds (1987), who edited an English translation of their most comprehensive reform study conducted in 1985, characterized the institute in a way that matches my observations from conversations with several of its members more than thirty years later:

> This fledgling organization, with a strikingly young staff (average age thirty-five), is lodged directly below the State Council ... and has won the strong patronage of Premier Zhao Ziyang. The enthusiasm of its members for sustained reform is clear. ... But tempering their proreform bias is an equally strong commitment to Deng Xiaoping's famous dictum: "Seek truth through facts."
>
> *(xvi)*

In parallel with Zhao Ziyang's tour in Anhui accompanied by Wang Xiaoqiang, a conference of young and middle-aged scholars took place on the Mogan mountain from September 3 to 10, 1984, with the support of the Zhejiang Academy of Social Sciences as well as several leading media outlets. Zhu Jiaming, one of the urban youths who returned from the countryside at the dawn of reform and became a leading reform intellectual, initiated the conference. I interviewed Zhu in his apartment in Beijing in 2016. After years in exile, having fled China in 1989, he had finally been allowed to return. Zhu stressed that his goal was to broaden the community of young scholars beyond Beijing and include young intellectuals concerned with the future of China across the country (Liu, 2016; Zhu, 2016). Zhu, together with Huang Jiangnan, Wang Qishan, and Weng Yongxi, had the privilege of the first dialogue of the young generation with the central leadership, in 1980. The dialogue followed the publication of a joint paper that argued that the crisis of the planned economy was a result of the nature of this economy and, as such, not incidental (ibid., Huang et al., 1981; Huang, 2016; Weng, 2016; Zhu, 2016).

Several members of the Rural Development Group, including Bai Nanfeng, Luo Xiaopeng, Lu Mai, and Zhou Qiren, as well as Wang Xiaolu and others from CASS, joined the organizing team for the Moganshan Youth Conference. More than 1,300 papers were submitted from all over China in response to the conference call, 124 of which were selected, primarily based on merit but also ensuring that authors from all over the country were to join the conference (Secretariat of the Meeting of Young Adult Economic Workers, 2003, 158; see Illustration 2 for the participants). The Moganshan Conference, the first national congress of young and middle-aged economists since 1949, turned out to be a key event in reform policy-making (Zhang, 2017, 440, 447).

Thanks to some of the young conference participants' connections with leading reform officials, it was known that price reform was the most pressing issue discussed by the leadership at the time. The Moganshan Conference was not organized based on presentations of papers, but in the form of discussion groups (Liu, 2010, 427–443). It included groups on all major reform topics. But, because the participants were eager to make a decisive contribution to reform and recognized the importance of price reform, this was the central topic of the plenary evening discussions (Hua, 2016; Luo, 2017; Zhang W., 2016; Wang X., 2016).

At the time, the debate among price researchers in Beijing was dominated by the question of how to achieve price adjustments based on computer calculations. The Price Research Center, which had been the coorganizer of the Moganshan World Bank conference, had by then been working for three years collecting data, calculating "optimal planned prices" based on input–output models, and trying to come up with feasible proposals (Lu and Li, 1991).[27] When the World Bank mission conducted research for their second report in April–May 1984, they found those working on price adjustments so occupied with finding the right theoretical prices that World Bank representative Edwin Lim warned the System Reform Commission in a meeting, along the lines of Hayek's critique of Lange, "you are looking for a perfect set of prices; but this is impossible, even with the biggest computer in the world your prices would be out of date before you published them." He urged them to take action, saying: "The swimmer on the edge of the pool with his clothes off, in the cold wind ultimately catches a cold."[28]

Tian Yuan, at the time a young researcher whose talents were appraised by Zhao Ziyang (Li, 2016b), represented the Price Research Center, of which he

ILLUSTRATION 2 Moganshan Young and Middle-Age Economists Conference, September 3–10, 1984. First row from the left: Zhao Ming, Cai Xiaopeng, Chen Yizi, Ding Wang, Ma Bin, Zhang Gang, Zhang Qi, Jia Chunfeng, Liu Youcheng, Zhu Jiaming, Bai Ruobing, Huang Jiangnan, Wang Qishan, Xu Jingan, Liu Jing, Ning Ke, Wei Xiaoan, Shi Shiming, Zhang Ronggao. Second row from the left: Zhang Hualong, Jiang Taiwei, Zhang Xukun, Chen Shenshen, Lu Lijun, Zuo Fang, Diao Xinshen, Ma Li, Shu Guozhen, Tao Hua, Cui Weide, Zheng Shaochang, Du Xia, Li Luoli, Chang Xiuze. Third row from the left: Tian Yuan, Lu Jian, Li Jiange, Hao Yisheng, Jin Yanshi, Ma Xiaofeng, Zheng Shiming, Luo Xiaopeng, Guo Fansheng, Yao Gang, Zhang Weiying, Li Qing, Yang Zhaohe, Fu Jianzhong. Fourth row from the left: Ma Kai, Jia Kang, Bai Nansheng, Jiang Yue, Wang Xiaolu, Zhou Qiren, Hua Sheng, He Jiacheng, Zhang Shaojie, Gao Liang, Xia Xiaolin. Courtesy of Liu Hong, Identification by Bai Nanfeng and Wang Xiaolu.

later became the deputy head at the conference (Hua, 2016; Zhang W., 2016). He argued that a calculation-based approach was feasible (Tian and Chen, 1984).[29] In his view, the argument—that large numbers of prices would have to be calculated simultaneously and that calculation-based price adjustments were thus impossible—was wrong. The state could let go of a large number of minor commodities, and it had the capacity to calculate and adjust the prices for a small number of key commodities, such as coal and crude oil. Those who argued that only free prices could guarantee economic efficiency were in Tian's eyes deceived by the equilibrium price theory. According to Tian, they overlooked the great harm free prices could do to economic development.

Tian reminded his audience that it was by then commonplace in Western economics that free prices could enter "cobweb cycles" instead of settling into an equilibrium. In a cobweb, dynamic prices are over- and undershooting the equilibrium price instead of settling in this resting point. If the prices of major commodities underwent such cycles, this would result in economic crisis, which Marx had identified as inherent to the capitalist system. To protect the people from violent price fluctuations, to implement a development strategy, and to prevent economic crisis, the state had to keep control over the prices of major products (ibid.). To overcome the problem of too-low prices of major producer goods, they should be adjusted in one step determined by calculation (Middle-aged and Young Economic Scientific Workers Conference, 1985a,b).

Zhou's and Lou's proposal for calculation-based price adjustment was presented by their collaborator, Li Jiange. Li, a fellow graduate student in economics at CASS, with a background in mathematics, served as deputy director of the Development Research Center of the State Council from 2003–2008 (Hua, 2016). The basic logic of their reform plan was similar to that of the Price Research Center, but they recommended adjustments in multiple small steps rather than one larger one (Middle-aged and Young Economic Scientific Workers Conference, 1985a,b). Li also took quite a different line of defense for the feasibility of price adjustments. Based on modern microeconomics, this group argued that the fear that price adjustments would create a burden for the state budget overlooked the overall efficiency gains resulting from rationalized prices that would occur as long as tight macroeconomic policies were enforced (Zhou et al., 1984).

This calculation-based price adjustment approach, which was the mainstream approach among professional economic researchers in Beijing at the time, was fiercely attacked at the conference. Everyone agreed that minor commodities, especially those in oversupply, could continue to be liberalized. But—in line with Wang Xiaoqiang's definition of the problem of price reform—the question was how to deal with the prices of energy, raw materials, and other important producer goods, which were currently too low but which were input prices for a large share of enterprises.

Zhang Weiying was at the time a master's student at Northwestern University. In our interview at Peking University, in his modest office in a classical

Chinese-style house, Zhang shared with me how he taught himself modern microeconomics and how he was impressed with Milton and Rose Friedman's *Free to Choose* (1980) (Zhang W., 2016).[30] Lu Liling, another participant in the conference, remembers that Zhang, a peasant's son, was unknown to the Beijing community of researchers and did not quite fit with their often-privileged backgrounds (Lu L., 2016). Zhang forcefully argued that the price distortions were inherent in the planned economy and could therefore only be overcome if the price system was liberalized and eventually all prices but those of monopoly producers would be determined by the market (Zhang, 1984b). Zhang stood out for his liberal position, but his analysis was in line with the prevailing practice. For him, the already operating dual-track price system was a mechanism that could achieve price liberalization in a controlled way and was, as such, superior to shock liberalization. With regard to the target model, Zhang was inspired by Friedman, but with regard to the method of reform, he derived his insights from the Chinese rural price policies and his on-the-ground experience of the unfolding of agricultural reforms.

Besides Zhang's criticism of principle, several objections were raised against the price-adjustment approach from a more pragmatic perspective. The small price increases suggested by Zhou, Lou, and Li would not provide a sufficient stimulus to either increase supply or to induce those using the raw materials to change to a more energy- or raw material–saving production technique (Keyser, 2003, 159). A larger increase, however, would be impossible to implement by simply applying calculated prices. The price changes would adversely affect the interests of enterprises, and those who would suffer from price increases would use all their political power to oppose such a plan. The only way to convince them would be to pay large subsidies to compensate for the price-induced cost increase, but this was not possible given the tight state budget (ibid., 160).

But even if enterprises were to agree to such a large price adjustment, the risk of chain reactions was incalculable and would "certainly shock the entire economy" (ibid., 160). The result could be inflation of more than 7 or 8 percent (ibid., 169). But the result would not only be monetary. A large increase in the prices of producer goods would "pull the production system off its customary track, compelling the production structure to rapidly reorganize, thus simply bringing about a comparative or even absolute decline in production standards and efficiency for a certain time period" (ibid.). If China had something to learn from the Eastern European and Soviet experience, it was that "there is in fact no one-time adjustment that results in an ideal rational situation" (ibid.). Thus, the conference report concluded that such a "'big step' price adjustment" puts the stability of the economy and society at risk and "is not the way to resolve the price problem" (ibid.). The plan for one big adjustment, which would have amounted to a big bang in planned prices, were rejected.

Among those arguing particularly eloquently and forcefully against both the price adjustment and overall price liberation was Hua Sheng. Hua was a graduate student in Nanjing and not yet acquainted with the Beijing circles of young reformers. Luo Xiaopeng, based on the experience with their price-liberation experiment, was also critical of both approaches (Chen, 2013, 311). The two were joined by He Jiacheng, Jiang Yue, Zhang Shaojie, and Gao Liang. Gao was the son of Gu Zhun, a famous pioneer of reform thinking (Hua, 2016; Luo, 2017). At the conference, the group gained the support of Chen Yizi and Wang Qishan for their stance on price reform (Zhang, 2017, 453). From then on, they came to form a powerful voice in China's reform debate. Essentially, the group defended China's current practice of a dual-track price system and proposed to expand it to all major producer goods as well as to combine it with gradual price adjustments. They too aimed to expand the scope of market prices, but they said that certain key goods—which might or might not be produced by monopolists—should continue to be regulated by the state. The approach was called "deregulation followed by adjustment, and adjustment accompanied by further deregulation" (Hua, Zhang, and Luo, 1993, 129).

In practice, there was already a dual-track price system with the official state price and grey or black market prices (Zhang, 2017, 444, 457).[31] A survey of 429 state-owned enterprises by the System Reform Institute showed that in 1984 those enterprises purchased on average 16.4 percent of their raw and other materials on the market (Diao, 1987, 35). At the same time, the mushrooming township and village enterprises did not receive any material allocations from the state and relied entirely on acquiring their inputs from markets, typically at prices higher than the ones set by the state. The proposal was now to legalize and promote this practice and enable the raw material producers to sell a certain amount at market prices (Hua et al., 1993, 129–130). Simultaneously, the amount of centrally allocated materials should be gradually reduced or fixed at a given amount, or the state should be granted a priority right to purchase the above-quota production—all depending on the concrete situation of specific commodities. The prices of some nonrationed producer goods had since May 1984 been allowed to fluctuate within a 20 percent upward or downward deviation from the state-set price (Cheng, 2006, 89). This cap should gradually or at once be abolished, depending on the concrete good (Hua, Zhang, and Luo, 1993, 130).

According to the Moganshan proposal, the organizations effectively implementing the dual-track price system would be those in charge of the material allocation at all administrative levels. In addition to continuing to operate the state allocation system, these organizations should "buy and sell *all* other materials at market prices or at floating prices, and making use of their advantages of access to information, finance and foreign trade, they should introduce the buyers to the sellers and vice versa" (ibid.). Thus, the state allocation system should not only implement the orders of the plan, but it should also become a system that creates market channels and facilitates market transactions actively. But, similar to the principles derived from the *Guanzi* (see Chapter 1), the role of these state commercial agencies should not be limited to such market creation and facilitation. They should also, as a third party on behalf of the state, "stabilize prices by buying and selling activities" (ibid.).

Once market prices for the major materials would be unified and stabilized, thanks to the activities of the state commercial agencies, the planned prices could be adjusted step by step (ibid.). At this point, the number of prices needing adjustment, as well as the range, would be greatly reduced, as compared with implementing adjustments immediately. The shortage of some crucial production materials would be reduced as the producers increased supply, responding to the high market prices, and as the supply would be more suitably distributed, thanks to the state facilitation of market transactions across the country. At the same time, the stabilized market prices would give a good indication of the degree of adjustment needed. Hence, there would no longer be a need to calculate target prices based on some theoretically derived formula. Instead, the market creation through state commerce would deliver the needed reference prices. The prices of those materials no longer in short supply would not need to be set by the state. Thus, after implementation of the dual-track price system, adjustments could follow an empirically identified path and would not be a major shock to the economy. Since the adjustment of the state price would also affect the market price, deregulation and adjustment should form a cycle until the gap between the two prices was closed (ibid., 131). Yet, as the experience in the countryside had shown, the market price could also undershoot, and so to protect the producers of the vital raw materials, the state's role in stabilizing prices would not be terminated.

Hua Sheng stressed that he presented the proposal to Zhang Jinfu, a revolutionary veteran in charge of economic work in Zhejiang in the post-liberation period, a former finance minister and then-director of the State Economic Commission (Editorial Board of Who's Who in China, 1989d; Hua, 2005, 23). The premier's personal secretary Li Xianglu, during our meeting in a Beijing coffeeshop, related how he subsequently presented the proposal to Zhao, who also came to support it (Li, 2016a). Li pointed out that "Zhao Ziyang was not academical. … The old generation of Communist cadres were not concerned with settling theoretical questions." The report rejecting price adjustments and proposing the dual-track price system was not of value because it presented a new theoretical insight. But the conference report provided the leadership a theoretical justification, a "good decoration" of a policy that the bureaucracy had worked out in practice (ibid.).

The 1984 "Decision"

On October 20, 1984, the Central Committee adopted the "Decision on Reform of the Economic Structure." This marked a breakthrough for economic system reform. Famously, China's socialist planned economy was redefined as "a planned commodity economy based on public ownership, in which the law of value must be consciously followed and applied" (The Research Department of Party Literature, 1991, 406). This meant that the aim was that prices should no longer be set in a voluntary fashion, but that market conditions should be systematically integrated in the price-fixing practice. Similarly, most goods were to be traded as commodities—that is to say, they should capture exchange value. In other words, production should be for the market and governed by exchange values and profitability considerations as far as possible in light of China's concrete conditions.

The core of this new model was essentially to "grasp what is heavy and to let go of what is light"—to borrow the *Guanzi*'s terminology (see Chapter 1):

> Mandatory planning will be applied to major products which have a close bearing on the national economy and the people's livelihood and which have to be allocated and distributed by the state, as well as major economic activities that affect the overall situation. Other products and economic activities which are far more numerous should either come under guidance planning or be left entirely to the operation of the market, as the case may require.
>
> *(ibid., 407)*

In terms of how to approach reform the decision held,

> As the decision-making power of enterprises grows, pricing will be increasingly important in regulating their production and operation. It is, therefore, all the more urgent to establish a rational system of pricing. ... Pricing is a most effective means of regulation, and rational prices constitute an important condition for ensuring a dynamic yet not chaotic economy. Therefore, reform of the price system is the key to reform the entire economic structure.
>
> *(ibid., 408)*

On October 21, 1984, Zhao Ziyang made a speech to the assembly of representatives of provinces, autonomous regions, and municipalities to explain what the implementation of the "Decision" would entail in practice (Zhao, 2016e). He said price reform would be the primary task and it would require four things: letting go, reforming, adjusting, and participating (放, 改, 调, 参) (ibid., 541). Zhao explained these four methods of reform as follows:

First, *letting go of prices* would apply to all "small" commodities, new products, and new services. But it had to be kept in mind that some commodities that might appear "small" are actually "big." For example, some places had let go of the price of pork but pork was a "big" commodity, and thus this practice had caused trouble (ibid., 535, 539–40). Second, reform would refer to the *reform of the price-management system*, mainly in the form of decentralization, transferring the price-setting rights of certain commodities to lower administrative levels (ibid., 540). Third, *price adjustment* would involve the change in the prices set by the state. This would primarily apply to production materials. But, in line with Lou and Zhou's proposal and with Wang's discussion with the premier, Zhao emphasized that adjustment could be done only in small, not big, steps to avoid chain reactions (ibid., 541). Last, but crucially, *market participation* would mean that "after having enlivened prices by letting them go, the state had to participate in the market to regulate the prices" (ibid., 540).

Zhao reminded his audience that this strategy had been very successfully applied in the first years after liberation, when state trading agencies had been used to stabilize prices. This would be a crucial lesson. The prices of the most important production materials, such as coal, oil, steel, and chemicals, should be regulated by the ministries in charge in two ways. The share under the state plan should continue to have state-set prices. Regarding the share for which prices were allowed to fluctuate on the market, the range of the fluctuations should be limited by market participation of state commercial agencies. The state should add supplies to the market when the price was rising too high and purchase them when the price was falling too low. This required adequate stocks. In addition, in very urgent situations, to avoid the market prices of critical materials from rising too high, imports could be acquired by the state and put on the market (ibid., 540–41).

In early 1985, this basic approach was turned into official policy. When the World Bank mission met with Zhao Ziyang on March 7, 1985, the premier thanked the foreign guests for their second report and advice and told them that China was implementing a dual-track price system for raw materials and fuel prices. As Zhao pointed out, China had experience in implementing dual pricing for thirty years in agriculture and for five years in coal. He expressed confidence that dual pricing "inflicts less of a shock on the people" than any of the alternatives for price reform.

Conclusion

As the account in this and the previous chapter shows, beginning in the early days of reform, two basic approaches to market reform in general and price reform in particular competed in China. One approach, inspired by modern mathematical economics and previous Eastern European reform attempts, aimed to reset the whole system and rebuild it based on ideal-type principles. Complex calculation seems to suggest that the approach has sophistication, but given the real complexities, it is often inconsistent and boils down to ad hoc rules put in practice. The second approach admits from the outset that it is impossible to build an ideal-type system. Instead, it departs from the given realities and tries to consciously use spontaneous tendencies already prevailing in the given workings of economy and society. This approach maintains the critical elements of the given system to maintain the stability of the society and the economy and to protect the people from violent economic shocks. It even uses the critical building blocks of the old system to regulate the newly emerging forces, as in the case of using the material allocation system to participate in the market to stabilize prices. But by letting go of the parts already moving, powers build up. These powers bear the potential to gradually and fundamentally transform the elements of the old system, which at first might have seemed untouched.

Let us consider the metaphor of rebuilding a tower. The first approach suggests we destroy the whole tower in order to build up a new tower based on a grand plan—no matter how much immediate pain results from the destruction. From this perspective, the given system must be destroyed in one big bang, to provide space to build the new utopia. The second approach is like the game of "Jenga," in which players take turns removing one block at a time from a tower, aiming to prevent its collapse. Only those blocks that can be pulled out without causing the structure to collapse should be removed—and only after cautious testing to determine whether they are loose enough not to destroy the tower's balance. The blocks so acquired can then be used to build on the given tower and transform its size, shape, and eventually its whole nature. Yet, since removing blocks changes the statics of the tower, this gradual approach cannot avoid the looming danger of collapse.

In these first years of reform in China, the economists aiming to adjust the price system based on a comprehensive package were trying to come up with the right plan for the crucial parts of the system. But it was determined that such an adjustment would be too dangerous, that it could result in a collapse of the whole economy, at least temporarily, and it was thus not implemented. While these researchers were dedicating great efforts to model building and calculations, the multitrack price system was slowly developing on the ground. Greatly boosted by the success of the rural reforms, this multimethod, multitrack approach gained the upper hand, and it was implemented as official policy. But some of those who had spent years searching for the perfect reform plan were not satisfied with the seemingly primitive approach now elevated to being the key to system reform. Thus, as soon as some weaknesses of the multi-tiered system became apparent, they were prepared to launch a counterattack—and gain the support of the central leadership desperate to bring reform to a success. This will be the subject of the next chapter.

Notes

1 See Key Chinese Reform Economists in the back matter.
2 I am following Liu Hong's definition of generations of intellectuals (Liu, 2010, 27, 189, 405) but have amended it by distinguishing young researchers who joined forces with middle-aged established intellectuals. For a more detailed overview of economists of different generations in China, see Cohn (2017, 69–76).
3 See Keyser (2003, 19–35) for a detailed discussion of this generation of reform intellectuals from a political science perspective.
4 See Xu (2019) for a social psychology analysis of the autobiographical memory of this large cohort of China's "sent-down youth," broadly conceived.
5 See Honig and Zhao (2019) for a detailed analysis, based on local archives, illustrating the conflicts between local party cadres and sent-down youth.
6 Those included so-called gray cover books (灰皮书), which were only printed for the use of a select circle, not published (ibid.). They got to read translations of some Western economists, such as Samuelson's famous textbook, a collection of writings of Joan Robinson, who was considered a friend of the Chinese people because of her positive evaluation of the Cultural Revolution (Robinson, 1969), and some of Keynes's and Galbraith's classics (Li, 2017). But, dedicated to the cause of socialism, their greatest interest at this time was in developing their own reading of

Marxist classics. These included publications banned from the Stalinist and Maoist orthodoxies, such as Mao's early writings, including the original edition of *On New Democracy* (1960 [1940]), Bukharin's writings of the 1920s articulating an alternative to Stalin's approach to industrialization, the letters of the late Lenin, Trotsky's *The Revolution Betrayed* (1937), but also neo-Marxist writings such as Baran and Sweezy's *Monopoly Capital* (1970) (Bai, 2016; Wang, X. L., 2016; Zhang M., 2016).

7 Zhang Musheng went with Chen Boda's son, Chen Xiao, to Linhe district in Inner Mongolia. Zhang's father had joined the Communist Party as early as 1931 and was secretary to both Zhou Enlai and Dong Biwu. His mother was a party intellectual who joined the party in 1936 (Zhang, 2009).

8 See Nolan (1988, 12–31) for a discussion of Bukharinism and Stalinism as alternative development paths in the Chinese context.

9 See Day (2013, 27–29) for a broader discussion of this reevaluation of historical forces and progress.

10 For an overview of the various household contracting experiments in Anhui see Chung (2000, 85-109).

11 By October 1981, an estimated 38 percent of production teams had introduced household contracting. By December 1983, this had risen to 94 percent (Bramall, 2004, 108).

12 See Fewsmith (1994, 19–54) for a more detailed account of the policy process that resulted in the decisive so-called Documents Nr. 1 (1982, 1983), which constituted the breakthrough for the household responsibility system and the contribution of the Rural Development Group in this process.

13 See Nolan (1988) for a systematic account of the evolution and the workings of the household responsibility system.

14 This was called "turning unified procurement into a tax" (统购改税) (Chen, 2013, 311).

15 The design, propagation, and evaluation of this experiment in Hebei province are documented in "Turning Unified Procurement into Tax" Experiment Leading Group (1987), Luo Xiaopeng (1987), and Song Guoqing (1987).

16 See Chapter 1 for the grain price regulation principles in the *Guanzi*.

17 For example, Milton Friedman (1988) invoked this interpretation of the dual-track price system as a tax in his speech at the International Studies Advisory Committee (ISAC) dinner upon his return from his second trip to China in 1988.

18 For the English translation, see Xue (1989).

19 Cheng Zhiping, at the time director of the State Price Bureau, reports that this plan was drawn up following the initiative of Zhang Jingfu, who was the State Council member in charge of price work. The plan suggested to decrease the retail price by 1.1 RMB and to increase that of cotton cloth by 0.3 RMB per meter. The plan was presented to the State Council for the first time on October 5, 1982, and subsequently intensely discussed in various leadership committees (Cheng, 2006, 54–59).

20 According to Cheng (2006), the state subsidies for cotton cloth was 460 million RMB in 1982 (54).

21 Adrian Wood noted, following a dinner with Ma Hong on April 4, 1984, that Ma had told him that people took the abolishment of cotton rationing as a signal that prices were about to rise, and the shops were emptied of cotton goods, which were often returned when prices remained stable.

22 For a partial English translation, see Lou and Zhou (1989).

23 A former research office under the State Council was transformed in 1982 into the System Reform Commission, a national organization with representations on all administrative levels. The commission was concerned with four key questions: the target model for system reform, the approach to price reform, the approach to ownership reform, and the definition of the government's role in the reform process (Wang H., 2016).

24 Wang (1998) published the respective graphs of sectorial profit rates for the period 1980–1989. It showed that the gradual price reform in fact greatly reduced the

variation in profit rates. See Figure 6.1. Figure 6.2 illustrates for the year 1979 that important raw materials typically had below-average profit rates, while light industry consumer goods and processed materials generated higher profits.

25 The World Bank, under the leadership of Gene Tidrick and William Byrd and in collaboration with the Economics Research Institute at CASS, in particular Chen Jiyuan, Xu Lu, Tang Zongkun, and Chen Lantong, had at the time just published a widely discussed study of the Chongqing Clock and Watch Company and the Qingdao Forging Machinery Plant, two enterprises that fall into this category (Byrd et al., 1984; Tang, 2016; Wang, 2017).

26 Note that Figure 6.2 for 1979 shows no enterprises with roughly average profit rates. In contrast, the second graph for 1980 shows several sectors with about-average profit rates. This is probably primarily due to the small selection of commodities in the figure for 1979, but it is also in line with the trend of increasing numbers of sectors generating about-average profit rates.

27 Lu Nan and Li Mingzhe (1991), who had both worked at the Price Research Institute and were part of the exchanges with the World Bank, reported,

> In 1981 we selected 1,200 categories of products, including 100 agricultural, 40 mineral, 600 manufactured, 100 light industrial, and 100 textile products, 200 wholesale and retail commodities, as well as 50 kinds of public service charges. In 1983, considering the actual need and difficulty in data manipulation, we reduced the categories to 750.
>
> *(83)*

They also showed that four kinds of sets of theoretical prices were calculated, based on the following price systems: a value price system, a production price system, a cost price system, and a two-channel price system (ibid., 84–85).

28 Quoted from Adrian Wood's notes on the meeting.

29 The *Economic Daily* published the most-discussed papers on price reform shortly after the conference. Those included Tian and Chen (1984), Zhang (1984a) and Zhou, Lou, and Li (1984). My analysis of the positions at the conference draws on interviews with participants, the official conference report (Middle-aged and Young Economic Scientific Workers Conference, 1985a,b [for an English translation, see Keyser, 2003, 158–176 as well as Hua et al., 1993, 126–131]), the articles published before the conference by Lou and Zhou (1984) and by Zhang (1984b) [for an English translation, see Zhang (2015, 265–282), as well as on the articles in the *Economic Daily*.

30 Zhang read Friedman (1980) in the freely available Chinese translation. Zhang reports that the National Economics Conference in 1984 (全国数量经济学会) was hosted by Northwest University in 1984, and he was assisting the conference organization. This was for him a big shock. In particular, Mao Yushi and Yang Xiaokai made him realize that what he had learned from his studies in Marxist economics was not useful, and he developed an eager interest in neoclassical economics (Zhang W., 2016). Yang Xiaokai was at the time studying at Princeton under Gregory Chow, a student of Milton Friedman and an influential figure introducing mainstream economics to China and remodeling the Chinese economics curriculum based on the American example (Chen, 2013, 311; Chow, 1994; Perkins, 2016). For a discussion of Zhang Weiying's intellectual formation, see Zhang Shuguang (2017, 444–446).

31 In China, the identity of the ultimate inventor of the dual-track price system is fiercely debated (see Zhang, 2017, 455–57 for a review of this debate). In my analysis, no individual invented the dual-track price system; it emerged from practical policy experimentation harking back to pre-revolutionary practices of price regulation and theorized collectively.

7

DEBUNKING SHOCK THERAPY

The Clash of Two Market Reform Paradigms

Introduction

> Two roads diverged in a yellow wood,
> And sorry I could not travel both
> And be one traveler, long I stood
> And looked down one as far as I could
> To where it bent in the undergrowth....

(Frost, 1920)

The 1984 decision instituted the dual-track price system as national policy. The logic of multi-tier pricing that kept the core of the system working while introducing markets from the margins had become the dominant reform approach. In January 1985, the State Price Bureau and the Material Allocation Bureau followed the instruction of the State Council and issued the "Notice on Deregulating the Self-Marketing of the Overproduction of Industrial Raw Materials" (Cheng, 2006, 89–90). The previous limit of 20 percent upward or downward deviation from the planned prices for above-quota sales of raw materials such as steel, wood, and cement was abolished (ibid.). This might sound like a technical detail, but it meant that the heart of the industrial economy was now officially under the dual-track price system and on its way to being marketized. Cheng Zhiping, director of the State Price Bureau at the time, remembered that the effect of this policy was like "letting a horse run" (ibid., 90). Once the most crucial industrial inputs were integrated into the marketization effort, the dual-track price system expanded quickly to other industrial goods. This rapidly increased the overall share of market-priced goods but also drove up the general price level, since market prices were above plan prices for scarce industrial goods (ibid.; see Figures 0.5–0.7 in the Introduction).

The government took another important step in gradual price reform in the spring of the same year. On April 12, 1985, Cheng Zhiping made an official announcement on state television:

> In 1985 the basic direction for price reform is: Combine adjusting with letting go and progress in small steps. … The centrepiece of reform will be liberalising the prices of live pig and pork and the rural purchase and sales prices for grain.…

(ibid., 76)

Cheng Zhiping's words have the tone of a mundane bureaucratic announcement. In fact, his statement marked the end of the backbone of the Maoist agricultural economy: The unified grain procurement system was abolished (see Chapter 4). The core of this system had been a compulsory quota of grain delivered by the rural communes to the state at a centrally set price. The massive increase in grain output in the early 1980s had brought this grain distribution system to its limits. Unified grain procurement had been designed in the 1950s to manage shortages and extract grain from the countryside for urban industrialization. No mechanism existed to deal with surpluses as China reached levels of grain output that would have been unthinkable only a few years earlier. The glut of grain meant the state procurement price was suddenly above the market price (see Chapter 6). The peasants wanted to sell more to the state than the state could store (Oi, 1986).

So, in 1985 the unified grain procurement was temporarily replaced by a system bearing some similarity to the imperial Ever Normal Granaries (see Chapter 1). The peasants could sell their grain directly on the private market, or they could enter into a contract with the state (Cheng, 2006, 76). This meant that the state's role switched from ordering quotas of grain from the peasants to participating in a market for crops. However, the prices for state procurement were not adjusted to current market conditions but were based on a weighted average of what used to be the quota and above-quota prices under the old system (ibid.). Song Guoqing and other former members of the Rural Development Group warned Zhao Ziyang that applying the same weighted average price to all procurement contracts resulted in harming poor, remote areas. Poor communities, which previously had a low quota, had sold large shares of their output to the state at the high above-quota price. Thus, for them the new price policy effectively resulted in a decrease of the state procurement price of grain. With new opportunities arising in the booming rural industries, this effective drop in the price for grain induced many peasants to leave their fields unworked (Luo, 2017). Soon, grain output began dropping (Lin, 1992, 35). Falling grain supplies and increasing rural incomes added to the inflationary pressures unleashed by the universalization of the dual-track price system.

The transformation of China's agricultural economy, the expansion of the dual-track reform to the heart of the industrial economy, and the upward pressure on prices provided the backdrop for a dramatic clash between the two marketization paradigms—gradual marketization and shock therapy—in the second half of the 1980s. By 1985, the dual-track price system regulated the core of the Chinese economy: grain and basic industrial inputs. Opening a market track while keeping state procurement intact, the dual-track price system allowed the possibility of both a return to a greater emphasis on the plan as well as a more radical shift to the market. In that year, the System Reform Institute conducted a study of the progress of market reforms on an unprecedented scale. The aim was to derive practical ways to improve on the existing institutions of the dual-track price system, so that China's economy would *grow into the market*[1] while maintaining state control over "heavy" goods and continuing state regulation of "light" commodities.

On the other hand, those who had long aimed for rationalizing the price system in one "big push" took an acceleration of industrial growth in 1985[2] and macroeconomic imbalance as signs of overheating caused by the dual-track price system and launched a forceful campaign to impose strict macroeconomic control to prepare for a big bang in price reform. Such a big bang would have been the first, decisive step of shock therapy. As explained in the Introduction, a big bang in price liberalization was the truly "shocking" element of shock therapy. All other measures in this policy package, such as trade liberalization and privatization, were acknowledged to be slow even by the most dedicated shock therapists. China's proponents of a big bang planned to first destroy the market track of the dual-track price system by returning to the approach of calculation-based plan prices. Once the plan prices were adjusted to what were thought of as equilibrium levels, those prices were to be liberalized in "one cut of the knife."

This chapter tells the widely overlooked story of how such a big bang was almost implemented in 1986 and how it was debunked and prevented by economists who were fully dedicated to marketization but subscribed to the alternative approach of "groping for stones to cross the river." This was a critical crossroads in China's reform. China's escape from shock therapy in 1986 occurred as the result of fierce debate among the foremost reform economists— not, as is often alleged, between anti-reform conservatives and market reformers. Following the 1984 "Decision on the Economic System Reform" (关于 经济体制改革的决定), China's leadership reached an unprecedented political consensus to pursue market reforms (Zhang, 2017, 530). At this juncture, the question was not whether or not to reform, but *how* to—whether by "feeling the way forward" by marketization from the margins, or by consciously imposing short-term pain, hoping for long-term gain by shocking the core of the system into marketization.[3] In 1986, the plan for a big bang was blocked as a result of the struggle between economists. In 1988, a renewed drive for radical price reform came from the highest political leadership desperate for a quick breakthrough. The second time, China escaped the big bang—but at historic social and political costs.

Preparations for "One Big Step"

> [I]f we don't take hard-hitting measures to supersede the dual-track system in a relatively short time and immediately establish a preliminary framework for the new system, problems will grow....
>
> *(Wu, 2013b [1988], 201)*

As soon as the dual-track price system became official policy, it was fiercely attacked by economists inspired by neoclassical economics, monetarism, and the approach of the Eastern European reformers. They argued along the lines of Šik's proposal for price reform but brushed aside his warnings regarding the limitations of his approach (see Chapter 5). In this view, China had to impose strict macroeconomic austerity, adjust prices to calculated equilibrium values, and then, finally, liberalize prices in "one big step." They thus argued for the core elements of the big bang—the first and decisive step in shock therapy.

Setting the Stage for a Big Bang in Price Reform

One of the leaders of the attack against the dual-track price system was Wu Jinglian. Wu's view was and is that the approach of "groping for stones to cross the river" was inevitable while China's leaders and advisors lacked knowledge of modern mainstream economics. But it had become obsolete by the mid-1980s, as Chinese economists had progressed to new levels of scientific economic knowledge thanks to the support of foreign advisors (Huang, 2004; Wu, 2016). Wu himself exerted great efforts to acquire knowledge of "Western economics." He was one of the pioneers among Chinese reform economists in the United States when he was a visiting scholar at Yale University (January 1983–July 1984). Wu studied comparative economic systems under Michael Montias and, when he was in his early fifties, attended undergraduate-level classes in macro- and microeconomics (Naughton, 2013, 116–117).

This was not Wu's first encounter with leading economists of the Western world. He had been engaged with the World Bank mission (see Chapter 5), and in 1981 he attended a conference on "The Economics of Relative Prices" organized by the International Economic Association in Athens, which included prominent participants such as the Soviet mathematician Leonid Kantorovich and the Oxford economist Sir John Hicks, both of whom had won the Nobel Prize in the 1970s, as well as Herbert Giersch, who was soon to become president of the neoliberal Mont Pelerin Society (Csikós-Nagi et al., 1984, i–ii). At this conference, Wu first met János Kornai. Kornai shaped Wu's thinking on reform, and Wu became Kornai's greatest advocate in China, promoting the translation of his works (Gewirtz, 2017, 98–100; Kornai, 2006, 250). Both men had been champions of the respective orthodoxies in Hungary and China earlier in their lives and were now in the process of becoming radical market reformers with Wu, following in Kornai's footsteps. This was before Kornai became a member of the Harvard University economics faculty, but by the time of their encounter in Athens, Kornai had already gained fame in the West (Kornai, 2006, 243). In contrast, Wu was still unknown outside of China.

Kornai had first gained an international reputation for his theoretical contributions to mathematical economics, and he had just published *Economics of Shortage* (1980). Written in his Stockholm home, the book, which was addressed to a Hungarian readership, made Kornai famous across the socialist world. As Kornai (2006, 244) writes in his memoir: "The book did not note that the cause of the general, intense, and chronic shortage economy was the Communist system and that a change of system was required before the shortage could be ended for good. The book did not state that the essential features of the system were not susceptible to reform." But Kornai had skillfully crafted his text such that "many readers clearly read that claim into it." Under a section titled "helping erode the system," Kornai (2006, 250–251) reflects on how his work "affected the thinking of intellectuals living under the socialist system." One of them was Wu Jinglian.

At the conference in Athens, Kornai clashed with V. R. Khachaturov, then-president of the Soviet Economic Association. Khachaturov held that shortages arose from planning errors and could be overcome by raising the standard of planning (Kornai, 2006, 250). Kornai, in contrast, took the position of his book and blamed shortages on the nature of the system of a socialist planned economy. It follows that the only way to overcome shortages, in Kornai's logic, is to get rid of central planning. Wu was familiar with the idea of economic reform as system change, through his encounters with Brus and Šik. In conversations with members of the World Bank mission, Wu had expressed that this vision was close to his heart (see Chapter 5). At the conference in Athens, Wu now heard the most sophisticated version of the view articulated by one of its most ardent and capable proponents. Kornai (2010) recalled that, after Khachaturov's attack, "Professor Wu stood up on my side in the controversy, explaining in much detail the systemic deficiencies of the centrally managed socialist system." At this moment, Wu entered the world stage of economics.[4]

Wu and Kornai were united in their conviction that reform could be achieved only as system change. But there was a crucial difference in analysis between Wu and Kornai. Kornai (1980, 1984) had argued that enterprises experienced a soft budget constraint under socialism. Since enterprises were not ultimately responsible for their losses, price signals were relatively ineffective in guiding the production decisions of socialist enterprises. In Kornai's (1984, 67) terminology, enterprises had low "price responsiveness." The softness of the budget constraint was like a tranquilizer, according to Kornai (1984, 69): "It leads to the economic managers hardly to be bothered by *any kind of* price signals." This meant that enterprises were demanding whatever inputs they could get hold of, largely independent of relative prices or financial constraints. This created shortages of inputs that exacerbated, in turn, the runaway demand. This vicious circle of shortages and price-inelastic demand made shortages a characteristic feature of socialism that was not accidental but systemic.

Wu (1984, 82) praised Kornai's paper. But a close reading of both of their contributions at the conference reveals a logical inconsistency between Kornai and Wu. Wu suggested, "The price system is a mechanism for replacing bureaucrats" and urged for price reform (Csikós-Nagi, Hague and Hall, 1984, 531). According to Kornai, enterprises under socialism did not actually care too much about prices; according to Wu, though, they should be guided by prices alone. Arguing in a somewhat Hayekian mode, Wu held that "The price mechanism simplified social organization. The Chinese economy was emphasizing the value of the decentralized use of information, replacing bureaucracy by decisions made by individual enterprises" (ibid.). But if, as Kornai had it, enterprises were not responsive to prices, replacing bureaucratic orders with price signals would have amounted not to the creation of a new economic mechanism; it would instead have left the economy without any coordination. From a careful reading of the Athens conference proceedings, it becomes apparent that with Kornai's insight, Wu's plan for price reform amounted to a recipe for disaster. In fact, some years later, China's gradualist market creators, debunking shock therapy, mobilized this argument of Kornai against Wu.

If one believed—as Kornai and Wu did—that reform must bring system change, risking such a meltdown of the economic mechanism might not have been entirely without benefit. In Chinese, the word *crisis* is composed of two characters: 危机. The first character, 危, means "danger." The second character, 机, means "opportunity." Hence, a crisis presents both danger and opportunity. This was precisely the script of shock doctrine captured by Naomi Klein (2007, 155–6) in numerous cases around the world. The shifts to neoliberalism in Chile, Bolivia, and Margaret Thatcher's United Kingdom were each preceded by a deep societal crisis. In Bolivia, this pivotal crisis took the form of hyperinflation. As discussed in Chapter 3, hyperinflation had helped the Communists win the revolutionary war.[5] No doubt China's reformers were acutely aware of the explosive powers of hyperinflation. Wu Jinglian's critics would later assert that his proposal for radical price reform created a risk of hyperinflation.

Wu represents a prominent example of a Chinese economist who joined the transnational network transcending the Cold War divide that Bockman (2011) has identified as the breeding ground for neoliberalism in Eastern Europe.[6] But Wu was by no means alone in his engagement with Western economics. A CIA (1986) report rightly observes that by the mid-1980s, "increased familiarity with Western economic concepts [was] not limited to one group of scholars or bureaucrats." The divide across these groups was not in their interest for Western economics but in their approach to this new knowledge—either as tools that China could use in carving out a feasible reform path or as the theoretical source for "reform blueprints" to manufacture system change. By the mid-1980s, efforts to design a target model to be implemented in one big push had already been going on for several years.[7]

In the summer of 1984, Wu returned to China from his studies at Yale and joined the State Council's Development Research Center (Fewsmith, 1994, 161–162; Liu

Hong, 2002, 248). He discovered that the young reform intellectuals had gained great influence since his departure to the United States. They were promoting a gradualist, experimental approach of "groping for stones to cross the river," which Wu considered an inferior method of reform, a makeshift solution that China had to rely on when it had lacked knowledge of "Western economics." Chen Yizi, Wang Xiaoqiang, and other young reform economists had acquired unusual institutional power. They had been put in charge of what some consider to be the first reform think tank in the socialist world. The System Reform Institute was highly regarded by the leader of economic reform, Zhao Ziyang. Their approach had won a great victory with the official institution of the dual-track price system. In fact, recognizing the influence of this new institution, Wu himself had attempted to join the System Reform Institute upon his return to China, but he was rejected due to his reputation as opportunist (Chen, 2013, 347–348). Subsequently, Wu was ever more dedicated to pushing his radical reform agenda.

Wu Jinglian propagated his view in various academic and popular publications. In May 1985, he expanded on a previous article in *People's Daily* (February 1985) in the prestigious journal *Economic Research* (经济研究) and laid out his vision for reform in one stroke (Wu, 1985a, 1985b). Wu (1985a) essentially summarized the presentations by Šik and Brus and drew on Kornai's (1980) *Economics of Shortage* to argue that the economic system would form an interrelated, organic whole and could, as such, only be reformed by a wholesale transition to a new system. Comparing a gradual to a package (一揽子) approach, Wu recommended the latter. A duality of elements of the old and the new systems was unavoidable in the transition, but it should be overcome as quickly as possible. Most importantly, price reform had to set an end to the dual-track price system. To make his main point, Wu quoted Friedman's 1981 talk in China, saying the "so-called economic miracle produced by Ludwig Erhard in 1948 was a very simple thing" (Friedman, 1990; Weber, 2020; Wu, 1985a, 4; see Chapter 5). According to monetarism and based on the post–World War II German experience,[8] Wu argued that it was crucial to tightly control the quantity of money and impose fiscal austerity. This was meant to prevent inflation, which Wu considered a sufficient condition for the implementation of swift price reform.[9]

Seeking to add more weight to the imperative of fiscal and monetary austerity as a starting point for long-term sustained growth and as necessary element in periods of structural transition, Wu promoted, in addition to the neoliberal myth of an Erhard Miracle (Weber, 2020), the so-called Dodge Line. Joseph Dodge, a Detroit banker and price-fixer during World War II, was a key architect of the West German currency reform as well as of Japan's postwar transition plan, which was named for him. In 1985, Wu arranged the publication of an article about the Dodge Line to propagate this second example of combining macroeconomic retrenchment with market liberalization among Chinese reformers (Wu, 2016; Xiao, 1985).[10]

Chinese reformers had studied the Japanese post–World War II transition since Deng Xiaoping's visit to Japan in 1978. Under the auspices of Okita Saburo, who had played an important role in Japan's economic transition from the war economy, and Gu Mu, Japanese and Chinese bureaucrats conducted annual metings (Vogel, 2011, 462–463). Beyond these bureaucratic exchanges, the Dodge Line was mobilized by package reformers such as Wu to justify their reform proposal. When I met Wu for our interview in 2016, he showed me a printout of the Wikipedia article on Joseph Dodge, in order to emphasize the importance of the Japanese postwar transition to China's 1980s reform debate. He pointed to the section on the "Dodge line." This section of the article explained that two key components of Dodge's cure for Japan were "balancing the consolidated national budget" and "decreasing government intervention into the economy, especially through subsidies and price controls." The message was clear, according to Wu: China should have combined austerity with overnight price liberalization.

To create an institution that would publicize the lessons from the Eastern European experience as articulated by Brus, Šik, Kornai, and others, Wu Jinglian, Zhao Renwei, and Rong Jingben founded a new journal called *Comparative Economic and Social Systems* (经济社会体制比较) in 1985 (Huang, 2004; Peng, 2016). An article published in the journal's inaugural issue by Guo Shuqing as lead author exerted immediate political impact.

Guo Shuqing later became the governor of China's industrial province Shandong (2013–2017), and he is currently the chairman of the China Banking Regulatory Commission. At the time, Guo was a doctoral student at the Institute for Marxism Leninism and Mao Zedong Thought of CASS, and he was thus well versed in orthodox Soviet views while studying Western mainstream economics. Together with his fellow students and coauthors Liu Jirui and Qiu Shufang, he forcefully promoted package reform with market-oriented price reform at its core (Wu, 2016; Zhang, 2017, 537–538; Zhang, 2015, 375). Guo Shuqing reported that they participated in a National Symposium on Theories of Pricing in late 1984 in Changzhou. There, they found themselves to be the only ones who suggested market-driven prices, with the plan taking a mere guiding role (Guo, 2012a, xxii). Guo mentioned that the mainstream view at the time was to separate goods into different categories and require "state pricing for certain key commodities and market-regulated pricing for lesser commodities" (ibid.). Other reformers, too, wanted more market. But the crucial difference between Guo and his collaborators and the Chinese mainstream view at the time was their argument that prices of these key commodities, too, should be left to the market. In their view, the market should regulate the core of China's economy.

Guo's views on price reform closely resembled those of the Eastern European visitors discussed in Chapter 5. Guo laid out, in January 1985, that the first step would be to clearly define the target model (Guo, 1985, 30).[11] He held that "truly [understanding] the Marxist approach to social value" would mean recognizing "that market value is the only concrete and realistic form of social value" and thus, market pricing was the only right target for reform (Guo, 2012b, 24). The only exception should be prices of those goods defined in neoclassical economics as public goods, such as transport, communication, and health, which should be set by the state (ibid., 23). But these goods should not include key industrial inputs such as steel or basic consumption goods such as rice. Those should be fully left to the free market.

Guo took an even more radical stance on the dual-track reform than Wu. He dismissed the dual-track price system as "not acceptable even as transitional model" (ibid., 26). Similar to the conclusion reached by the foreign experts at the Moganshan World Bank Conference, Guo believed that "allowing one product to have multiple prices is absolutely incompatible with the commodity economy" (ibid., 25). More generally, he reckoned the Eastern European experience had proven that "trying to maintain the old system by simply mending it is absolutely pointless" (ibid.). In the same vein, Guo brushed aside the extant achievements in economic reform that had occurred by the mid-1980s by categorizing China's system at the time as a "fairly traditional model" (ibid., 22). Guo's starting point was thus an idealized vision of the old system. The target model was an idealized model of a market economy. His reform package promised to facilitate the swift transition from one to the other.

In April 1985, Guo, Liu, and Qiu published their views on "comprehensive reform" with price reform at its core in the new journal *Comparative Economic and Social Systems* and proposed their recommendations to the State Council in a letter (Guo, 2012a, xxiii; Guo et al., 1985, 21).[12] Like Wu describing the "economic system as an organic whole," they stressed that the price system "is the whole economic system from one angle" (Guo et al., 2012, 29). They argued that "comprehensive reform is a huge task of social system engineering" and as such would require an "overall plan" to move toward the "target model" (ibid., 28). They attacked the gradualist experimentalist approach up front, denying the validity of lessons from pilot projects and rural reform for urban industrial reform (ibid., 31–32). The dual-track price system was again at the center of their criticism. The dual-track price system would simply induce commodities within the plan to flow out on the market, being sold and resold multiple times, generating private profits for the officials in command of the cheap plan allocations. This, according to Guo and his coauthors, encouraged corruption and resulted in a "conflicted transitional system" (ibid., 29–30).

Furthermore, in their view, as long as the old system prevailed, "investment hunger" and excess aggregate demand manifested in shortages must prevail. Rapid economic growth and economic system reform were incompatible. The Eastern European reform had shown that the only way was to strictly control aggregate demand and then implement a "comprehensive" package of reforms (ibid., 31).

They added a negative case to the list of the West German and Japanese miracles crafted to support the "mantra" of macroeconomic austerity plus price liberalization. The Polish case of the 1970s would prove that gradual reform must fail. The Poles failed to carry out their plan of wholesale price reform and instead limited the scope to about 40 percent of the industrial products. Initially, this brought about very fast growth fueled by uncontrollable aggregate demand. However, "[w]hen Poland was at last forced to reform prices, the result brought on a social crisis" (ibid., 33). Examinations by the Polish Communist Party had shown the problem to be that the reforms had taken "an experimental and wrong-minded path" (ibid.). Thus, foreign scholars including Šik, Kosta, and Brus now agreed that the only way was following an overall plan. Guo, Liu, and Qiu added that this approach was also encouraged by János Kornai, who had noted to Chinese students abroad that "if China's reform continues to focus on local experience and to ignore the overall situation, if it continues to make merely fragmentary changes, eventually it will have to return to the traditional system" (ibid.).

Finally, they called on the World Bank's authority to lend further weight to their urging to part with the gradual approach and implement an overall plan for reform. They quoted a report, stating, "In some aspects, although there exists the risk of making wrong decisions, we had better implement a whole set of fundamental reform measures simultaneously" (ibid.). The message from Guo, Liu, and Qiu was clear: Gradual reform that kept the core of the old system running could do only harm, not good. The only way forward was full-out market reform pushed through by wholesale price liberalization. With regard to the immediate course of action, Guo, Liu, and Qiu agreed with Wu Jinglian: Impose strict macrocontrol and draw up a comprehensive plan to prepare for an overall price reform to be implemented once the economic environment was suitable.

Zhao Ziyang read their report on May 19, 1985, and said that it could only be beneficial, and not harmful, to further explore this line of reasoning (Guo et al., 2012, 28; Wu, 2016). The State Council ordered a working group to be set up under the State Commission for Restructuring the Economic System, which worked throughout June 1985 to draft a reform program along the lines proposed by Guo Shuqing, Liu Jirui, and Qiu Shufang (2012, 28; Lou, 2011[13]).

The program proposal was testing new waters in at least two regards: According to Wu Jinglian (2016), it was the first comprehensive reform program that met the standards of modern economics. In Guo Shuqing's (2012a) view, it was also the first to explicitly confirm that the direction should be "marketization" (xxiii). Lou Jiwei was appointed to be one of the conveners of the working group, and Guo Shuqing and his coauthors joined the participants (Guo, Liu, and Qiu, 2012, 28).[14] Looking back on their work, Lou remarked that while he and his collaborators used computers to apply the Program Evaluation and Review Technique (PERT), Guo Shuqing and his coauthors used Marxist classics and concepts from philosophy and political economy. Yet, they arrived at very similar priorities for reform (Lou, 2011). Joining forces and combining those two approaches lent them modern scientific as well as ideological authority.

One of their key priorities was the unification of the multiple price tracks into a single track for each commodity, which was believed to be crucial for establishing a market economy (Research Group for an Overall Plan, 1986).[15] Three approaches were considered to achieve such a price unification. First, the plan prices could be gradually raised such as to eventually close the gap with the market prices. This approach resembled most closely Lou Jiwei's previous proposal at the Moganshan Youth Conference (see Chapter 6; Lou and Zhou, 1984;

Zhou et al., 1984). But the working group rejected this reform on the grounds that it was too slow. It would postpone for too long other important reforms that were dependent on price reform. Futhermore, each small plan price adjustment would induce a myriad of other adjustments in taxes and public finance, which made this approach too complicated.

Second, a mixed price system could be instituted as an intermediate step to price liberalization. Under this approach the dual-track prices would be unified in only one track, either a free market or a plan price. This would involve the liberalization of all prices of goods that were in excess supply. The prices of goods in short supply should be corrected by a large upward adjustment of plan prices to abolish the prevailing high market prices and thus close the two tracks. The next step would be to abolish the plan prices altogether and let all prices be determined by the market. The authors found this approach superior to the first, but they also noted drawbacks. Because the enterprises were accustomed to selling their goods at market prices, it would require high enforcement costs to return to a unified plan track. The negative sides of the inflexible system of planned prices would also prevail, and the transition period would be prolonged under this plan.

The third, and preferable, approach, according to the authors of the reform proposal, was to liberalize in one stroke all prices then under the dual-track price system. This clearly anticipated a later push for a big bang price reform. Critically, the proposal included prices of essential raw materials that were in short supply. As a concession to more cautious reformers, the proposal held that this could possibly be combined with an upper limit for the market prices of certain commodities, which would be abolished once prices had stabilized.

For the second and third approaches, the authors acknowledged that compensationary subsidies were necessary for enterprises suffering losses due to the price changes and in order to equalize profit rates. Furthermore, they pointed out that in order to prevent the rising costs of increased raw material prices from affecting consumers, the value added tax should be decreased. Nevertheless, the authors acknowleged that an overall increase in the price level would be inevitable, and they recommended austerity. The only way to effectively limit inflation, in their view, was to impose strict monetary policies, including interest rate rises and a control over the total volume of credit. Rapid, simultaneous reforms undertaken in one big step would be quite demanding, the authors admitted. But, full of youthful optimism, they argued that meticulous scientific planning could overcome such challenges (Research Group for an Overall Plan, 1986).

The working group presented their results to the State Council on July 27–29, 1985 (Guo et al., 2012, 28). Just a few months after the official implementation of the dual-track price system, this was not the ideal moment to make a sharp turnaround and go for overall price reform in one stroke. Yet, the young intellectuals, with the support of their older-generation counterparts, had managed to put the possibility of a planned, overall reform in one go into the minds of the leadership. In only a couple more months, preparations to realize the grand plan for one big bang were undertaken.

Foreign Tailwind: The Bashan Boat Conference

The campaign for macroeconomic restraint and wholesale price reform gained support of great symbolic value from participants in a second major conference jointly organized with the World Bank, which was held on the MS Bashan cruising the Yangtze River from September 2 to September 7, 1985 (Liu and Zhang, 1985, 3; Guo, 1985). In February 1984, when the World Bank mission visited China for their second report, Liao Jili, one of the high-ranking participants in the Moganshan World Bank Conference, had suggested planning another reform conference (Wood, 1984). When the mission came again to China in March 1985 to discuss their report, this idea was transformed into a concrete plan. The World Bank economists met with Dong Fureng, Gao Shangquan, and Liao Jili to discuss who should be the international experts. They agreed that there should be three participants from socialist countries, at least two Nobel Prize winners in economics, and three others, including one French and one Japanese (ibid.).[16] The ambition to invite Nobel Laureates indicated that this conference was not to be "under the radar" (Lim, 2016) like the Moganshan World Bank Conference but that a group of world-renowned experts should help draw public attention and create further momentum for market reforms. In fact, up till today, the Bashan Conference remains a widely known and celebrated event among certain circles of market reformers in China and internationally (Gewirtz, 2017; Kornai, 2006; Lim, 2008).[17]

The setting of the Bashan boat conference was in stark contrast to the young intellectuals' meetings in parks and empty offices at austere Chinese research institutes in the 1980s, such as the Institute of Economics of CASS. (When I visited the former building of the Institute of Economics in 2016, it still had a strong cachet of the old days.) The Bashan Conference took place on a luxurious tourist boat with a pool on the deck. In the group photograph of the conference participants, the pool takes up about as much space as the esteemed economists and reformers, who are mostly wearing fashionable, Western-style clothes. The boat provided a secluded setting. Cut off from the outside world, internationally leading experts and high-ranking Chinese reformers were brought together to discuss the future of China's economic system. The boat toured one of China's most iconic sceneries: the Three Gorges. The modern, Western comforts provided to the elites on the boat symbolized the aspirations for a new kind of China.

Upon their arrival in Beijing, the delegation were invited to dine with Prime Minister Zhao Ziyang on September 1, 1985. Besides Lim, Wood, and Brus, Cairncross—who played an important role in the United Kingdom's postwar transition to a peace economy (see Chapter 2)—was part of the delegation. Cairncross (1985) noted in his diary that day,

> The visit to the Prime Minister was remarkable in many ways. We formed the usual crocodile [i.e., a long queue of international delegates] which

I led, as the most elderly, and shook hands with a succession of Chinese before lining up for the customary photograph.

Other members of the foreign "crocodile" who stood out for their contributions to the pivotal question of price reform included the Nobel Prize–winning New Keynesian James Tobin;[18] Otmar Emminger, the former director of the Bundesbank (1976–1979) who had helped shape the German monetary policy of central bank independence since 1950 (Der Spiegel, 1986); Aleksander Bajt, the Yugoslav reform economist who would later argue vigorously for privatization (Bajt, 1992) and who had also attended the 1981 Athens Conference; and János Kornai, the Hungarian star economist (China Economic System Reform Research Conference, 1986).[19] Some prominent Chinese participants included An Zhiwen, Gao Shangquan, Xue Muqiao, Ma Hong, Liu Guoguang, Zhao Renwei, and Wu Jinglian, as well as Tian Yuan, Lou Jiwei, Guo Shuqing, and Luo Xiaopeng from the younger generation (see Illustration 3 of conference participants).[20] Remarkably, no economists from the System Reform Institute nor any other prominent proponent of gradual marketization from the margins were invited.

Cairncross noted in his diary that at the dinner, wage and price reform were the "cardinal issue raised by the Prime Minister" (Cairncross, 1985). Tobin cautioned, "China should do better than any of us and devise new institutions." In

ILLUSTRATION 3 On the boat of the Bashan Conference, Yangtze, September 1985. All participants, without their wives. Courtesy of Adrian Wood.

contrast, Emminger suggested China should follow the German path (ibid.). In line with Friedman and Wu Jinglian, Emminger "emphasised Erhard's bold stroke in abolishing price control at one go in 1948" (ibid.). The so-called Erhard Miracle was invoked in China to argue for a form of neoliberal shock doctrine, just as Sachs, Balcerowic, and others did later in Poland (Weber, 2020).

Later, during the boat conference, Cairncross[21] contrasted the British post-war experience under Clement Attlee's Labor government with the German "miracle" and called for a *gradual* decontrol of prices (Liu et al., 1987, 14; also see Chapter 2). Cairncross pointed out that relying on monetary control as a means of macroeconomic regulation required a highly developed fiscal and currency system (ibid., 24). In China, the banking sector was still rudimentary and there was no developed money market. Under these conditions, in Cairncross's view, "monetary policy will be impotent and the effect of budgetary control will also be limited" (ibid.). All the calls by Wu Jinglian, Guo Shuqing, and others to impose monetary restraints to prepare for a big step in price reform would be futile, by his analysis.

According to Cairncross's conference input, stabilizing the overall price level by macroeconomic means was impossible under China's specific circumstances. In addition, prices were hardly suited to be a means of economic coordination. Market regulation relies on quantity adjustments in reaction to price changes. But if, as in China, Cairncross argued, "supply and demand are inelastic in terms of price changes, then administrative control can achieve what the price mechanism cannot" (ibid.). Hence, a free movement of prices would not equilibrate supply and demand. Instead, in Cairncross's view, while the institutional changes enabling enterprises and consumers to react more readily to price changes were still in the early stages, administrative controls over quantities and prices were needed. In sum, Cairncross warned, "Indirect control relies on a perfectly competitive market. If there is no perfect competition or if the market is not competitive, then administrative measures [such as price controls] are necessary" (ibid.).

With these straightforward arguments, Cairncross debunked the idea that China could revert to indirect macrocontrol under the given institutional reality as well as the notion that swift price liberalization would solve the problem of aggregate excess demand. Cairncross cautioned that adjustments to the wage structure could easily result in wage-induced cost-push inflation (ibid., 34):

> When the prices of some commodities go up, it does not *necessarily* lead to a general price rise for all commodities, but when wages are raised in one sector or department, it will very quickly affect other sectors and departments. The trend toward income equality will lead to a general upsurge of the wage scale.
>
> *(ibid., 24–25, emphasis added)*

Brus, whose arguments during his first visits were frequently cited by Wu, Guo, and others in favor of wholesale price reform, had arrived at a slightly more accommodating position than he had held at the Moganshan World Bank Conference (see Chapter 5). Brus explained that when reflecting with other Eastern European reformers on the failure of their reforms, they had reached the conclusion that only reforms of all aspects of the economic system, including enterprise and price reforms in one fell swoop, could be successful (Guo, 1985, 9; Guo and Zhao, 1986, 19). But his visits to China had taught him that there was some scope for gradual reform in particular, in light of the successes in China's large agricultural sector. Furthermore, the Eastern European countries had "given up half way as a result in the changes in the political circumstances," but in Brus's eyes "such a threat does not exist in China" (Liu et al., 1987, 13).

Brus also acknowledged that China was the first country to adopt a dual-track price system for raw materials. Other socialist countries had had multiple prices for consumer goods, but the dual-track price system for industrial producer goods had been a Chinese invention (ibid., 16). Brus was so impressed with the Chinese reform success and disillusioned with the Eastern European attempts of the 1950s and 1960s that he advised Chinese economists against seeking inspiration from his own writings (Lim, 2008). Nevertheless, in his conference presentation, Brus warned that the dual-track price system could only be a transitory mechanism and should by no means be applied for too long, or it would cause very detrimental effects overall (Guo and Zhao, 1986, 21). Regarding the next steps for price reform, Brus ultimately came to agree with Kornai's and Emminger's stance—that it had to be imposed in one big package, including a liberalization of raw material prices.

Brus's somewhat more cautious stance was overshadowed by Kornai, the self-described "radical reformer" (Kornai, 1986, 1733). I interviewed Edwin Lim in a pleasant London pub some thirty years later. Lim, who had at the time of the conference been the World Bank's lead economist in China, stressed that Kornai was critical of the World Bank's activities in China in the 1980s due to their focus on economics rather than politics. In fact, it is remarkable that amidst the global neoliberal shift, the World Bank took a relatively balanced approach in China, bringing in a diverse set of views while leaving the judgment to the Chinese side. This practice is clearly reflected in the famous Bashan Conference. Cairncross, Tobin, Kornai, and Emminger—to name just a few international participants—did not see eye to eye when it came to the question of China's economic system reform. Lim (2016) pointed out that the World Bank was considered naïve by Kornai for their hope to contribute to economic reform in China without promoting a change in the political system. According to Lim, Kornai's view was that economic reform without political change would get stuck.

In an article on the Hungarian reform experience published in the *Journal of Economic Literature,* a year after the boat conference—and with some resemblance of Kornai's speech on the Yangtze River—Kornai articulated his skepticism of what he called "naïve reformers." They would be caught in a "stubborn inner contradiction" in their hope to "get the active participation of the very people who will lose a part of their power if the process [of market reforms] is successful" (Kornai, 1986, 1729). Kornai (1986, 1728–1729) described this naïve reform approach as dominant in China's official writings and challenged the "faith placed in the harmonious, mutually correcting duality of 'plan' and 'market'."

On the boat, Kornai plainly expressed his criticism of such a duality of plan and market. He told his audience that "the gradualist style of reform is likely to lead to a problem of the disuniformity of 'traffic regulation', and this would cause confusion in economic operations" (Liu et al., 1987, 13). This same example was later invoked by Jeffrey Sachs in his arguments against gradual reform, which he described as "the rough equivalent of the British shifting from right-hand to left-hand driving by just switching over the trucks at first" (Sachs, 1992, 36). Kornai acknowledged at the boat conference that in some realms, such as the ownership system, a gradualist reform was in place (ibid., 14, 15). Nevertheless, he insisted, "it would be necessary to adopt the mode of 'all-out' reform *at once*, that is the various reform measure are synchronized, coordinated, and kept in step with one another" (ibid.).

Price reform was at the heart of Kornai's "'all-out' reform *at once*." Both Emminger and Kornai argued, "On the whole it will not be possible to complete China's reform within a short period of time, but the implementation of flexible market prices should not be delayed." Guo Shuqing and Zhao Renwei noted in their report on the conference that the advice was to "fight for carrying out a fairly all-encompassing price reform as quickly as possible" (Guo and Zhao, 1986, 21). Or, to use Kornai's words after he criticized the Hungarian government for taking thirty years to implement price and wage reform instead of pushing them through in one package, "I personally feel that things would have been a good deal better if the price system had undergone one brave 'surgery'" (Kornai, 1986, 93). Kornai pushed his radical liberalization stance to the point where Cairncross (1985) noted in his diary, "I found Kornai's constant assumption that all State intervention in economic affairs, and especially pricing, was for the bad and to be suppressed, very unrealistic."

It has recently been argued that the "advice that Kornai offered at the Bashan Conference differed in subtle but significant ways from the views for which he was widely known around the world" (Gewirtz, 2017, 149). This suggested Kornai was behaving as a two-faced reform economist, with "one face for Hungary and one other face for China" (Kornai in Gewirtz, 2017, 149).[22] Kornai's intellectual journey was marked by radical turnarounds reflecting different phases of his life and stages of the socialist experiment in Hungary (Kornai, 2006). But from the above-cited reports on the Bashan Conference, it becomes apparent that regarding China, Kornai emerged as a radical reformer consistent with his agenda of 1990.

The "views for which [Kornai] was widely known around the world" to which Gewirtz refers in the above quote were crystalized in Kornai's (1990) *The Road to a Free Economy*. Kornai (1990, 17) calls the title of his book "an echo of the Hayek title" (1944) *The Road to Serfdom*. The book is a neoliberal manifesto for shock therapy. Kornai promises nothing less than to show how "to overcome the roadblocks" on the way to "a free society" after decades of "tight central planning" and an "overwhelming power of the state." Kornai's ambition goes far beyond his native Hungary. The book is meant to provide a universal blueprint from serfdom to freedom. He notes in the foreword, "I am confident that the core of ideas presented here is applicable not only in Hungary, but in *all* other countries in transition from a socialist regime to a free economy" (ibid., 13).

Kornai's reform blueprint had a "Surgery for Stabilization" at its core (ibid., 102). This surgery was the quintessence of shock therapy as applied in many socialist countries. Just as at the boat conference, Kornai (1990) warned that "the execution of *some* of the required tasks should not be prolonged, and cannot be accomplished by a series of small steps. Instead, these measures must be taken in *one stroke*" (ibid., first emphasis added). But, entirely in accordance with his position at the Bashan Conference, Kornai argued that some other parts would take time to be implemented. Kornai (1990, 80) asserted, for example, that privatization, which he identified as a key element of system reform in addition to price reform, "can be achieved only through an organic process of development and social change" and as such had to be more gradual.

In contrast, Kornai emphasized, consistent with his advice in China, that price reform belonged to the set of measures that must be taken at one stroke: He (1990) held that "*total liberalization of prices* is necessary in the state sector. ... *The sooner the operation achieves this goal, the better*" (146, second emphasis added). The "surgery," both in the eyes of the "Chinese" Kornai and the globally acclaimed Kornai (1990), had to be prepared by creating a beneficial macroeconomic environment, by the means of "stopping inflation" (ibid., 105–13), "restoration of budgetary equilibrium" (ibid., 114–37), and "managing macrodemand" (ibid., 138–44). In sum, both Kornais were in perfect agreement. Or, in other words, there is only one Janós Kornai when it comes to market reforms from the mid-1980s onwards. This Kornai is a shock therapist. The great admiration that Kornai reaped for his advice at the Bashan Conference by some Chinese reform economists also shows that shock therapy was very much "in the cards" in China.

The mode of reform that had emerged as dominant in China by the mid-1980s and that was attacked by the one-stroke reformers was based on marketization through growth. I call this process "to grow into the market" rather than "to grow out of the plan" (Byrd, 1988; Naughton, 1995) because the most important aspect of the dual-track system was not a decline in absolute terms of the plan share, but the growth in relative terms of the market share. Marketization from the margins unleashed a fundamental transformation of the planned economy. But the process of reform meant, initially, growing into the market. And high growth rates indicated that the increase of the market share did not necessarily have to be at the expense of the planned economy. Thus, this mode of reform was driven by growth and development.

In sharp contrast, those arguing for a package reform of the shock therapy type looked at the economy from a viewpoint of zero-sum games. The planned

economy had to be cut out in order to make space for the market. As in a surgery, the patient had to take an anesthetic. This meant growth had to be sacri-
ficed for some time in order to get the necessary, if painful, adjustments under
way. At the Bashan Conference, Kornai warned of the trade-off between reform
and high growth—very much in agreement with Wu's (1985a, 1985b) Kornai-
inspired arguments earlier in 1985.

Bajt supported this line, arguing that Yugoslavia's problem had been the failure to impose macroeconomic controls (Cairncross, 1985; Liu et al., 1987, 33).
Kornai explained that if the economy was allowed to "overheat," the reaction
would typically be recentralization, which would ultimately result in a reversal
of reform. So, whereas from the reform paradigm of marketization from the
margins, high growth was a powerful tool to transform the economy, Kornai
emphasized the danger of overheating and a falling back on the plan. Kornai
thus advised strict controls over total investment as well as over the amount of
currency in circulation to avoid a rise in the general price level and make price
reform safe (Guo, 1985, 9–10; Liu et al., 1987, 19–21).

But it is not clear that those measures would, in fact, have stabilized the price
level and made price reform safe. Some participants at the conference expressed
concerns about the problem of microeconomic limits to macroeconomic controls. For example, Tobin advised that the experience of many developing countries had shown that macroeconomic policies such as those proposed by Kornai
are hardly effective if they lack the necessary microeconomic conditions, and
they could thus not serve to stop inflation caused by price reform (ibid., 38–39).
Based on Kornai's own logic, one should not expect those macroeconomic controls to be effective in a socialist economy. At the Bashan Conference, Kornai ran
into a similar inconsistency in his argument, which we spotted in Wu Jinglian's
comments in Athens (see "Setting the Stage for a Big Bang in Price Reform,"
earlier in this chapter).

Kornai implicitly delivered arguments as to why the control over investment
as well as over the general price level were hardly compatible with the rapid
price liberalization he promoted under China's given institutional arrangements.
One of Kornai's most famous insights is the problem of a "soft budget." Due
to the "paternalistic" relationship between the state-owned enterprises and the
"higher authorities," enterprises can rely on a "helping hand" when they get into
financial difficulties—for example, due to high investment expenditures. At the
boat conference, Kornai added that if tight controls prevent this "helping hand"
from stepping in, the enterprises "shift budget difficulties away by raising prices"
(Liu et al., 1987, 40). The greater the enterprises' power to set prices, the more
they would tend to escape their difficulties by charging higher prices. The price
liberalization recommended by Kornai would leave it fully to the enterprises to
set prices. Thus, given that Kornai acknowledged that enterprise reform must be
a slow process, the combination of strict budget controls with no possibility to
go bankrupt on the part of the enterprises meant that price liberalization would
result in rising price levels. Faced with rising prices and a strict budget constraint

but no way to discontinue business, the only way forward for enterprises was to raise prices. If this is taken into account, Kornai's policy prescription appears to be not for stabilization, but for destabilization.

Kornai himself did not point to this contradiction between his prediction of enterprises' behavior and the overall outcome of price reform, and neither did the conference reports, but all the elements of such a critique of radical price reform were presented. This contradiction in Kornai's recommendation became the core of the warning against price reform issued by the leaders of the System Reform Institute shortly thereafter.

Irrespective of these logical pitfalls, those on the boat who had long argued for macroeconomic retrenchment and rapid price reform took Kornai's recommendation for "surgery" at face value and were pleased to find Emminger reiterate the "Erhard Miracle." Lim (2016) remembered that, after the boat conference and the many contacts with Eastern European reform economists that the World Bank had organized, China's economists "realized that a fundamental reform of the system was required." According to Lim, they now understood that instead of tinkering around with the old system, "they had to dismantle the central planning system,"

The Chinese participants had, in essence, been familiar with the arguments presented by the foreign scholars at the conference. As Cairncross (1985) noted in his diary, "Brus [who worked closely with the World Bank and had by then been several times to China] said they knew it all and wanted not diagnosis, but prescription." To be sure, there were some new insights on practices of macroeconomic regulation in Western economies, and spelling out policies of indirect economic governance enhanced the prospects for marketization. Yet, the most immediate impact of the conference was to create momentum for the so-called package reform. In the months to come, the proponents of rapid price reform could enhance their position on the right prescription for China by citing conversations with world-renowned experts. One young conference participant opposed to rapid price reform, Luo Xiaopeng (2017), suggested that this followed the old Chinese strategy of "using a foreigner to enhance one's own position" (挟洋自重).

The 1986 Program Office

Shortly after the Bashan meeting, the national Conference of Party Delegates convened in late-September 1985 to adopt the "Proposal for the Seventh Five Year Plan," which was to commence in 1986 (Wu and Ma, 2016, 215). Parts of the proposal reflected the package approach to reform. It stated that changing from direct control over enterprises to indirect macrocontrol was necessary to "establish a new system for the socialist economy" (Hua, Zhang, and Luo, 1993, 132).

Wu Jinglian and some of his opponents saw this as a sign that the package reform approach was gaining support (ibid.; Wu, 2016). The leadership decided to continue strict controls over credit quotas and tight financial policies, which had been implemented earlier in 1985 in reaction to the high growth and rising prices (Zhao,

2009, 127–128). This continuation of macroeconomic retrenchment was consistent with the logic that there was a trade-off between reform and growth and that in order to prepare for reform, aggregate demand had to be constrained.

In early 1986, preparations for a shift in the approach to reform became more apparent. Zhao Ziyang had long been torn between his experience with rural reforms and enterprise reform in Sichuan, which had taught him to "grope for stones to cross the river," and plans to jump over to a modern market economy with help of the magic of economic science.[23] As the challenges of reform became ever more apparent, the promise of an easy, clear-cut solution gained in attraction to the point that China came very close to a big bang.

In his January 1986 speeches to the economic leadership and the State Council on the tasks in the year ahead, Zhao still emphasized that no major step should be taken in price reform—and in particular, the dual-track price system for steel should be continued for the time being (Zhao, 2016a, 250; 2016b, 262). At the same time, however, macroeconomic control should be strengthened such as to create a good environment to launch the next step in reform (Zhao, 2016a, 251). The year should be used to prepare a program for this next step by conducting thorough research (Zhao, 2016f, 263).

By March 1986, Zhao had crystalized his vision for this next step: "Package reform is superior to reform by individual measures," Zhao told his Personal Secretaries Bao Tong and Bai Meiqing (Zhao, 2016a, 305; Zhang S., 2017, 538). The most important task was to straighten out the prices of sixty-six major producer goods (Zhao, 2016a, 304). This would have to be accompanied by adjusting the tax system—and, consequently, the system of public finance—and would affect the system of foreign trade and the financial system (ibid.). To tie all these reforms together "will be a major battle," since it affected the interests of enterprises, local and central government, as well as consumers immediately (ibid.). But—in line with the arguments of the Eastern European reformers and their Chinese partners—Zhao warned pretty much in Kornai's style that the basic problem was the coexistence of the old and the new systems. This caused a lot of friction. If China continued to proceed gradually, the contradictions between the two systems would become very severe, Zhao cautioned. In particular, Zhao suggested, just as Brus had at the boat conference, the situation of the coexistence of two very different prices for the same good could not last too long. If the conditions were found to be ripe, China should "take a decisive step in the next two years, and basically transition to a primacy of the new system" (ibid).

But despite this clear endorsement of package reform, Zhao also cautioned, "This could be the line of thought [for further reform], we can also consider other lines.... The key is to design a good program, thoughtful and comprehensively" (ibid.).

Four days after his conversation with his secretaries, on March 15, 1986, Zhao addressed the National Work Conference on Urban Economic System Reform along the same lines. A package reform was the right approach, Zhao proclaimed, but out of the package, the reform of the prices of raw materials, energy, and other important producer goods was the most crucial step to be taken first, in a decisive manner (Zhao, 2016g, 313). To ensure success, Zhao argued, it was necessary to prevent changes to people's real incomes. If prices were rising too much, this should be achieved by indexing wages to the consumer price index. Even if such compensations incurred short-term financial losses, price reform had to be implemented determinedly, Zhao told his audience. Just as the proponents of macroeconomic restraint as a first step toward package reform had argued, Zhao suggested that to prepare for the reform of producer prices, investments had to be sharply limited. Whatever short-term pain this might cause was better than suffering from the "chronic diseases" of the old system (ibid., 314–315). To push ahead with this package of short-term pain based on the promise of long-term gain, Zhao called for "drawing on the collective wisdom of practitioners and theoreticians, comrades from central departments and local authorities, old and young to design a good program" (ibid., 314).

Zhao managed to generate the necessary political support for his preparations for a "decisive step." On March 25, 1986, the State Council established the Economic System Reform Program Design Office (usually referred to as 方案办, henceforth Program Office) to draw up a reform plan (Wu, 2005, 78; Zhang, 2017, 538). The same month, Deng Xiaoping endorsed the go-ahead for price reform. Deng told a delegation from Hong Kong,

> Reform will certainly involve risks, it can also cause some turbulences, but it will not work without determination. If we want to reform, we have to be prepared to take risks. In the past few years our reforms have borne fruit thanks to careful consideration. If we now manage to adjust prices, we will have passed through an important pass in economic system reform.
>
> *(Cheng, 2006, 93)*

These statements by Zhao Ziyang and Deng Xiaoping show that by the mid-1980s the idea of a trade-off between short-term and long-term pain that necessitated sacrifices now to prepare for a better future was on the minds of China's leadership. This logic of inducing suffering by policy action now, in hopes of creating a future, superior economic system, is at the heart of shock therapy.

The Program Office had representatives from all levels and relevant departments of the state and party to ensure its legitimacy in imposing drastic measures. Yet, those who had long pushed for package reform dominated intellectually.

The office was led by Zhao Ziyang's trusted protégé Tian Jiyun, who had come from Sichuan with Zhao and was at the time vice premier (Fewsmith, 1994, 149, 177, 185). The executive head was Gao Shangquan, a vice minister of the System Reform Commission (Wu, 2016), who had also been the commissioned director of the System Reform Institute before Chen Yizi and Wang Xiaoqiang took over and played a critical role in granting the institute's autonomy (Wang, 2017). Yet, since Gao Shangquan was about to lead a delegation of the System Reform Institute to Hungary and Yugoslavia, Wu Jinglian was among those substituting temporarily for Gao in his capacity of deputy director (Wu, 2016; Zhang, 2017, 543).[24] Other notable members included An Zhiwen, Cheng Zhiping, Ma Hong, Tian Yuan, Xu Jingan, and Zhang Jinfu, as well as Zhu Rongji, who became vice premier in 1993 and premier in 1998 and is known for his neoliberal reform agenda (Zhang, 2017, 540). Zhu, an engineer by training, was at the time a deputy minister of the State Economic Commission, the founding director of Tsinghua's School of Economics and Management (modeled on US business schools), and had maintained a working relationship with the World Bank since their first mission to China (Andreas, 2009, 229, 244; World Bank, 1983).

The prominent proponents of package reform who now joined the Program Office included Lou Jiwei, who had previously joined forces with Guo Shuqing to draft a proposal for radical price reform; Zhou Xiaochuan, Lou's coauthor at the Moganshan Youth Conference; as well as Liu Guoguang, who had worked closely with the World Bank to bring Eastern European economists such as Brus and Šik to China in the first years of reform (Lou, 2011; Wu, 2016; Zhang, 2017, 541–543).[25] Wu (2016) pointed out that this was the beginning of a close cooperation among this group that came to fruition under the presidency of Jiang Zemin and the pre-miership of Zhu Rongji in the 1990s and early 2000s, the period of China's most neoliberal market reforms. Zhou Xiaochuan aptly summarized the main charac-teristics of their group as "radical reform economists applying basic market theory" and noted that since they were seeking to derive market-oriented reforms from these basic theories, they were "often criticized for 'the divorce of theory from practice', 'idealism' and 'book worship'" (Zhou, 1992, 180).

The first reform proposal of the Program Office, titled "Basic Outline for Reform in the Next Two Years" (dated April 25, 1986) was drawn up within twenty-two days (Program Office, 1986, 1). The Program was an expansion on the 1985 draft proposal and reflected the basic logic previously supported by Wu, Guo, Lou, and others[26] as well as promoted by the Eastern European reformers and proponents of the "Erhard Miracle." The Program was fully in accord with Zhao Ziyang's March 15 speech in which he had urged for the necessity of short-term pain for long-term gain.

The Program argued for the "necessity and possibility of one big step" in reform within the next two years, stressing that the success or failure of reform would be decided in the course of the Seventh Five Year Plan (1986–1990) (ibid.). The approach was once more labeled a "package" (配套). The need for coordina-tion was stressed, to create synergies between the different elements of reform, yet the implementation was meant to be split into separate, planned steps (ibid., 4, 15). In the past years, the autonomy of enterprises had been greatly strength-ened, yet no complementing measures had been taken to create a competitive market (ibid., 12-13). A competitive market was thereby defined as a rational price structure that would guarantee equal profit rates and hence fair competi-tion. Thus, for 1987 and 1988, the "big step" should be price reform with com-plementary tax and public finance reform (ibid., 14–15).

More concretely the proposal stated, "The reform of energy and raw material prices is the starting point and key link of this package reform" (ibid., 6). The distorted price signals were to be corrected in one big, upward adjustment. Depending on the concrete conditions of the commodities, this would either be one big adjustment, or a big adjustment followed by one or two smaller ones (ibid.). Crucially, the proposal expected that stable market conditions would arise from this exercise relatively swiftly. So, prices should be liberalized within a short period of time, unifying the dual prices into one track (ibid., 6–7). Tax reductions should serve to stabilize retail prices, while important investment projects should receive subsidies to compensate the increased input prices (ibid., 14). Then, in 1988, the reform of the producer goods prices and taxes should be followed by a reform of the public finance system and the state allocation and investment system, which were both directly affected by the previous two reform measures (ibid., 14–15). Later, wage reform and reform of the international trade system should follow.

Wu, as one of the architects, stressed that this plan with price reform at its core followed Šik's basic model of adjusting first and then letting go (先调后放) (ibid., 6; Wu, 2016). However, in light of the discussion in Chapter 5, it is clear that the Program also departed in critical ways from Šik's recommendations. Šik had pointed out that calculation-based adjustments would make price liberalization safe, but only under certain restrictions. First, Šik explicitly warned that the prices of basic producer goods should continue to be state planned as long as these goods were in very short supply, which was still the case in China at the time—manifested in the very large gap between the market and planned prices for these goods. Second, Šik saw it as a precondition that the state allocation system of mandatory planning would be dismantled before price liberalization, since this old system was, in his eyes, incompatible with the market mechanism. The 1986 Program, in contrast, saw the reform of the state allocation and investment system as the second step, after price liberalization (ibid., 15). Third, Šik warned that, besides a sellers' market —aggregate excess supply, which the Program Office's plan sought to achieve by further macroeconomic retrenchment, just as Kornai and others had recommended at the boat conference (ibid., 18)—the monopolistic state-owned enterprises had to be broken up prior to price liberalization. Šik had put forward the case of Yugoslavia to caution that if monopolies prevailed, the result of price liberalization would be inflation and turmoil.

The plans of the Program Office aroused strong opposition from China's gradualist reformers. Warnings of the dangers arising from price rises and social instability caused by a big bang in price reform were issued by the reform economists at the Economic System Reform Research Institute, based on fieldwork in Yugoslavia and Hungary. These economists were dedicated to reform but opposed to this one-stroke program. Their interventions fueled skepticism among government officials and state-owned enterprise leaders concerned about the high costs and political risks of the Program Office's plan.

As these critical voices were becoming more forceful, the economists in the Program Office once more relied on "foreign tailwind." On June 21, 1986, Edwin Lim, as World Bank representative, met with Zhao Ziyang and urged, "I think you can speed up reform, in particular price reform" (Zhao and Lim, 2016, 415).[27] Repeating once more Brus's position at the Bashan conference, Lim said that the dual-track price system was a transitory measure and as such should not last too long. Lim advised that China could not simply copy the method of rural reform in the cities but should adopt the combined program of price, tax, and public finance reforms (ibid.).

The same month, one of China's most important elderly reform economists spoke out in favor of the Program Office: prompted by Wu Jinglian, Xue Muqiao wrote a letter to Zhao Ziyang and Tian Jiyun, supporting the plan for radical price reform (Xue M., 2011a, 115). Xue wrote, "I was told that what was going on was not a single reform, but a total overhaul in prices, tax revenues, finance and credit. I believe this is encouraging progress" (Xue M., 2011a, 115). Xue also encouraged prioritizing the reform of the prices of the means of production and believed that the risk could be reduced to a reasonable level if capital construction could be strictly controlled (ibid., 115–17). Elsewhere, Xue explained the critical difference between his thinking and Kornai's. Xue pointed out that he did not agree with Kornai (1980) that the budget constraint was necessarily "soft" and "investment hunger" was an "incurable chronic disease in socialist countries" (Xue M., 2011b, 119). In Xue's view, capital construction could be brought under control and inflation must not be a logical result of price reform. Xue thus avoided the inconsistency in Kornai's argument. Yet, it remains remarkable that Xue, in his eighties, underwent such an intellectual turnaround—from a cautious reformer drawing lessons from his decades of experience in practical economic work to an endorser of package reform.

Despite these influential voices rallying behind the Program Office, the plan for a "big step" in price reform was ultimately aborted.

Debunking the Big Bang

In theory, for any given good, utility will be increased by eliminating price distortions. In practice, however, the nature of the goods could be decisive if one was waiting for expected responses from supply and demand after implementing the big bang.... If price distortions were primarily concentrated in consumer goods, such as bikinis and mini skirts, the big bang would be a little bang, and vice versa: the big bang would be really big if price distortions were concentrated in energy and material goods, such as oil and steel.

(Wang, 1998, 25)

As the proponents of the package approach were gaining influence and the preparations for a big bang were advancing, different groups of reform-minded economists gathered forces to oppose this drastic measure. The opponents of shock therapy differed in their views on what would be the right next step in economic system reform, but they all agreed that a big bang would have disastrous consequences for the Chinese economy and people and, ultimately, for the prospects of reform.

Some young economists who had emerged from the Moganshan Youth Conference as influential reform thinkers, such as Hua Sheng, He Jiacheng, and Luo Xiaopeng, but also Zhou Qiren, Zhang Weiying,[28] and others, saw the core contradiction between the old and the new systems not in the persistence of two different prices but in the loosely defined ownership relations (Hua, He, Zhang, et al., 1986;[29] Luo, 2017; Zhang M., 2016; Zhou, 2016). For instance, establishing clearly defined property rights over the enterprises' assets in the form of an "asset management responsibility system" was the recommendation of Hua Sheng and his group (1986) for the next step of reform. One of China's most eminent senior economists, Li Yining, argued for establishing a socialist stock market (Li, 1989). Others, like Wang Xiaoqiang, the leader of the China Economic System Reform Research Institute, and Ji Xiaoming, promoted enterprise reform but thought that China should "transcend the logic of private ownership" rather than simply emulating Western capitalist organizational forms not suited for China's realities and socialist path (Wang, 1989, 1998; Wang and Ji, 1985[30]).

The debate between the proponents of different versions of enterprise reform and those in favor of a big bang in price reform has typically been labeled as a debate of enterprise or ownership reform first, versus price reform first (Brødsgaard and Rutten, 2017, 81; Fewsmith, 1994, 184; Naughton, 1995, 188; Hsu, 1988, 1225; Stiglitz, 1994, 262). But the confrontation between the different views was deeper than just a question of sequencing. Those in favor of a big bang were drawing on the Lange tradition of applying the logic of Walrasian equilibrium theory. For them, the market was essentially represented by a vector of prices, and the most crucial thing for China to move to a market economy was to "get the prices right." Those who challenged this view were deeply versed in the institutional reality of China and the complex historical processes that had given rise to market economies in the capitalist world. For them, the market was much more than price signals and could only emerge from the interplay between suitably structured enterprises facilitated by the state in some way. From this perspective, letting go of the prices of essential producer goods—with or without previous adjustment—would result not in an equilibrium but in chaos, inflation, and political instability.

A Big Bang in Price Reform Is No Solution to Structural Disequilibrium: Li Yining's Challenge

Li Yining used a speech commemorating the sixty-seventh anniversary of the 1919 May Fourth movement at Peking University to debunk, on theoretical grounds, the plans for a big bang.[31] Rebecca Karl (2019, 379) aptly characterized May Fourth as an anti-imperialist "intellectual and activist program of resistance and opposition to the corrupt domestic governmental systems [of the Republican era], global institutions, [and] local organizations." The May Fourth program, in important ways, reshaped China's political and intellectual landscape of the twentieth century. Peking University students were an important force in this movement. Some thirty years later, Li Yining had been introduced to Western economics at Peking University in the 1950s by Chen Daisun and Luo Zhiru, who had earned PhDs from Harvard in 1925 and 1937, respectively, and were among China's leading authorities on foreign economic thought (Li Yining, 2012, vi; Trescott, 2012, 343, 357). While some of the economists of the middle generation, who now pushed for radical price reform, had been fully integrated into China's emerging orthodoxy of Soviet-style economics at the time, Li kept a critical distance and a vibrant interest in Western economic thought throughout the Mao years (Fewsmith, 1994, 185–186). Due to his research, Li was repeatedly and for prolonged periods banned to the countryside for hard manual labor before and during the Cultural Revolution (Li, 2012, vi).

With the beginning of reform, Li finally became a full professor at Peking University in 1979 at age forty-nine, and he became a Party member in 1984 (Fewsmith, 1994, 186). Li Yining organized a weekly lecture series on Western economics at Peking University beginning in 1979 (Gewirtz, 2017, 79–81). It drew great attention, including from young intellectuals who had returned from the countryside and were at the time beginning their own studies of foreign economics (Bai, 2016; Wang, 2017). The proponents of package reform were inspired by the Eastern European reformers and ultimately in the intellectual tradition of Oskar Lange's neoclassical vision of market socialism. In contrast, Li Yining had broken with Lange in the 1970s, dissatisfied with his ignorance of human behavior and institutional realities (Lu, 2002, 53–54).

Back at Peking University and back at academic work, Li drew on two decades of reading and reflection to publish a number of books introducing contemporary currents in economic thinking (ibid., 56–57). The first of his monographs, *Galbraith's Institutional Economics*, criticizes Galbraith's bourgeois frame of reference (Li, 1979, 18). To argue from the standpoint of critique when discussing Western economics was still customary in China at the time. Through his in-depth study of Galbraith's life and work, it is clear that Li was familiar with the Galbraithian stance on American price controls and monopoly capitalism (see Chapter 2). Li's second major work was *The British Economy in the Twentieth Century* (Luo and Li, 1978). He set out to find the reasons for the "British Disease" and was critical of the British postwar mode of economic regulation and welfare policies. Yet, through this work, Li was an expert on the British transition from a wartime to a peacetime economy and must have been acquainted with the arguments in favor of maintaining a degree of price controls in the transition, as also put forward by Cairncross at the Bashan Conference. These books served as prepatory works for Li's theoretical systematization of his forceful challenge to the feasibility of a big push in price reform, which resulted in what Li considers his most important academic contribution (Li, 2014, vi, x): *Chinese Economy in Disequilibrium*[32] (1990).

In his 1986 May Fourth anniversary speech, Li Yining coined what Fewsmith (1994) found to be "perhaps the best-known sentence to be penned in the course of debate over economic reform" (186):

> Economic reform can fail because of the failure of price reform, but its success cannot be determined by price reform but only by ownership reform.[33]
>
> *(Li, 1986)*

Although the proponents of a "big push" had promised that rapid reform of crucial input prices would bring a breakthrough, Li now warned that its failure could ruin the whole reform project, while even its success could not bring the promised advance in reform. When they invoked the need for short-term pain to achieve long-term gain, China's political leaders acknowledged that the risk and fiscal costs of a major step in price reform would be high. Li now added that, while the pain was certain, in contrast to the promises of the package reformers, the gains, even in the best case scenario, would be low. According to Li and in contrast to Milton Friedman, Wu Jinglian, and many others, China could not hope to replicate the West German postwar "Erhard Miracle" (Li, 2014, x). All that imposing such a shock in pursuit of a miracle would do would be to undermine the social and economic foundations of succesful reforms.

At the core of Li's argument was that China was in a state of structural diequilibrium—an argument clearly reminiscent of Galbraith's (Galbraith, 1980, 28) "disequilibrium system" (see Chapter 2). Li defined his notion of disequilibrium in contrast to the Walrasian equilibrium concept. Li saw a Walrasian *dis*equilibrium as a deviation from the Walrasian *equilibrium*. The Walrasian disequilbrium is a state when price and quantity adjustments that are automatically forthcoming have not yet been completed. This assumes fully developed markets in the form of perfect competition, perfect information, and fully flexible prices. Hence, in this conception, disequilibrium is not a resting point but a transitionary state before equilibrium is reached.

However, China at the time, in Li's view, was in a state of disequilibrium understood as a "balance condition under which there is neither a fully developed market nor a flexible price mechanism" (ibid., 1). Li warned that overcoming aggregate excess demand under China's conditions was not a matter of adjusting prices but of developing enterprises' competitiveness. In a Galbraithian mode, Li argued, this could not be achieved by breaking up monopolies. Instead, Li urged fostering of management capacities and transferring the socialist enterprises into public stock companies.

Li's main concern was with instituting horizontal market relations between enterprises and professionalizing the government's regulatory capacities (Li, 1986). Hence, in Li's analysis, a market would not emerge by destroying the plan and liberalizing prices. Instead, a slow process of institutional change had to be initiated by the state to create markets. As long as these institutional changes that were meant to create, essentially, an emulation of capitalist enterprises were ongoing, a dual system of prices and modes of economic regulation must prevail, in Li's view.

Moreover, Li cautioned, China was to face an absolute scarcity of certain key inputs for some time. Those scarcities could not be overcome by liberalizing prices. Instead, direct government regulation continued to be necessary, including certain price controls. In the government's regulation of prices, prices prevailing on the market track of the dual-track system must be the starting point. This did not mean that the government would equate plan and market prices; rather, Li suggested, the government would regulate the market through the deviation of the two prices. In Li's approach, maintaining the dual-track price system for a long period was an essential part of China's market reforms (ibid.; Li, 2014, 104). Li acknowledged that the dual-track price system caused frictions. But he found that under China's conditions there was no choice but to stick with this "second best solution" for the time being (Li, 2014, 104).

Crucially, for Li, equilibrium is not a goal in itself but an analytical tool to assess the conditions of China's economy. It would be easy to achieve a low equilibrium by suppressing demand to the low level of supply. But this would mean creating an equilibrium of poverty. Even if imposing macroeconomic austerity and letting go of prices would create a stable equilibrium—as the package reformers seemed to think—this would not be a desirable state for the society and economy. Creating a good environment for reform must mean something different than such a low equilibrium, in Li's vision. The outcome of the short-term pain imposed by package reform, according to Li, was not expected to enhance China's economic development.

Li stressed that the government's reform policies should not impose shocks but be designed to enhance continuity and stability, putting people at ease. If individuals and firms sensed the kinds of sudden changes that overnight price liberalization would bring, they would react by rushed precautionary measures, up to the point of political unrest (Li, 1986). Thus, a swift, "big step" in price reform would create social and political dangers for the overall reform project without solving China's economic challenges in moving toward a prosperous market economy. The "price reform first" proposal sounded very appealing in theory, Li argued, but in practice, given China's reality, the only way was to stick with the dual-track price system and gradually go ahead with ownership reform (Li, 2014, 114).

Lessons from Reform Practice: The System Reform Institute's Surveys in China, Hungary, and Yugoslavia

Li Yining's challenge to the package reform program had authority, thanks to his status as one of China's foremost scholars of foreign economics at the time. The reputation of the Chinese Economic System Reform Research Institute (CESRRI), henceforth referred to as the System Reform Institute, was derived from the pioneering scale of their empirical research and the sharpness of their interpretation. Their work had gained these young researchers the leadership's, in particular Zhao Ziyang's, trust and support since the rural reforms. In 1985, the newly founded System Reform Institute, under the leadership of Chen Yizi and Wang Xiaoqiang, conducted a large-scale study[34] to evaluate the progress of reform in the urban industrial economy and to delineate possible ways forward (CESRRI, 1986).[35] This was "arguably the most extraordinary empirical investigation undertaken in twentieth-century China" up to that point (Reynolds, 1987b, xv). The quality of the study was uncontested, and it impressed the State Council, especially Zhao Ziyang, and many fellow economists. Even those who disagreed with the study's conclusions, such as Wu Jinglian, endorsed the high standards of research (Bai, 2016; Cao, 2016; CESRRI, 1986; Wu, 1987).

In the preface to the publication of this ground-breaking study, Chen Yizi summarized the System Reform Institute's research approach. Chen argued that as reform progressed, the economy would become more difficult to control and reform harder to sustain. In sharp contrast to the package reformers, who took the planned economy as a starting point for their analysis, Chen observed that, at this stage, "China's economy is quite different from both the Soviet model and the Western market economy" (ibid.). While China had to learn from the experiences of other countries, Chen insisted, China could not simply copy: "The answer does not lie in books or in other countries' models ... only through practice can we find the best way to build a socialist country with Chinese characteristics" (ibid.). In Chen's view, China's researchers from all social science disciplines were challenged to cooperate in "integrating theory with practice" to achieve a "systematic investigation into the actual situation" (Chen Yizi, 1987, xxiii).

Zhao Ziyang read the 1985 System Reform Institute survey and once more asked Wang Xiaoqiang to join one of the premier's study tours (Wang, 2017). This provided an opportunity to discuss the institute's findings at a time when the package reform approach had already gained great attention. Wang and the researchers at the System Reform Institute agreed with the basic goal of marketization and with the liberalization of the prices of goods in excess supply, as was already underway in 1985. The major disagreement, Wang pointed out to the prime minister, was on *how* to achieve the creation of a market economy: whether the prices of scarce key inputs should be liberalized in one go despite the great risks and costs, or the dual-track price system should continue until market relations had developed to a sufficient degree, enterprises had become more independent entities, and supply had increased enough to open the bottlenecks. Wang strongly supported the second option. He and his colleagues agreed with the shortcomings of the dual-track price system, with its tendency to divert inputs from the plan into the market that harmed the plan's fulfillment, and the problem of corruption. But they thought that the dual-track system was still a better solution than trying to destroy the planned economy through overnight liberalization. They warned Zhao that package reform would destroy the core of China's industrial economy without creating a market.

The proponents of the package reform approach frequently emphasized its comprehensiveness, pointing to the coordination of the reform of prices, taxes, and public finance. Yet, comprehensiveness in the reform approach was not what set the two sides apart in the eyes of the researchers at the System Reform Institute. It was commonplace among market reformers at the time that changes to the price system would necessitate changes in the tax and wage system, and thus also in public finance. Wang Xiaoqiang saw the decisive difference in whether the core of the planned economy should be reformed in one package with price reform as the first "big step" or whether the economy should grow gradually and experimentally into a socialist market by letting the dual-track price system prevail.

The System Reform Institute's study demonstrated that the dual-track price system was showing remarkable results only months after its official adoption in 1984, but it also warned that adjustments within the system were required. One part of the study was a questionnaire survey on the public response to price reform, conducted in more than 2,000 households all over the country in February and July 1985—before and after the abolishment of the unified purchase and sale system for grain and the letting go of the prices of a range of non-staple agricultural products (Yang, Yang, and Xuan, 1987, 59). The survey showed that a large majority of respondents reported rising living standards and increasing or constant levels of food consumption, as well as an increasingly positive attitude to a partial market regulation of prices, despite these price liberalizations (ibid., 59–75). The clear message of the survey was that the dual-track price system was a success in the public's perception.

Another part of the study evaluated the economic outcomes of the dual-track price system for raw materials, by surveying 429 industrial enterprises (Diao, 1987, 35). It demonstrated that once the price liberalization at the margins for raw materials exceeded a certain threshold, it had a great effect on the enterprises' behavior. Raw material producers expanded production to meet demand, and downstream enterprises economized on raw materials (ibid., 35–46). This demonstrated that under the dual-track price system, enterprises had begun to tailor their activities to market conditions.

But, besides these positive findings on the expansion of the dual-track price system to the industrial economy, the study also warned of macroeconomic imbalances driven by structural wage inflation. The spiraling up of wages would result in a hidden expansion of the consumption fund, an excessive expansion of the light industry, and a softening of the bank constraint (Chen et al., 1987).

The System Reform Institute researchers asserted that the "problem lies in the micromechanism" (ibid., 3). Enterprises faced "extremely uneven operational conditions," for example, with regard to fixed assets (Chen et al., 1987, 9). Thus, labor productivity and profits were primarily determined by these uneven conditions rather than by the efforts of the workers. Enterprises with good initial conditions had high profits and used them to raise their workers' wages and bonuses. This kicked off a wage hike. In the absence of a labor market and given the lifelong socialist bond between enterprises and workers, workers in other enterprises and sectors pressed for matching wages (ibid., 9–10). The overall result was a rapid expansion of the consumption fund. This again exerted inflationary pressures but also induced a swift proliferation of small-scale, consumption-oriented investments in light industry, diverting resources away from investment in more upstream projects necessary for China's long-term industrial development. These investments were fueled not only by the traditional "investment hunger," as the package reformers would have it, but also by a "softening" of the "bank constraint" (ibid., 13).

A survey among factory directors showed that they faced a hardened fiscal constraint but had access to lax bank lending. This soft bank constraint, the System Reform Institute argued, posed an even greater danger than Kornai's soft budget constraint. In a very Keynesian fashion, the System Reform Institute study states,

> [T]he banks possess unlimited power to create money.... Nowadays, it has become common practice for enterprises to pay bonuses and welfare expenses from their own funds and carry on construction projects on borrowed funds. The profit retained by the enterprise is mainly earmarked for consumption, which generates additional investment demand through the accelerator mechanism. The resulting effects—a shortfall in productive investments ... in turn exert a two-pronged pressure on bank financing, compelling the banks to grant loans and finally compelling the central bank to issue currency.
>
> *(ibid., 14)*

In the analysis of the System Reform Institute researchers, this accelerating process of bank lending was underlying the inflationary tendency in the mid-1980s. To overcome this upward pressure on the general price level, however, it would not be enough to simply rely on indirect macroeconomic control of the kind that the package reformers prescribed. The effectiveness of such indirect control was determined by the state of the microeconomic base, the System Reform Institute study argued (ibid., 27–28). Such indirect macrocontrol was thus not suited to prepare for reform but could only be developed by reforming the microeconomic base. The interviews with enterprise mangers had shown that imposing fiscal constraints did not work to harden the budget constraint when they had access to practically unlimited bank lending. But, just as James Tobin had argued at the boat conference, they suggested that monetary policy was also relatively ineffective under Chinese specific conditions. The soft banking constraint was in the nature of the Chinese banking system at the time and could not easily be overcome by reducing money supply, since money was endogenously created.

The underlying force driving prices up, the System Reform Institute researchers found, was an overexpansion in wages and small-scale, consumption-oriented investment in the light industry that was enabled by the banks' money creation.

Thus, to ensure reform as well as the foundations for long-term development, which required large-scale coordinated investments in heavy and chemical industries, infrastructure, and so on, some of China's most radical reformers argued for a temporary recentralization. Wages had to be recontrolled, investment priorities had to be imposed, and bank lending had to be curbed by planning (ibid., 19). In the meantime, the introduction of a labor market and capital market should be pursued gradually such as to establish competitive constraints on excessive wage and investment expansion (ibid., 19–27). Once those market constraints were in operation, the temporary recentralization could be relieved.

In parallel to this partial recentralization, the System Reform Institute authors maintained, the dual-track price system should be transformed into contracting fixed quotas to the enterprises rather than adjusting the quotas regularly based on the enterprises' output, as was the policy when they conducted their survey. A fixed quota would ensure that profitability considerations for investment decisions were internalized, and the enterprises would be made responsible for their long-term development. As the enterprises grew beyond the fixed quota, they became ever more reliant on the market, a process facilitated by the gradual expansion of the labor and capital markets (Diao, 1987, 45–46).

This fixed-quota approach, which kept the size of the plan constant and encouraged the enterprises to grow into the market, was at the heart of the System Reform Institute's reform strategy. They posed this as an alternative to the package reform approach. The "readjustment of prices" promoted as the first step in the "big push" was rejected as necessarily arbitrary. Such a price readjustment should be prepared by calculations, argued the proponents of package reform. The System Reform Institute researchers held against this, arguing that those calculations must be based on a static analysis of the situation at one point in time. Only by looking at a "frozen" image of the economy could a complete set of prices be calculated. However, as a result of China's ongoing reform efforts, China's economic system was evolving dynamically. In essence, such a price adjustment would mean a forced return to the old, unified system of 'irrational' planned prices, initially. The System Reform Institute study recommended instead to "lift control step by step," depending on the specific conditions of each commodity (ibid., 45).

When it became clear, in early 1986, that Zhao Ziyang was actively considering taking a "big step" in price reform, the System Reform Institute researchers faced a political dilemma. On the one hand, their political influence was built on being "Zhao's Institute." On the other hand, their extensive research was making them ever more aware of the dangers of a rapid reform of the prices of raw materials and other key inputs. Although they were not challenging Zhao publicly, a fierce debate arose among China's reform economists, who agreed on marketization as the direction to take but violently disagreed on *how* to reform.[36]

Wang Xiaoqiang was most articulate in his critique of the big bang (Bai, 2016; Lu, 2016; Zhang M., 2016; Wang, 2016). Alarmed by the dangers involved in pursuing such a shock approach, Wang personally went to the home of Zhao's

Senior Secretary Bao Tong in early 1986. Bao Tong held Wang in high regard and welcomed the opportunity to discuss the next step in reform with him (Li, 2016). Wang warned of the high risks and low prospects of success of taking the planned "big step" in price reform, hoping to influence Zhao Ziyang through his trusted secretary. Wang also directly raised his concerns in discussions with the proponents of the Program Office's plan (Wang, 2017). Wang (2017) pointed out that his argument against the big bang was very simple:

> There is no question that enterprise reform is a very slow process. But if you cannot have a big bang in enterprise reform, you cannot succeed with a big bang in price reform.

Wang's basic point is that China's major industrial enterprises, at that time, were still socialist production units that formed a part of the state planning apparatus. They were not set up to respond to price signals, and they were, by design, monopolists or oligopolists. These enterprises had been created not to compete with other enterprises but to implement orders from higher-level planners. Given this institutional structure, liberalizing prices would not result in prices converging to equilibrium. There were also no forces in place that would sustain calculated equilibrium prices, no matter how correct those prices might be. Under the given institutional arrangement, giving up price control could not create equal competition, as the proponents of a big bang promised. Horizontal links between producers were only emerging under the dual-track price system. Most transactions between providers and customers were handled by the administrative distribution system, and enterprises often did not even know their suppliers or customers.[37]

Wang cautioned that this system was built on administrative relations with administratively set prices and was not prepared to adjust to market signals—no matter whether they were "correct" or "distorted." Furthermore, Wang pointed out that the state-owned enterprises could not fire workers and could not go bankrupt. Wang put forward an argument, like that presented by Kornai at the Athens Conference, on price responsiveness. If the prices of inputs such as basic raw materials were rising as a result of upward adjustments of prices or liberalization while the budget constraint was hardened—as the package reformers recommended—enterprises had no other choice but to use their monopoly position and also raise their output prices. Wang warned that under China's given institutional structure, this was the only way for enterprises to generate sufficient revenues to pay the wages of their workers. Since there was no competition, more downstream enterprises would pay those higher prices, and they would hand down the price increase to consumers for the same reasons. The result would thus be inflation and not perfect competition or equilibrium (ibid.). Under China's given institutional arrangements, Wang argued, liberalizing prices of industrial goods in short supply—with or without prior price adjustments—would result in accelerating inflation, undermining the foundations of reform.

This debate was not an academic argument in which the proponents of "one decisive step" in price reform would have been prepared to be convinced by the challenges to their plan based on empirical facts or theoretical analysis—or vice versa. It was, rather, a battle over influence on China's leaders. As has been derived, the package reform approach drew on the insights of Eastern European reform economists and the lessons they drew from their countries' reform attempts. The System Reform Institute, for their part, decided to see for themselves what China could learn from the frequently referenced cases of Hungary and Yugoslavia, applying their methods of on-the-ground investigation (Zhang, 2008, 261).

In late 1984, Chen Yizi had met Márton Tardos, one of the architects of the Hungarian New Economic Mechanism of 1968 and at the time head of the Department for Economic Mechanism under the Institute of Economics of the Hungarian Academy of Science, during the latter's visit to China (Chen, 2013, 348). Tardos told Chen that his friend George Soros had great interest in China's reforms and would like to invite a Chinese delegation. Soros, according to Tardos, was dissatisfied with the course Hungary's reforms were taking and thought that change in a big country such as China could attract greater attention from the world than a small country such as his native Hungary (ibid.). Soros's hope might have been that if China pushed ahead with radical market reforms, that would "break the dike" and create an opening for other socialist countries to follow. He Weiling, an old friend of Chen Yizi who was studying in the US, reiterated Soros's invitation until the System Reform Institute leadership finally decided to take up this opportunity (ibid.).[38]

From May until mid-June 1986, a delegation under the leadership of Gao Shangquan, the head of the Program Office, with Chen Yizi and Wang Xiaoqiang as deputies, visited Hungary and Yugoslavia, sponsored by George Soros (ibid., CESRRI, 1987; Zhang, 2008, 261; see Illustration 4 of meeting with Soros in Hungary). Members of the delegation included not only the heads of several departments of the System Reform Institute, but also Ma Kai, the director of the Beijing City Price Bureau (Vice Premier from 2013 to 2018); Lu Mai (today, secretary general of the China Development Research Foundation) of the State Council's Rural Development Research Center, sent on behalf of Wang Qishan (today, vice president); Li Jiange, of the State Council's Technological and Social Development Research Center, who was a coauthor with Wu Jinglian, Zhou Xiaochuan, and Lou Jiwei and seen as a proponent of package reform; Zhao Ming of the State Planning Committee; and others (ibid.; Bai, 2016; Lu, 2016).

They held 111 discussion meetings in Hungary and Yugoslavia with the countries' leaders of reform programs from the government, the party, and academia, with representatives of enterprises and government departments affected by the reform, to study the "friction, contradictions, and the general problematic areas that emerged in the transition from an old to a new system" (Gao et al., 1987, 15).[39] Among their discussion partners were, for example, several vice prime ministers, the "father of Hungary's economic reforms" Reszö Nyers, Soros himself, economists Tardos and Kornai, as well as high-ranking planners (Chen, 2013, 349).

ILLUSTRATION 4   Wang Xiaoqiang meets George Soros in Hungary, 1986. Wang
Xiaoqiang (left, standing) greets George Soros on behalf of the
System Reform Institute in the center. Courtesy of Wang Xiaoqiang.

On the most basic level, the delegation brought home the lesson that the
Hungarian and Yugoslav leaders stressed that reform was a "difficult gradual process
in which it was impossible to reach a goal in one step" (ibid., 16). Hungary had been
reforming for twenty years and Yugoslavia for forty years, and the final breakthrough
had still not been achieved. Reform was a unique historical process and could only
be approached as such (ibid.). This message of the reform leadership ran counter
to the interpretation of academic economists such as Brus, Šik, Kornai, and others.
Rather than suggesting that gradual reform must fail, those operationally in charge
of reform in Hungary and Yugoslavia saw gradual reform as the only possible way.
From the viewpoint of the reform practitioners, there was no alternative to gradual
reform. All attempts they had launched in trying to pursue reform in a big push
had failed. This finding questioned the logic of any "one decisive step" on the most
fundamental level. At the same time, the investigations in Hungary and Yugoslavia
showed specifically that the "one decisive step" in price reform that China was then
preparing was more likely to bring difficulties than a reform breakthrough.

The investigation was structured in an open-ended way, open to the point
that Zhou Xincheng, a professor of the People's University of China, asked Chen
Yizi why they were starting the investigation from such basic questions (Chen,
2013, 349). This open process of investigation generated decisive evidence for
the System Reform Institute's warning against pushing ahead with price liberalizations in China.

The survey showed that both Hungary and Yugoslavia had gone through a "golden age" of reform that closely resembled the initial reform years in China (Gao et al., 1989, 85–86; Wang 2017). When enterprises had first been granted greater autonomy and the prices of processing and consumer goods industries were largely liberalized, while the prices of raw materials and energy remained controlled at a low level, the profit motive served to generate very high growth. When it was at that stage, Yugoslavia was even propelled to rank third in the world, in terms of growth rates from 1956 to 1964 (ibid.). The pre-reform industrial structure had been skewed toward heavy industry. This provided the foundation for a rapid growth of light industry. Light industry quickly became a highly competitive sector, thanks to its low investment requirements and high turnover rate. Traditionally, high prices of industrial consumer goods made processing industries very profitable, while high demand was the result of years of chronic shortages (ibid., Wang, 1998, 34–35). Thus, industry was growing rapidly, and living standards were rising at a high pace.

This simple combination of price liberalization and profit incentives proved insufficient, however, as a reform approach for the more capital- and technology–intensive, large-scale heavy and extracting industries. The high investment requirements and degree of concentration, long gestation periods, and central position in the distribution system of the planned economy led to these basic industries being inflexible in their response to the market (Gao et al., 1989, 86). The supply elasticity for critical inputs such as energy and raw materials was very low, while at the same time the demand of the industries processing these inputs was also relatively inelastic. In the absence of the possibility to go bankrupt, all enterprises had to keep running, buying inputs and selling their outputs at whatever price allowed them to pay the wages of their workers (Wang, 1998, 14–15). With the demanders and suppliers unable to adjust to the price signals, both Hungary and Yugoslavia experienced that liberalizing the prices for these critical goods did not adjust their industrial structure. They entered an "inflationary spiral in which commodity prices and wages [took] turns going upward" (ibid., 85).

As Kornai had pointed out to the Chinese delegation in his analysis of the Hungarian experience, the result of an upward adjustment of the prices of production goods would be a reversion to the initial relative prices at a higher general price level. Due to the inelasticity of supply of producer goods, more or less the same quantity would be offered at the higher price, thus increasing the input costs for the processing industries. The processing industries, in turn, would hand down the price increases to the consumers. During the "golden age" of reform, workers had become accustomed to higher living standards and would now react to price rises by demanding higher wages. The lesson the delegation drew from the Hungarian and Yugoslav experience was directly opposed to the recommendation that the package reformers had drawn from the writings of Eastern European reform economists. As a result of one "big step" in price reform, the delegation warned, the economy would enter into a spiral of price and wage hikes endangering its internal stability and external competitiveness (ibid., 87–88).

A Warning to Zhao Ziyang

The delegation sent back a telegram to Zhao Ziyang with their warning (Bai, 2016; Chen, 2013, 251; Wang, 2017). The survey of the two socialist pioneers of economic reforms showed that the result of a big bang in producer goods prices would be inflation and a threat to social stability (ibid., Zhang, 2008, 262). What was required for China to move toward a market economy was a slow and complicated process of "reindustrialization" turning the socialist factories from subordinate production units into competitive enterprises (Wang, 1998, 24–25; Wang, 2017). A big bang in price reform would, however, endanger the institutional foundations for such a gradual reform.

The telegram carried great weight, both because it came from Zhao's trusted young economists and because it was based on historical experience and a clear analysis. More critically, the leader of the delegation and main signatory of the telegram, Gao Shangquan (Gao Shangquan, 1987), was also the leader of the Program Office (Lu, 2016; Wu, 2016). The Program Office had been established to draw up a plan for a big push in price reform, combined with wage and tax reform, that would have resembled the first step of shock therapy. Now, the reform cadre, who had been put in charge to spearhead this program for a "decisive step," had come around to warning the leadership not to implement this same plan (Lu, 2016; Wang, 2017). On the second day after the delegation's return to Beijing in mid-June, they met Zhao Ziyang (Chen, 2013, 351–352). In all their interactions with him, they had never seen Zhao in such a state of despair (Wang, 2017).

Shortly before receiving the delegation, Zhao had met with the senior reform officials and economists An Zhiwen, Ma Hong, Tian Jiyun, and Yao Yilin for a two-day discussion on the Program Office's plan (Fang, 2004; Zhao, 2016m). Ma Hong expounded his view on the basic dilemma they faced. There were two plans for price adjustments of raw materials. One was a large plan with price adjustments to the levels that had been calculated as equilibrium prices. This involved an estimated cost of 60 billion RMB for subsidies to compensate enterprises and citizens for the price rises. A smaller plan, estimated to cost 30 billion RMB, would entail only smaller adjustments. Those at the Program Office, with whom Ma Hong basically agreed, argued there was no point in implementing the smaller plan, since the reason for the adjustment was to prepare for liberalization, which would require the calculated adjustments. The finance department, however, held against this that all the economy could handle was the smaller plan. Yao Yilin agreed with Ma Hong, recommending the larger plan (Fang, 2004, 72; Zhang, 2017, 547).

In contrast, An Zhiwen, who had previously supported package reform, cautioned that the plan should be reevaluated prudently. An made clear that he was not alone with this view. He reported that there was great anxiety within the System Reform Commission about the Programme Office's plan. An added, the closer comrades were to practical work, the greater their worries about this plan. But, An pointed out, warnings were not limited to officials in charge of economic work. Li Yining, one of Chinese leading theoretical economists, had also cautioned that price reform could not bring about a success in system reform (Fang, 2004, 73, 79; Zhang, 2017, 547).

Zhao Ziyang, too, brought up several objections and alternative plans that had been raised to him (Fang, 2004, 73). This included Hua Sheng's plan for an asset management responsibility system, which Zhao, however, criticized as too idealistic and impractical. Zhao's greatest concern regarding the Program Office's plan was its prospects of success. The key question, in Zhao's eyes, was not that there were risks involved, but to gauge the advantages of a realistic outcome of this plan. The short-term costs and risks of the plan could be handled, but if it could not actually deliver a breakthrough for reform, it had to be discarded (Fang, 2004, 77).

Before meeting with the delegation, Zhao was already at the tipping point in his decision, pondering his doubts about the long-term benefits of package reform. The delegation to Hungary and Yugoslavia now delivered a thorough assessment of the prospects for success of the "big step" in price reform, based on the concrete lessons of the two countries with the greatest experience in socialist reform. The delegation concluded that experience proved that the plan was not suited to deliver a breakthrough in economic system reform and was likely to do more harm than good. The findings of the survey in Hungary and Yugoslavia, which delivered a clear, experience-based answer to Zhao's question regarding the prospects for success, were critical in convincing Zhao to stop the plan for overnight price liberalization that he had pushed with all his political capital (Bai, 2016; Chen, 2013, 352; Lu and Feng, 2012, 40).

If any further evidence regarding the uncertainty about the advantages of rapid liberalization, especially of key input prices, was required, it was furnished by the visit to Beijing of the West German economist Hans-Karl Schneider in October 1986. As I have described, besides the Eastern European experience, a second important historical reference, first promoted by Friedman and frequently cited by the Chinese proponents of a big bang, was the so-called "Erhard Miracle."

Schneider, a West German ordoliberal who had completed his PhD with a dissertation on price determination in the gas sector inspired by Walter Eucken, was then-chair of the German Council of Economic Experts and could count among his credentials that he had worked in the 1950s under Ludwig Erhard in the West German ministry for economic affairs (Loeffler, 2002, 78). During his visit to China, Schneider warned vigorously against rapid liberalization of the prices of energy and raw material that were still in short supply. He stressed that these prices were not deregulated as part of Erhard's overnight liberalization after the war in West Germany. Steel and coal remained subject to price control until the 1970s (Cheng, 2006, 97; Zhao, 2016l, 460).

Schneider reiterated a warning that the Swiss ordoliberal Wilhelm (Willy) Linder of the University of Zürich had delivered to China's leading reformers a month earlier. Linder had cautioned against the same ripple effect that the survey in Hungary and Yugoslavia pointed to and suggested, based on the West German experience, that prices of production goods should only be liberalized when supply was no longer short of demand (Zhang, 2017, 553–554). This debunked the reading of the Erhard Miracle by Milton Friedman and his Chinese followers. As we have seen, Friedman infamously pronounced, during his first visit to China, that the Erhard Miracle was a very simple thing that produced more-or-less instant success. Linder and Schneider, with the authority of detailed knowledge of the West German case, now warned that Erhard's price reform did not involve the liberalization of the prices of essential production inputs such as energy. This must have added to Zhao's doubts about the benefits of the short-term pain he had been about to impose on the Chinese economy.

Conclusion

By the late summer of 1986, what had started under the label "coordinated, comprehensive package reform" was watered down to an adjustment of only the important and symbolic price of steel, combined with a partial tax and financial reform. In the fall, the last remnants of the shock treatment were condemned (Cheng, 2006, 95–96; Zhang S., 2017, 548–550). On September 15, 1986, in a speech at Peking University on "Comparing the Two Schools of Reform Thought" (两种改革思路的比较), Li Yining (1988) reiterated his warning that price reform would not solve the challenge of economic system reform. He stressed once more the dire propects for success.

The decisive question remained, of whether a chance for succcess of the Program's Offices plan for price liberalization warranted the uncertain effects on the overall price level and the economy as a whole. Zhao consulted An Zhiwen once more for his evaluation of competing inflation estimates. An admitted that it was impossible to calculate the ripple effect of a price increase—even if it was for only one price, that of steel. The only experience China had was the adjustment of textile prices (see Chapter 6), but textiles were a semifinished product, so it was much easier to foresee the resulting inflation. In contrast, for an indispensable upstream product in short supply such as steel, An pointed out, it was out of the question to predict the impact of a sudden price increase on the general price level (Zhang, 2017, 550–551).

In 1986, China narrowly escaped a big bang. Confronted with diverse, authoritative warnings about the unforeseeable risks of imposing the shock of price reform and the uncertainty about its benefits, Zhao Ziyang ultimately gave up on package reform. This plan had appeared like a comprehensive solution in theory, but it proved infeasible in practice. Zhao came around to arguing that the basic challenge of economic reform was enlivening enterprises.

This, Zhao realized, could not be achieved in parallel with a radical price reform that endangered the stability of economy and society while bearing little prospect for success (Cheng, 2006, 97; Zhang S., 2017, 550). The first, most shocking element of shock therapy, overnight price liberalization, was aborted. Instead, the reform approach of marketization from the margins prevailed that left the core of the old industrial system in place but froze its size. At a meeting in January 1985, Wang Xiaoqiang and Song Guoqing had presented enterprise reform with output-contracting at its core to Zhao Ziyang in a discussion of the Seventh Five-Year Plan (Liu, 2010, 396-7). A full-scale contract responsibility system enhancing the dual-track price system, along the lines proposed in the 1985 System Reform Institute survey, was now implemented (Brødsgaard and Rutten, 2017, 82). For the time being this settled the fierce contestation among China's competing reform economists in favor of gradually growing into the market. But the struggle over China's reform approach was by no means over.

Notes

1 I use *grow into the market* rather than *grow out of the plan* (Byrd, 1988; Naughton, 1995) because the most important aspect of the dual-track system was not the decline in absolute terms of the plan share, but the growth in absolute terms of the market share. The process of change was, in the first instance, growing into the market without yet changing the plan. Because China's economy at the time was growing at high rates, the growth of the market share did not necessarily have to be at the expense of the planned economy in order for the market to increase its relative importance rapidly. Thus, this terminological reversal from *growing out of the plan* to *growing into the market* stresses that growth and development drove reform in the early years.

2 Overall real GNP grew from 4.5 percent in 1981, the year of the first major retrenchment of the reform period, to 14.7 percent in 1984 and 12.8 percent in 1985 (Naughton, 1995, 329). Growth of the industrial sector surpassed 15 percent in 1984 and 20 percent in 1985 (Zinser, 1991, 113).

3 My interview partners, despite their fierce disagreements regarding the right approach to reform, agreed nonetheless that the decisive controversy at the time was over the question of how to reform, not whether or not to reform. On this point also see Zhang S. (2017, 440, 530).

4 The conference symposium states: "The conference has witnessed an unusual event, an intervention at an IEA conference by a Chinese economist" (Csikós-Nagy et al., 1984, 530).

5 See Hirschman (1985, 71–72) for a list of other cases where hyperinflation has preceded regime change, including Brazil in 1964, Ghana and Indonesia in 1966, Chile in 1973, and Argentina in 1975.

6 For an analysis of this "actor-network" from a Latourian perspective, see also Bockman and Eyal (2002).

7 The first major research report was published in China's leading social science journal 中国社会科学 in 1984, titled "On the Question of the Target Model for China's Economic System Reform" (关于我国经济体制改革的目标模式问题). It was edited by Liu Guoguang and drew on research conducted under his leadership by the Economic Systems Research Group at the Economics Institute of CASS jointly with Cheng Jiyuan, Rong Jingben, and Wu Jinglian. The basic logic in this and subsequent studies arguing for a target model for reform was that first, the macroeconomy had to

be balanced and then, all economic leverages had to be deregulated to ensure flexible adjustment and overcome distortions. See Zhang S. (2017, 531–37) for an overview of this research project.

8 For a detailed discussion of the role of the so-called Erhard Miracle in China's reform debate, see Weber (2020b, 2021).

9 The stress on macroeconomic tightening was in part a response to Zhu Jiaming's forceful argument that China's high growth and relatively high rate of inflation, compared with that of previous periods, was not a sign of "overheating" but resulted from China's transformation from an essentially nonmonetary economy to a monetary economy, which involved a process of deep change that could not be grasped by the static analysis of most of modern mainstream economics (Zhu, 2016; Zhu, 1989 (English translation of Chinese 1985 original; the same issue of *Chinese Economic Studies* also contains translations of other important contributions to the debate on "overheating").

10 Joseph Dodge, "a Detroit banker of liberal views" (Galbraith, 1981, 251–252), joined the American economists Raymond Goldsmith and Gerhard Colm to derive a plan for currency reform in Germany, which—more or less by historical accident—was later credited to Ludwig Erhard (Hagemann, 1999). Dodge went on to Japan to become the "Financial Adviser to the Supreme Commander for the Allied Powers" (Thorsten and Sugita, 1999, 297). In this capacity, he imposed strict austerity measures on the Japanese postwar economy (ibid.).

11 For an English translation of this article, see Guo Shuqing (2012b), which I henceforth reference.

12 For an English translation of this article, see (Guo et al., 2012), which I henceforth reference.

13 The transcription of Lou Jiwei's lecture on the 1985 program office in September 2011 was provided to the author by Peng Xiaomeng.

14 The second convener was Gong Zhuming. Other participants included Xu Meizheng, Jia Heting, Li Hong, and Wang Qin (Guo et al., 2012, 28; Luo, 2011).

15 The lead author of the report drafted in June 1985 was Guo Shuqing (Guo et al., 2012, 28). The report was published in March 1986 (Research Group for an Overall Plan, 1986).

16 The participants considered for this meeting included Goodhart as a central banker, Giersch from the Institute of International Economics in Kiel, Gutowski (who had visited China as a government advisor in 1979 (Kulke, 2007; Merklein, 1980), Tobin, Schultz, Meade, and Mason (Wood, 1985). Gewirtz (2017), who places the Bashan Conference at the center of his narrative, suggests with regard to the list of invitees that Lim had "immediately thought of his friend Cairncross" (139). However, Cairncross is not included in Adrian Wood's notes. Evidence from the Cairncross papers at the University of Glasgow (file DC106/2/14) furthermore shows that Cairncross was first approached by Edwin Lim's brother Cyril Lin, not Lim himself. More importantly, Gewirtz writes, "Lim was committed to expanding beyond economists with backgrounds in socialist countries," whereas it becomes apparent from Wood's notes that this was not Lim's personal commitment but rather the result of joint consultation with the Chinese counterparts. There are several other infelicities in Gewirtz's account. For example, Gewirtz (2017) writes, "In 1982, several of the same economists [now participating in the Bashan Conference], including Xue Muqiao, Wu Jinglian, and Zhao Renwei, had participated in the much smaller World Bank conference with Eastern Euro" (330). However, as we saw Chapter 5, Wu Jinglian opted not to participate in the conference (Lim, 2016; Wu, 2016; Wood 2016).

17 In 2015, a high-profile event was hosted by the China Economic System Reform Research Association, the National Development and Reform Commission and the World Bank to celebrate the thirtieth anniversary of the conference.

18 Tobin had previously visited China together with John Kenneth Galbraith and Wassily Leontief in September 1972, just seven months after Nixon's visit. Galbraith

was, at the time, president of the American Economics Association, and Leontief and Tobin joined the delegation as predecessors (Galbraith, 1973, 3–4; Tobin, 1973).

19 The other international experts were Michel Albert, the former director of the French national planning authority; Leroy Jones, an American Korea expert; and Kobayashi, a board member of the Industrial Bank of Japan, (China Economic System Reform Research Conference, 1986; Liu, 2009b).

20 Luo Xiaopeng was the only participant formerly from the Rural Development Group. He and his collaborators, in particular Hua Sheng, cooperated with the World Bank in their research on enterprise reform (Luo, 2017).

21 For Cairncross's role in the post–World War II transition in the United Kingdom, see Chapter 3. Cairncross had previously visited China in 1979 as part of a British Academy Mission (Cairncross, 1979, 1998, 282–287).

22 On the question of whether Kornai was or was not two-faced, also see my review of Gewirtz (2017) for the *China Quarterly* (Weber, 2019, 2021).

23 This ambiguity in the attitude of Zhao Ziyang to reform was pointed out to the author by many interview partners.

24 For details of the institutional setup of the Program Office, see Fewsmith (1994, 185), Hua, Zhang, and Luo (1993, 133), and Zhang S. (2017, 539–543). Zhang points out that the role of Wu Jinglian in the Fanganban has frequently been overstated (ibid.).

25 When the Program Office was in operation in 1986, Guo Shuqing was a visiting scholar in Oxford. At the Bashan Conference, Lim had approached Cairncross to arrange a stay for Guo in Oxford (Cairncross, 1985). Guo became the pioneer participant of an Economics Training Program for young Chinese officials sponsored by the Ford Foundation and the United Nations Development Program and run by Cyril Lin under Cairncross's patronship (Chen Xindong, 2013, 2016).

26 Two further articles published that year and arguing along similar lines were, for example, Zhou Shulian (1986) and Dai Yuanchen (1986). Dai Yuanchen was an important contributor to the 1950s and 1960s law of value debates and challenged the accounting interpretation. See Brødsgaard and Rutten (2017, 43) and Lin (1981, 27).

27 The authenticity of this transcript was confirmed to the author by Edwin Lim.

28 Zhou Qiren and Luo Xiaopeng were among those who, after the founding of the CESRRI and the termination of the Rural Development Group, moved on to the the State Council's Rural Development Research Centre, which was headed by Du Runsheng (Luo, 2017; Zhou, 2016). Hua Sheng and He Jiacheng were at the CASS Economic Research Institute (Hua, 2016). Zhang Weiying had joined the CESRRI after the Moganshan Youth Conference, but his position on ownership was in conflict with that of the institute's leadership (Zhang M., 2016; Wang, 2017).

29 For an English translation, see Hua Sheng, He Jiacheng, Zhang Xuejun, Luo Xiaopeng, and Bian Yongzhuang (1987).

30 For an English translation, see Wang Xiaoqiang and Ji Xiaoming (1988).

31 Li Yining's speech was presented on April 25, 1986, and published on May 19 in *Beijing Daily* (Li, 1986) and later in a collection of essays, which Peng Xiaomeng edited in parallel with a collection of the competing writings of Wu Jinglian and his collaborators (Li, 1989; Peng, 2016; Wu and Zhou, 1989).

32 For an English translation, see Li Yining (2014).

33 Translation as in Fewsmith (1994, 186).

34 Wang Xiaoqiang and Zhang Gang reported that

> With participation from 21 units, including ministries, research institutes, and colleges and universities, the investigation employed a work force of 447 people including statisticians and college undergraduates and postgraduates. Fourteen million data were collected and 156 reports totaling 1.3 million words were written in the investigation.
>
> *(1987, xxv)*

35 The study was translated into English in Reynolds (1987a). All references henceforth will be to the English edition. Reynolds became acquainted with Chen Yizi, Wang Xiaoqiang, and Cao Yuanzheng at a conference with influential Chinese, American, and European scholars held at the Ardenhouse Conference Center, in New York, in October 1986, sponsored by the Ford and Rockefeller foundations to review China's economic reforms. Impressed with the high quality of analysis and the wealth of data of this survey, Bruce Reynolds edited the translation (Cao, 2016; Reynolds, 1988).

36 This debate, at times, also set apart economists within the CESRRI—in particular, with regard to the question of ownership reform.

37 On this point, see also Wang Xiaoqiang (1998, 38–39).

38 Soros's support of this delegation was important for the course China's reform took. The collaboration between the CESRRI and Soros that evolved from this visit in 1986 soon showed the difference in agenda, however. In 1987, the Fund for Reform and Opening of China (改革开放基金会), which Soros had set up to fund projects in China, moved its support to the China International Cultural Exchange Foundation in Beijing (Keyser, 2003, 78). Soros found that his Chinese counterparts behaved too much like bureaucrats aiming to serve the government (Li, 2016). Nevertheless, acceptance of these foreign funds was one of the accusations raised against Zhao Ziyang, Bao Tong, and Chen Yizi in the context of the crackdown on the 1989 Tiananmen movement (Keyser, 2003, 78–79).

39 Translation as in Gao Shangquan, Chen Yizi, and Wang Xiaoqiang (1989), a partial translation of the report

8

ESCAPING SHOCK THERAPY

Causes and Consequences of the 1988 Inflation

When discussing the question of price reform Deng Xiaoping said: "We have to take a big risk here, but we can accomplish it. ... We have to take the possibility of big risks as our starting point and prepare countermeasures from the outset. This way, even if we face a major hazard, the heavens will not fall."

(People's Daily, June 4, 1988a, p. 1)

Introduction

In 1986, wholesale price liberalization was debunked by reform economists who believed in marketization but opposed a big bang. After Zhao Ziyang gave up on the reform blueprint, his program in 1987 and early 1988 was to combine enterprise contracting with a new coastal-development strategy. This constituted an internationalized version of gradual marketization from the margins and the dual-track system. But in the early summer of 1988, radical price reform suddenly became the agenda of the day. China once more came within a hair's breadth of a big bang. This time, the cost was dramatic. For the first time since the 1940s, inflation spiraled out of control. People across the country reacted to the announcements of a big push in price reform with panic buying, bank runs, and local protests, in an unprecedented popular backlash against market reforms. The Chinese leadership had no choice but to halt the plans for price liberalization in the fall of 1988. Instead of pushing through with price reform, austerity and retrenchment became the order of the day.

The events of 1988 and 1989 led up to the imprisonment or exile of many protagonists of reform, some of whom I have interviewed. A number of the reform economists who emerged relatively unharmed from the turmoil were quick to come up with their interpretations of the events of 1988. Conversely, many of those exiled abroad, imprisoned, or withdrawn into private business had difficulties making their stories heard.

Confronted with various conflicting accounts and with little reliable evidence at hand, it is hard to make sense of the precise dynamic of the 1988 breaking point of reform. With this caveat in mind, I present here my reading of China's escape from shock therapy in 1988. The synthesis of my thoughts is based on the wide-ranging interviews I conducted. My account cannot be attributed to any single one of my interviewees. Given the politically charged nature of the events in 1988, I have decided to not include references to individual interviews in this chapter but to instead exclusively refer to published material.

China's painful escape from a big bang in 1988 is part of the larger background to the uprisings and the massacre on Tiananmen Square. English-language literature basically presents two interpretations for why radical price reform was attempted in 1988. One stresses the importance of Deng Xiaoping. According to this account, Deng personally took initiative and pushed for price reform, anxious to achieve a reform breakthrough before his powers would become frail.[1] The other interpretation emphasizes the policy advice presented to Zhao Ziyang by a delegation to Latin America, who allegedly suggested that inflation was not to be feared. By that account, the delegation's policy advice led to a bold move on price reform.[2] This interpretation resonates with the widespread sentiment among intellectuals in China's 1990s—which was also prevalent among the 1980s package reformers—that Western science constitutes the only legitimate source of knowledge (Wang, 2011, 43). It appears, from this perspective, that the deeper reason for the mistake was to follow the example of a "backward" country.

These two interpretations roughly coincide with the explanations provided by economists who were competing over the right market reform approach in the 1980s. For example, Chen Yizi (2013, 512–15) and Zhu Jiaming (2013, 44) stress that Deng Xiaoping initiated the attempt to push through with price reform, and Zhao Ziyang had to follow. In contrast, Wu Jinglian (2005, 368; Wu and Ma, 2016, 216) argues that Zhao Ziyang took the lead and followed the advice of the delegation to Latin America that was headed by Zhu Jiaming and Chen Yizi. It will probably have to wait until historians have access to the relevant archives before this matter can be settled.

I aim to take both interpretations into account. On balance, my reading is closer to the first interpretation. But rather than focusing on Deng Xiaoping individually, I situate the decision to implement wholesale price reform in the context of the clash among China's political leadership at the time and the increasing social tensions resulting from marketization. I therefore begin by laying out the political impasse that reform had reached in late 1987. The previous chapters in this book show that by 1988, China's reformers had been grappling with the question of price reform for about a decade. This is important in interpreting Deng's impatience in 1988. Furthermore, I have derived how the question of price reform divided China's reform economists broadly in two camps: those arguing for gradual marketization from the margins under the dual-track system and those promoting wholesale price liberalization in one package. Understanding the formation and intellectual orientation of these groups provides important background in considering competing interpretations of the looming inflation and corruption that led to the spiral out of control in the summer of 1988.

Impasse of Reform

To understand the course of events in the summer of 1988, we must begin by considering the broad political constellation. The Thirteenth Party Congress, in October 1987, marked a consolidation of China's market reform agenda. It unleashed an increasing tension between reformers such as Zhao Ziyang and Deng Xiaoping, who were prepared to do whatever it would take to reform China's economic system, and leaders such as Chen Yun, who thought that reform should not overrule the primacy of socialist planning. As I discussed in Chapter 4, the beginning of China's reform era was underpinned by a reevaluation of historical progress. Under Mao, revolution was conceptualized as a continuous political struggle. Establishing socialist relations of production was perceived both as a goal in itself and as a means to achieve material development. In contrast, under reform, economic development became the all-encompassing goal, and social relations of production were evaluated based on how much they contributed to achieving this goal—largely independent of how socialist they were. The development of the forces of production was from this point forward China's foremost project. When the fight over the boundaries of reform among China's leaders was mounting in the second half of the 1980s, the old debate over the nature of China's socialism and the role of economic development was revived. The Thirteenth Party Congress settled this debate in favor of economic reform at all costs (Schram, 1988).

Zhao Ziyang, who later became General Secretary, proclaimed in his political report to the Party Congress,

> with the productive forces lagging far behind those of the developed capitalist countries we are destined to go through a very long primary stage. During this stage, we shall accomplish industrialization and the commercialization, socialization, and modernization of production which many other countries have achieved under capitalist conditions.
>
> *(Zhao, 1987)*

Zhao spelled out what being in the primary stage of socialism should mean in terms of the party's agenda:

> Whatever is conducive to the growth [of the productive forces] is in keeping with the fundamental interests of the people and is therefore needed by socialism and allowed to exist. Conversely, whatever is detrimental to

this growth goes against scientific socialism and is therefore not allowed to exist. (ibid.)

This implied a new kind of "whateverism" that contrasted sharply with that of Mao's designated successor, Hua Guofeng. Hua had famously said, in 1977, "We will resolutely uphold whatever policy decisions Chairman Mao made, and unswervingly follow whatever instructions Chairman Mao gave" (Research Department of Party Literature, 1991, 887). According to the logic proclaimed by Zhao at the Thirteenth Party Congress, as long as China was in this primary stage, defined as economic underdevelopment, everything that served economic growth should be considered necessary for socialism. This was an "anything goes" paradigm of market reforms. Versions of the concept of a primary stage of socialism had been discussed since the late 1970s. In 1979, Su Shaozhi and Feng Lanrui published an influential article arguing that China was still at a stage of "undeveloped socialism" (不发达的社会主义) (Chang, 1988; Sun, 1995, 185–186). At the time, this formulation was judged as too dismissive of China's socialism. The 1986 "Resolution on Certain Questions in the History of our Party" acknowledged that China's "socialist system [was] still in its early phase of development" but also emphasized that "China [had] undoubtedly established a socialist system and entered the stage of socialist society" (section 33). Now the concept was elevated to state doctrine. This implied that all boundaries to reform should be shattered. Throughout the "very long primary stage of socialism," China should do whatever was needed to catch up with the achievements in modern production that other countries had reached under capitalism.

Deng's perspective was fully consistent with the logic of the primary stage of socialism that Zhao had articulated at the Party Congress. Some months earlier, in April 1987, Deng had famously pronounced, in a conversation with the Czechoslovak premier,

> Poverty is not socialism. We must support socialism, but we must move ahead in building a socialism which is truly superior to capitalism. We must first rid ourselves of the socialism of poverty (pinkun shehuizhuyi); although everyone now says we are creating socialism, it is only in the middle of the next century, when we have reached the level of the moderately-developed countries, that we will be able to say with assurance that socialism is really superior to capitalism and that we are really building socialism.
>
> *(People's Daily, 1987)[3]*

In Deng's view, the sole leadership of the party had to be preserved to guide China to the stage of economic development that would allow the creation of a fuller version of socialism. This was a strict limit to the new "whateverism." But on this path, Deng found fearless market reforms necessary, even if it required unraveling core socialist institutions for the time being. In response to the first major student protests of the reform era in 1986, Deng had shown his readiness to defend the Communist state's authority by all means. Deng called upon the younger generation of political leaders—including Hu Yaobang, Zhao Ziyang, Wan Li, Li Peng, and others—that protests had to be responded to with a "firm clear-cut stand" and warned that "otherwise bourgeois liberalization will spread unchecked." Copying Western democracy was not a way forward for China, in Deng's eyes (Vogel, 2011, 579). Deng's intervention was an unmistakable message to General Secretary Hu Yaobang. Hu had been a key reform leader from the early days onward, and Hu's 1978 essay "Practice Is the Sole Criterion for Judging Truth" had laid out a foundational principle for economic reform. In 1987, Deng accused Hu of "taking a laissez-faire attitude towards bourgeois liberalization" and forced Hu to submit his resignation (Pantsov and Levine, 2015, 401). In Deng's view, China's stage of development dictated that democracy could only be considered a viable option half a century hence (Schram, 1988, 182). As much as Deng was violently opposed to Western style democracy and the separation of powers, he was dedicated to market reforms at all costs.

Deng's vision clashed with that of Chen Yun, who refused to go as far as Deng in dismantling existing state socialism (Bachman, 1986). In the second half of the 1980s, Deng's approach became dominant. Marketization had moved to the core of the urban industrial system in 1984. The full embrace of the concept of a primary stage of socialism was in sharp contrast with Chen Yun's famous "birdcage logic" (ibid., 297; Vogel, 2005). Chen Yun was an important initiator of reform in the early days. Since the revolutionary war, Chen had gained experience in using the market as a weapon in the Communists' struggle (see Chapter 3). He had a deep practical understanding of the powerful dynamic unleashed by the market. Chen thought that while the market could be used as a means, it should not become the dominant force. Although he was a reformer, Chen did not believe this action would negate the achievements of socialism to that date—as the concept of China still being in a "primary stage" implied. For Chen Yun, the market should operate within the boundaries of a socialist planned economy, like a bird flying inside a cage. In Chen's eyes, China was about to let the bird free in the late 1980s.

In the approach articulated by Zhao at the Thirteenth Party Congress, market forces were welcome to whatever extent they served economic development. Note, however, that for Zhao too, development—not marketization—was the goal. At the Thirteenth Party Congress, the market was elevated to the dominant economic mechanism, yet it was not meant to be free but to be regulated through the state. This was captured in Zhao's famous slogan: "The state intervenes in the market, and the market drives the enterprises" (Zhao, 2009, 122). The free, unfettered market was not expected to deliver development, but at the same time, some of the core economic institutions of state socialism were considered expendable in the name of economic progress. In his report to the Thirteenth Party Congress Zhao called to "speed up the establishment and cultivation of a socialist market system." This involved expanding the market to the means of production, technology, labor, and finance (Wang, 2019, 97). Including the factors of production in the commodification agenda meant a decisive step away from planning. When Zhao began to make his opening remarks at the Congress, Chen stood up and walked out. Chen, the senior leader who had guided the initial economic reforms, expressed his disapproval for everyone to see (Zhao, 2009, 122–123).

Before the Thirteenth Party Congress, revolutionary veterans who had led reform with widely varying degrees of principledness and pragmatism had announced their semiretirement. Deng Xiaoping, Chen Yun, and Li Xianian officially stepped down. But they continued to compete over defining China's path through informal channels (Pantsov and Levine, 2015, 403–404). When in 1988 reform reached an impasse, the battle among China's leadership was led by these semiretired veterans. Seeking a way out of the deadlock, Deng decided to push ahead with price reform. Hoping to defend his vision, Deng decided that the decisive task of reform was to "break through the barrier of prices" (闯价格关) (Liu, 2011).

Looming Inflation, Corruption, and Competing Reform Paradigms

The increasing political confrontation occurred when the mood in the population at large was at a tipping point. As a result of marketization, corruption was increasingly rampant. Social tensions heightened and exacerbated the clash between the two sides of China's leadership. China was experiencing high inflation by its own postrevolutionary standards even before the the summer of 1988, when inflation spiraled out of control. Output growth was high in 1987 and early 1988, at about 11 percent, but the long-standing privilege of China's urban population to access basic goods at low prices began to be threatened. The growth of the consumer price index (CPI) had reached a new height at 8.8 percent in 1985 before falling to 6 percent in 1986 as result of Chen Yun's retrenchment policies of 1985 to 1986. Inflation was back on the rise in the second half of 1987 with a year-on-year increase of the CPI of 9.1 percent in December (see Figure 8.1 for monthly price data; Geng and Zhou, 1998, 543; Vogel, 2011, 469).

State bank credit had been growing at an annual rate of 20 to 25 percent since mid-1986, far outpacing the growth of output (Naughton, 1989, 270). The question was not primarily about whether or not money was oversupplied. Instead, the question was about the drivers of this money supply and the inflationary trend. Was it a matter of central bank policy and government spending—fiscal and monetary policy in the conventional macroeconomic sense? Or was some dynamic ingrained in the workings of the economy endogenously creating money, in which case further institutional innovation, gradual rebalancing, and reform were the way out? Competing and complementary explanations for China's looming inflation in 1987 and early 1988 broadly align with the opposed reform approaches I described in previous chapters.

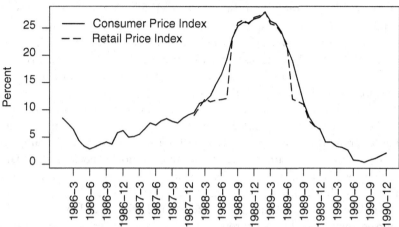

FIGURE 8.1   Inflation in China, 1986–1990. Source: Retail Price Index includes retail commodities, service products, and producer goods (Burdekin and Hu, 1999, 69, 81). Consumer Price Index as in Geng and Zhou (1998, 543).

Package reformers such as Wu Jinglian argued that inflation was the result of aggregate excess demand (Wu and Reynolds, 1988, 464) and in a monetarist fashion saw the "root cause of inflation [in] the accelerated money supply after 1986" (Wu and Ma, 2016, 217). Wu's junior collaborator Zhou Xiaochuan, later appointed governor of the People's Bank of China by Zhu Rongji, was broadly in line with the macroeconomic view that focused on fiscal and monetary policy. He unpacked what he saw as problems in the banking sector that undermined effective monetary policy. Zhou stressed that China did not yet rely on an independent central bank (Zhou and Zhu, 1987). The role of the People's Bank of China, Zhou pointed out, was to implement the State Council's credit plan, while commercial banks had to respond to direct requests by local governments and government departments. It follows, from this perspective, that money supply could be adjusted only by changing the demands of the central and local government on the banking sector. Hence, what was needed was fiscal restraint combined with banking reform toward central bank independence. Zhou's view was broadly consistent with the larger package reform paradigm that projected the economic problems of the reform process on partial reforms and a perceived insufficient separation of the state and the market.

As I have shown in previous chapters, the dual-track price system did not directly abolish the existing planning institutions. But as it took hold of the core of China's economy, it unleashed a powerful market dynamic that served to both transform and erode the existing state socialist institutions. The dual-track price system was meant to turn socialist production units into market-oriented enterprises. With it came a new logic of operation: the pursuit of profit and individual incentives. The proponents of a more shock-like form of market reforms were quick to attribute the spreading of corruption and official profiteering (官倒) to the friction between the old and the new systems inherent in the dual-track approach rather than the market per se. In fact, trying to erase the friction between the two systems by leaping to the market as Russia did turned out not to prevent but to accelerate corruption (Popov, 2007, 3).

Chinese proponents of shock therapy began to employ Virginia School public choice theory and new institutionalist theory, in particular the concept of rent-seeking, to argue their case against dual-track reforms. They were catching up with the latest neoliberal attack against state intervention. Neoclassical welfare economics saw the state a benevolent agent with the capacity to fix market failures. Public choice theory posited against this that the state would be constituted of politicians and bureaucrats who are controlled by special interest groups and pursue their own benefit through corruption and rent-seeking (Chang, 2002; Madra and Adaman, 2010; Fischer, 2009, 325–26). Nicholas Lardy introduced rent-seeking theory to China's reform debate in 1988 in the new journal *Comparative Social and Economic Systems* (Lardy, 1988; Wu, 1988, 1). The journal published a series of contributions throughout 1988 to popularize rent-seeking as an analytical tool in China's market reform debate. Wu Jinglian and Rong Jinben, the driving forces, collected these articles in the book *Corruption: Exchange of Money and Power* (Editorial Board of Comparative Social and Economic Systems, 1989). It included translations of leading neoliberals like Buchanan (1980) as well as of Koford and Colander (1984) and surveys of the recent English-language literature, including, for example, Anne Krueger's contributions.

Rong Jingben's preface to the book illustrates how rent-seeking theory was mobilized against the dual-track price system. From the vantage point of public choice theory, corruption resulted not from marketization but from the lack of a perfectly competitive market. Rong (1989) argues that some people would associate the rampant corruption with the increasing role of the market. Contrary to this view, Rong held, it would be obvious that official profiteering was in fact the result of the divergence between plan and market prices under the dual-track price system, which provided opportunities for rent-seeking. This, in turn, would create a vicious circle, where officials were taking advantage of the dual-track price system and therefore opposed real reforms.

Rong issued yet another call for wholesale price liberalization as the only way forward for reform. In Rong's (1989, 6) words,

> If we want to break out of this vicious circle, we can no longer control the economy, we have to stop exclusive sales [under the plan] and price controls. The only way to establish fair competition is to separate enterprises from the state bureaucracy and liberalize prices to achieve full marketization.

The policy implication of the rent-seeking analysis turned out to be fully aligned with the aborted big bang of 1986. In line with their monetarist analysis of the underlying reason for rising inflation, Wu Jinglian and other package reformers now put even greater emphasis on the need for macroeconomic restraint to bring aggregate demand below aggregate supply as a necessary step in preparing price liberalization. The so-called package reformers' (see Chapter 7) common slogan was "Control the money supply, reform prices" (管住货币, 改革价格) (Lin, 1988; Wu, Zhou, Lou, et al., 1988). In a proposal for the next seven years of reform (1988–1995) submitted to the System Reform Commission in May, Wu Jinglian and his group—Zhou Xiaochuan, Li Jiange, Lou Jiwei, Guo Shuqing, and others—once more fleshed out their vision for reform in two steps: monetary control followed by comprehensive price liberalization, importantly including the prices of essential raw materials and industrial inputs. Once again, they referred to the West German and Japanese postwar liberalization to legitimize their strategy (Wu, Zhou, Li, et al., 1988, 202). Urging that a decisive step had to be taken sooner than later, they employed typical shock therapy rhetoric:

> Both controlling the money supply and liberalizing prices are not easy to implement and require taking a considerable risk. … Although it is difficult to launch price reform at the right time, there is no way around it and the longer one waits the more difficult and riskier it gets. …As long as we put a comprehensive package of reform measures in place, we can absolutely crash through the barrier (i.e. price reform).
>
> *(ibid., 202–203)*

According to Wu and his coauthors, the inflationary trend in the first half of 1988 only added to the urgency:

> When inflation starts, it usually accelerates. There have been very few examples in the world of gradual control of inflation; usually one must stomp on the brake at some point. We need to cross this pass eventually, so better sooner than later. A long-lasting pain is worse than short sharp pain, so it is important to decide quickly.
>
> *(Wu, Zhou, Li, et al., 1988 as in Wu, 2013c, 196)*

The basic orientation of the 1988 proposal remained the same as in the plan of the 1986 Program Office. But the tone had further radicalized, and the scope of reform had moved from combining price, tax, wage, and finance reform to include ownership reform, a reform of the government system to be compatible with a market economy, financial liberalization, and the commodification of land and labor. As Wu (2013b, 200–201) made clear in a paper later that year, he was calling for a "completely new economic system" as the only way to improve efficiency. This would require "hard-hitting measures to supersede the dual-track system in a relatively short time." Small state-owned enterprises should be sold off while bigger ones should be turned into joint-stock companies. This privatization strategy should "reform the legal governance structure of state-owned enterprises ... [such that] the government will only retain the role of overall management of society and the economy" and would "no longer be the direct agent of public ownership, let alone interfere in the internal affairs of enterprises." In this paper, Wu articulated the full shock therapy script. China's radical market reformers had evolved beyond calling for the first and decisive step of shock therapy—that is, a big bang in price liberalization. They were now proposing the full shock doctrine that was sweeping the developing and socialist world.

An alternative perspective on the growing inflationary pressure and aggregate excess demand to that of the package reformers emphasized the long-standing question of the relationships between agricultural expansion, investments, and urban consumption. This was—as I will discuss in the next section—broadly Zhao Ziyang's approach. In early 1988, the emphasis on food prices and agriculture was also a common take among price officials. For example, Cheng Zhiping, then the director of the General Administration of Commodity Prices, in a speech in February 1988 stressed that food price increases explained about two-thirds of the consumer price index rise in 1987. The underlying problem was both a heightened demand, thanks to growing incomes, and a lack of supply of agricultural goods. In Cheng's (2006, 284) words, "When grain, meat and vegetable are plentiful, it is easy to stabilize prices." This condition was not in place in the late 1980s.

Agricultural reform had delivered quick results in the first years of their inception but increasingly ran into difficulties. When grain output reached unprecedented levels in the early 1980s, the old problem of how to industrialize without aggregate excess demand (see Chapter 4) was temporarily eased to some extent. By 1988, grain output had not again surpassed the 1984 level that had prompted the abolition of the unified purchase and sales system for grain (Han et al., 1998, 519; Naughton, 1989, 271). In 1984, the state fixed the prices of 67.5 percent of agricultural goods. By 1988, that share had declined to 24 percent (Han et al., 1998, 493). But—as Song Guoqing and others had warned—it turned out that the switch to voluntary contracting did not yield enough grain procurement for the state to keep prices stable (see Chapter 7). The unified system of purchase and sales had been abolished since it could not handle large grain surpluses (Oi, 1986). When faced with a tight supply of grain, the government reverted to compulsory contracts (Naughton, 1989, 271).

But the government had to raise the grain-procurement prices also for these compulsory grain contracts in order to compete with new economic opportunities in the flourishing rural industries and sideline production. Rising grain-procurement prices exacerbated the challenge of keeping the cost of grain low for urban workers (see Chapter 4). Since 1985, this had been achieved through a combination of low retail prices for grain and by means of subsidies. These urban consumption subsidies were part of the wage bill. Increasing these subsidies set off an upward spiral for a wide range of prices. A higher wage bill exerted pressure on industrial prices. Higher prices for industrial inputs, in turn, reduced returns on agricultural production and encouraged more farmers to move into rural industry, hence exacerbating the upward pressure on agricultural prices. The need for government subsidies to keep agricultural procurement prices up and retail costs down caused a growing government deficit. In the face of limited access to international and domestic lending, this deficit was largely financed by printing money that went to peasants in the form of a higher price for their produce and to urban workers in the form of subsidies (ibid., Gang, 1990, 40–47). As a result, aggregate demand exceeded supply and exerted pressure on the general price level. In this interpretation of the causes of the growing inflation, it would not be enough to simply tighten monetary policy. Rather, the rural–urban relation had once more to be rebalanced.

An additional dimension to cost-push inflation originated from the imbalance across different industrial sectors. The System Reform Institute researchers attributed the imbalance to the behavior of enterprises and continued to urge for enterprise reform. They had called the underlying mechanism of credit expansion the "soft bank constraint" in their 1986 study, which gave rise to overinvestment or excessive wage payments (see Chapter 7). This study had also warned of a "minisculization of investment," with most funds going into highly profitable light industries and consumer goods instead of raw materials, energy, and heavy industry. This trend continued in 1987. Light industry grew at a faster pace than key industrial inputs such as energy, thus exacerbating shortages (Gang, 1990, 52–53). The first years of reform marked a shift from a heavy industry–oriented development model to a light industry–oriented one (see Chapter 4). Eventually, this created bottlenecks in upstream industries. The combination of bottlenecks and increasing demand due to a rapid expansion of light industry caused the market prices of essential inputs such as coal, oil, and steel to diverge sharply from the state-planned prices (Geng and Zhou, 1998, 545–46). By 1987, the number of producer goods rationed by the central government had declined from 256 categories in 1984 to 26 in 1987, and the rationed goods, too, were sold on the market under the dual-track system (Gang, 1990, 36). The government announced in 1987 that 50 percent of all producer goods were allocated by the market (Han et al., 1998, 496).

It turned out that the rapid and chaotic increase of market prices for producer goods set off a limited version on the market margin of the kind of cost-push inflation that the System Reform Institute, Li Yining, and others had warned Zhao Ziyang of in 1986, when they intervened to stop the implementation of wholesale price liberalization. Market prices rapidly inflated in relation to plan prices. In 1987, the market prices of thirteen basic producer goods were 115 percent above plan prices. Rising prices of industrial inputs put upward pressure on all other goods.

At the same time, the tremendous divergence between market and plan prices in highly concentrated upstream industrial sectors such as energy provided unprecendented opportunities for profiteering and corruption (ibid., 496, 499). Many officials with access to the resources that were in short supply did not manage them as stewards of the national or local economy or their production unit. Instead, according to numerous accounts, they abused their power, diverting some of the revenue from the skyrocketing market prices into their own pockets, accepting cigrattes and alcohol as bribes, or granting relatives and acquaintances access to the precious resources.[4] Corruption was one of the reasons for the Chinese students' dissatisfaction that resulted in major protests in 1986. One of their leaders, Fang Lizhi, a brilliant phycisist, called for "complete modernization" and "complete Westernization" in response (Pantsov and Levine, 2015, 400–401; Vogel, 2011, 577–578). As I have argued, package reform economists saw widespread official profiteering as yet another ground to attack gradual reform and call for complete marketization.

In sharp contrast, the researchers at the System Reform Institute continued to vehemently oppose the logic of shock doctrine. In 1987, after the implementation of the nationwide production contracting system for state-owned enterprises, they conducted another large-scale survey mirroring their efforts in 1986 to evaluate the state of reform (CESRRI, 1986; see Chapter 7). They were concerned by corruption but once more argued that wholesale price liberalization and a jump to the free market would not serve to solve the underlying problem of shortages in essential raw materials, energy, and heavy industrial goods (Wang, 2019, 89–90).

From the perspective of the economists at the System Reform Institute, given China's low level of development, the state was the only actor that had the capacities to organize these crucial upstream industries essential for China's economic progress. In their view, a separation between bureaucracy and enterprises in these critical sectors was not compatible with China's development goals. Instead, what was needed was an industrial restructuring in these upstream industries; it would involve mergers under public ownership to enlarge the scale of production and enhance technology, aiming to stimulate higher levels of output and overcome the prevailing shortages. The problem of official profiteering, in the opinion of the economists, could not be solved simply by abolishing the plan. Instead, new organizational structures and institutional innovation were needed to overcome excessive power in the hands of individual cadres and establish a system of accountability that would effectively prevent corruption (ibid.).

After 1986, Zhao's reform approach was broadly aligned with that of the System Reform Institute. Zhao's mission was to continue reform through development. This increasingly involved not only domestic marketization but also a gradual reintegration into global capitalism. At the core of Zhao's approach was enterprise contracting combined with a coastal-development strategy. In working out these policies, Zhao relied on survey work by the System Reform Institute (Wang, 2019, 90).

The coastal-development strategy is not to be confused with the Special Economic Zones that had been launched in the very early days of reform as islands of opening up (Macfarquhar, 2009, xx). In Zhao's own words, his new strategy "meant allowing the 100 million to 200 million people in the coastal regions, and the enterprises in the regions, to integrate into the global market" (Zhao, 2009, 150). From the autumn of 1987 to 1988 Zhao Ziyang, who had built his career in the 1960s in Guangdong, toured this coastal province along with Jiangsu, Zhejiang, and Fujian (ibid., 149–150; Zhao Ziyang, 2016k). On this extended investigation, he was once more joined by Du Runsheng and Wang Xiaoqiang, on whose research Zhao had relied since the agricultural reforms of the early 1980s (Wang Xiaoqiang in Deng, 2017, 195; see Illustration 5 of Zhao and the delegation). On their travels, they held long discussions with local cadres on the county, district, and provincial levels to evaluate whether the export-led development strategy of the "Asian Tigers"—Hong Kong, Singapore, South Korea, and Taiwan—could be adopted to China's coasts (Zhao, 2009, 150).

Upon their return from the study tour, Zhao (2016k, 342–343) summarized the coastal-development strategy in January 1988: "Labor-intensive industries always go where labor costs are lowest," Zhao observed. "From the perspective of the Asia-Pacific region, we see that these industries first relocated from the US to Japan, and later to Taiwan, South Korea, Hong Kong, and Singapore." Zhao remarked that "during these two big waves of relocation, China's economy had

ILLUSTRATION 5   Delegation led by Premier Zhao Ziyang to study prospects for Coastal Development Strategy, winter 1987. Zhao Ziyang (left front), Wang Xiaoqiang (middle back), Du Runsheng (middle front), Zhao's secretary Li Shuqiao (right front) on investigation tour in Guangdong, Jiangxi, Shanghai and Jiangsu. Courtesy of Wang Xiaoqiang.

not yet opened up. Currently, another big shift is under way." But the current time, he suggested, was the ideal moment to bring this production to China: "China's coastal regions should be very attractive this time."

We can think of the coastal-development strategy as an internationalization of the gradual dual-track marketization. The idea was not to integrate all of China at once into global capitalism or to loosen state control over core upstream and technology-intensive industries. Rather, as Zhao (2016k, 354) pointed out, coastal development was to be pursued in a way that would not drain China's domestic resources. The slogan "extend both ends abroad" (两头在外) meant that raw materials should come from abroad to be processed by cheap Chinese labor for export.

This strategy would channel the abundant investments in light industry by township and village enterprises into exports. In Zhao's vision, small enterprises engaging in export industries could be privatized to free up funds that could be invested into technology-intensive upstream industries. The expansion of upstream industries, in turn, would help to overcome the shortages in industrial inputs—one of the key drivers of cost-push inflation. Revenues from light industry exports could also finance the import of industrial inputs and further ease the pressure on prices. Foreign indebtedness should be avoided, according to Zhao. Instead, China's coastal enterprises should attract foreign direct investment. This would not only prevent the risks of being dependent on foreign creditors, but it would also bring the advantage of acquiring new management techniques, thus contributing to enterprise reform (ibid., Zhao, 2009, 145–147).

The domestic version of the dual-track system transformed China's socialist production units into market-oriented enterprises (see Chapters 6 and 7). The coastal-development strategy extended this approach to the global market. China's enterprises were to be not just marketized; they were to catch up with global capitalism. The reformers and economists involved in devising this strategy saw it as another step in the gradual marketization process from the margins. Wang Xiaoqiang (as in Deng, 2017, 195), who advised Zhao on this strategy, reminds us when looking back more than two decades later, "We never guessed that the economy of the coast would become the engine of Chinese economic growth."

To be sure, by far not all of the young reform economists who had entered the market reform debate as proponents of the dual-track price system continued to argue for a gradual reform approach in the late 1980s. An article widely discussed both in China and internationally merits mentioning in this regard. Authored by Hua Sheng, one of the claimants to be originator of the dual-track price system (see Chapter 6), and his coauthors Zhang Xuejun and Luo Xiaopeng, the article describes the first decade of reforms. The authors posited that the dual-track system had been effective in opening up markets and disintegrating the old planning system but that it had failed to create a functioning market economy (Hua et al., 1988, 21).

Hua, Zhang, and Luo continued to oppose proposals for radical price reform, arguing that they would fail to establish market competition. Instead, they claimed "that reform in socialist countries had reached a dead-end unless the system of state ownership was dismantled and property and civil rights re-established" (Hua et al., 1993, viii). Hua and his coauthors saw the reason for the failure of the dual-track system in its tendency to reproduce and expand the power of officials. In their view, the official authority could not be broken by abolishing planned prices—as those in favor of rent-seeking suggested. Rather, for Hua, Zhang, and Luo, the only way to move to a market economy was to undermine official power by guaranteeing property rights and civil rights to China's citizens. They pioneered proposals for voucher privatization and effectively demanded a wholesale change in the political system.

It might seem as though Hua Sheng and his group and Wu Jinglian and other package reformers had converged in their demands for wholesale marketization and with the System Reform Institute in their desire to reintegrate China into global capitalism. In truth, however, the separate groups of reform economists remained fierce opponents. They were deeply divided in their view of how market creation could succeed. In fact, Hua, Zhang, and Luo's 1988 article in large part is framed as an attack against the reform proposals by Wu Jinglian, Lou Jiwei, Zhou Xiaochuan, and other package reformers. This reflects the heated debate at the time. While this ever-fiercer struggle among market reform economists was raging over the question of *how* to move forward, the looming inflation and rampant corruption created a new momentum among those who were opposed to further reform altogether.

Zhao Ziyang's Stance and Critiques

Zhao had already been severely criticized by planning proponents and cautious reformers such as Chen Yun in 1987 and early 1988 for allowing prices to rise moderately (Vogel, 2011, 471). He also faced increasing criticism from the same direction for not bringing corruption under control (Fewsmith, 1994, 220). Trying to defend his reform approach against radical reformers and reform opponents alike, Zhao made remarks that were later interpreted as saying that some degree of inflation and corruption was inevitable in the process of reform (ibid., Cheng, 1995, 191). Zhao (2009, 157) reflects on this criticism in his prison notes. He writes,

> After June Fourth, when Li Peng and his associates were criticizing me, they accused me of saying that corruption was unavoidable in the reform process and therefore that I had a laissez-faire attitude toward corruption.

Zhao reports that in one of his letters of appeal against his imprisonment, he had explained that "[t]hough inflation hit in 1988, I believed that the condition was neither all that grave, nor so difficult to resolve" (Zhao, 2009, 57). In Zhao's account, he did not think that inflation or corruption were unimportant, as his political opponents alleged, but that both were solvable problems that could be overcome in the process of reform and that there was no need to bring rapid growth to a temporary halt. In Zhao's eyes, development and stability could go hand in hand (Zhao, 2016n, 405–407). In addition, the fact, that Zhao decided in 1986 to stop his own push for price liberalization in response to warnings against the dangers of inflation shows that he was fully aware of the risks involved in rapid price rises (see Chapter 7). Yet Zhao's awareness of the dangers of inflation has not been widely recognized. One of the most detailed accounts available of this juncture suggests that "Zhao now [spring 1988] began to signal that he did not regard inflation as a serious risk" (Gewirtz, 2017, 198).

After the Thirteenth Congress of the Communist Party of China (CPC), in October 1987, Zhao Ziyang had become General Secretary. In his new position, he was no longer directly in charge of the economic policy. The new premier was Li Peng—an engineer by training and Zhou Enlai's foster son, considered to be a protégé of Chen Yun and Li Xiannian (Pantsov and Levine, 2015, 405). In January, Li Peng, along with leading cadres of several departments of the State Council—including Yao Yilin, who soon afterward became vice premier—warned that the economic situation was dangerously deteriorating. In particular, they worried that rising prices would be alarming. They called for bringing prices under control as the most urgent task of the year 1988 (Fang, 2014, 281–295). Premier Li Peng summarized the takeaway points of the State Council's consultation: "The focus of our attention must be the price question," he pleaded. "Every [economic] challenge is related to prices and prices have an impact on every aspect [of our economy]" (ibid. 291). In light of the looming inflation, Li Peng stated, "Stabilize the economy and adhere to the policy of deepening reform. There is no way forward without reform but if the reform steps are too big, there is no way to achieve stability" (ibid., 295). To achieve stability, the State Council called for austerity. The root cause of inflation, in their view, was aggregate excess demand and the overheating of an increasingly export-oriented economy. Macroeconomic balance should be reestablished by reducing the growth rate and bringing down the money supply (ibid., 281–295, 307; Zhao, 2009, 146).

Strikingly, the policy recommendations of Li Peng and other skeptics of further reform were quite similar to the preparatory step suggested by the package reformers; both those who thought reform was going too fast and those who thought it didn't go far enough agreed that macroeconomic restraint was needed in 1988. To be sure, they violently disagreed on the steps to be taken after macroeconomic stability would have been achieved, but in calling for macroeconomic control at all costs they were united against Zhao Ziyang.

Li Peng, Yao Yilin, and others warned that China would be at the verge of economic collapse if strict stabilization measures were not imposed. Zhao held against this, saying that it was "not seeing the forest for the trees" (Zhao, 2016i, 358; Fang, 2014, 307–308). Zhao insisted that the economic pressures that had built up over the previous years were easing and that the overall economic situation, as well as the rising general price level, were good. Zhao pushed to continue the same strategy as in 1987. In his view, stability and rapid development could be combined. There was no need to separate the two. While Zhao agreed with the need to stabilize the macroeconomy, he argued that stability should not be confused with retrenchment or contraction (ibid.; Zhao, 2016n, 407). Instead, his approach was what he called a "soft landing," a method he considered superior to Li Peng's traditional adjustment policy. Zhao agreed that infrastructure construction and consumption needed to be controlled but held that overall production should not be reduced.

The challenge, in Zhao's eyes, was to restore balance across different sectors of the economy, not to simply reduce aggregate demand indiscriminately. Zhao advocated gradual rebalancing to be implemented over several years instead of "stepping on the brakes" in a sudden manner (Zhao, 2009, 128–129). The key driving force behind inflation, in Zhao's view, was the increase in agricultural prices and the need to compensate urban consumers with subsidies. This, in Zhao's eyes, had to do with the question of how to move forward with agricultural reform as well as with changing urban consumption patterns. Zhao Ziyang (2009, 128) explained in his secret journal that in addition to increased grain prices, the expansion of the money supply was driven by local governments using up their credit quotas for their preferred projects such as construction. This forced the central government to allocate additional credit to fund essentials such as grain procurement. Zhao thought of these drivers of inflation as solvable problems that required careful empirical study and experimentation. Simply reducing aggregate demand, according to Zhao, was ill-fit to solve this imbalance. The key was increasing supply, especially of the goods that showed an upward trend in prices (Zhao, 2016i, 359–360).

Zhao's coastal-development strategy aroused opposition from the same quarters that opposed the dual-track price system. Chen Yun expressed concerns that China had to import raw materials first. If it did not succeed in exporting its processed products in turn, China would run the risk of a foreign deficit. Yao Yilin and Li Peng warned that such an export orientation would further fuel overheating. Against this, Zhao insisted that the Asian Tigers had proven that his strategy worked. They began their labor-intensive exports at a time of high inflation, and they achieved growth and a decrease in the overall price level as a result of this strategy. Zhao stressed the importance of price stability. In his view, though, inflation was not a matter of high or low development but of balance across sectors (Zhao, 2009, 146–148; Zhao, 2016k, 354–355). After reading Zhao's January 1988 report, Deng Xiaoping noted, "I fully agree. Let's implement this boldly and swiftly" (Zhao, 2016k, 342). The Politburo later adopted the coastal-development strategy.

Zhao's "soft landing" was the Party's original strategy for the year 1988. This meant gradual stabilization, deepening enterprise reform, and coastal development. In January, Zhao had once more laid out his view on the price question. He stressed that food accounted for 60 percent of consumer spending. Therefore, solving the food price inflation, he argued, would go a long way in addressing overall consumer price inflation. The prices of agricultural goods had to be raised gradually and the relative prices of vegetable, grain, meat, and eggs had to be adjusted. The increase in procurement prices had to be compensated by subsidies for urban consumers. In Zhao's mind, this was a long-term plan, possibly taking decades. He warned this had to be done slowly to avoid distress among the people (Zhao, 2016i, 359–360).

In mid-March, Zhao again expressed a similar view and added that gradual price adjustments could be effective only if they were complemented by measures that would increase the production of agricultural goods. To balance market fluctuations, Zhao once more highlighted the critical role of state commerce (see Chapter 6). The commerce system for agricultural products had to be improved and funds were to be set up that enabled the state to balance prices by adding or withdrawing demand and adjusting exports. Solving the problem of agricultural prices was the key to solving the overall price problem, according to Zhao (2016n, 407–408). Zhao's approach to price stabilization was also still the official line of the Price Bureau: Cheng Zhiping reported to the National People's Congress, which took place from March 25 to April 13, 1988, that bringing the prices for subsidiary agricultural products under control would be essential to stabilizing the overall price level. If necessary, even prices of agricultural goods that had already been liberalized would need to be guided by the state to ensure overall stability (Cheng, 2006, 447–448).

However, at the same National People's Congress, Deng Xiaoping urged that price reform was the most pressing issue and had to be accelerated (Yang, 1998, 390). Zhao's approach was sidelined. In sharp contrast to Zhao's warning against chaotic price rises for agricultural goods, on April 5 the State Council announced that the prices of pork, eggs, sugar, and vegetables would be liberalized and price controls would be replaced by subsidies (Yang, 1998, 391). This was based on Deng Xiaoping's idea (Han, Wu, Ding, and Geng, 1998, 511). The result was immediate, steep price rises for these goods, highest for pork at 50 to 60 percent (Yang, 1998, 391). These four goods were by no standards "light" or unessential commodities; they were essential to the ordinary diet, making up about one-third of the average urban household's expenditure (Naughton, 1991, 140–146).

The first months of 1988 saw a rise in the overall consumer price index unprecedented in the reform period (see Figure 8.1), with non-staple food prices rising faster than the average prices of other consumer goods. In 1985, during a previous episode of heightened inflation, the consumer price rises had on average been compensated by rises in incomes. Compensatory subsidies were paid to urban workers in 1988. Nevertheless, urban real incomes fell (Geng and Zhou, 1998, 546; Naughton, 1991, 140–146). Sporadic panic buying and hoarding began to occur in several places (Zhang, 2017, 575). The consumer subsidies also did not cover the rising number of industrial workers still holding peasant status. Migrant workers were the ones most severely affected by the new policy. They reacted with strikes and protests. For example, workers in Tianjin's factories, who had formerly worked in the fishing trade but had been in the city for many years, by 1988 had shut down more than 5,700 township enterprises (Yang, 1998, 392).

Losing out on the question of how to manage the prices of subsidiary agricultural products was an important setback for Zhao, given the great importance he had attributed to this set of prices for overall price stability. At the same time, Zhao was confronted with increasingly severe criticism by leading package reformers such as Liu Guoguang and Wu Jinglian, who were supported by China's legendary economist Xue Muqiao. Wu and Liu disagreed on the precise time horizon, but they both warned Zhao that a period of strict macroeconomic restraint and tight monetary policy was urgently needed to bring inflation back under control and to prepare the conditions for price liberalization. This was, in their view, the only way to finally render the law of value operational in China. The short-term loss in terms of growth that such an austerity program would bring about was small compared with the long-term harm of overheating, they argued (Zhang, 2017, 568–571; Xue, 1996, 411–412).[5] Confronted with the calls for austerity from package reformers and planning proponents alike, as well as with Deng's move toward price liberalization, Zhao was fighting a losing battle for his approach of adjustment through growth and reform through development.

It was in this context that the Latin American experience of opening up, industrialization, and inflation became relevant to China's reform debate. This Latin American connection has led to the interpretation that in 1988, Zhao Ziyang "proposed to bring China down the road of Brazilian hyperinflation" (Shih, 2008, 125). It therefore merits careful analysis.

The Latin American Connection

It is important to remember that in the late 1980s, China's reformers looked up to the Latin American modernization success of the postwar era and aspired to achieve similar levels of infrastructure development, industrialization, and urbanization (Zhu, 2009, 524). Amidst the mounting tensions over how to move forward with economic reforms, Zhu Jiaming organized an investigation tour to Brazil, Venezuela, Chile, Mexico, and Argentina (Chen, 2013, 505; Zhu, 2009, 524, 2013, 45). Once more, George Soros helped to fund the trip. By then, the Open Society Foundation had set up a subsidiary, the China Reform and Opening Up Foundation, thanks to the help of He Weiling, Li Xianglu, and Zhao Ziyang's secretary Bao Tong and with the support of the System Reform Institute. It is a widespread interpretation in the recent English-language literature on the 1988 reform impasse that the reports sent back by the delegation to Latin America caused the inflationary episode in 1988 that set the stage for the uprising of 1989 (see, e.g., Gewirtz, 2017, 199–200; Shih, 2008, 131–133; Wu, 2005, 368; Wu and Ma, 2016, 216).

In 1988, Zhu Jiaming had just moved from the Henan Province Economic System Reform Commission to the International Office of the China International Trust Investment Corporation (CITIC), where he worked with Zhao's former secretary, Li Xianglu. Both were also involved with the Open Society Foundation's China branch. The CITIC International Office had been set up to engage in soft diplomacy on behalf of the State Council. A central aim of this new institution was to establish relations with the Middle East and Latin American countries to facilitate the import of raw materials, first and foremost oil (Zhu, 2013, 41–42). These were the industrial inputs that had experienced rising prices. They were essential to the coastal-development strategy and China's industrialization effort more broadly. Zhu encouraged Chen Yizi to join the investigation with a delegation of the System Reform Institute that included Song Guoqing, the director of the macroeconomics department (Chen, 2013, 505). The focus of the study tour was Brazil, in particular the Brazilian economic take-off under the military dictatorship in the late 1960s, since it promised to hold lessons for China's reforms (Zhu, 2009, 524–528; Chen, 2013, 506).

The Brazilian so-called "economic miracle" (*milagre econômico*) of 1968–1973 was unleashed by a heterodox, developmentalist policy (Macarini, 2000). Brazil's rapid expansion in this episode relied on a combination of low wages, foreign capital inflows, and rapidly rising exports. The basic mechanism was similar to the coastal-development strategy, but in Brazil foreign capital came mostly in the form of foreign credit, not foreign direct investment as envisioned by Zhao. One observer notes, "[I]n principle, the system was magical: foreign finance boosted industrial production, and enough of this production was exported to cover interest and principal payments" (Frieden, 1987, 95). This set Brazil on a high growth trajectory. Between 1965 and 1980, real GDP more than tripled, industrial production quadrupled, and exports rose more than tenfold (ibid.). In Brazil, this growth success is closely associated with Antônio Delfim Netto, the young minister in charge of the development strategy. Delfim Netto coined what is commonly referred to as the "cake theory" (Folha de S. Paulo, 2008), a Brazilian version of Deng Xiaoping's slogan "let some people get rich first". It held that the cake had to grow before it could be distributed. The cake did grow, but it was not shared equally later on.

Chen Yizi's (2013, 506) memoir expresses the Chinese delegation's fascination with Brazil's "large cake"—the modernist capital Brasilia, highways, stylish buildings and factories, up-to-date housing, and small cars for masses of people. Chen notes that Brazil's GDP per capita was around USD 3,000 at the time, about ten times that of China. He acknowledges the great income inequality but suggests that it is mitigated by Brazil's poverty-alleviation program. Poor people receive social benefits that cover all their basic needs.

The highlight of this trip was a meeting with the architect of Brazil's miracle, Delfim Netto. In the 1980s, when Brazil was suffering from a balance of payment crisis and high inflation, Delfim Netto was called back into office to devise a way out. He could not replicate his success of the late 1960s (Frieden, 1987, 117–119). Even so, he was delighted to lecture the Chinese delegation about the Brazilian take-off experience. Before the miracle, Delfim Netto said, Brazil suffered from capital shortages. Opponents of opening to capital inflows had argued that they would make the country dependent on imperialist powers—an argument that resonated with the Chinese opponents of Zhao's coastal-development strategy. Proponents including Delfim Netto, to the contrary, saw that foreign capital would accelerate development. This, according to Delfim Netto, had been proven true by Brazil's experience (Chen, 2013, 506; Zhu, 2009, 524–528).

When asked about inflation, Delfim Netto pointed out that in periods of rapid growth and industrialization, inflation was inevitable. Inflation could have a stimulating effect on growth, but it had to be controlled within certain limits (ibid.). His emphasis on the need for such limits to inflation is not surprising. After all, Delfim Netto had returned to office in 1979 to solve the dual crises of foreign indebtedness and inflation. But he tried to bring the situation under control without relying on austerity. This approach is reflected in Zhu Jiaming's report on the trip (Zhu, 2009, 524–528): the Latin American experience would show that the anti-inflationary monetarism that might work in developed countries was not suitable for poor countries unable to absorb sharp economic declines due to their low level of development. The lesson in this is not that inflation does not matter but that it should be brought under control by means other than austerity and monetary restraint.

During the trip, the delegation sent telegrams back to Beijing (Chen, 2013, 507; Zhu, 2013, 45). Upon their return, Chen immediately went to speak to Zhao Ziyang to report Delfim Netto's view on foreign capital and inflation. Chen told Zhao, "In every country, in the period of high-speed development, there will be inflation. In socialist countries, there will also be inflation in the process of market reforms." He explained that "structural inflation caused by the expansion of both consumption and investment is inevitable, in particular when enterprises have not been reformed." Yet Chen immediately cautioned, "Of course we are not advocating inflation but we have to acknowledge this objective truth and make sure to keep inflation within certain limits."

We have to remember that Chen, as the leader of the System Reform Institute, was an important voice in the warning against implementing wholesale price liberalization in 1986 on the grounds that it would risk high inflation. Zhao had broadly pursued the reform approach advocated by the System Reform Institute in 1987 and 1988. But China still experienced an increase in inflation. Delfim Netto's judgment that some degree of inflation is inevitable during rapid industrialization thus matched with the experience of Zhao and the System Reform Institute. They did consider inflation as dangerous but thought it was a manageable problem as long as a gradual reform was pursued.

In the context of the purges after June Fourth, planning proponents accused Zhao and his so-called brain trust (智囊团), the System Reform Institute, of propagating the notion that inflation was harmless (Chen, 2013, 509; Zhu, 2013, 44–45). The delegation did report back that people in Brazil had been accustomed to high levels of inflation and that what mattered to Brazilians was real incomes more than money wages (ibid., Zhu, 2009, 526). But they also warned that the tolerance in China for high levels of inflation was much lower, after decades of almost absolute price stability (ibid.).

The accusation against Zhao and the young reformers came not only from opponents of further reform. It was also propagated by China's package reformers and became a common interpretation. Xue Muqiao (1996, 411) notes in his memoir that "Zhao Ziyang was influenced by the wrong ideas and wavered at the idea of curbing inflation." Wu Jinglian (2005, 368) claims, in his textbook on China's economic reforms,

> According to their observations of economic situations in Latin America, these economists believed that even inflation rates of a thousand percent or more would not necessarily throw obstacles in the way of economic prosperity. As a result, government leaders concluded that crashing through the pass of price reform could be achieved despite hyperinflation and high growth rates.

First of all, it is important to notice that inflation spiraled out of control only after the later attempt to push through price reform—as we will see in the account below. But we also have to see the struggle over the story of the 1980s that is entailed in Wu's statement and other readings along similar lines. Zhu Jiaming, in his reflections on the reform period, directly addresses Wu Jinglian's interpretation. He writes, "After June Fourth, we lost the right to speak and history was written by those who monopolized its interpretation. Wu Jinglian is a classic example for this." Zhu further explains that since the early 2000s, Wu and others had exerted great efforts to tell the story of the 1980s in a self-serving manner (Zhu, 2013, 45).

Countering the accusation that he downplayed the potential harm of inflation, Zhu takes the same line of defense as Chen: "We did not say that inflation is harmless. We stressed that inflation is inevitable in new market economies and transition countries like China. The key issue in our view was how to face inflation" (ibid.). Zhu and Chen were both exiled after June Fourth. Their memoirs, from which I quote here, were published by small presses in Taiwan and Hong Kong, with little reach into mainland China and English-speaking academia. In contrast, Wu Jinglian's perspectives were published by Oxford University Press (Wu and Ma, 2016), MIT Press (2013), and leading Chinese presses with prestigious endorsements. The struggle over the interpretation of China's experiences in 1988 is not over. Here, I try to take both sides into account and situate Zhu's and Chen's arguments in the larger political and economic context.[6]

While Zhu and Chen both belonged to the same broad movement of young reform intellectuals, they did not see eye to eye on many reform questions. By 1988, what had begun as a broad, fluid movement of young reformers who were meeting in parks and empty offices to discuss China's future (see Chapter 6) had developed into established institutions and distinct groups. Zhu Jiaming, from his early interventions together with Weng Yongxi, Wang Qishan, and Huang Jianan, considered the question of the nature of the economy. Since the mid-1980s, Zhu (2013, 45; Zhu, 1985; Zhu, 1989; see Chapter 7) had developed the idea that in the course of transitioning from a planned to a market economy the process of monetization and commodification had to involve a certain degree of inflation. He now found this view confirmed by the Latin American experience. In contrast, Chen Yizi pursued a more pragmatist approach, preoccupied with working out feasible solutions for the next step in reform. In 1988, they went on the joint research journey to Latin America. But their viewpoints diverged on the critical question of whether China should or should not push through with price liberalization. Zhu Jiaming was in favor of a big bang in 1988 (Zhu, 2013, 44). In his report on their study tour in Latin America, Zhu stressed the lessons of Pinochet's Chile. Ironically, Zhu had come very close to Wu Jinglian's take on reform, with their views diverging, however, on timing and the need for austerity measures. Zhu (2009, 526–27) reports,

> The lesson of the Chilean experience is that price, exchange rate and wage liberalization can be implemented without excessive inflation as long as they are part of a suitable package of economic policies that ensures stable economic growth and expanding exports.

Chen Yizi had come a long way since his attempts to contribute to the improvement of collective farming in Henan. Chen, too, admired Pinochet's economic success, Chile's social stability, and the tapping of the economic expertise of the "Chicago boys" by the military regime. Salvador Allende's agenda of nationalization and central economic control were a failure, according to Chen, and gave rise to widespread dissatisfaction. In contrast, the people he spoke to in Chile told him "they would love to have Pinochet's economic program without Pinochet" (Chen, 2013, 508). Chen's worldview had largely become compatible with neoliberalism. But he had not turned into a proponent of shock therapy (Chen, 2013, 5009–5015; Wang, 2019, 90).

Pushing Through with Price Reform

Several weeks before the delegation from Latin America returned to China in late May, Deng Xiaoping had begun to lobby for radical price reform. On May 7, during a meeting at his home, Deng called for "breaking a path for price reform" (Fewsmith, 1994, 220; Cheng, 1995, 192). He contended that "China was in a critical period of reform and should meet the stormy waves head-on while trying to complete price reforms in three to five years" (Cheng, 1995, 192). On May 15, Deng Xiaoping met with Rául Alfonsín, the first democratically elected president of Argentina after the end of the military dictatorship (Li Jingwei, 1988). The officially retired Deng used this meeting to proclaim his commitment to push ahead with reform. He told Alfosin that China's ten years of reform and opening up were overall a success. Deng remarked—in what sounds like a signal to competing Chinese leaders who thought that reform had gone too far—that

China's reform policy was not going to stop there but that China was getting ready for the next step. Deng added,

> This is a risky enterprise and there will be twists and turns on the way. We might even commit mistakes. But we have to face the waves heads on, while exerting every effort to avoid major mistakes. If we do this, there is hope for our reform. (ibid.)

Deng had made it clear that his approach to breaking out of the impasse that reform had reached was to forge ahead. Some speculate that Deng was influenced by Li Tieying, who earlier that month had delivered Deng's message on price reform to the System Reform Commission, of which Li was the director at the time (Cheng, 1995, 191–192; Fewsmith, 1994, 222). Li was the son of Jin Weiying, a veteran revolutionary and Deng's ex-wife and was about to become the youngest member of the Politburo (Vogel, 2011, 28–29; Pantsov and Levine, 2015, 529). Li had argued in April that inflation was an acceptable cost of price reform and that the longer the dual-track price system prevailed, the greater the political risk (Cheng, 1995, 191–192). It might be true that Deng was influenced by Li. Certainly, by 1988, Deng must have been aware of the package reform approach that was built on the logic of creating a market in one bold stroke from a wide range of sources – including the prominent economists who had promoted this approach for years.

Wu Jinglian, the leader of this approach, received congratulatory notes from other economists once the Politburo officially approved Deng's push for price reform (Chuang, 1988). But although package reformers remained committed to their project, as I have argued above, they also continued to warn China's leadership from April through June 1988 that retrenchment would be needed prior to wholesale price liberalization (Fang, 2014, 347). As I noted, with regard to the immediate course of action, the package reformers agreed with those cautioning against more reform. So, from Deng's perspective, following the full package would have amounted to giving in to Chen Yun. It would not have constituted a decisive signal toward more reform, and it left open the possibility of reversing some of the reform steps. An alternative gradual approach left open the possibility of restrengthening the old system. Continuing to grope for stones was not a signal that the battle over China's path had been decided in favor of Deng's marketization agenda. In this context, Deng advocated taking a big step in price reform, even at the high risk of inflation and unrest. Zhao decided to follow Deng.

In his memoir, Zhao (2009, 18–19) reflects on his turnaround. He writes, "Deng Xiaoping had repeatedly urged us to be decisive in price reform, which he believed required a breakthrough, saying, 'a quick sharp pain is better than prolonged pain.'" This led Zhao "to be swayed away from incremental steps and toward the all-at-once idea. Though fixed prices had risen, the situation with incorrect pricing had not changed, so perhaps it was better to make a major adjustment all at once."

At the Politburo Standing Committee's meetings on May 16 and 19, Zhao Ziyang joined Deng's call for price reform. Everybody now had to gather strength to push through with price reform, Zhao urged. If prices were finally straightened out, that would lay the necessary foundation for future reform. Echoing the rhetoric of Kornai and other Eastern European reform economists, Zhao warned that China should avoid getting stuck with reform, as had happened to Yugoslavia, Poland, and Hungary. Prices should be corrected over the course of five years. This would involve a planned inflation level of about 10 percent, for which wage earners would be compensated. A comprehensive package was needed for the next years; it would entail not only price but also wage and tax reform and would be implemented step by step, in a planned manner (Zhao, 2016d; Fang, 2014, 335–339). Clearly, this was the same logic that had been advocated by the aborted 1986 Program Office plan (see Chapter 7).

Zhao's speech shows that he was fully aware of the resistance that such a package would arouse and the repression required to push it through. After all, in 1986 he had decided against such a package, not least because of this danger. In his 1988 address, Zhao made it clear that to ensure political stability, a new public security law was required that the State Council could invoke in an emergency. Zhao argued that Poland's experience of social uprisings had shown such a law to be necessary (Fang, 2014, 339). Just eleven days before this Standing Committee meeting, on May 5, special troops of the Polish Interior Ministry had cracked down on a major strike wave that was sweeping the country in reaction to falling real incomes (George, 1988). This, in my eyes, erases any doubts about whether Zhao anticipated that inflation would be harmless. He recognized the possibly explosive consequences of rising prices. But in the spring of 1988, he seems to have been prepared to use force, if necessary, to finally make marketization happen.

Yao Yilin expressed agreement with the plan laid out by Zhao during that meeting. A committee was formed to work out the operational details headed by Yao. Chen Yun intervened. Chen warned of the public reactions following announcement of the plan. He also pointed out that indexing wages to planned price rises would not compensate China's peasant majority (Fang, 2014, 339–340; Zhang, 2017, 573). Some accounts hold that while Yao Yilin was preparing plans for price reform, he secretly also worked with Chen on measures to be put in place in the case of a failure of price reform (Chen, 2013, 514; Cheng, 1995, 194). But for the time being, the direction was set by Deng.

Notwithstanding the inflationary tendency resulting from the price liberalizations in Spring 1988, Deng Xiaoping accelerated his public rhetoric, campaigning for a breakthrough in price reform (Cheng, 1995; Fewsmith, 1994, 220–221). Deng invoked a strategy of one of China's greatest historical novels, the *Romance of the Three Kingdoms* (Luo, 1959). This fourteenth-century novel compiles oral traditions depicting the turbulent transition period (220–280 AD) between the fall of the Han and the reunification under the Jin dynasty and has served as a reference for China's rulers throughout the centuries, including Chairman Mao (Lam, 2011). On May 19, 1986, Deng told a North Korean delegation,

> Only once prices have been straightened out will we be able to step up reform. ... Doesn't China have the tale of Lord Guan 'Slaying Six Generals to Force Through Five Passes' (过五关斩六将)? We might have to force through even more 'passes' than Lord Guan, slaying even more 'generals'. To force a pass is not at all easy and requires taking great risk. We have to be at the same time cautious and conscientious, bold and careful towards each step, synthesizing experience, adjusting our actions when we encounter problems, and accord with the actual circumstances. But we <u>cannot not</u> carry out price reform, we have to face the risks and difficulties head–on. ... I always tell my comrades we must not be afraid of risks and be even more courageous. If we fear wolves ahead and tigers behind, we will not get anywhere.
>
> *(Deng, 2004, 1232–1233)*

To the Chinese audience familiar with the famous tale of Lord Guan, there could have been no doubt of Deng's determination to push ahead with radical price reform. Guan is commonly known for having slayed all generals who opposed him on his path through a mountain pass (Luo, 1959).

On June 4, 1988, following a renewed call for price reform by Deng (Fang, 2014, 343), the *People's Daily* (1988a) reported on the push for the reform in plain language. Employing a rhetoric very similar to that of Kornai and others who prescribed a big bang a few years later in the Soviet Union and some Eastern European countries, Deng stated, with regard to price reform, "Long-term pain is worse than short-term pain." If price relations were not put in order now, Deng argued, the long-term goal of China catching up with the developed nations fifty years into the twenty-first century would be endangered. Deng admitted once more that risks were great, but he was optimistic that they could be brought under control: "as long as countermeasures[7] were well prepared, heaven would not collapse even in face of great risks" (ibid.). Deng repeated his call for bracing the risk and pushing through with price reform at subsequent meetings with foreign guests, for example, with the Ethiopian President Mengistu Haile Mariam on June 22 (Yu and Feng, 1988).

Far from being responsible for this attempt at shock therapy – as some observers have alleged, the System Reform Institute mobilized once more against this reform program. In a last attempt to stop implementation of the plan, Chen Yizi and Wang Xiaoqiang accepted an invitation from the Social Democratic Friedrich Ebert Foundation. On June 12, they left for West Germany. But they could not replicate the success of their 1986 investigation in Hungary and Yugoslavia (CESRRI, 1987; Chapter 7). The justification for the 1988 price-reform push was rooted in the logic of package reform—even though Wu Jinglian, Liu Guoguang, and other package reformers criticized that it did not include sufficiently strict austerity measures, as I stressed above. Invoking the West German Erhard Miracle had been core to the rhetoric of package reform, at least since Friedman's first visit to China (Weber, 2020a, 2020b, 2021). The delegation of the System Reform Institute now traveled to West Germany to consult local economists about their understanding of the country's postwar economic transition and the lessons it held for China (ibid., Chen, 2013, 509–512).

Wang argued against the proposal to try an "Erhard Miracle" in China, rationalizing that the conditions of West Germany in the 1940s and China in the 1980s were too different (Wang, 1998, 148). Wang and Chen received a strong confirmation of this view from Herbert Giersch. Giersch, then-president of the global neoliberal thought collective the Mont Pelerin Society and of the Kiel Institute for the World Economy, had attended the Athens Conference with Wu and Kornai (see Chapter 7; Csikós-Nagy et al., 1984, ix; Giersch, 2006, 207–221; Mont Pelerin Society, 2019). Giersch counted among his credentials relating to the West German postwar economic reconstruction that he had received his PhD under Alfred Müller-Armack's supervision. Müller-Armack is considered to be one of the intellectual fathers of the ordoliberal idea of a social market economy (Ötsch, Pühringer, and Hirte, 2018, 146). When Chen cautiously raised the possibility of combining tight macroeconomic control with price liberalization in China, following Ludwig Erhard's example, Giersch replied the action would induce a catastrophe equivalent to suicide. The West German currency and price reform had relied on market-oriented enterprises and a legal system designed to sustain a market economy, Giersch argued. Neither was in place in China (Chen, 2013, 510).

Wang Xiaoqiang and Chen Yizi returned to China on June 28 (Chen, 2013, 512). In addition to the study tour in West Germany, the System Reform Institute had conducted fieldwork in China to evaluate the potential consequences of pushing through with price reform. They submitted six reports to the leadership that demonstrated that the price-reform program would result in disaster (see, for example, CESRRI, 1988a, 1988b; Wang, 2019, 90). As in 1986, they urged that liberalizing prices without preceding institutional reforms would not solve the problem of correcting relative prices or the mechanisms of endogenous money creation (ibid.; Chen, 2013, 514; see Chapter 7). The operational logic of enterprises, the banking sector, and the system of welfare provisioning could only be gradually reformed and had to go hand in hand with gradual price reform (Chen, 2013, 514). Liberalizing prices could give rise to panic buying and unrest. It would not resolve the challenges of reform; it would instead undermine the conditions for working out solutions.

Li Yining (1988a, 1988b), too, once more issued a warning against wholesale price liberalization.[8] He stressed that there were only two competing market reform paradigms in China, and they differed in substance: wholesale price liberalization versus slow reform of ownership and enterprises. It follows that the logic underpinning the renewed attempt at pushing through with price reform was that of the package reformers—the same group of economists who had drawn up the plans of the Program Office in 1986. Li explicitly attributes the economics of price reforms to János Kornai and Western mainstream economics. According to Li, they were caught up in the ideal of perfect competition and were blind to China's economic reality. Li reiterated that China was a disequilibrium system (see Chapter 7). Under such conditions, price liberalization could only do harm and risked high inflation. Wilhelm Linder, the ordoliberal economist who had cautioned against price reform in 1986, also issued another warning against shock therapy in a meeting with Zhao Ziyang on July 30, 1988, pointing out the implications for social and economic stability of too-rapid price liberalization (Zhao, 2016b).[9]

The warnings by opponents of shock therapy against the logic of price liberalization as well as the cautions of package reformers that austerity and monetary restraint had to precede price reform remained unheard in the summer of 1988. Yao Yilin, Li Peng, and Chen Yun also intervened, trying to water down the price-reform plans (Fewsmith, 1994, 225–26). But the agenda was ultimately set by Deng, with Zhao's loyal support. More product-specific price deregulations followed. The prices of color TVs and, in July, of branded alcohol and cigarettes were liberalized, resulting in instant exorbitant price rises (ibid., 392–93; Zhang, 2017, 575). These goods were luxury goods, but with the improvement of living standards, people had found them increasingly within their economic reach and did not take these price rises lightly. Nevertheless, the price-reform campaign went ahead.

From August 15 to 17, the Politburo of the Central Committee of the Communist Party held a plenary meeting in Beidaihe, discussing a "Preliminary Plan for Price and Wage Reform" (关于价格、工资改革的初步方案) (Hu, 1989; Zhang, 2017, 574–575). China's leadership decided to basically abolish the dual-track price system and gradually liberalize the prices of core industrial products such as steel and energy, as well as of all consumer goods (Fang, 2014, 355). The plan predicted a rise in consumer prices of 70 percent over five years, for which wage laborers were to be compensated. This decision constituted the attempt to give up on the strategy of marketization from the margins and state control over the core of the economy. It marked a shift toward marketizing the industrial core and commodifying the basic livelihoods. On August 19, 1988, state TV and the *People's Daily* reported that the Politburo had adopted, in principle, a plan for price and wage reform (*People's Daily*, 1988; Yang, 1998, 393). The announcement did not contain any information on the timing and details of the plan, but it was enough to break the people's trust in the stability of the economy, the protection of their income and savings by the state, and the value of their money.

Panic buying, bank runs, and worker protests immediately began to spread outward from big cities all over the country. Rising incomes in the 1980s had resulted in increasing savings. People now rushed to withdraw their money and exchanged it against whatever durable commodities they could get hold of, culminating in riots in some places (Brødsgaard and Rutten, 2017, 83; Burdekin and Hu, 1999; Burdekin, 2000; CIA, 1988; Song, 1995; Yang, 1998, 393–394; Zhang, 2017, 575–577; Zhao, 2009, 131).[10]

For the first time since 1978, the savings rate dropped in China (Burdekin and Hu, 1999, 67). Previously, specific items for which a price adjustment or liberalization had been announced had become subject to hoarding. But in the summer of 1988, the general exchangeability of money was uncertain, and all sorts of durable goods were snatched up, regardless of their immediate usefulness, brand, or quality (Zhang, 2017, 575). For example, in Kunming, dubbed the "city of spring" due to its year-round mild climate, people began hoarding air conditioners (Geng and Zhou, 1998, 547). The more prices rose, the more people rushed to buy whatever they could get. Panic-buying, in turn, fueled price rises (Zhang, 2017, 576).

China spiraled into accelerating inflation for the first time since the revolution. The total retail price index, which includes consumer goods, services, and producer goods, shot up from 12 percent in July to 23 percent in August 1988, peaking at around 28 percent in April 1989 (Burdekin and Hu, 1999, 81). In 1988, the growth in the consumer price index outpaced the growth in real GDP—an occurrence unprecedented in China's first decade of reform (Brødsgaard and Rutten, 2017, 89; Burdekin, 2000, 224).

Russia's shock therapists asserted, "The collapse of communist one-party rule was the sine qua non for an effective transition to a market economy" (Lipton and Sachs, 1990, 87). To Deng Xiaoping, in contrast, the leadership of the CPC was a cardinal principle that he considered essential for China in its pursuit of catching up. After listening to Li Peng's and Zhao Ziyang's report on the explosive reactions across the country to the announcements of the price-reform plans on September 12, Deng said that the Central Committee had to assert its authority. There was no way to govern without authority; both economic and political controls were now needed (Fang, 2014, 377). When the push toward radical price reform shook the political and social stability, the government rolled back the program, called for recentralization of power, reintroduced price controls over important commodities, and imposed a strict retrenchment policy to regain control.[11]

In the same month, the economists in support of a big bang rallied once more in hope that a second meeting between Friedman and Zhao could help them restart their radical reform agenda. (See Illustration 6 of Zhao and Friedman, with Wu Jinglian and Zhou Xiaochuan in the background.) Friedman issued the same call for shock therapy that China's package reformers had advocated. Limit the money supply by printing less money, and then liberalize prices, he told Zhao, adding that liberalizing prices would help bring inflation under control (Friedman, 1990; Zhao, 2016c, 514–515).[12]

In October, Chen Yizi met the former Hungarian Premier Jenő Fock, who had held this position from 1967 to 1975. Fock had presided over attempts to introduce market elements under the New Economic Mechanism. Fock warned Chen that economic imbalances had to be resolved in the process of reform instead of trying to first achieve macrobalance and then reform—a view that

ILLUSTRATION 6   Milton Friedman meets Premier Zhao Ziyang, October 1988. Zhao
Ziyang shaking hands with Milton Friedman with Wu Jinglian (left)
and Zhou. Xiaochuan (right) in the back and Rose Friedman by
her husband's side. Courtesy of Hoover Institution Archives, Stanford,
California.

resembled Zhao Ziyang's stance prior to May 1988. Chen shared Fock's lessons
with Zhao, but Zhao remained silent (Chen, 2013, 515).

The window of opportunity for a foreign tailwind from either direction had
closed. Zhao remained General Secretary for the time being but lost his influence on economic policy, which was now in the hands of Li Peng and Yao Yilin.
Chen Yun and Li Xiannian regained their influence (Zhao, 2009, 233–234). Not
pushing ahead with reform but bringing the economy back under control was
the order of the day.

The director of the Price Bureau, Cheng Zhiping, stressed that in late 1988
lessons of the 1940s and of the aftermath of the Great Leap Forward were key to
regaining control over the economy (see also Chapter 3). According to Cheng
(2006, 119), the stabilization effort was guided by Chen Yun's assertion that the
degree of the government's control over the market is decided by its control over
the most essential goods on the market (see also Chapter 3). Applying a logic that
is strikingly similar to the *Guanzi*'s light–heavy principles of price stabilization
(see Chapter 1), Cheng argues that the key was to focus the price work on the
important, or "heavy" (重), points.

In the 1940s price stabilization, the "two whites and one black" (两白一黑),
referring to rice, cotton, and coal, were the most essential goods for feeding and clothing the people and for industry. In the 1960s, the list of prices

had been refined, reflecting China's more diversified economy, to include 18 essential goods. The 1988 price stabilization effort now targeted the prices of 383 goods. These goods were identified, based on survey work, as critical to people's livelihoods and agricultural and industrial production. The prices of these goods were stabilized through a concerted effort: production was expanded to increase their supply; the commerce system was enhanced to overcome bottlenecks in circulation; the price control system was used to reimpose price controls; and the macroeconomic regulation system was used to adjust the overall plan, credit expansion, and investments (Cheng, 2006, 119–121). These measures were complemented with another 1940s anti-inflationary tactic. Government bonds indexed to a set of essential commodity prices were issued to re-create trust in monetary assets (Burdekin, 2000; Burdekin and Wang, 1999; see Chapter 3).

The Chinese state reestablished control over the core of the economy. Inflation was overcome in about a year's time (see Figure 8.1), but the political consequences of the 1988 aborted big bang shaped the fate of China and the world. The combination of the aborted push for radical reform and the subsequent drastic reversal in course deepened the social and political tensions that had built up in the second half of the 1980s, creating an explosive situation. The runaway inflation of 1988 undermined the trust in money-market relations for many urban residents and added to the anxieties unleashed by an increasing commodification of life. On the other hand, those who benefited from the growing profit opportunities and mushrooming markets felt threatened by the tightening of control. This formed the background for the broad and diverse social movement of 1989, which demanded not only democratic rights but also an end to corruption, social securities, and price stability (Wang, 2011, 21–30).

Conclusion

Opinions continue to diverge as to what caused the short-term pain with its long-term detrimental effects and what lessons are to be learned from the crisis of 1988. Lou Jiwei, who together with Guo Shuqing, Zhou Xiaochuan, and others rose to powerful positions in the 1990s, stated recently, after retiring from the post of minister of finance,

> Certainly 1988 saw a high rate of inflation. Later some people attributed this inflation to comrade Deng Xiaoping's "crashing through the barriers of prices" (价格闯关), this turns things on its head. Comrade Xiaoping's target was the corruption and economic disorder created by the dual track price system, this required uniting the two tracks and obeying to the market. There is nothing at all wrong with this. Necessary conditions for the market to determine prices are tight fiscal and monetary policies and avoiding inflation by any means, even given these conditions, there will be mild price increases as result of the corrections to the price distortions. If

something was a mistake, its root lies in the suppressed inflation from the time when all-round contracting was implemented [in 1987].

(Lou, 2017)

The World Bank economist Adrian Wood, who was part of the first mission to China, comes to a similar conclusion as Lou Jiwei. In a *Financial Times* article of October 1990, he writes:

China's economic reform in the second half of the 1980s got on to the wrong track, with the premature relaxation over state enterprise expenditures, and the universalisation of two-tier (fixed and market) pricing. The result was accelerating inflation and massive corruption, which were deeply unpopular… Economic anger, rather than a wish for democracy, was what moved most demonstrators in May 1989.

(Wood, 1990, 25)

Wood sees in the harsh austerity imposed in the fall of 1988 the potential for "real progress." In his view, "severe deflation of the sort which China has lately undergone provides ideal conditions for price liberalisation." Wood also sees a "silver lining" in "China's political conservatism"; it would make it easier to impose the pain necessary for further economic reforms.

Zhao Ziyang, while imprisoned in his own house, came to a quite different conclusion on the causes of the 1988 crisis. Zhao wrote in his journal,

[T]he proposed pricing reform was not in line with the gradual reform strategy but relied on large-scale government-administered price adjustments. This reflected the sentiments of the time: to rush through price reforms, and to eliminate the two-track pricing system to unify or at least reduce the gap between set prices and market prices. This was not the correct way to carry out price reform, because ultimately it was not a shift from price controls to market mechanisms. It was using planning methods to adjust prices. It was still the old way of planned pricing. It is clear now that if high inflation had not occurred, and this price reform plan had been carried out, it would not have resolved the problem….

(Zhao, 2009)

My interviewees strongly disagreed on the course and causes of the crisis of 1988. But they agreed that the disastrous failure of the push for price reform in 1988 was critical for the political crisis that culminated on June 4, 1989, with the massacre on Tiananmen Square. In 1988, Zhao had urged that a public security law was necessary to push ahead with reform. In 1989, Zhao tried to transcend the same logic of state repression that eventually led to his downfall and imprisonment. The young economists Zhao had nourished were openly loyal with the protesters. They were aware that the troops were on their way to Tiananmen

Square and that martial law would soon be imposed. They sensed that a disaster was about to happen.

On May 18, the day Gorbachev ended his visit to China and when the world's eyes were on Beijing, Zhao Ziyang went to Tiananmen Square in the early morning to address the hunger-striking students. The famous image of Zhao with a microphone surrounded by protesters shows him appealing to the students to stop their fasting. He stood there as General Secretary of the party and apologized that it had taken the leadership so long to reach out to the protesters. The students should live to see China complete the Four Modernizations, he urged. "[W]hen you end your fast," Zhao pledged, "the government will never close the door to dialogues, never" (Beijing Television Service, 1990). The next day, Zhao returned to the square and reiterated his call on the students to end the hunger strike (*China Daily*, 1990). Zhao was aware that Deng was making provisions to impose martial law and was willing to use the military to crack down on the students. Zhao prepared to resign. He knew that this was the end of his career (Zhao, 2009, 27–32).

Still, on May 19, the young economists who had risen to influence under Zhao decided to make their own statement. These economists were based at the System Reform Institute, the Agriculture Research Center at the Development Research Institute, and the International Office of CITIC and were organized in the Beijing Economics Youth Association—the "three institutes and one association" (三所一会). In the name of their organizations, they endorsed the social movement as the most brilliant chapter in China's history of democratic movements and thus responded to the protesters' demand for the state to recognize the legitimacy of their movement. They pronounced that since the founding of the People's Republic, the leadership of the party and the government had never been as divided from the people and as opposed to the popular will as it was now. Echoing Zhao's dialogue with the students, they called on the leadership to organize an extraordinary meeting of the National People's Congress as the legitimate assembly to resolve the crisis, on the people to support the protesters, and on the hunger strikers to end their strike, since they were needed for China's future. They sent their statement to media organizations, universities, and the protesters. Tens of thousands of copies were produced and posted all over Beijing (Chen, 2013, 601–604; Zhu, 2013, 46–47).

On May 28, Zhao was put under house arrest, where he remained until his death in 2005. On June 4, the military cracked down on the protests. The bloodshed against which the young reform intellectuals lobbied also marked the end of their era in China's reforms. Many of the young economists had to flee the country or were imprisoned. Many did not return to policy-making or research institutes. Some became rich in private business; many disappeared into private business without making a fortune. Some returned to China; others, like Chen Yizi, died in exile.[13]

In contrast, Liu Guoguang, Xue Muqiao, and Zhou Xiaochuan, who had converged to promote shock therapy in the second half of the 1980s, chose not to publicly support the protests and instantly turned against Zhao Ziyang. On June 14, Wu (1989) had completed a first draft of their criticism under the title "Our Worries and Proposals—Viewpoints of Several Economists" (我们的忧思和建议：几位经济学者的意见), which was published in August in the compilation "Essential Reports" (要报) by the Chinese Academy of Social Sciences. These reports are issued for consideration by the central leadership. Wu and his collaborators accused Zhao of having betrayed the 1978 decision on the direction of reform and development. Zhao would have made big mistakes, resulting in economic chaos. Most importantly, he would have installed a dual-track system in prices and other economic mechanisms, resulting in a distortion of social accounting and corruption (Zhang, 2017, 612–5). Many package reformers enjoyed stellar careers in China throughout the 1990s and until today, while most of the economists who debunked shock therapy in the 1980s are now largely forgotten inside and outside of China.

Notes

1 See, for example, Fewsmith (1994, 220–232), Cheng (1995), Vogel (2011, 470–471).
2 See, for example, Gewirtz (2017, 198–200) and Shih (2008, 124–135).
3 Translation as in Schram (1988, 180)
4 See, for example, (Myers, 1989) for an account of how corruption was at the time discussed in the Chinese press and Oi (1989) for a systematic account of corruption in the rural economy.
5 For a detailed account of Liu Guoguang's, Wu Jinglian's and other package reformer's interventions urging for macroeconomic restraint see Gewirtz (2017, 197–198, 205) and Zhang (2017, 568–571).
6 Also see my review (Weber, 2019a) of Gewirtz (2017) on the issue of telling the 1980s reform debate from more than one side.
7 I have been told that the contemplated countermeasures included military control, which one of my interviewees compared to Pinochet's approach to enforcing his drastic "shock therapy."
8 Also see Gewirtz (2017, 205) on Li Yining's intervention.
9 See Linder (1990) for a discussion of his analysis of reform from a planned economy.
10 The cancellation of savings was an intended consequence of high inflation induced by shock therapy (International Monetary Fund (IMF), World Bank, Organisation for Economic Co-Operation and Development (OECD), and European Bank for Reconstruction and Development, 1990; Reddaway and Glinski, 2001, 180).
11 For a meticulously detailed analysis of the political dynamic around inflation in 1988, see Holbig (2001).
12 For a discussion of how Milton Friedman's engagement with Chinese reformers speaks to the broader question of China's relation with neoliberalism, see Weber (2020b).
13 See the list of biographies for a more detailed overview.

CONCLUSION

Wanderer, your footprints are the path, and nothing else; wanderer, there is no path, the path is made by walking.

Antonio Machado

The economic transformation China experienced during its period of reform beginning in 1978 was inconceivable at its outset. The country's historic economic growth in the decades of neoliberal globalization stands in sharp contrast with the fate of most economies in the global south. In the period 1950–1980, most developing economies enjoyed high rates of economic growth, outpacing China's. But their relative standing has been turned upside down in the decades since (Amsden, 2007, 6–7). In the 1980s, most African countries endured negative GDP growth, while in Latin America, the golden age of industrialization gave way to twenty-five years with only 10 percent cumulative growth. By comparison, in the first two decades of reform, China's economy grew annually, on average, by more than the growth recorded by Latin America over a quarter of a century (ibid.). Although the East Asian "tigers" and India fared far better than the rest of the world, China's average annual growth rate of more than 10 percent stands at double that of these other high-performing countries. With the benefit of hindsight, we now know that China was, in the late 1970s, on the cusp of an economic expansion often described as unprecedented in scope, pace, and scale—just as the developing world as a whole was falling behind.

GDP growth is, of course, a crude indicator. However, it does provide an approximate measure of the changing position of a given country in relation to the world economy. When China's economists returned to Beijing after the Cultural Revolution to join the reform effort, China was poor and attempting to carve out a path toward economic prosperity. The ambition of continuous revolution under Maoism was replaced by an all-encompassing primacy of economic development.

China's rise is now a fact of life. From the vantage of the struggles among China's economists over the right reform path, this historic outcome was a daring hope, if not altogether implausible. When young reform intellectuals returned to Beijing after years in remote villages and flocked to empty lecture halls to discuss China's future, the explosive growth of subsequent decades—albeit with all its severe social and environmental consequences—was unimaginable. In their study exchanges on economic system reform with Eastern European émigré economists and with World Bank and other international dignitaries, the economists of China's revolutionary generation and its establishment intellectuals could only marvel at the prosperity and advanced state of the applied sciences abroad. The System Reform Institute's delegations toured Hungary, Yugoslavia, Brazil, and other Latin American countries, in the hope of learning from the achievements (as well as mistakes) of what were then model national economies for China.

What was at stake in China's reform debate of the 1980s was nothing less than a common understanding of the economy's basic mechanisms. Early on, the dominant position within the Chinese economic intelligentsia reflected the view that market forces had to play a greater role in society and that this would necessitate price reform. Fundamental disagreements arose among China's economists around the question of *how* such reform would take place. Competing reform approaches expressed themselves in the disagreements over the continued use of the dual-track price system and mobilization of existing institutions to create markets; this was countered by some with a strategy of shock, in which the economy was to be subjected to wholesale and sudden liberalization. The fact that the two sides clashed over this next step of reform rather than over the economy's basic direction might suggest that its focus was highly technical, without deeper ideological significance. In fact, as in the Soviet industrialization debate of the 1920s—the focus of which was also the speed and pattern of development, but not the retreat from War Communism to the New Economic Policy per se—"the basic differences between two ideological tournaments became visible" (Erlich, 1967, xvii). Such differences manifested themselves in two different approaches to the economics of reform.

China's reform economists shared one common goal above all others: economic progress. They also agreed that marketization would be necessary in the pursuit of economic development. But the two basic schools of thought clashed over how to move forward. One position was in accordance with what came to be known as the shock therapy doctrine of transition—a quintessentially neoliberal policy prescript that swept the socialist world (see the Introduction). This side held that the desired economic model would be posed axiomatically and that a shock to the old system would transform it in one go. This approach assumed that the most desirable future economic system as well as the means of establishing it could be derived from economic models. According to this view, a blueprint was to be drawn up to map a comprehensive package of measures that would redesign the entire system according to one unified concept.

The alternative school of thought, by contrast, acknowledged an essential ignorance of both the end—the ultimate configuration of the Chinese economy—as well as the path to get there. This second vision took as a basic premise the absence of any blueprint or comprehensive plan that could deliver a general answer to the challenge of reform. From this viewpoint, the mechanism of reform and the specifics of the new system had to be worked out through experimentation and theoretically guided empirical research. From this latter perspective, there was simply no way to divine China's future on a drawing board. "Armchair economics" was deemed to fail. In the following sections, I recapitulate the core reform prescripts of these two competing approaches.

The Idealism of Package Reform

The Chinese proponents of a so-called package reform, like the shock therapists around the world (see the Introduction), promoted an initial big bang in price reform. The package was to include price adjustments, in one step, for critical producer goods such as raw materials and energy, followed by liberalization. The package reformers' basic approach was to begin by choosing a target model for reform and to contrast this ideal target model with a schematic version of the old command economy. In the ideal target model, the market mechanism was carried out primarily through flexible prices. One of the fundamental differences between the desired target and the old system was a lack of price flexibility in the latter. These reformers located the most severe price distortions in the producer goods sector, which were traditionally priced low in the Soviet approach to development. The most effective approach to reform, in their view, would require first tackling these exaggerated deviations from the target model, overcoming the distortions in the prices of raw materials and energy simultaneously. Such a dramatic step in reform had to be prepared, however, by first "cooling" the economy. This meant, in practice, enforcing harsh austerity with the aim of overcoming macroeconomic imbalances.

The package approach to reform held that the coexistence of the obsolete old and the desired new systems would create harmful frictions, resulting in the ineffectiveness of both the old and the new regulating mechanisms. From the vantage of package reformers, the dual-track price system was at best acceptable as a temporary, transitory measure, but it had to be overcome as quickly as possible. The big bang proponents invoked an argument structurally similar to Hayek's warning of the "slippery slope" toward a planned economy that might result from any move in favor of price controls (see Chapter 2). In their eyes, if the dual-track price system prevailed, along with the confusion and corruption they attributed to it, the result would be a harmful reversal. As long as core elements of the old system persisted—such as central control over the prices of crucial producer goods—the possibility of a relapse would be ever present. They thus recommended that the price system be introduced rapidly and universally, arguing that only the destruction of the core of the old system could realize the target model. They acknowledged that this approach would cause short-term pain. But in their eyes, the only alternative was long-term suffering.

The proponents of such radical price reform recognized that their proposal entailed one grave risk, namely, an increase in the general price level. However, as with Friedman's (1966, 20) metaphor of the overfueled furnace that can be defused only by letting all its heat out at once (see Chapter 2), they argued that suppressed inflation could not be overcome unless direct price controls were removed. As a necessary evil, they argued, it would be better to get on with it without delay. As Brus put it, "the day of reckoning" would arrive eventually, and so it would be better to confront and overcome its challenges sooner rather than later (see Chapter 5). As long as tight fiscal and monetary controls were in place, a one-time increase in prices to compensate for suppressed inflation would not detonate an ongoing inflationary process. To return to Friedman's metaphor: the overfueled furnace, having released its heat, would exhaust itself. As with the pain accompanying surgery, removing price controls was therapeutically necessary and temporary. Seen from this perspective, inflation was a monetary, not structural, phenomenon and could be controlled by the government; aggregate excess demand was only the result of the pathologies of socialism. Such thinking is best captured by concepts such as Kornai's "investment hunger" and "soft budget constraint" (see Chapter 7)—which do not concern themselves with the challenges of industrialization. In this view, the Chinese inflation of 1988 was the result of the government's failure to impose sufficiently strict macro controls and not the consequence of Deng Xiaoping's failed attempt at shock therapy (see Chapter 8).

As I explore in Chapters 4, 5, and 6, the package reformers found inspiration in Eastern European émigré economists who had abandoned market socialism, neoclassical mainstream economics, and monetarism. The younger generation also drew on concepts of optimal design and control from engineering.[1] Most of the package reformers were academic economists, and many had been adherents to Soviet orthodoxy in the early years of the People's Republic. In fact, we may observe a parallel between the idealization of the planned economy in Soviet Marxism, where the whole national economy was imagined to function as one centrally planned factory, and the idealization of a market economy underlying the shock therapy approach. While the two theoretical approaches oppose one another on the question of the superiority of a plan or a market as a regulating mechanism, they are united in striving for an optimal, rational economy. This methodological commonality between those believing in the omnipotent power of the visible and the invisible hands was observed by one of the foremost general equilibrium theorists, Frank Hahn (1981, 2):

> [Both sides] take it for granted that somewhere there is a theory, that is a body of logically connected propositions based on postulates not wildly at variance with what is the case, which support their policies.

This quest for representing the whole economy in one closed model was also a common ground between the planning and the market proponents of the Socialist Calculation Debate. From the technocratic stance of both sides, the economic problem boils down to finding a set of rational prices. Or, as Paul Samuelson (as in Foley, 2011) observed,

> [I]t doesn't really matter whether capital hires labor or labor hires capital, or both are allocated by a central planner: the important goal is the allocation of productive resources and final products consistently with the principle of equating marginal cost and marginal benefit.

The Chinese package reformers adhered to the same kind of economics. They saw the task of market creation as drawing up a comprehensive policy blueprint that had to ensure, first and foremost, rational prices. From the reformers' perspective, rational prices could be achieved only by applying either the market or the plan as a pure form, and the dual-track price system was condemned as an incoherent hybrid. Whereas a multitrack price system had been used to overcome hyperinflation after the civil war, the subsequent pursuit of Soviet-style planning involved the ambition to suppress price tracks other than planned prices, at least for important goods (see Chapters 3 and 4). The dual-track price system would be an unavoidable evil over the course of the market transition, but it was to be abolished as soon as possible. At the outset of reforms, package reformers saw the task before them as precisely the opposite of that from the days when China had emulated the Soviet model. Now, all prices should be unified under the market track.

Resemblances between the paradigms of pure market orthodoxy and pure planning can also be detected in the concrete steps suggested by the Program Office in 1986, with the aim of generating a breakthrough in China's price reform. According to the 1986 agenda, prices would first be unified into planned equilibrium prices determined by calculation, after which they would be fully liberalized. This reform proposal assumed that both the calculation and forces of the market would bring about the same, or at least sufficiently similar, equilibrium prices. Thus, calculation-based planning and the market were taken to be means to the same end. As with Hayek's and Robbins's judgments in the Socialist Calculation Debate,[2] the problem presented by calculating prices within the logic of the Program Office approach was that it was too time-consuming to be practical as a sustainable form of regulation. Nevertheless, the Program Office economists believed calculation from the center could prepare the wholesale transition to a superior market mechanism. Market determination of crucial input prices, from this point of view, did not require a process of institution building. As the *natural* order of things, market prices were expected to emerge instantly and spontaneously once the *artificially* imposed control over prices was removed. Instead of envisioning a slow, historical evolution toward a new political economy, shock therapy suggested a rapid move into an ideal market, following planned steps from the theoretically derived blueprint.

In this regard, the so-called "Erhard Miracle" was invoked as anecdotal evidence for the practicality of the theory. However, proponents of emulating the West German example did not analyze in any great depth the actual economic history of Erhard's price and currency reforms or whether, indeed, these policies were suitable for addressing the challenges China confronted in the 1980s. Rather, they subscribed to the neoliberal mystification of Erhard's price reform and saw it as a "miracle" (Weber, 2020). Similarly, they cited the supposed lesson of Eastern Europe—that gradualism would fail. They relied on the authority of famous economists. Systematic historical inquiry, however, might have posed the question of why attempts at overnight price liberalization in Eastern Europe repeatedly provoked social and political turmoil and were ultimately (partially) reversed. This history, in any case, had been well known in China since the Moganshan World Bank Conference of 1982, if not earlier (see Chapter 5).

As for their idealism, those academic economists in favor of a comprehensive reform package showed some striking resemblance to the scholar officials in the *Salt and Iron Debate*, despite the radically different contexts and the two millennia that separated them. The scholars of the ancient debate began from a vision of an ideal state in the past, which they aimed to reinstate, rather than from the specific challenges facing the new emperor in the context of a deep economic crisis (see Chapter 1). The ancients held that if the ritual order and righteousness were to be reestablished, the state could withdraw from direct intervention into the economy—in particular, from controlling salt and iron monopolies, as well as from regulating prices of essential agricultural products by dampening the supply and demand fluctuations. As long as morality ruled, they believed, the state's interventions could remain minimal, and the retreat of bureaucrats from economic activities would guard against corruption.

The big bang proponents of the 1980s also advanced an argument about the state's withdrawal from the economy; they saw the state's role as a market player under the dual-track price system as the main source of corruption. They too envisioned a minimalist state that would regulate society indirectly by macroeconomic means and rule-setting rather than through righteousness. But here, the parallels end. In sharp contrast with the ancients, reformers held that morality was to be replaced by free competition among individuals. Left to develop spontaneously on its own, this competition would translate the pursuit of self-interest into the best outcome for society. The ancient scholar officials held that markets were to be subordinate to the moral order of society. For the shock therapists, all realms of society were to be subordinate to a universal market.

The Pragmatism of Dual-Track Reformers

Just as in the ancient *Salt and Iron Debate*, practically minded scholars and commerce officials challenged the idealist approach in China's price reform debate of the 1980s (see Chapters 5 through 8). Rather than aiming to move toward a theoretically derived target model in one push, they conducted in-depth empirical research guided by theorizing but unconstrained by the quest for one all-encompassing model of the economy. Their aim was to discover a means for the gradual improvement of China's economy and to examine the place of markets in this endeavor—not to project an ideal future state. Dual-track reformers took an approach that identified and harnessed transformative forces already emerging in prevailing commercial and industrial activity. With regard to price reform, this meant an imperative to improve the dual-track price system rather than destroy it. In their analysis, wholesale liberalization could not solve the problems of China's price system. Investigations using a large sample of Chinese state-owned enterprises, as well as a survey of the Yugoslavian and Hungarian reform experience, for example, indicated that a big bang would result in a reversion to the initial relative prices instead of the sought-after adjustment of the price structure.

Closer scrutiny of the postwar West German transition amplified the gradualists' skepticism about reproducing an "Erhard Miracle" in China, as the big bang was dubbed. The mere removal of price controls could not transform the state-owned enterprises into market enterprises. They remained socialist production units insofar that they had no power over the magnitude of capital and labor they employed. Workers could not be fired, and state-owned enterprises did not draw upon any capital market; they were forbidden from going bankrupt. The state-owned enterprises had no choice but to use their monopolistic position and to carry on, no matter the circumstances. According to the logic of the big bang, an increased input price should have induced adjustments in production technology or even have arrested the production of certain goods. But in reality, the state-owned enterprises could only react to input price increases by passing them on to producers further along in the production chain. The result would thus ultimately be consumer price inflation, which would in turn fuel wage increases. The opponents of a big bang predicted that shock therapy would generate runaway inflation rather than a convergence at some desired equilibrium. The outcome would be destruction of the core of the old economy, without creating a functional market economy. Such a development would put China's social and political stability at risk and thus endanger the project of reform altogether.

The defenders of the dual-track price system predicted that the prescription of rapid price liberalization would lead to failure, even on its own terms. In their view, neither pure central control nor overnight liberalization could address the challenge of catching up with the advanced capitalist world and increasing overall living standards. They did not infer from this that there was no prospect for reform, however. Rather, the gradualists suggested that the prevailing system of multiple prices—along with certain practical adjustments—was well suited for gradually transforming both China's price structure and its price-determining system and, with it, the economy's regulating mechanism at large.

In the view of the gradualist experimentalists, market determination of prices was not achieved simply by abolishing price controls. The gradualists contended that the manner in which prices are determined depended on the mode of operation at the micro level. In a similar vein, inflation was not understood as a purely monetary phenomenon, especially under conditions such as China's. From the viewpoint of these pragmatic economists, familiar as they were with the living conditions of the overwhelmingly rural population of China, aggregate excess demand was not to be achieved by suppressing demand, but rather by boosting supply.

For the dual-track defenders, the challenge facing the Chinese economy was to be understood as a "reindustrialization." Reindustrialization required overcoming certain bottlenecks, for example, in critical producer goods and in energy, by increasing production but not by raising prices. The process was complex and required delicate intervention. It could not be accomplished in a single blunt act. China's revolutionary history had shown that industrialization could not be attained simply by state command. The gradualist reformers argued that faith in a market miracle was likewise a delusion. The only sensible approach, they said, was a gradual, experimental one in which market forces would be created and harnessed by the state in a controlled manner. In their eyes, the dual-track price system, which had emerged from bureaucratic practice and the experience of rural reform, was well suited to achieve this and could be expanded to apply to critical producer goods such as steel and coal.

The essence of the dual-track price system can be captured by the perspective of the Guanzian principle of controlling the "heavy," or essential, and letting go of the "light," or unimportant (see Chapter 1). It is critical to understand that the relative importance of commodities was determined not only by their physical characteristics but also by the specific local conditions of their markets and social contexts of their production. What was determinative was whether a good was the product of a major, centrally controlled production facility or the productive efforts of a minor local enterprise. Even within the output of one major producer, the state-mandated quota was important for keeping the core of the industrial economy running. Surplus production, by contrast, could be left to the discretion of the enterprise. The basic principle of the dual-track price system therefore was to relinquish the price controls of inessential goods produced by minor suppliers. It also relinquished the price controls on surplus products of major producers of essential industrial inputs such as raw materials and energy. The system of material balancing along with planned prices thus was initially kept intact. At the same time, the high prices of surplus products of scarce raw materials and energy marketed to producers outside the industrial command system—such as township and village enterprises (TVEs) as well as other state-owned enterprises—produced strong incentives for the enterprises to economize their planned production and to squeeze out a surplus for the market. In this way, the state-owned enterprises grew into the market as the industrial core of the Chinese economy was marketized. The state commercial system, too, was not abolished but was used to integrate the national market and balance prices across regions.

Exactly who is to be credited as the originator of the dual-track price system remains a matter of dispute. I have argued throughout the second part of this book that the reform mechanism was not, in fact, invented by any single individual. Rather, the dual-track price system emerged through the gradual relaxation of control in the areas most peripheral for the functioning of the industrial economy. Such a relaxation of controls was achieved by careful experimentation, followed by systematic evaluation of this practice through empirical research. The structure of gradual price releases thereby reflected the logic of the Maoist price system, under which the most essential prices for industrialization and livelihood were the most tightly controlled (see Chapter 4). Importantly, the dual-track price system was defended through unorthodox reform economics that theorized and refined the prevailing reform practice. The decisive reform question in the mid-1980s was therefore whether to maintain and improve the dual-track price system or to abolish it. Defenders of the dual-track price system acknowledged that corruption was a problem, but they did not see abolition of the system as an acceptable solution. In pursuing reforms, they instead advocated for systematic interdisciplinary, social-scientific inquiry. These gradualist reformers believed that an easy solution to the colossal challenge of China's economic transformation could not be deduced from pure theoretical analysis. China could make its own way cautiously, and it had to use a range of theories and experiences—both foreign and domestic—to assess its progress and trajectory of development.

There is a surprising parallel with the *Salt and Iron Debate* (see Chapter 1). The basic outlook of the defenders of the dual-track price system resembles, to some extent, that of Sang Hongyang. Both focused on their respective given realities, such as (natural) monopolies, seasonal fluctuations, and the structures of a command economy, and how they could be mobilized to improve the workings of the economy; a supposed ideal state or target model was to be excluded from consideration. An emphasis on the feasible rather than on the ideal might be misunderstood as avoidance of fundamental change. However, the dual-track price system brought forth historic transformations of rare intensity and scope. The basic logic of the dual-track price system was at the heart of China's transformation from a poor agricultural country with revolutionary ambitions to one of global capitalism's manufacturing powerhouses.

This pragmatic stance vis-à-vis economic policy is certainly not uniquely Chinese. As the vigorous debates recounted in this book demonstrate, China's tradition is itself anything but internally uniform. We saw in Chapter 2 that the war economies of the major belligerent powers of the Second World War relied on a pragmatic approach similar to that advocated by China's gradualist reform economists decades later. As John Kenneth Galbraith has argued, in the case of the United States, price control relied to a large extent on the use of prevailing economic practices, such as the customer relations of monopolistic or oligopolistic suppliers. The successful general price freeze worked because it used empirically observed rather than theoretically derived prices. With regard to the transformation from a planned war economy to a postwar market economy, it was structurally similar to the challenge of market reforms in a socialist command economy. The pragmatic, gradual approach of the United Kingdom, as recounted by Alex Cairncross during his visit to China, presented an alternative to the overnight liberalization of the type that had been implemented in the United States, against the best advice of some of the most famous American economists of the time. In postwar West Germany too, the ordoliberal approach of wholesale price liberalization competed with a dual-track approach similar to the one that prevailed in China in the 1980s.

Throughout this book, I showed that China's gradualist and pragmatic approach to economic policy-making has been forcefully and repeatedly contested by those in favor of a sudden leap into an unregulated market economy. Gradualist experimentalism was by no means a foregone conclusion; it was defended over the course of fierce intellectual and political struggles. At the crossroads of the 1980s, China escaped shock therapy. Instead of experiencing severe economic decline and deindustrialization, as did Russia and several other transition economies, China's dual-track reforms laid the institutional and structural foundations for its economic ascent under tight political control by the party and the state.

The Path Was Set

The 1980s set in motion the process of China's marketization. Many of the young economists who emerged as strategic defenders of the dual-track approach of adjusting to the market in the 1980s fell out of favor, along with Zhao Ziyang, in 1989. After the military crackdown on Tiananmen Square and the imprisonment of Zhao (then General Secretary of the Communist Party of China), some of China's brightest reform economists vanished from the scene of policy-making (see Chapter 8). The reform approach they helped to shape and defend has survived and has continued to be contested. Throughout the 1990s, the economics profession in China was remodeled to align with the international neoclassical mainstream (Cohn, 2017). Neoliberal reformers made deep inroads in the arenas of ownership, the labor market, and the healthcare system, among others. But the core of the Chinese economic system was never destroyed in one big bang. Instead, it was fundamentally transformed by means of a dynamic of growth and globalization under the activist guidance of the state.

In October 1992, after Deng Xiaoping had restarted the reform agenda with his Southern Tour, the 14th CPC National Congress made the formal decision to establish a Socialist Market Economy with Chinese Characteristics. Jiang Zemin, Zhao Ziyang's successor as General Secretary, explained this new so-called leading concept:

> Whether the emphasis was on planning or on market regulation was not the essential distinction between socialism and capitalism. This brilliant

thesis has helped free us from the restrictive notion that the planned economy and the market economy belong to basically different social systems, thus bringing about a great breakthrough in our understanding of the relation between planning and market regulation.[3]

This decision marked a political breakthrough for a forceful restart of the marketization agenda. The official declaration of a socialist market economy signaled that the Chinese leadership of the 1990s was willing to shatter all remaining boundaries to the operation of market forces, in the name of economic progress. Their first step in this direction was the far-reaching price liberalization of 1992–1993. On the surface, this price liberalization resembled the big bang agenda that had been avoided in the 1980s. Controls over essential consumer and producer goods were now dismantled step by step. Among those targeted were key commodities such as grain, steel, coal, and oil. However, because of the drastically different status of the early-1990s Chinese economy—when compared even with the dynamics of the late 1980s—the relative impact of this big bang was far smaller than it would have been only a few years earlier.

As Naughton (1995, 289–290) argues in his classic account of China's economic reform, the economy had already been deeply marketized when several essential plan prices were abolished: "The plan had already become an island surrounded by an ocean of market price transactions" (ibid., 290). This is evidenced in Figures 0.5–0.7 of the Introduction. We observe that for retail, agriculture, and producer goods the share of government-set prices resembles the shoulder of a mountain. The market share in all three sectors increased as a result of the universalization of the dual-track system, and government-set prices diminished in their importance. A big bang in 1986—or even in 1988—would have been catastrophic. By 1992, this same liberalization effort was akin to jumping off a low-standing rock at the base of a mountain from which one has just descended.

The 1992 and 1993 price liberalizations gave rise to the only episode in China's reform period in which inflation outpaced economic growth (see Figure 0.4 of the Introduction). But it was not the kind of hyperinflation that had swept Russia (see Figure 0.3 of Introduction). The combination of deep and gradual marketization that had preceded liberalization, as well as the assertion of state power in 1989, ensured that the "small bang" of 1992 was constrained enough to preserve core economic institutions. The state maintained its control over the "commanding heights" of China's economy as it switched from direct planning to indirect regulation through the state's participation in the market.[4] China grew into global capitalism without losing control over its domestic economy.

Notes

1 This finding is consistent with Bockman (2012, 2011) and Bockman and Eyal (2002), who have shown the roots of neoliberal transition in neoclassical socialist economics.

2 Hayek (1935a, 1935b) and Robbins (1934) retreated from von Mises's claim of the impossibility of a rational socialist economy to a "second line of defense" (Lange, 1936, 36). They did not deny the *theoretical* possibility of a rational allocation of resources in a planned economy. But they doubted the possibility of a satisfactory *practical* solution to the problem.

3 Jiang Zemin, "Full Text of Jiang Zemin's Report at 14th Party Congress, 1992," online: www.bjreview.com.cn/document/txt/2011-03/29/content_363504.htm, last updated March 29, 2011.

4 For detailed accounts of the more recent evolution of state-market relations and reform policy making in China see Ang, 2016, Eaton, 2016 and Zheng and Huang, 2016.

KEY CHINESE REFORM ECONOMISTS[1]

An Zhiwen (安志文, 1919–2017)

An Zhiwen studied at the Anti-Japanese University in Yan'an, where he joined the Communist Party. After the revolution, he held leadership positions at the Policy Research Office and the Ministry of Industry in Dongbei. He became deputy director of the State Planning Commission in 1956 and returned as economic reform leader in the 1980s, first at the Ministry of Machinery and Industry and then at the National Economic System Reform. By the time An entered the core circles of economic reform policy-making, he had long-standing practical experience in industrial policy and economic planning. In 1984, An proposed to Zhao Ziyang to set up a research institute staffed with young intellectuals, reflecting the important contribution to agricultural reform of the Rural Development Group. This resulted in the founding of the Chinese Economic System Reform Research Institute. An participated in the Bashan Conference in 1986 and was a leading member of the Program Office. Although he initially supported the so-called "package reform" that had shock liberalization of prices at its core, An cautioned against its implementation in 1986, warning that it would be impossible to predict the inflationary effect of overnight price liberalization.

Bai Nanfeng (白南风, 1952–)

Bai Nanfeng was a member of both the Rural Development Group and the System Reform Institute. He was one of the leading young reform intellectuals of the 1980s. A sent-down youth in Shaanxi during the Cultural Revolution, he identified with the problem of rural poverty and the challenge of poverty alleviation. During our interviews in 2016, he stressed that his lifelong eating habits and living rhythm had been shaped by his years in the countryside. Along with his elder brother Bai Nansheng, another important researcher of the young generation of reformers, he entered Renmin University in 1980. Bai had very wide interests, sat in on lectures in advanced mathematics and philosophy, and participated in Li Yining's study group on Western economics. Bai's main contributions to the work of the Rural Development Group were in survey design and methodology. He also brought a long-term perspective of comparative civilization study to the group's work on rural reform. Bai participated in the writing of several important reports on urban and industrial reform, in the Moganshan Youth Conference, and in study tours to Japan and Eastern Europe. Together with Wang Xiaoqiang, he conducted fieldwork in Tibet and authored *Poverty of Plenty* (1986) out of their concern for the imbalance in economic development between China's coastal and Western provinces. Bai pioneered the research of public attitudes to reform in China and briefly, in 1988–1989, coproduced a TV show about reform. After June Fourth, both the Bai brothers were imprisoned. They did not return to formal research work in the 1990s but instead pursued private business activities.

Bao Tong (鲍彤, 1932–)

Bao Tong joined the Communist Party while in high school in 1949. Between 1954 and 1966, Bao was the director of a department of the Communist Party of China (CPC) Central Committee and worked as a researcher, deputy team leader, and deputy director of the research department. During the Cultural Revolution, he was sent for reeducation to the May Seventh Cadre School and labored there until 1975. Bao served as Zhao Ziyang's secretary in charge of political issues from 1980 to 1989. In 1986, he was entrusted by Zhao with plans for package reforms. He also served as deputy director of the National Economic System Reform Commission. He was in close exchange with the young reform intellectuals emerging from the Rural Development Group. He helped set up the China International Cultural Exchange Foundation in Beijing, funded by George Soros. From December 1987 until July 1989, Bao served as the director of the Political System Reform Research Office of the CPC Central Committee. He was arrested in 1989 and imprisoned until 1996.

Chen Yizi (陈一咨, 1940–2014)

Born into a family of intellectuals, Chen spent 1959–1969 at Peking University as a student of physics and Chinese literature as well as a leader in the Communist Youth League. Purged as an "anti-revolutionary element" during the Cultural Revolution, he was sent to Henan (1969–1978). During that time, Chen conducted in-depth studies of the conditions of peasants and became a cadre at an agricultural education institute, where he was joined by Deng Liqun's son, Deng Yingtao. During the Cultural Revolution, Chen discussed the shortcomings of collective agriculture with Deng Liqun and Hu Yaobang. With their support, he emerged as a leader of the young reform intellectuals of the 1980s dedicated to agricultural reform and became the head of the Rural Development Group. Chen and the Rural Development Group contributed important research to the breakthrough of the household responsibility system. Chen was appointed by Zhao Ziyang as director of the System Reform Institute, which reported directly to the State Council. Chen was one of the most outspoken opponents of the big-push price liberalization and a proponent of market reform through commercialization and reindustrialization. Together with Wang Xiaoqiang, he spearheaded the 1985 survey of the state of urban-industrial reform, led the delegation to investigate reform efforts in Hungary and Yugoslavia in 1986, and traveled to West Germany in 1988 to study the "Erhard Miracle." During the 1989 Tiananmen protests, Chen organized public support for Zhao Ziyang. He lived in exile in the United States until the end of his life.

Cheng Zhiping (成致平, 1926–2015)
Cheng joined the Communist Party in 1949 and worked in state commerce, such as the Gansu Trading Company and the Southwest Silk Company, before becoming a price administrator. In 1955, Cheng was promoted to director of both the National Price Committee and the Finance and Trade Price Group of the State Planning Commission. He returned to leading positions in the price administration after the Cultural Revolution in 1977, until his retirement in 2003. In the 1980s, Cheng was a leading reform cadre in charge of prices. He served as the deputy director general of the State Price Administration, executive officer of the Economic Research Center of the State Council, and, notably, director of the State Price Bureau. As director, he released this nationwide television announcement to publicize the dual-track price system: "In 1985 the basic direction for price reform is: Combine adjusting with letting go and progress in small steps." Cheng was also the deputy leader of the Price Group of the State Council and a member of the 1986 Program Office, which was charged with devising a plan for rapid wholesale price liberalization.

Deng Liqun (邓力群, 1915–2015)
Deng Liqun studied economics at Peking University but dropped out to join the Communist Party in his first year. During the civil war, he was sent to the Northeastern Communist base area, where he got to know Chen Yun. In 1965, Deng was purged as a "capitalist roader" for being Liu Shaoqi's secretary and was sent to the countryside for reeducation by labor. During that time, he became acquainted with Chen Yizi through his son Deng Yingtao, and he and Chen engaged in conversations on the shortcomings of collective farming. In 1975, Deng returned to Beijing to work in Deng Xiaoping's Political Research Office of the State Council, where he was mainly in charge of education, science, and economic questions. When Deng Xiaoping again returned to the center of power in 1977, Deng Liqun joined him and drafted some of Deng Xiaoping's speeches. Deng Liqun helped to create momentum around the reinstatement of college entrance exams in 1977 that allowed many sent-down youth to take up university studies. In his capacities as deputy director of the Chinese Academy of Social Sciences and head of the Policy Research Office of the Central Secretariat, Deng

Liqun provided crucial resources for the founding of the Rural Development Group. He listened to the young volunteer researchers' findings and disseminated their reports to Chen Yun and Deng Xiaoping. Deng was involved in the drafting of key reform documents such as "Resolution on Several Historical Issues of the Party Since the Founding of the People's Republic of China." From April 1982 to July 1985, he served as the minister of the propaganda department of the CPC Central Committee, and from September 1982 to October 1987, as secretary of the Secretariat of the CPC Central Committee. In these roles, Deng was responsible for the Party's propaganda as well as ideological and cultural work, and he played an important role in the campaigns against "spiritual pollution." In the aftermath of the Tiananmen massacre, Deng once more rallied against "bourgeois liberalization" and argued for "people's democratic dictatorship" against Zhu Rongji and others, who emphasized peaceful evolution and further opening up and reform. Nevertheless, several Rural Development Group members report they received help from Deng Liqun after June Fourth, despite their public support of the protests.

Dong Fureng (董辅礽, 1927–2004)

After earning a first degree in economics at Wuhan University, Dong moved to Moscow in 1953 and received a doctorate from the Moscow National Institute of Economics in 1957. Upon his return to China, Dong joined the Institute of Economics at the Chinese Academy of Social Sciences (CASS) as an associate researcher; he became the director of the CASS graduate school in the early 1980s. Between 1957 and 1958, Dong served as a lecturer for the Wuhan University's economics department and was the deputy leader of the National Economy Balance Group until 1976. He was a critic of the Stalinist development strategy after the Great Leap Forward, and during the Cultural Revolution, he was purged as one of Sun Yefang's "Eight Lieutenants." Between 1977 and 1988, Dong rose through the ranks of the CASS Institute of Economics, becoming its head in 1985. He stood out for his radical views on ownership reform in the late 1970s. Dong was active in the World Bank mission to China and participated in the Moganshan and Bashan Conference. Between 1988 and 1993, he was the deputy chairman of the Financial and Economic Committee of the National People's Congress. From 1989 until his death in 2004, Dong was the honorary director of the CASS Institute of Economics.

Du Runsheng (杜润生, 1913–2015)

Du once described himself as an "intellectual who came from the countryside." He is considered to be the "father of rural reform" in China. Du began studies at Beijing Normal University's Department of Literature and History in 1934 and joined the Communist Party in 1936. He was involved in economic warfare in the civil war, supporting Deng Xiaoping's troops by leading peasant movements to implement land reform. After the founding of New China in 1949, Du continued work on land reform and in 1952 was transferred to the rural work department of the CPC Central Committee. After the Cultural Revolution began in 1966, he was purged and later sent to the May Seventh Cadre School of the Chinese Academy of Sciences in Qianjiang, Hubei, for manual labor. Du returned to his work on agricultural policy in the era of reform and in 1981 became the director of the Central Rural Policy Office. Together with Deng Liqun, Du was a crucial supporter of the Rural Development Group and facilitated the rise of young reform intellectuals. He was entrusted by the Central Committee to draft a summary of the National Rural Work Conference. This document became the so-called "No. 1 Document" and formally established the legitimacy of the household contracting system in agriculture, settling a nearly thirty-year debate over China's agrarian question. In 1983, Du became the director of the Rural Policy Research Office of the Secretariat of the CPC Central Committee and director of the Rural Development Research Center of the State Council. He withdrew from these positions in 1989 due to his support of Zhao Ziyang. Du nevertheless continued his research on rural economy and policy.

Gao Shangquan (高尚全, 1929–)

Gao graduated from the Department of Economics of St. John's University in Shanghai in 1952. He has been engaged in economic policy research throughout his life. From the 1950s to the 1980s, he worked in the First Ministry of Machinery Industry, the Ministry of Agricultural Machinery, and the State Machinery Industry Commission on economic policy research. After the reform and opening up, Gao participated in the drafting of several important documents of the Central Committee, including the decisions of the Third Plenary Session of the 12th Central Committee in 1984 that sanctioned the expansion of reform to the urban-industrial economy and of the 14th Central Committee in 1993 to establish a socialist market economy. Gao joined the State Commission for Restructuring the Economy in 1982 and served as its deputy director from 1985 to 1993. He advised the World Bank mission to China, participated in the Bashan Conference, and was later a senior visiting scholar at the World Bank, Harvard University, and Stanford University. Gao served as executive head of the Program Office, which was charged with drafting a plan for wholesale price liberalization combined with tax and wage reform. Additionally, he was the leader of the System Reform Institute's delegation to Hungary and Yugoslavia in 1986, which led him to send a telegram warning against the reform plan of the Program Office, which he headed. Gao continued to be engaged in economic reform throughout the 1990s, and in 1999, he became the president of the China Economic System Reform Research Association.

Guo Shuqing (郭树清, 1956–)

Guo majored in philosophy at Nankai University from 1978 to 1982 and received a master's degree in science and socialism from the Chinese Academy of Social Sciences Graduate School. In 1985, Guo, with coauthors Liu Jirui and Qiu Shufang, proposed package reform with price liberalization at its core in a letter to the State Council, which subsequently ordered a working group to draft a reform program. Their approach was inspired by the insights of Eastern European émigré economists. From February 1985 to September 1988, Guo was an assistant researcher at the Institute of Marxism-Leninism of the Chinese Academy of Social Sciences and pursued postgraduate studies in science and socialism at the Institute of Marxism-Leninism of the Chinese Academy of Social Sciences, obtaining a doctorate in law. In 1986, he joined the Program Office to contribute to the drafting of a plan for wholesale price liberalization combined with wage and tax reform. Guo participated in the Bashan Conference and, thanks to an invitation arranged by Alec Cairncross on a recommendation by the World Bank team, he was a visiting scholar at Oxford University from 1986 to 1987. From 1988 to 1993, Guo was a deputy group leader at the Economic Research Center of the State Planning Commission. Between April 1993 and September 1995, he served as the director of the Comprehensive Planning and Pilot Division of the National Economic System Reform Commission. From 2013 to 2017, Guo was the governor of Shandong, and he is currently the chairman of the China Banking Regulatory Commission.

He Weiling (何维凌, 1944–1991)

He graduated from the technical physics department of Peking University in 1968, specializing in nuclear physics. During the Cultural Revolution, he contributed to the writing of the "Manifesto of the Communist Youth Society" and was first jailed as a counterrevolutionary and then sent to Qinzhe farm for "reform by labor." He was a close friend of Chen Yizi, with whom he shared dissenting views of China's development path during the Cultural Revolution. In the late 1970s, he returned to Peking University to teach. He was a cofounder of the China Rural Development Research Group, provided leadership when Chen Yizi fell ill, and brought methodological training and systemic thinking to the group. He had to leave the group for unknown political reasons but stayed in close touch with its members. From 1985 to 1987, he visited Princeton University, Hopkins University, and the Atlantic Commission to study and prepare for the establishment of the "China Reform and Opening Up Foundation," sponsored by George Soros. He helped establish a connection between George Soros and Chen Yizi to fund the System Reform Institute study tour to Hungary and Yugoslavia. Bringing together his concern for economic reform and his background in science, he made important contributions in the 1980s to the introduction of control theory, systems theory, cybernetics, and the study of dynamic economic systems to China. He died in a car accident in Mexico in 1991. His classmate Deng Pufang, the son of Deng Xiaoping, gave the graveside speech.

Hua Sheng (华生, 1953–)

During the Cultural Revolution, Hua spent ten years in Huai'an in Northern Jiangsu province. He received a first degree in economics from the Nanjing Institute of Technology, and from 1982 to 1985, he studied in the Department of Finance of the graduate school of the Chinese Academy of Social Sciences. In 1984, Hua participated in the Moganshan Youth Conference and began a long-standing collaboration with He Jiacheng, Luo Xiaopeng, Jiang Yue, Zhang Shaojie, and Gao Liang. Together, they argued for a dual-track price system and, later, for ownership reform in the form of an "asset management responsibility system." After the conference, Hua was invited to attend the State Council meeting to talk about urban-industrial reform. He began working at the Institute of Economics of the Chinese Academy of Social Sciences in 1985, served as the director of the Microeconomic Research Office and a member of the China Youth Federation, and participated in the work of the Office of the Economic System Reform of the State Council. He received his doctorate from Wuhan University, where he was advised by Dong Fureng. In 1987, Hua went to Oxford University to study. With coauthors Zhang Xuejun and Luo Xiaopeng, he published the research article "Ten Years of China's Reform: Review, Reflection, and Prospects" in 1988, which reached the conclusion that reform had reached a dead end without the dismantling of the socialist ownership system and the establishment of civil liberties. In the early 1990s, Hua was based at Cambridge University.

Huang Jiangnan (黄江南, 1949–)
In 1978, Huang was a graduate student in economics at the Chinese Academy of Social Sciences. In 1980, articles on the systemic economic crisis of the planned economy that he coauthored with Weng Yongxi, Wang Qishan, and Zhu Jiaming resulted in a first dialogue between young intellectuals and the central leadership, including Premier Zhao Ziyang. He and his coauthors were subsequently referred to as the "four gentlemen" of reform. They were active in organizing meetings that had more than 1,000 participants, mainly other university students. In 1984, Huang Jiangnan, Zhu Jiaming, Liu Youcheng, and Zhang Gang initiated the Moganshan Youth Conference, which was critical in establishing networks among young reform intellectuals and helping them rise to influence. At the time, Huang was an economist and assistant researcher at the Technology and Economic Center of the State Council. After 1989, he had to end his career as a policy researcher, and he subsequently became a businessman.

Li Jiange (李剑阁, 1949–)
Li obtained his master's degree in economics from the graduate school of the Chinese Academy of Social Sciences from 1982 to 1984. His background in mathematics drew him to mathematical economics. At the Moganshan Youth Conference, Li proposed adjustment of prices in planned, calculation-based steps. From December 1984 until June 1988, he worked as a researcher in the Development Research Center of the State Council. Li coauthored with Zhou Xiaochuan and Lou Jiwei and collaborated with Wu Jinglian and other more senior economists to further the package reform agenda. Nevertheless, he participated in the 1986 delegation to Hungary and Yugoslavia, which warned against

the implementation of the Program Office's plan for wholesale price liberalization. Between 1988 and 1992, Li served as deputy director of the department of reform and regulation of the State Planning Commission and deputy director of the Policy Research Office. He subsequently served as the deputy director and, later, director of the department of policies and regulations of the State Economic and Trade Commission. From 2003 to 2008, Li was the deputy director of the Development Research Center of the State Council.

Li Xianglu (李湘鲁, 1949–)

After graduating from high school in Beijing in 1968, Li joined the army in rural Hebei. In 1975, Deng Liqun recruited him to join the Research Office under the State Council, when Deng Xiaoping had temporarily returned to Beijing. In 1978, Li entered Renmin University to study economics but continued his work at the Research Office. From 1980 to 1984, he served as Premier Zhao Ziyang's youngest secretary. Li played an important role as the interlocutor between Zhao Ziyang, the Rural Development Group, and the young reform intellectuals more broadly. He participated in the 1984 Moganshan Youth Conference to report the insights of the young scholars back to Zhao. Li helped facilitate the founding of the System Reform Institute and the selection of Chen Yizi and Wang Xiaoqiang as its leaders. He was in charge of the China Reform and Opening Foundation, funded by George Soros, in the second half of the 1980s. In 1987, he left for graduate studies at Columbia University and subsequently returned to China in January 1989. Since the 1990s, Li has worked for investment firms.

Li Yining (厉以宁, 1930–)

Li Yining entered the Department of Economics at Peking University in 1951 and graduated in 1955. There, he was introduced to Western economics by Chen Daisun and Luo Zhiru, who had gained their doctorates from Harvard University in 1925 and 1937, respectively. Li maintained a critical distance from orthodox Soviet-style economics and demonstrated a vibrant interest in Western-style economics. Due to his research, Li was repeatedly and for prolonged periods banished to the countryside for hard manual labor, before and during the Cultural Revolution. With the beginning of reform, Li finally became a full professor at Peking University in 1979, at age forty-nine, and he became a Party member in 1984. Beginning in 1979, Li organized a weekly lecture series on Western economics at Peking University that attracted a wide range of young reform intellectuals. He made an important contribution in disseminating knowledge of Western economics in China. In 1980, he began teaching his first major course in Western economics at Peking University; the same year he published his book *Macroeconomics and Microeconomics*. His course was popular, and his lectures were ultimately compiled into *An Introduction to Modern Western Economics*, published in 1983. From 1985 to 1992, Li served as the first dean of the Guanghua School of Management at Peking University. From 1988 to 2002, he served as a member of the Standing Committee of the National People's Congress, vice chairman of the Finance and Economics Committee of the National People's Congress, and vice chairman of the Legal Committee of the National People's Congress. Li was an outspoken opponent of wholesale price liberalization and an advocate of ownership with what he called a "socialist stock market" at its core; he has been dubbed "Stock Market Li." Li Keqiang, China's Premier since 2013, is among Li Yining's notable disciples.

Liao Jili (廖季立, 1915–1993)

Liao was involved in economic policy work in China beginning in the 1940s and reemerged as a leading economic reformer in the 1980s. He entered the journalism department of Fudan University in Shanghai in 1936 and joined the revolution a year later, moving to Yan'an in 1938 to join the Anti-Japanese University. In 1940, Liao joined the Ministry of Finance and Economy of the Central Committee of the Communist Party of China, contributing to the economic warfare of the civil war. Following the founding of the People's Republic of China in 1949, Liao served as the head of the Secretariat of the Financial and Economic Commission of the Central Committee, the Finance and Trade Department, and the National Bureau of Statistics. In 1954, he joined the Comprehensive Planning Bureau of the State Planning Commission. In the reform era, Liao, along with Xue Muqiao and Lin Zili, was among the early advocates for a commodity economy. In 1979, he became a leader within the Restructuring Group, which had been established under the Financial and Economic Commission of the State Council to research the economic system reform. In 1980, the State Council established an Office of Economic System Reform and made Liao the deputy director. After the National Economic System Reform Commission was established in 1982, Liao served as a member and consultant. Later, he worked as the deputy director general of the Economic and Technological Development Research Center of the State Council and vice president of the China Economic System Reform Research Association. Liao participated in discussion rounds with Ota Šik at the Moganshan World Bank Conference, and he helped plan the Bashan Conference.

Liu Guoguang (刘国光, 1923–)

During the war with Japan, Liu studied in the Department of Economics of the Southwest Associated University—a wartime merger of Tsinghua, Peking, and Nankai universities that featured many of China's leading economists as faculty. In 1951, Liu was among the first researchers from the People's Republic of China studying in the Soviet Union, and in 1955, he obtained an associate doctorate degree from the Moscow School of Economics. Upon his return to China, Liu began working at the Chinese Academy of Sciences Institute of Economics. In the aftermath of the Great Leap Forward, Liu spoke out against the Stalinist development model, along with Dong Fureng, Chen Yun, and others. Sun Yefang's early reflection on the planned economic system had a profound impact on Liu. In 1979, Liu, together with Zhao Renwei, pioneered the rethinking of the relationship between planning and market in the socialist economy. From 1981 to 1982, Liu served as the deputy director of the National Bureau of Statistics, and from 1982 until 1993, he was the vice president of the Chinese Academy of Social Sciences. He was an influential promoter of exchange with Western economists and the World Bank. He helped organize the visits of Włodzimierz Brus and Ota Šik, suggested the Moganshan World Bank Conference, participated in the Bashan Conference, and fostered the introduction of mathematical economics and the establishment of comparative economic systems as a subfield in China. In the 1980s, Liu Guoguang was an important proponent of combining macroeconomic austerity with wholesale price liberalization.

Liu Zhuofu (刘卓甫, 1911–1993)

Liu graduated from the biology department of Peking Normal University in 1936. That same year, he participated in the Olympic Games, held in Berlin, as a member of the Chinese basketball team. Two years later, he joined the Communist Party and was involved in the economic warfare of the civil war. He served, among other posts, as deputy manager of the Shanxi Suiyuan Trading Corporation, vice president of the Northwest Farmers' Bank, and deputy director of the Department of Industry and Commerce of the Shaanxi-Gansu-Ningxia border area. Liu contributed to price stabilization in the strategically important provinces of Shaanxi, Gansu, and Ningxia in the decisive year of the civil war and the immediate postliberation period. In the most severe inflationary period of the Maoist period, resulting from the disasters of the Great Leap Forward, he joined the State Price Regulation Commission to support Xue Muqiao in stabilizing prices. Liu served successively as deputy minister of the Ministry of Commerce and the Ministry of Agricultural Products Procurement. From 1979 to 1982, he served as director of the State Price Administration, and in this capacity, he shaped early attempts at price reform. Liu participated in an exchange with the World Bank mission and participated in the Moganshan World Bank Conference.

Lou Jiwei (楼继伟, 1950–)

During the Cultural Revolution, Lou was a soldier in the navy and a worker at the Beijing Institute of Automation. He later attended Tsinghua University and graduated in February 1982 with a degree in computer science. Lou continued his education at the graduate school of the Chinese Academy of Social Sciences Department of Quantity and Technology Economics. He received his master's degree in economic system analysis in December 1984. That year, Lou, together with Zhou Xiaochuan and Li Jiange, published a paper on price reform that was widely discussed, including at the Moganshan Youth Conference. From December 1984 until June 1986, Lou was a member and then deputy leader of the Finance Group of the Research Office of the State Council, assigned to research financial system reform. One of the young proponents of package reform, he joined the 1986 Program Office as head of the finance and tax group. From February 1989 until January 1992, Lou was the deputy director of the Shanghai Economic System Reform Office as one of (later Premier) Zhu Rongji's protégés; Zhu was at the time the city's mayor. Throughout the 1990s, Lou rose through the ranks as a reform official, working mainly on finance and taxation. From 2013 to 2016, he was the finance minister, and he currently serves as the chair of the National Council for Social Security Fund.

Lu Mai (卢迈, 1947–)

Lu studied at the Beijing College of Economics and was a member of the Rural Development Group. He joined the organizing team of the Moganshan Youth Conference and was an active member of the circles of young reform intellectuals. In the late 1980s, Lu became the director of the Rural Reform Experimental Area Office of the Research the State Council's Rural Development Research Centre. Substituting for Wang Qishan, he joined the 1986 study tour to Yugoslavia and Hungary of the System Reform Institute and was one of the lead authors of the report that warned against wholesale price liberalization, based on the experiences of these two countries. In 1989, Lu left China and studied at the John F. Kennedy School of Government at Harvard University, thanks to Dwight Perkins's invitation. After research fellowships at Harvard and in Hong Kong, Lu returned to China. Since 1998, he has led the China Development Research Foundation under the State Council, one of China's most important reform policy research organizations.

Luo Xiaopeng (罗小朋, 1947–)

Luo Xiaopeng is the son of Luo Peng, a revolutionary of the first generation who was ousted in 1959 and sent to Jiangxi. Deng Xiaoping was sent to the same place during the Cultural Revolution, so he and Luo Peng were acquainted. After undergraduate training in Beijing, Luo Xiaopeng worked as a technician in the Ministry of Aerospace Industry in Jiangxi. Due to his specialization in engineering, he was not sent to the countryside during the Cultural Revolution, but he decided voluntarily to join his friends Chen Yizi and Deng Yingtao at the Agricultural Education Institute in Chumaodian prefecture in Henan. After the resumption of the university entrance exam in 1977, Luo entered Renmin University as a graduate student in industrial economics and became a founding member of the Rural Development Group. He led research on the reform of the unified purchase and sale system in agriculture and rural price-liberalization experiments. Luo helped to organize the Moganshan Youth Conference, and he was the only participant in the Bashan World Bank Conference who had been a member of the Rural Development Group. In the second half of the 1980s, Luo joined the Center for Research on Rural Development, under the State Council, which was headed by Du Runsheng. He collaborated with Zhang Xuejun, Hua Sheng, He Jiacheng, and others on proposals for a dual-track price system and, later, radical enterprise reform. In 1989, Luo briefly moved to the UK before pursuing a PhD in the United States. Later, Luo worked on poverty alleviation for an international NGO, as a consultant for the World Bank, and as a guest professor at Zhejiang University.

Ma Hong (马洪, 1920–2007)

Ma, born to an impoverished family, self-taught himself the middle school curriculum. An autodidact in progressive literature, he joined the Communist Party at age seventeen after participating in anti-Japanese student protest and union organizing at the railway. At age eighteen, he traveled to Yan'an, where he studied political economy at the Party School of the Central Committee and the Marxism-Leninism Institute. In 1941, he joined the Political Research Office of the Central Research Institute. Ma had direct working relationships with several revolutionary leaders, including Mao Zedong, Chen Yun, Deng Xiaoping, and Hu Yaobang. He participated in large-scale survey work in the northwestern Communist base areas. After the founding of the People's Republic, Ma contributed to the drafting of the first Five-Year Plan and was involved in devising the planning system and industrialization strategy. After serving as director of the Northeast Bureau Policy Research Office, Ma transferred to the Central Committee as a member and secretary general of the National Planning Committee. He was implicated in the purge of Gao Gang and demoted to deputy manager of the Beijing Construction Company. In 1956, he was promoted to director of the Research Office of the State Economic Commission, in charge of major surveys. During the Cultural Revolution, Ma held positions at the Ministry of Chemical Industry and the Beijing Petrochemical Plant. In 1978, he was asked to establish the Institute of Industrial Economy of the Chinese Academy of Social Sciences. In 1979, Ma became vice president of the Academy, and in 1982, he became its president. In 1985, Ma was appointed as the director general of the Research Center for Economic, Technological, and Social Development of the State Council. Along with Xue Muqiao, he was part of the leadership of the newly founded Price Research Center; Ma and Xue advised the State Council and the Central Finance and Economics Leading Group on price questions and reform plans. An ardent supporter of young intellectuals, Ma was one of the most influential Chinese reform economists in the 1980s and 1990s, combining a broad outlook on questions of the economic system with dedicated empirical work. He was an important interlocutor with foreign economists, including Japanese, Korean, and American counterparts, as well as the World Bank. Ma was one of the pioneers to promote a socialist market economy, a concept that was adopted as China's model in 1992.

Song Guoqing (宋国青, 1954–)

Song, a peasants' son, served as a brigade leader before enrolling at Peking University, from which he graduated in 1977. He majored in geometry but combined his mathematical skills with his interest in political economy to study modern microeconomics. In the early 1980s, Song was accepted as a member of the Rural Development Group after the group read an article he had written proposing agricultural reform. Song later became the architect of the Rural Development Group's experiments with rural price liberalization. He participated in several of the group's rural investigations. Song later transferred to the System Reform Institute, where he led the Department of Macroeconomics. Jointly with Zhang Weiying, he worked on price reform, monetary policy, and economic growth and with Wang Xiaoqiang on state-owned enterprise reform. From 1991 to 1995, Song earned his PhD in economics at the University of Chicago, and he became a professor of economics at the National School of Development at Peking University.

Sun Yefang (孙冶方, 1908–1983)

Sun Yefang was one of China's most influential economists of the twentieth century. In the 1920s, Sun Yefang was engaged in both the Student Movement and the Workers' Movement and joined the Communist Party. In November 1925, he was sent to Zhongshan University in Moscow. After graduating in the summer of 1927, he worked as a translator for lectures on political economy in the Communist University of the Toilers of the East in Moscow. Upon his return to China in 1930 he joined research on the rural economy. In the 1940s, Sun worked at the Central Party School, the Jiangsu Anhui Regional Goods Management Bureau, and the East China Finance Office in Shandong. After the founding of the People's Republic of China, Sun served as the vice minister of industry of the East China Military and Political Commission before becoming the dean of the Shanghai Institute of Finance and Economics (now Shanghai University of Finance and Economics), the deputy director of the National Bureau of Statistics, and the director of the Institute of Economics of the Chinese Academy of Sciences. In 1955, Sun Yefang, Xue Muqiao, and Yu Guangyuan were tasked with writing a textbook on political economy. All three were prominent participants in the debates over the law of value in the 1950s and 1960s. Sun Yefang argued that the law of value was in operation under socialism and suggested to use profits instead of physical targets to guide enterprises. During the Cultural Revolution, Sun was labeled "China's biggest revisionist in economics circles." In April 1968, he was arrested and served time in Qincheng prison until 1975. Red Guards circulated his writings on pamphlets that criticized his revisionist interpretation of Marx. Prison did not stop Sun from writing. He developed his reform proposals and scarcity interpretations of value. In the late 1970s, Sun's writings served as an influential starting point to China's market reform debate. Sun also pioneered the publication of mortality data of the Great Famine. After 1977, Sun served as honorary director of the Economic Research Institute of the Chinese Academy of Social Sciences and as a consultant to the Economic Research Center of the State Council. In 1979, Sun was diagnosed with liver cancer, and he passed away in 1983. China's most important prize in economics is named after him.

Tang Zongkun (唐宗焜, 1933–)

Tang graduated with a degree in economics from Peking University and, in 1957, began working as an editor at the Institute of Economics. In 1979, he attended the groundbreaking Wuxi Conference. Between 1983 and 1989, as the executive deputy editor of *Economic Research*, he played a key role in reforming this leading journal. Tang realized that articles had been either unoriginal, too practical, and lacking a high theoretical level, or too general, lacking practical implications. Under his editorship, the journal became an important outlet for reform thinking and published a range of competing views. The journal also added new columns featuring review articles of foreign research and case studies of reform. Previously, most economic research came from the same well-established group of older Chinese economists. Tang made an effort to promote newer, younger voices. Though he received demands that the opinions of young economists be censured, Tang stated his support of publishing their work in an article in 1986. Tang's research focused on enterprise reform, and he collaborated with the World Bank. When we met there in 2016, he was still affiliated with the Institute of Economics.

Tian Yuan (田源, 1954–)

During the Cultural Revolution, Tian worked in agriculture in Henan as a sent-down youth and then as a soldier in the political department of the Kunming Military Region. In August of 1975, he joined the economics department at Wuhan University. After he graduated in 1981, he remained in the department as a member of the faculty. Between 1983 and 1991, Tian Yuan served as the executive officer and director of the Development Research Center of the State Council. As a young researcher, his talents were praised by Zhao Ziyang. He attended the Moganshan Youth Conference, representing the Price Research Center. Tian Yuan also attended the Bashan Conference and served as a member of the Program Office. From 1990 to 1991, Tian Yuan studied at the University of Colorado as well as the Chicago Futures Exchange. Upon his return to China in 1992, he was appointed director of the Department of Foreign Economic Cooperation of the Materials Ministry but left shortly afterward to pursue a career in private asset management.

Wang Qishan (王歧山, 1948–)

Wang was a sent-down youth in Yan'an (Shaanxi) before studying history at Northwest University and working at the Shaanxi provincial museum. In 1979, Wang joined the Institute of History of the Chinese Academy of Social Sciences and joined the circles of young intellectuals engaged in rural reform. In 1980, Wang, Weng Yongxi, Huang Jiangnan, and Zhu Jiaming jointly authored an article that argued that the crisis of the planned economy was a result of the nature of this economy. This article was well received by Premier Zhao Ziyang, and the so-called "four gentlemen" of reform were able to conduct one of the first dialogues between the younger generation and central leadership. This key event prepared the way for younger economists to play a role in shaping the economic reforms of the 1980s. Wang was put in charge of the State Council's Rural Development Research Center. In 1988, he became the general manager of the China Rural Trust and Investment Corporation and throughout the 1990s rose through the ranks of China's major state-owned banks. Wang was the vice governor of Guangdong and mayor of Beijing before becoming vice premier. Since 2018, Wang has been China's vice president.

Wang Xiaolu (王小鲁, 1951–)

During the Cultural Revolution, Wang was a sent-down youth in Fenyang, Shanxi province. Like Wang Xiaoqiang, he worked on the editorial board of the Chinese Academy of Social Sciences working paper series "Unfinished Drafts." Wang was part of the reform movement of young intellectuals and worked closely with the Rural Development Group. He served as a member of the organizing team of the Moganshan Youth Conference. In 1985, Wang transferred to the newly founded System Reform Institute and became the director of the Development Research Office. Before June Fourth, Wang left China to pursue a PhD at the Australian National University. Upon his return to China, he became an assistant professor at Peking University. He later became the deputy director of the National Economic Research Institute and the managing director of the National Economic Reform Research Association.

Wang Xiaoqiang (王小强, 1952–)

Wang was a sent-down youth in Yan'an (Shaanxi) before studying mechanics at the Henan University of Science and Technology. In 1978, he was part of the writing group of the Chinese Academy of Social Sciences (CASS). In 1979, Wang worked as a fitter in a Beijing neighborhood factory and spent every free minute reading. He wrote an essay titled "Critique of Agrarian Socialism" that presented a reevaluation of the People's Communes and was widely discussed among theoretical circles. Wang joined the editorial board of the working paper series "Unfinished Drafts" at CASS, an important outlet for unorthodox contributions. He was a founding member of the Rural Development Research Group, one of the deputy leaders managing the group during Chen Yizi's illness, and the group's intellectual backbone. As part of the group, he conducted investigations into Chuxian county, Anhui province, Ji'an county, Jiangxi province, Wuzhou city, and Guangxi province and theorized the household responsibility system. Wang was a leading author of reports and articles that paved the way for household contracting. In 1984, he went on his first study tour with Premier Zhao Ziyang. With Bai Nanfeng, he conducted extensive fieldwork in Guizhou and Tibet that resulted in the book *The Poverty of Plenty*. Wang became the founding deputy director of the System Reform Institute and, in 1985, jointly with Chen Yizi, led a large-scale survey to assess urban-industrial reform. On behalf of the System Reform Institute, in 1986, Wang proposed an enterprise-contracting reform to Zhao Ziyang.

In the same year, he was the deputy head of a delegation studying reform in Hungary and Yugoslavia. The delegation warned Zhao Ziyang against implementing wholesale price liberalization. Wang was one of the pioneers of studying the Wenzhou model of private enterprises but advocated enterprise reform beyond the logic of private ownership. In late 1987 and early 1988, he joined Zhao Ziyang for the last time on an investigation tour to evaluate the feasibility of a coastal-development strategy. In 1988, Wang and Chen Yizi traveled to West Germany to study the postwar price reform and warned once more against wholesale price liberalization. After June Fourth, Wang left China, first to study English in Boulder, Colorado, and later to pursue a PhD at the University of Cambridge. Upon his return to China, Wang briefly joined the Institute of Management Studies at the National Reform Commission as a researcher and later moved to Hong Kong.

Weng Yongxi (翁永曦, 1948–)
During the Cultural Revolution, Weng Yongxi was a sent-down youth in Inner Mongolia. Weng moved to Beijing in the late 1970s to work at the *Peasants' Newspaper*. Weng was one of the organizers of the movement of young reform intellectuals. In 1980, Weng, Wang Qishan, Huang Jiangnan, and Zhu Jiaming emerged as "four gentlemen" of reform and were the first young economists to have a dialogue with Premier Zhao Ziyang. In May 1984, Weng became secretary of the Fengyang County Party Committee. He participated in the Moganshan Youth Conference. Du Runsheng promoted him to be deputy director of the Agricultural Research Office under the State Council, skipping various ranks. Weng later started his own business.

Wu Jinglian (吴敬琏, 1930–)
Born to a family that included generations of industrialists and intellectuals, Wu graduated in 1954 from Jinling University in Nanjing and was assigned a highly competitive position at the Institute of Economics of the Chinese Academy of Sciences. In the 1957 anti-rightist campaign, Wu was targeted. In reaction, Wu dedicated himself to an orthodox left worldview to the extent that in the 1960s, he supported an attack against Sun Yefang, his superior at the Institute, for the latter's economic reform ideas. During the Cultural Revolution, Wu joined the group "Criticism Headquarters." Later, Wu and the whole Institute of Economics were sent to May Seventh Cadre Schools for reeducation. Subsequently, Wu was singled out as a "counterrevolutionary." During his forced labor, Wu became acquainted with Gu Zhun, one of China's leading reform economists of the Mao era. At the dawn of reform, Wu returned to the Institute of Economics and became one of the keenest students of Western economics. When he was in his fifties, he learned English; engaged with the World Bank mission; learned from the Eastern European reform émigré economists Włodzimierz Brus and Ota Šik and Milton Friedman during their visits to China; and became one of

the first Chinese economists to study economics in the United States during his visit to Yale University in 1983, where he sat in on undergraduate macro- and microeconomics classes and studied comparative economic systems with Michael Montias. By the mid-1980s, Wu had evolved into one of the most enthusiastic proponents of "package reform" and one of the architects of the 1986 Program Office's proposal for wholesale price liberalization combined with tax and wage reform. Wu emerged from the political crackdown in 1989 unharmed and continued to be an influential voice of reform under Jiang Zemin and Zhu Rongji. Since the early 2000s, Wu has evolved into a widely known pro-market economist with frequent TV appearances.

Xue Muqiao (薛暮桥, 1904–2005)

Xue Muqiao is one of China's best-known economists of the twentieth century. Xue was self-taught in history, philosophy, and economics during his time in the Nationalists' prison, where he was held for his activism in the railroad workers' movement. In the 1930s, Xue participated in rural survey work and served as editor of *China's Countryside*. His writings became important instruction materials for soldiers and cadres. In the 1940s, Xue emerged as a key strategist of economic warfare and managed to stabilize prices and drive out competing currencies in the Shandong revolutionary base area. This solidified Xue's reputation as a leading authority on financial and economic works. In 1948, under the leadership of Zhou Enlai, Xue began to work on strategies for the creation of a planned economic system in China. Following the founding of the People's Republic of China in 1949, Xue became secretary general of the Finance and Economics Committee of the State Council; the director of the Bureau of Private Enterprises, the National Bureau of Statistics, the National Price Commission, and the Economic Research Center of the State Council; and the deputy director of the National Planning Commission. After the failure of the Great Leap Forward, Xue contributed to the renewed price-stabilization effort. Throughout the 1950s and 1960s, Xue was also a prominent contributor to the debate over the law of value and, together with Yu Guangyuan and Sun Yefang, was part of a project charged with writing a new political economy textbook that was not published. In 1969, Xue was sent to the countryside to be "reeducated by labor." In the late 1970s, Xue published his reform thinking. In 1979, his research was published in the book *China's Socialist Economy*, which exerted great influence on China's economic reform debates. As one of China's leading economists and the leader of the Price Research Center, Xue was also a key interlocutor with foreign guests. Xue engaged in exchanges with Eastern European émigrés and the World Bank and, among other events, participated in the Moganshan and Bashan Conference. Xue initially argued for gradual state creation of markets but later came to support package reform, and he spoke out in favor of the Program Office. After 1989, Xue helped to revive the market reform agenda. He was an eminent economist until the end of his long life, which lasted for more than a century.

Yu Guangyuan (于光远, 1915–2013)

Born to a family of intellectuals and officials, Yu Guanyuan was one of the most prolific economists and philosophers of twentieth-century China. Yu graduated from the Tsinghua University Department of Physics in 1936. After being part of the December Ninth Movement, he joined the CPC. In 1939, Yu became the director of the Yan'an Zhongshan library and was one of the cofounders of the Anti-Japanese University. Subsequently, he served as the director of the library of the CPC Central Committee and professor of the library department of Peking University. Beginning in 1941, Yu studied the economy of the Shaanxi-Gansu-Ningxia border area and later taught in the Department of Finance and Economics of Yan'an University. From 1948 until 1975, Yu worked in the propaganda department of the CPC Central Committee. In 1955, he was elected to membership in the philosophy and social sciences department of the Chinese Academy of Sciences. Jointly with Sun Yefang and Xue Muqiao, Yu authored the attempt at a political economy textbook and pursued subsequent textbook projects in the 1960s. In 1957, Yu was attacked in the "anti-right" movement. In 1958, he returned to his research and published the first volume of *Political Economies and Socialist Exploration*, which later evolved into six additional volumes. A close ally of Deng Xiaoping, Yu was rehabilitated near the end of the Cultural Revolution and became the director of the Economic Research Institute of the State Planning Commission in early 1975. Yu was an early initiator of reform and an advocate of distribution according to labor and the compatibility of socialism with a commodity economy. In 1978, he was the deputy head of a delegation to Yugoslavia that was crucial in promoting the recognition of non-Stalinist models of socialism in China. The same year, Yu contributed to Hu Qiaomu's article that called on policy makers to "Act in Accordance with Economic Laws." Both helped to pave the way for the breakthrough toward reform in 1978. Together with Lin Zili, Yu argued for the importance of productive forces and for a plurality of ownership arrangements. In 1979, Yu was appointed director of the Marxism-Leninism and Mao Zedong Institute of the Chinese Academy of the Social Sciences and the Academy's vice president. From 1982 to 1992, Yu served as advisor to the Central Committee.

Zhang Musheng (张木生, 1948–)

Zhang Musheng was born to a family of Communist revolutionaries. Zhang's father was secretary to Zhou Enlai and his mother was a party intellectual. At the start of the Cultural Revolution in 1965, Zhang Musheng (only seventeen years old) went with Chen Xiao, the son of Chen Boda, to the Linhe district of Inner Mongolia. They published a series of articles on the history of agricultural development, based on their experience and investigations, and articulated ideas for rural reform. Zhang stayed there until a book-length study that was circulated as an internal publication—arguing that agricultural output could only be increased through household contracting—landed him in prison in 1972. After his release in 1973, Zhang studied philosophy at the Inner Mongolia University and then taught at the Inner Mongolia Business School until 1980. Zhang was one of the founding members of the agricultural development group and, from 1980 to 1984, served as a researcher of the Chinese Academy of Social Sciences Institute of Agricultural Economics. He was then transferred to the Rural Policy Research Office of the Secretariat of the Central Committee, where he worked as a researcher until 1990. From 1990 to 1993, he was the president and editor in chief of the *China Baiye* information newspaper, which later became known as the *China Tax News*. In the 1990s, Zhang went to Tibet and served as the executive officer of Linzhi district.

Zhang Weiying (张维迎, 1959–)

Zhang Weiying was born to a peasant family and attended Northwestern University between 1979 and 1984, graduating with a master's degree. He participated in the Moganshan Youth Conference thanks to his paper on price reform being selected by the organizing team. At the conference, Zhang emerged as an articulate voice in the discussion arguing for a dual-track price system as a mechanism for reform. His contribution to the conference and the subsequent publication of his paper enabled Zhang to become a member of the System Reform Institute, where he mainly worked on macroeconomic questions. In 1989, Zhang went to Oxford University, where he obtained a PhD in economics under the supervision of Nobel Memorial Laureate James Mirrlees. Upon his return to China, Zhang joined Peking University, where he cofounded the China Center for Economic Research. He later moved to the Guanghua School of Management and then to the National School of Development, where he holds the Sinar Mas Chair of Economics. In his own account, Zhang at some point realized that his thinking was close to that of the Austrian school of economics and became interested in Hayek. He attended the 2014 Mont Pelerin Society annual meeting in 2014.

Zhu Jiaming (朱嘉明, 1950–)

Originally from Beijing, Zhu Jiaming was a sent-down youth in Heilongjiang, Tibet, and Shandong provinces. In 1978, he began graduate studies at the Institute of Industrial Economics at CASS and earned a PhD. Zhu, together with Huang Jiangnan, Wang Qishan, and Weng Yongxi, broke new ground for young reform intellectuals when they entered a dialogue with China's leadership as the famous "four gentlemen" of reform. Zhu initiated the 1984 Moganshan Youth Conference and was an organizer of the Beijing Young Economists Association. He participated in the establishment of the Technology and Economics Research Center of the State Council. Zhu served as deputy director of the Henan Economic System Reform Commission before moving to the International Research Institute of the China International Trust and Investment Corporation (CITIC). As the deputy director of this institute, he organized several study tours and foreign relations projects, including an investigation trip to Latin America in 1988. In May 1989, Zhu was one of those organizing a statement, trying to facilitate a dialogue with the student protesters in Tiananmen Square. Later that year, Zhu was exiled to the United States, where he organized the overseas democratic movement. He was a visitor at the Harvard University Fairbank Center and obtained an MBA at the Sloan School of Business of the Massachusetts Institute of Technology. Zhu then moved to Austria, where he taught economics at the University of Vienna and was engaged in NGO and private business work around environmental issues.

Note

1 I have limited the individuals in this list to Chinese economists, since information on their biographical background is mostly not readily available in English. This list is not comprehensive by any standards; it is intended to provide the readers with the broad biographical contexts of the 1980s economists covered in this book.

AUTHOR'S INTERVIEWS

Bai Nanfeng (2016). Beijing, October 12 and November 20.

Cao Yuanzheng (2016). Beijing, November 22.

Chen Xingdong (2016). Beijing, November 22.

Cui Zhiyuan (2017). Beijing, January 11.

Fan Shitao (2016). Beijing, September 23.

Galbraith, James (2016). Cambridge, England, June 23.

Hu Jiyan (2016). Beijing, December 28.

Hua Sheng (2016). Beijing, September 28.

Huang Jiangnan (2016). Beijing, November 23.

Jiang Chunze (2016). Beijing, December 28.

Jiang Dongsi (2016). Beijing, November 22.

Kende, Peter (2017). Paris, July 13.

Li Fan (2016). Beijing, December 6.

Li Shi (2016). Beijing, October 17.

Li Xianglu (2016a). Beijing, December 24.

Lim, Edwin (2016). London, England, June 13.

Lin, Cyril (2016). Oxford, England, January 19 and March 15; Beijing, November 22.

Lin Chun (2015, 2016). London, England, October 28, 2015, and February 4, 2016; Cambridge, England, March, 2, 2016.

Lin (Justin) Yifu (2016). Beijing, December 27.

Liu Hong (2016). Beijing, August 31.

Lu Liling (2016). Beijing, September 24 and October 19.

Lu Mai (2016). Beijing, December 21.

Luo Xiaopeng (2017). Hong Kong, January 5; via Skype, May 29 and July 6.

Peng Xiaomeng (2016). Beijing, September 21.

Perkins, Dwight (2016). Cambridge, Massachusetts, April 25.

Song Guoqing (2017). Beijing, January 2.

Sun Fangming (2016). Beijing, December 18.

Tang Zongkun (2016). Beijing, December 22.

Tian Yucao (2016). Cambridge, England, March 2.

Tidrick, Gene (2016). Edinburgh, Scotland, June 28.

Toporowski, Jan (2016). Cambridge, England, June 21.

Wang Haijun (2016). Beijing, July 29.

Wang Xiaolu (2016). Beijing, September 27.

Wang Xiaoqiang (2017). Hong Kong, January 9 and January 10.

Wei Zhong (2016). Beijing, September 20.

Wen Tiejun (2016). Beijing, December 9.

Weng Yongxi (2016). Beijing, October 28 and November 18.

Wood, Adrian (2016). Brighton, England, May 30 and July 7.

Wu Jinglian (2016). Beijing, July 29.

Xue Xiaohe (2016). Beijing, September 23.

Yang Mu (2016). Beijing, November 15.

Zhang Jun (2016). Beijing, November 24.

Zhang Musheng (2016). Beijing, October 26.

Zhang Shuguang (2016). Beijing, November 22.

Zhang Weiying (2016). Beijing, November 24.

Zhang Zhuoyuan (2016). Beijing, October 13.

Zhao Renwei (2016). Beijing, December 20.

Zhou Qiren (2016). Beijing, December 30.

Zhu Jiaming (2016). Beijing, August 31.

Zhu Ling (2016). Beijing, September 20.

Zuo Xuejin (2016). Shanghai, November 1.

BIBLIOGRAPHY

Abelshauser, W. (2004). *Deutsche Wirtschaftsgeschichte Seit 1945*. Munich: Verlag C.H. Beck.

Adler, S. (1957). *The Chinese Economy*. London: Routledge & Kegan Paul.

Alvaredo, F., L. Chancel, T. Piketty, E. Saez, and G. Zucman (2017). World Wealth and Income Database (WID). Retrieved July 1, 2017, from http://wid.world/data/

Amsden, A. H. (2007). *Escape from Empire: The Developing World's Journey Through Heaven and Hell*. Cambridge, MA: The MIT Press.

Amsden, A., J. Kochanowicz, and L. Taylor (1998). *The Market Meets Its Match: Restructuring the Economies of Eastern Europe*. Cambridge, MA: Harvard University Press.

Andreas, J. (2009). *Rise of the Red Engineers: The Cultural Revolution and the Origins of China's New Class*. Stanford: Stanford University Press.

Ang Yuen Yuen (2016). *How China Escaped the Poverty Trap*. Ithaca, NY: Cornell University Press.

Ash, R. (2006). Squeezing the Peasants: Grain Extraction, Food Consumption and Rural Living Standards in Mao's China. *The China Quarterly, 188*, 959–998.

Åslund, A. (1989). Soviet and Chinese Reforms: Why They Must Be Different. *World Today, 45*(11), 188–191.

Åslund, A. (1992). *Post-Communist Economic Evolutions: How Big a Bang?* Washington, DC: Center for Strategic and International Studies, c1992.

Åslund, A. (1995). *How Russia Became a Market Economy* (Brookings Institution, Ed.). Washington, DC: Brookings Institution, c1995.

Bachman, D. (1986). Differing Visions of China's Post-Mao Economy: The Ideas of Chen Yun, Deng Xiaoping, and Zhao Ziyang. *Asian Survey, 26*(3), 292–321. https://doi.org/10.2307/2644194

Bai Nanfeng (2016). Interview with author, Beijing.

Bajt, A. (1992). The Scope of Economic Reforms in Socialist Countries. In J. M. Kovács and M. Tardos (Eds.), *Reform and Transformation in Eastern Europe Soviet-type Economics on the Threshold of Change* (pp. 191–202). London: Routledge.

Baran, P. A., and P. M. Sweezy (1970). *Monopoly Capital: An Essay on the American Economic and Social Order*. Harmondsworth: Penguin.

Barkley, F. R. (1942). Wickard Blights Farm Group Hope for Higher Prices. *New York Times*, February 1, 1, 43.

Bartels, A. H. (1983). The Office of Price Administration and the Legacy of the New Deal, 1939–1946. *The Public Historian*, 5(3), 5–29.

Baruch, B. (1960). *The Public Years*. New York: Holt, Rinehart and Winston.

Bauer, T. (1990). Success and Failure: Emergence of Economic Reforms in Czechoslovakia and Hungary. In K. Dopfer and K.-F. Raible (Eds.), *The Evolution of Economic Systems: Essays in Honor of Ota Šik* (pp. 245–264). New York: St. Martin's Press.

Beijing Television Service. (1990). Zhao Ziyang and Li Peng Visit Fasting Students at Tiananmen Square. In M. Oksenberg, L. R. Sullivan, and M. Lambert (Eds.), *Beijing Spring, 1989, Confrontation and Conflict: The Basic Documents* (pp. 288–289). Armonk, NY: M. E. Sharpe.

Belik, Y. (1998). Price Reform—The Missing Link? Vox Populi. In M. Ellman and V. Kontorovich (Eds.), *The Destruction of the Soviet Economic System: An Insiders' History* (pp. 159–162). New York; London: Routledge.

Bell, S. (2013). *Rise of the People's Bank of China: The Politics of Institutional Change.* Cambridge, MA: Harvard University Press.

Bockman, J. (2011). *Markets in the Name of Socialism: The Left-Wing Origins of Neoliberalism.* Stanford, CA: Stanford University Press.

Bockman, J. (2012). The Long Road to 1989: Neoclassical Economics, Alternative Socialisms, and the Advent of Neoliberalism. *Radical History Review*, 2012(112), 9–42. https://doi.org/10.1215/01636545-1416151

Bockman, J., and G. Eyal (2002). Eastern Europe as a Laboratory for Economic Knowledge: The Transnational Roots of Neoliberalism. *American Journal of Sociology*, 108(2), 310–352.

Bodde, D. (1951). *Peking Diary: A Year of Revolution*. London: Jonathan Cape.

Bol, P. K. (1993). Government, Society, and State: On the Political Visions of Ssu-ma Kuang and Wang An-shih. In R. P. Hymes and C. Schirokauer (Eds.), *Ordering the World: Approaches to State and Society in Sung Dynasty China* (pp. 128–193). Berkeley: University of California Press.

Bonefeld, W. (2013). On the Strong Liberal State: Beyond Berghahn and Young. *New Political Economy*, 18(5), 779–783. https://doi.org/10.1080/13563467.2012.753046

Bonefeld, W. (2017). *The Strong State and the Free Economy*. London: Rowman and Littlefield.

Bramall, C. (2004). Chinese Reform in Long-Run Perspective and in the Wider East Asian Context. *Journal of Agrarian Change*, 4(1), 107–141.

Bresciani-Turroni, C. (1937). *The Economics of Inflation: A Study of Currency Depreciation in Post-War Germany, 1914–1923*. Northampton: John Dickens & Co. Ltd.

Brødsgaard, K. E. (1983a). Paradigmatic Change: Readjustment and Reform in the Chinese Economy, 1953–1981, Part I. *Modern China*, 9(2), 37–83.

Brødsgaard, K. E. (1983b). Paradigmatic Change: Readjustment and Reform in the Chinese Economy, 1953–1981, Part II. *Modern China*, 9(2), 253–272.

Brødsgaard, K. E., and Rutten, K. (2017). *From Accelerated Accumulation to Socialist Market Economy in China: Economic Discourse and Development from 1953 to the Present.* Leiden: Brill.

Brunet, G. (2018). *Stimulus on the Home Front: The State-Level Effects of WWII Spending.* Retrieved May 1, 2019 from https://berkeley.box.com/s/5fwkm24om69xvbzowv eaepg5jx79yo3c.

Buchanan, J. M. (1980). Rent Seeking and Profit Seeking. In J. Buchanan, R. D. Tollison, and G. C. Tullock (Eds.), *Toward a Theory of the Rent-Seeking Society* (pp. 3–15). College Station: Texas A&M University Press.

Burawoy, M. (1996). The State and Economic Involution: Russia Through a China Lens. *World Development*, *24*(6), 1105–1117. https://doi.org/10.1016/0305-750X(96)000 22–8

Burdekin, R. C. K. (2000). Ending Inflation in the People's Republic of China: From Chairman Mao to the 21st Century. *The Cato Journal*, *20*(2), 223–235.

Burdekin, R. C. K. (2008). *China's Monetary Challenges*. Cambridge: Cambridge University Press.

Burdekin, R. C. K., and F. Wang (1999). A Novel End to the Big Inflation in China in 1950. *Economics of Planning*, *32*(3), 211–229.

Burdekin, R. C. K., and X. Hu (1999). China's Experience with Indexed Government Bonds, 1988–1996: How Credible Was the People's Republic's Anti-Inflationary Policy? *Review of Development Economics*, *3*(1), 66–85.

Burgin, A. (2012). *The Great Persuasion: Reinventing Free Markets Since the Depression*. Cambridge, MA: Harvard University Press.

Brus, W. (1972). *The Market in a Socialist Economy*. London: Routledge & Kegan Paul.

Brus, W., and K. Laski (1989). *From Marx to the Market: Socialism in Search of an Economic System*. Oxford: Oxford University Press.

Byrd, W. A. (1988). Impact of the Two-Tier Plan/Market System in China. *Journal of Comparative Economics*, *11*(3), 295–300.

Byrd, W., G. Tidrick, Chen Jiyuan, Xu Lu, Tang Zongkun, and Chen Lantong. (1984). *Recent Chinese Economic Reforms: Studies of Two Industrial Enterprises*. World Bank Staff Working Papers, 652.

Cagan, P. (1956). The Monetary Dynamics of Hyperinflation. In M. Friedman (Ed.), *Studies in the Quantity Theory of Money* (pp. 25–117). Chicago: Chicago University Press.

Cai Huimei (1981). The Substance of the Soviet Bureaucratic Regime: "The Communist Power System" – A Book Review (苏联官僚统治的实质 — 《共产主义政权体系》一书简介). *Soviet and Eastern European Issues*, *1*, 56–57.

Cairncross, A. (1979). *Papers of Alec Cairncross. Diary of British Academy Visit to China 1979 [File GB248DC10690/12]*. Glasgow: University of Glasgow.

Cairncross, A. (1985). *Papers of Alec Cairncross. Typescript of Visit to China in 1985 [File GB248DC1062/14]*. Glasgow: University of Glasgow.

Cairncross, A. (1985). *Years of Recovery: British Economic Policy 1945–1951*. London: Methuen & Co.

Cairncross, A. (1998). *Living with the Century*. London: Lynx.

Campbell, C. D., and G. C. Tullock (1954). Hyperinflation in China, 1937–1949. *Journal of Political Economy*, *62*(3), 236–245.

Central Committee of the CPC Research Department of Party Literature (Ed.) (1991). Decision of the CPC Central Committee on Reform of the Economic Structure (Adopted at the Third Plenary Session of the Twelfth CPC Central Committee on October 20, 1984). In *Major Documents of the People's Republic of China: Selected Important Documents Since the Third Plenary Session of the Eleventh Central Committee of the Communist Party of China (December 1978–November 1989)* (pp. 395–427). Beijing: Foreign Language Press.

Central Intelligence Agency. (1952). Price Control in Communist China, 1950–1951, Price Indexes. Distributed May 1954. Sanitized Copy Approved for Release, October 19, 2011: CIA-RDP80-00809A000600150188-7.

Central Intelligence Agency, CIA (1986). China's Economists: Soundings on Reform. CIA Online Archive. Retrieved from https://www.cia.gov/library/readingroom/document/cia-rdp86t01017r000706920001-6

Central Intelligence Agency, CIA (1988). Memorandum for Director of Central Intelligence, 18 October 1988. Retrieved on April 21, 2019 from Memorandum for Director of Central Intelligence.

CESRRI (Chinese Economic System Reform Research Institute) (1986). *Reform: China's Challenges and Choices* (改革：我们面临的挑战与选择). Beijing: China Economics Press.

CESRRI (China Economic System Reform Research Institute) (1987). *A Difficult Exploration: An Investigation of the Reforms in Hungary and Yugoslavia* (艰难的探索：匈牙利，南斯拉夫改革考察). Beijing: China Economic Management Press.

CESRRI (Chinese Economic System Reform Research Institute) (1988a). First Objection Against Storming the Fortress and Crushing Through the Barrier of Reform: On the Deep Seated Meaning of Crushing Through the Price Barrier in the Fortified Position on Economic System Reform (对改革攻坚，过关的意见之一：过价格关意味着深层次的体制改革攻坚). *Internal Documents of System Reform Research*, *23*, July 30.

CESRRI (Chinese Economic System Reform Research Institute) (1988b). Fourth Objection Against Storming the Fortress and Crushing Through the Barrier of Reform: Price Liberalization Requires a Reform of the Circulation System for Goods and Materials (对改革攻坚，过关的意见之四：价格放开的同时必须进行物资流通体制改革). *Internal Documents of System Reform Research*, *26*, August 2.

Chang, G. H. (1988). Interview with Su Shaozhi, December 1985. *Bulletin of Concerned Asian Scholars*, *20*(1), 12–17.

Chang, H.-J. (2002). Breaking the Mould: An Institutionalist Political Economy Alternative to the Neo-Liberal Theory of the Market and the State. *Cambridge Journal of Economics*, *26*(5), 539–559.

Chang, J. L. Y. (1987). History of Chinese Economic Thought: Overview and Recent Works. *History of Political Economy*, *19*(3), 481–499.

Chang Kai-Nagu (1958). *The Inflationary Spiral: The Experience in China, 1939–1950*. New York: The Technology Press of Massachusetts Institute of Technology and John Wiley & Sons, Inc.

Chang Yifei (1969). Several Problems of Commodity Pricing Under the Socialist System. *Chinese Economic Studies*, *3*(2), 146–176.

Cheek, T. (2016). *The Intellectual in Modern Chinese History*. Cambridge: Cambridge University Press.

Chen Huan-Chang (1911a). *The Economic Principles of Confucius and His School, Vol. I*. New York: Columbia University Press.

Chen Huan-Chang (1911b). *The Economic Principles of Confucius and His School, Volume II*. New York: Columbia University Press.

Chen Nai-Ruenn (1966). The Theory of Price Formation in Communist China. *The China Journal*, *27*, 33–53.

Chen Xikang (1979). Input-Output Techniques in Economic Work - Use and Development Directions (投入产出技术在经济工作中的应用情况及发展方向). *Chinese Economic Issues*, *(4)*, 46–53.

Chen Xijun (1978). Lecture 15: Price Planning. In N. Lardy (Ed.), *Chinese Economic Planning* (pp. 89–99). New York: M. E. Sharpe.

Chen Xingdong (2013). Encounters with Alumni from Greater China. Retrieved June 10, 2016, from http://www.oxforduchina.org/chen-xingdong.html

Chen Yizi (1987). Social Scientific Research Serves Reform. In B. L. Reynolds (Ed.), *Reform in China - Challenges and Choices: A Summary and Analysis of the CESRRI Survey*

Prepared by the Staff of the Chinese Economic System Reform Research Institute (pp. xxii–xxiv). Armonk, NY: M. E. Sharpe.

Chen Yizi (2013). *Memoirs of Chen Yizi* (陈一咨回忆录). Hong Kong: New Century Media and Consulting.

Chen Yizi, Wang Xiaoqiang, Zhang Gang, Zhang Xiaojie, Diao Xinshen, Li Jun, … and Liu He (1987). Summary Report. In B. L. Reynolds (Ed.), *Reform in China - Challenges and Choices: A Summary and Analysis of the CESRRI Survey Prepared by the Staff of the Chinese Economic System Reform Research Institute* (pp. 3–32). Armonk, NY: M. E. Sharpe.

Chen Yun (1956). Speech by Comrade Chen Yun. In Eighth National Congress of the Communist Party of China, *Vol. II, Speeches* (pp. 157–176). Beijing: Foreign Language Press.

Chen Yun (1983a). Methods of Solving the Tensions in Supplies of Pork and Vegetables, September 1956, Speech at the Eighth National Party Congress of the CPC. In *Chen Yun's Strategy for China's Development: A Non-Maoist Alternative* (pp. 23–29). Armonk, NY: M. E. Sharpe.

Chen Yun (1983b). *Chen Yun's Strategy for China's Development: A non-Maoist Alternative* (N. Lardy and K. Lieberthal, Eds.). Armonk, NY: M. E. Sharpe.

Chen Yun (1986). Uphold the Principle of Proportion in Regulating the National Economy, 21 March, 1979 (坚持按比例原则调整国民经济). In *Selected Works of Chen Yun (1956–1985)* (pp. 226–234). Beijing: People's Publishing House.

Chen Yun (1986a). *Selected Works of Chen Yun, 1956–1985* (陈云文选). Beijing: People's Publishing House.

Chen Yun (1986b). The Question of Planning and the Market (计划与市场问题). In *Selected Works of Chen Yun* (陈云文选) (pp. 220–223). Beijing: People's Publishing House.

Chen Yun (1999). Address to the 1978 CPC Work Conference. In *Selected Works of Chen Yun, Volume 3 (1956–1994)* (pp. 236–241). Beijing Foreign Language Press.

Chen Yun (2000). *Chen Yun Chronicle, Vol. II* (陈云年谱, 中). Beijing: Central Document Publishing House.

Cheng Lin, T. Peach, and Wang Fang (Eds.) (2014). *The History of Ancient Chinese Economic Thought*. Abingdon: Routledge.

Cheng Lin, T. Peach, and Wang Fang (Eds.) (2019). *The Political Economy of the Han Dynasty and Its Legacy*. Abingdon: Routledge.

Cheng Xiaonong (1995). Decision and Miscarriage: Radical Price Reform in the Summer of 1988. In C. L. Hamrin and S. Zhao (Eds.), *Decision Making in Deng's China: Perspectives from Insiders* (pp. 189–207). Armonk, NY: M. E. Sharpe.

Cheng Zhiping (1993). Forever a Model of Ceaseless Struggle - Deep Grieve for Comrade Liu Zhuofu (奋斗不息 风范长存——深切悼念刘卓甫同志). *Price: Theory and Practice*, 3, 42–44.

Cheng Zhiping (1998). *50 Years of Chinese Commodity Prices: 1949–1998* (中国物价五十年: 1949–1998). Beijing: Chinese Price Press.

Cheng Zhiping (2006). *30 Years of Price Reform, 1977–2006* (价格改革三十年, 1977–2006. Beijing: China Market Press.

Chin, Tamara (2014). *Savage Exchange: Han Imperialism, Chinese Literary Style, and the Economic Imagination*. Cambridge, MA: Harvard University Asia Center.

China Daily (1990). Zhao, Li Visit Hunger Strikers in Tiananmen. In M. Oksenberg, L. R. Sullivan, and M. Lambert (Eds.), *Beijing Spring, 1989, Confrontation and Conflict: The Basic Documents* (pp. 290–291). Armonk, NY: M. E. Sharpe.

China Development Research Foundation (2011). About the Author. In China Development Research Foundation (Ed.), *Chinese Economists on Economic Reform - Collected Works of Xue Muqiao* (pp. x–xi). London: Routledge.

China Economic System Reform Research Conference (1986). Introduction of Foreign Economists Who Participated in the International Conference on Macroeconomic Management (参加宏观经济管理国际讨论会的外国经济学家简介). In China Economic System Reform Research Conference (Ed.), *Macroeconomic Management and Reform: Selected Speeches of the Macroeconomic Management Symposium* (pp. 260–276). Beijing: Economic Daily Press.

China Rural Development Issues Research Group, Deng Yingtao, He Weiling, Luo Xiaopeng, Sun Fangming, Wang Yan, and Chen Xintao (1981). On Strategy Research (论战略研究). *Countryside, Economy, Society: Collected Papers of the China Rural Development Issues Research Group, 1*, 386–395.

China Vitae (2017). Lou Jiwei (楼继伟): Member, 18th CPC, Central Committee; President, National Council for Social Security Fund. Retrieved June 1, 2017, from http://www.chinavitae.com/biography/Lou_Jiwei/career

Chou Shun-Hsin (1963). *The Chinese Inflation, 1937–1949*. New York: Columbia University Press.

Chow, G. C. (1994). *Understanding China's Economy*. Singapore: World Scientific Publishing.

Chuang Jae Ho (2000). *Central Control and Local Discretion: Leadership and Implementation During Post-Mao Decollectivization*. Oxford: Oxford University Press.

Chuang, Ming (1988). Zhao Ziyang's Makes Ten Points on Creating a New Order (赵紫阳为建新秩序提出十条). *Mirror Monthly Newspaper*, July, 22–27.

Clark, C. (1940). *The Conditions of Economic Progress*. London: Macmillan.

Cohn, S. M. (2017). *Competing Economic Paradigms in China: The Co-Evolution of Economic Events, Economic Theory and Economic Education, 1976–2016*. Abingdon: Routledge.

Coit, M. (1958). *Mr Baruch*. London: Victor Gollancz.

Colander, D. (1984). Galbraith and the Theory of Price Control, *Journal of Post Keynesian Economics, 7*, 77–90.

Cole, R. W. (2018). *"To Save the Village": Confronting Chinese Rural Crisis in the Global 1930s*. Ph.D. Dissertation, New York University, Department of History.

Cooper, R. (2005). *A Half-Century of Development*. Harvard Center of International Development Working Paper No. 118, March.

Common Program of The Chinese People's Political Consultative Conference, Adopted by the First Plenary Session of the Chinese People's PCC on September 29, 1949, in Peking. (1949). *In The Important Documents of the First Plenary Session of the Chinese People's Political Consultative Conference* (pp. 1–20). Beijing: Foreign Language Press.

Communique of the Third Plenary Session of the Eleventh Central Committee of the Communist Party of China (Adopted on December 22, 1978) (1986). In *China's Socialist Economy: An Outline History* (1949–1984) (pp. 564–577). Beijing: Beijing Review.

Cottrell, A., and W. P. Cockshott (1993). Calculation, Complexity and Planning: The Socialist Calculation Debate Once Again. *Review of Political Economy, 5*(1), 73–112.

Csikós-Nagy, B., D. Hague, and G. Hall (1984). *The Economics of Relative Prices: Proceedings of a Conference Held by the International Economic Association in Athens, Greece*. London: Macmillan Press.

Dai Yuanchen (1986). Dual Prices in the Process of Transition of the Economic Model (经济体制模式转换过程中的双重价格). *Economic Research, 1*, 43–48.

Davies W. (2018). The Neoliberal State: Power Against 'Politics'. In D. Cahill, M. Cooper, M. Konings, and D. Primrose (Eds.), *SAGE Handbook of Neoliberalism* (pp. 273–283). London: SAGE.

Day, A. (2013). *The Peasant in Postsocialist China: History, Politics, and Capitalism.* Cambridge: Cambridge University Press.

Deng Liqun (1981). Speech at the Symposium of the China Rural Development Issues Research Group (在中国农村发展问题研究组讨论会上的讲话). *Agricultural Economics Periodical, 3,* 4–9.

Deng Liqun (2005). *Deng Liqun's Own Account: 12 Times Spring and Autumn (1975–1987)* (邓力群自述十二个春秋). Unpublished manuscript.

Deng Xiaoping (1992). Restore Agricultural Production, July 7, 1962. In *Selected Works of Deng Xiaoping (1938–1965), Vol. I.* Beijing: Foreign Languages Press. https://dengxiaopingworks.wordpress.com/selected-works-vol-1-1938-1965/

Deng Xiaoping (1984a). Emancipate the Mind, Seek Truth from Facts and Unite as One in Looking to the Future, December 13, 1978, Speech at the Closing Session of the Central Working Conference in Preparation for the Third Plenary Session of the Eleventh Central Committee of the Communist Party. In *Selected Works of Deng Xiaoping* (1975–1982) (pp. 151–165). Beijing: Foreign Language Press.

Deng Xiaoping (1984b). Hold High the Banner of Mao Zedong Thought and Adhere to the Principle of Seeking Truth from Facts, September 16, 1978. In *Selected Works of Deng Xiaoping* (1975–1982) (pp. 141–144). Beijing: Foreign Language Press.

Deng Xiaoping (2004). *Deng Xiaoping Chronicle, Vol. II, 1975–1997* (邓小平年谱). (Office for Research on Documents of the Central Committee of the Communist Party of China, Ed.). Beijing: Central Document Publishing House.

Deng Yingtao (2017). *New Development Model and China's Future.* London: Routledge.

Der Spiegel (1986). Otmar Emminger †. *Der Spiegel*, August 11, 80.

Diao Xinshen (1987). The Role of the Two-Tier Price System. In Bruce Reynolds (Ed.), *Reform in China - Challenges and Choices: A Summary and Analysis of the CESRRI Survey Prepared by the Staff of the Chinese Economic System Reform Research Institute* (pp. 35–46). Armonk, NY: M. E. Sharpe.

Dobb, M. (1933). Economic Theory and the Problems of a Socialist Economy. *The Economic Journal, 43*(172), 588–598.

Dong Fureng (1986). China's Price Reform. *Cambridge Journal of Economics, 10*(3), 291–300.

Donnithorne, A. (1967). *China's Economic System.* London: C. Hurst & Co.

Donnithorne, A. (1978). The Control of Inflation in China. *Current Scene, XVI* (4 and 5), 1–11.

Du Runsheng (1981). Speech at the Symposium of the China Rural Development Issues Research Group (在中国农村发展问题研究组讨论会上的讲话). *Agricultural Economics Periodical, 3,* 1–3.

Du Runsheng (2014). Author's Preface. In C. D. R. Foundation (Ed.), *Chinese Economists on Economic Reform: Collected Works of Du Runsheng* (pp. xvii–xiv). Oxon: Routledge.

Dunstan, H. (1996). *Conflicting Counsels to Confuse the Age: A Documentary Study of Political Economy in Qing China, 1644–1840.* Ann Arbor, MI: University of Michigan Press.

Dunstan, H. (2006). *State or Merchant? Political Economy and Political Process in 1740s China.* Cambridge, MA: Harvard University Asia Center.

Eaton, S. (2016). *The Advance of the State in Contemporary China: State-Market Relations in the Reform Era.* Cambridge: Cambridge University Press.

Eberhard, W. (1977). *A History of China* (4th ed.). London: Routledge & Kegan Paul.

Eckstein, A. (1977). *China's Economic Revolution.* Cambridge: Cambridge University Press.

Economic Report of the President (1950). Washington, DC: United States Government Printing Office.

Economic Report of the President (1958). Washington, DC: United States Government Printing Office.

Edelstein, M. (2015). The Size of the U.S. Armed Forces During World War II: Feasibility and War Planning. *Research in Economic History, 20,* 47–97.

Edgerton-Tarpley, K. (2008): *Tears from Iron: Cultural Responses to Famine in Nineteenth-Century China.* Berkeley: University of California Press.

Editorial Board of Who's Who in China (Ed.) (1989). Chen Yun (b. 1905). In *Who's Who in China Current Leaders* (中国人民大词典现任党政军领导人物卷) (pp. 67–70). Beijing: Foreign Language Press.

Editorial Board of Who's Who in China (Ed.) (1989a). Gao Yang (b. 1909). In *Who's Who in China Current Leaders* (中国人民大词典现任党政军领导人物卷) (pp. 159–160). Beijing: Foreign Languages Press.

Editorial Board of Who's Who in China (Ed.) (1989b). Hu Yaobang (b. 1915). In *Who's Who in China Current Leaders* (中国人民大词典现任党政军领导人物卷) (pp. 234–235). Beijing: Foreign Languages Press.

Editorial Board of Who's Who in China (Ed.) (1989c). Wan Li (b. 1916). In *Who's Who in China Current Leaders* (中国人民大词典现任党政军领导人物卷) (p. 662). Beijing: Foreign Languages Press.

Editorial Board of Who's Who in China (Ed.) (1989d). Zhang Jinfu (b. 1914). In *Who's Who in China Current Leaders* (中国人民大词典现任党政军领导人物卷) (pp. 930–931). Beijing: Foreign Language Press.

Editorial Board of Who's Who in China (Ed.) (1989e). Zhao Ziyang (b. 1919). In *Who's Who in China Current Leaders* (中国人民大词典现任党政军领导人物卷) (pp. 986–987). Beijing: Foreign Languages Press.

Editorial Board of Comparative Social and Economic Systems (Ed.) (1989). *Corruption: Exchange of Money and Power* (腐败：货币与权力的交换). Beijing: China Prospect Book Company.

Encyclopædia Britannica (2011). Bernard Baruch - United States Government Official. Retrieved April 30, 2017, from https://www.britannica.com/biography/Bernard-Baruch.

Erlich, A. (1967). *Soviet Industrialization Debate, 1924–1928.* Cambridge, MA: Harvard University Press.

European Bank for Reconstruction and Development (1999). *Transition Report 1999: Ten Years of Transition.* https://doi.org/10.1016/j.jpowsour.2010.04.050

Eyferth, J. (2009). *Eating Rice from Bamboo Roots: The Social History of a Community of Handicraft.* Cambridge, MA: Harvard University Press.

Eyferth, J. (2012). Women's Work and the Politics of Homespun in Socialist China, 1949–1980. *International Review of Social History, 57*(3), 365–391.

Fairbank, J. K. (1983). *The United States and China* (4th ed.). Cambridge, MA: Harvard University Press.

Fan Shitao (forthcoming). 薛暮桥年谱 (Xue Muqiao Chronicle). Beijing.

Fang Weizhong (2004). 11–12 June: Zhao Ziyang's Hearing of the Report on the Comprehensive Reform Approach of Combing Price Tax and Fiscal Reform (赵紫阳听取经济体制改革总体思路，价税财改革思路汇报). In *Forward in the Storm: Chronology of China's Reform and Development, 1977–1989, Vol. 9* (1986) (在风浪中前进：中国发展与改革编年记事) (pp. 72–82). Unpublished manuscript.

Fang Weizhong (2014). *Record of Thirty Years, 1977–1989, Volume 2 (*十三年纪事, *1977–1989,* 下卷*)*. Beijing: China Planning Press.

Fewsmith, J. (1994). *Dilemmas of Reform in China: Political Conflict and Economic Debate.* Armonk, NY: M. E. Sharpe.

Filatochev, I., R. Bradshaw, and R. O. Y. Bradshaw (1992). The Soviet Hyperinflation: Its Origins and Impact Throughout the Former Republics. *Soviet Studies, 44*(5), 739–759.

Fischer, K. (2009). The Influence of Neoliberals in Chile before, during, and after Pinochet. In P. Mirowski, and D. Plehwe (Eds.), *The Road from Mont Pelerin: The Making of the Neoliberal Thought Collective* (pp. 305–346). Cambridge, MA: Harvard University Press.

Foley, D. (2011). Socialist Alternatives to Capitalism I: Marx to Haye. Lecture at the Havens Institute, University of Wisconsin, Madison, April 6–7. http://www.havenscenter.org/files/FoleySocialismMarxtoHayek.pdf

Folha de S. Paulo (2008). Antonio Delfim Netto. Retrieved October 10, 2019, from Folha de S. Paulo website: https://www1.folha.uol.com.br/folha/treinamento/ho tsites/ai5/personas/delfimNetto.html

Frieden, J. A. (1987). The Brazilian Borrowing Experience: From Miracle to Debacle and Back. *Latin American Research Review, 22*(1), 95–131.

Friedman, M. (1952). Price, Income, and Monetary Changes in Three Wartime Periods. *American Economic Review, 42*(2), 612–625.

Friedman, M. (1966). What Price Guideposts? In George Shultz and Robert Z. Aliber (Eds.), *Guidelines, Informal Controls, and the Market Place: Policy Choices in a Full Employment Economy.* Chicago: The University of Chicago Press.

Friedman, M. (1973). Monumental Folly. *Newsweek*, June 25, 64–65.

Friedman, M. (1977). *Friedman on Galbraith and on Curing the British Disease.* London: Institute of Economic Affairs.

Friedman, M. (1981). Money and Inflation (货币与通货膨胀). *Comments on International Economics, 1,* 9–23.

Friedman, M. (1988). Friedman Speech at International Studies Advisory Committee (ISAC) Dinner. Hoover Institution on War, Revolution and Peace Records.

Friedman, M. (1990). *Friedman in China.* Hong Kong: Chinese University Press.

Friedman, M., and A. J. Schwartz (1963). *A Monetary History of the United States.* Princeton: Princeton University Press.

Friedman, M., and R. Friedman (1980). *Free to Choose: A Personal Statement.* New York: Harcourt Brace Jovanovich.

Frost, R. (1920). The Road Not Taken. In *Mountain Interval* (pp. 9–10). New York: Henry Holt and Company.

Fuchs, J. R. (1974). Oral History Interview with Arthur N. Young. Harry S. Truman Library and Museum, 1–44. Retrieved from http://www.aaa.si.edu/collections/i nterviews/oral-history-interview-john-yeon-12428.

Fuhrmann, U. (2017). *Die Entstehung der "Sozialen Marktwirtschaft" 1948/9: Eine historische Dispositivanalyse.* Konstanz: UKV Verlagsgesellschaft.

Fukuyama, F. (1989). The End of History? *The National Interest*, 16(Summer 1989), 3–18.

Fuller, P. (2019). *Famine Relief in Warlord China.* Cambridge, MA: Harvard University Asia Center.

Fung, K. K. (1982). Editor's Introduction. In *Social Needs Versus Economic Efficiency in China: Sun Yefang's Critique of Socialist Economics* (pp. xiii–xxx). New York: M. E. Sharpe.

Gale, Esson M. (1930). Public Administration of Salt in China: A Historical Survey. *The Annals of the American Academy of Political and Social Science, 152,* 241–251.

Gale, Esson M. (1931). Introduction. In Esson M. Gale (Ed.), *Discourses on Salt and Iron* (pp. XV–LI). Leyden: Late E. J. Brill Ltd.

Galbraith, J. K. (1941). The Selection and Timing of Inflation Controls. *The Review of Economics and Statistics, 23*(2), 82–85.

Galbraith, J. K. (1943). Price Control: Some Lessons from the First Phase. *American Economic Review, 33*, 253–259.

Galbraith, J. K. (1973). *A China Passage*. New York: Paragon House.

Galbraith, J. K. (1980). *A Theory of Price Control*. Cambridge, MA: Harvard University Press.

Galbraith, J. K. (1981). *A Life in Our Times*. Boston: Houghton Mifflin Company.

Galbraith, J. K. (1990). The Rush to Capitalism. (October 25, 1990). Retrieved April 30, 2017, from http://www.nybooks.com/contributors/john-kenneth-galbraith/

Galbraith, J. K. (1992). Revolt in our Time: The Triumph of Simplistic Ideology. In G. Prin (Ed.), *Spring in Winter: The 1989 Revolutions*. Manchester: Manchester University Press.

Gang Yi (1990). The Price Reform and Inflation in China, 1979–1988. *Comparative Economic Studies, Winter*, 28–61.

Gao Shangquan (1987). The Revelation We Received from the Economic System Reform in Hungary and Yugoslavia (匈牙利，南斯拉夫经济体制改革给我们的启示). In CESRRI (China Economic System Reform Research Institute) (Ed.), *A Difficult Exploration: An Investigation of the Reforms in Hungary and Yugoslavia* (pp. 1–14). Beijing: Economic Management Press.

Gao Shangquan, Chen Yizi, and Wang Xiaoqiang (1987). Report on the Investigation in Hungary and Yugoslavia (匈牙利，南斯拉夫改革考察报告). In CESRRI (Chinese Economic System Reform Research Institute) (Ed.), *A Difficult Exploration: An Investigation of the Reforms in Hungary and Yugoslavia* (pp. 15–30). Beijing: Economic Management Press.

Gao Shangquan, Chen Yizi, and Wang Xiaoqiang (1989). Investigation of Reforms in Hungary and Yugoslavia. *Chinese Economic Studies, 22*(3), 80–88.

Gao Wangling (2011). A Study of Chinese Peasant "Counter-Action." In Kimberley M. and F. Wemheuer (Eds.), *Eating Bitterness: New Perspectives on China's Great Leap Forward and Famine* (pp. 274–278). Vancouver: University of British Columbia Press.

Garms, E. (1980). Vorwort. In E. Garms and A. Mixius (Eds.), *Wirtschaftsreform in China – Chinesische Beitraege zur Theoriediskussion von Sun Yefang u.a.* (pp. 7–30). Hamburg: Mitteilungen des Instituts Fuer Asienkudne.

Geng Chongyi, and Zhou Wangjun (1998). The 1988 Intensifying Price Increases and the Process of Calming Down Panic Buying (1988 年物价上涨加剧与平息抢购风经过). In Cheng Zhiping (Ed.), *50 Years of Prices in China, 1949–1998* (中国物价五十年, *1949–1998*)) (pp. 542–556). Beijing: China Price Publishing House.

George, K. (1988). *1988 Polish Crisis: Worse Than 1980–81. 15*(20), 32–34.

Gewirtz, J. (2017). *Unlikely Partners: Chinese Reformers, Western Economists, and the Making of Global China*. Cambridge, MA: Harvard University Press.

Giersch, H. (2006). *Die Offene Gesellschaft und Ihre Wirtschaft: Aufsätze und Kommentare aus fuünf Jahrzehnten*. Hamburg: Murmann.

Gittings, J. (2006). *The Changing Face of China: From Mao to Market. Journal of Chemical Information and Modeling*. Oxford: Oxford University Press.

Goldsmith, R. W. (1955). *A Study of Saving in the United States*. Princeton: Princeton University Press.

Gottschang, T. R. (1995). Introduction. In Du Runsheng (Ed.), *Reform and Development in Rural China* (pp. 1–19). New York: St. Martin's Press.

Government of the PRoC (2017). Zhou Xiaochuan (周小川). Retrieved June 1, 2017, from http://www.gov.cn/guoqing/2013-03/11/content_2583176.htm

Graham, A. (1964). The Place of Reason in the Chinese Philosophical Tradition. In R. Dawson (Ed.), *The Legacy of China* (pp. 28–56). Oxford: Oxford University Press.

Guo Shuqing (1985). Famous International Scholars and Experts Discuss China's Economic Reforms (国际知名学者和专家谈中国经济改革). *Comparative Economic and Social Systems*, *3*, 6–11.

Guo Shuqing (2012a). A Brief Note on Each Article. In China Development Research Foundation (Ed.), *Chinese Economists on Economic Reform: Collected Works of Guo Shuqing* (pp. xxi–xxxiii). Oxon: Routledge.

Guo Shuqing (2012b). On the Target Model of Price Reform (January 1985). In China Development Research Foundation (Ed.), *Chinese Economists on Economic Reform: Collected Works of Guo Shuqing* (pp. 22–27). Oxon: Routledge.

Guo Shuqing, Liu Jirui, and Qiu Shufang (2012). Comprehensive Reform is in Urgent Need of Overall Planning. In China Development Research Foundation (Ed.), *Chinese Economists on Economic Reform: Collected Works of Guo Shuqing* (pp. 28–36). Oxon: Routledge.

Guo Shuqing, and Zhao Renwei (1986). Target Model and Transition Measures (目标模式和过渡步骤). In China Economic System Reform Research Conference (Ed.), *Macroeconomic Management and Reform: Selected Speeches of the Macroeconomic Management Symposium* (pp. 16–23). Beijing: Economic Daily Press.

Hagemann, H. (1999). Colm, Gerhard. In Harald Hagemann and Claus-Dieter Krohn (Eds.), *Biographisches Handbuch der Deutschsprachigen Wirtschaftswissenschaftlichen Emigration nach 1933* (pp. 104–113). Munich: K.G. Sauer.

Hahn, F. (1981). Reflections on the Invisible Hand. In *Fred Hirsch Memorial Lecture*. University of Warwick. https://warwick.ac.uk/fac/soc/economics/research/workingpapers/1978-1988/twerp196.pdf

Halpern, N. (1985). *Economic Specialists and the Making of Chinese Economic Policy*, 1955–1983. Ann Arbor: University of Michigan.

Halpern, N. (1986). Making Economic Policy: The Influence of Economists. In Joint Economic Committee Congress of the United States (Ed.), *China's Economy Looks Toward the Year 2000, Volume I: The Four Modernizations* (pp. 132–146). Washington, DC: U.S. Government Printing Office.

Halpern, N. (1988). Social Scientists as Policy Advisers in Post-Mao China : Explaining the Pattern of Advice. *The Australian Journal of Chinese Affairs*, *19*(20), 215–240.

Halpern, N. (1993). Review of Economic Theories in China by Robert C. Hsu. *Pacific Affairs*, *66*(2), 267–268.

Hamm, P., L. P. King, and D. Stuckler (2012). Mass Privatization, State Capacity, and Economic Growth in Post-Communist Countries. *American Sociological Review*, *77*(2), 295–324. https://doi.org/10.1177/0003122412441354

Han Zhirong, Geng Chongyi, He Jianyu, Li Keding, and Ye Ruixiang (1998). The Decision on Economic System Reform" and the Task of Price Reform (《关于经济体制改革的决定》和价格改革的任务). In *50 Years of Prices in China, 1949–1998* (中国物价五十年, *1949–1998*) (pp. 487–502). Beijing: China Price Publishing House.

Han Zhirong, Wu Xiaojiang, Ding Jie, and Geng Chongyi (1998). The Overall Unfolding of the Reform of Prices of Agricultural Goods and Agricultural Production Materials (农产品和农用生产资料价格改革全面展开). In Cheng Zhiping (Ed.), *50 Years of Prices in China，1949–1998* (中国物价五十年, *1949–1998*) (pp. 503–519). Beijing: China Price Publishing House.

Hansen, A. H. (1941). Defense Financing and Inflation Potentialities. *The Review of Economics and Statistics*, *23*(1), 1–7.

Harris, S. E. (1945). *Price and Related Controls in the United States*. New York: McGraw-Hill Book Company.

Hayek, F. A. (1935a). The Nature and History of the Problem. In F. A. Hayek (Ed.), *Collectivist Economic Planning* (pp. 1–40). London: Routledge and Kegan Paul Ltd.

Hayek, F. A. (1935b). The Present State of the Debate. In F. A. Hayek (Ed.), *Collectivist Economic Planning* (pp. 201–244). London: Routledge and Kegan Paul Ltd.

Hayek, F. A. (1940). Review: How to Pay for the War by J. M. Keynes. *The Economic Journal, 50*(198/199), 321–326.

Hayek, F. A. (1944). *The Road to Serfdom*. London: George Routledge and Sons.

Hebei Province "Turning Unified Procurement into Tax" Experiment Leading Group (1987). Report on the Progress and Situation of the "Turning Unified Procurement into Tax" Experiment (关于统购改税试点进行情况的报告). In *Research on Grain Issues in China* (中国粮食问题研究) (pp. 224–228). Beijing: Economic Management Press.

He Weiling (2015). *He Weiling Manuscript: The Legend* (传说中的何维凌手稿). Hong Kong: Strong Wind Press.

Heilmann, S., and E. Perry (2011). Embracing Uncertainty: Guerrilla Policy Style and Adaptive Governance in China. In Sebastian Heilmann and Perry Elizabeth J. Perry (Eds.), *Mao's Invisible Hand: The Political Foundations of Adaptive Governance in China* (pp. 1–29). Cambridge, MA: Harvard University Asia Center.

Hibbs, D. A. (1976). On the Political Economy of Long-Run Trends in Strike Activity. *British Journal of Political Sciences, 8*, 153–175.

Hirschman, A. (1985). Reflections on the Latin American Experience. In L. Lindberg and C. Maier (Eds.), *The Politics of Inflation and Economic Stagnation* (pp. 53–57). Washington, DC: Brookings Institution.

Hoff, T. J. B. (1949). *Economic Calculation in the Socialist Society*. London: William Hodge and Company Limited.

Holbig, H. (2001). *Inflation als Herausforderung der Legitimation Politischer Herrschaft in der VR China: Wirtschaftspolitische Strategien in den Jahren 1987–1989*. Hamburg: Mitteilungen des Instituts für Asienkunde.

Holt, R. P. F. (Ed.). (2017). *The Selected Letters of John Kenneth Galbraith*. Cambridge: Cambridge University Press.

Honig, E., and Zhao Xiaojian (2019). *Across the Great Divide: The Sent-Down Youth Movement in Mao's China, 1968–1980*. Cambridge: Cambridge University Press.

Hsia, Ronald (1953). *Price Control in Communist China*. New York: International Secretariat Institute of Pacific Relations.

Hsiao, K. H. (1971). *Money and Monetary Policy in Communist China*. New York: Columbia University Press.

Hsu, R. C. (1988). Economics and Economists in Post-Mao China: Some Observations. *Asian Survey, 28*(12), 1211–1228. https://doi.org/10.1525/as.1988.28.12.01p0217m

Hsu, R. C. (1991). *Economic Theories in China, 1979–1988*. Cambridge: Cambridge University Press.

Hu Bading (1989). The Tenth Plenary Meeting of the Political Bureau of the Central Committee Adopted the Preliminary Plan for Price and Wage Reform (中央政治局第十次全体会议原则通过价格、工资改革初步方案). *China Price Yearbook*, 12–13.

Hu Jichuang (2009). *A Concise History of Chinese Economic Thought*. Beijing: Foreign Language Press.

Hu Qiaomu (1978). Act in Accordance with Economic Laws, Step Up the Four Modernizations (按照经济规律办事，加快实现四个现代化). *People's Daily*, October 6, 1.

Hu Qiaomu (1995). Act in Accordance with Economic Laws, Step Up the Four Modernizations. In J. T. Myers, J. Domes, and M. D. Yeh (Eds.), *Chinese Politics: Documents and Analysis. Volume IV, Fall of Hua Kuo-Feng (1980) to the Twelfth Party Congress (1982)* (pp. 169–199). Columbia, SC: University of South Carolina Press.

Hua Sheng (2005). The Complete Story of the Dual-Track Price System (双轨制始末). *China Reform*, 1, 22–25.

Hua Sheng, He Jiacheng, Zhang Xuejun, Luo Xiaopeng, and Bian Yongzhuang (1986). A Restructuring of the Microeconomic Foundation: More on China's Further Reform and Some Related Thoughts (微观经济基础的重新构造：再论中国进一步改革的问题和思路). *Economic Research*, 3, 21–28.

Hua Sheng, He Jiacheng, Zhang Xuejun, Luo Xiaopeng, and Bian Yongzhuang (1987). A Restructuring of the Microeconomic Foundation: More on China's Further Reform and Some Related Thoughts. *Chinese Economic Studies*, XX(4), 3–26.

Hua Sheng, Zhang Xuejun, and Luo Xiaopeng (1988). 10 Years of Reform in China: Review, Reflections and Prospects (中国改革十年：回顾，反思和前景). *Economic Research*, 9, 13–37.

Hua Sheng, Zhang Xuejun, and Luo Xiaopeng (1993). *China: From Revolution to Reform.* London: Macmillan Press.

Huan Kuan (1931). *Discourses on Salt and Iron: A Debate on State Control of Commerce and Industry in Ancient China* (Esson McDowell Gale, Trans. and Ed.). Leyden: Late E. J. Brill Ltd.

Huang Jiangnan, Zhu Jiaming, Wang Qishan, and Weng Yongxi (1981). On China's Current Economic Situation and Several Views on the Adjustment of the National Economy (关于我国当前经济形势和国民经济调整问题的若干看法). *Internal Manuscript - Red Flag Magazine Publisher*, 1, 1–22.

Huang Peijian (2004). The Comparative School of Thought and China's Economic Reforms (比较经济学派和中国经济改革). *Economic Observer*, August 2.

Huang Yanjie (2013). *Constructing a National Oikonomia: China's Great Monetary Revolution, 1942–1950.* EAI Working Paper, 161, January.

Hymes, R. P. (1993). Moral Duty and Self-Regulating Process in Southern Sung Views of Famine Relief. In R. P. Hymes and C. Schirokauer (Eds.), *Ordering the World: Approaches to State and Society in Sung Dynasty China* (pp. 280–310). Berkeley: University of California Press.

Hymes, R. P., and C. Schirokauer (Eds.) (1993). *Ordering the World: Approaches to State and Society in Sung Dynasty China.* Berkeley: University of California Press.

International Monetary Fund (IMF), World Bank, Organisation for Economic Co-Operation and Development (OECD), and European Bank for Reconstruction and Development (1990). *The Economy of the USSR: Summary and Recommendations.* Washington, DC.

International Monetary Fund (IMF) (2017). World Economic Outlook Database. Retrieved June 1, 2017, from https://www.imf.org/external/pubs/ft/weo/2017/01/weodata/index.aspx

International Monetary Fund, World Bank, Organisation for Economic Co-Operation and Development and European Bank for Reconstruction and Development (1991). *A Study of the Soviet Economy: Vol. 1.* Paris.

Jessop, B. (2002). Liberalism, Neoliberalism, and Urban Governance: A State-Theoretical Perspective. *Antipode*, 34(3), 458–478.

Jessop, B. (2018). Neoliberalism and Workfare: Schumpeterian or Ricardian? In *SAGE Handbook of Neoliberalism* (pp. 347–359). London: Sage.

Johnson, Paul, and Chris Papageorgiou (2020). What Remains of Cross-Country Convergence? *Journal of Economic Literature*, 58(1), 129–175.

Jiang Zemin (1992). Full Text of Jiang Zemin's Report at 14th Party Congress, 1992. http://www.bjreview.com.cn/document/txt/2011-03/29/content_363504.htm, updated March 29, 2011.

Kalecki, M. (1947). *Survey of Current Inflationary and Deflationary Tendencies*. New York: United Nations Department of Economic Affairs.

Kalecki, M. (1949). *Inflationary and Deflationary Tendencies, 1946–1948*. New York: United Nations Department of Economic Affairs.

Karl, R. E. (2017). *The Magic of Concepts: History and the Economic in Twentieth-Century China*. Durham, NC: Duke University Press.

Karl, R. E. (2019). The Shadow of Democracy. *The Journal of Asian Studies, 78*(2), 379–387.

Katona, G. (1945). *Price Control and Business: Field Studies Among Producers and Distributors of Consumer Goods in the Chicago Area, 1942–1944*. Indianapolis: Cowles Commission for Research in Economics.

Keynes, J. M. (1912). Review: The Economic Principles of Confucius and his School by Chen Huan-Chang. *The Economic Journal, 22*(88), 584–588.

Keynes, J. M. (1936). *The General Theory of Employment, Interest and Money*. New York: Harcourt, Brace and World.

Keynes, J. M. (1940). *How to Pay for the War: A Radical Plan for the Chancellor of the Exchequer*. New York: Harcourt, Brace and Company.

Keynes, J. M. (1980). Letter to Professor F. A. Hayek, 28 June 1944. In D. Moggridge (Ed.), *The Collected Writings of John Maynard Keynes, Vol. XXVII. Activities 1940–1946 Shaping the Post-War World: Employment and Commodities* (pp. 385–388). London: Macmillan Cambridge University Press for the Royal Economics Society.

Keyser, C. H. (2003). *Professionalizing Research in Post-Mao China : The System Reform Institute and Policymaking*. Armonk, NY: M. E. Sharpe.

King, F. H. H. (1965). *Money and Monetary Policy in China 1845–1895*. Cambridge, MA: Harvard University Press.

Klein, N. (2007). *The Shock Doctrine: The Rise of Disaster Capitalism*. New York: Picador.

Koford, K., and D. C. Colander (1984). Taming the Rent Seeker. In D. C. Colander (Ed.), *Neoclassical Political Economy: The Analysis of Rent-Seeking and DUP Activities* (pp. 205–216). Cambridge: Ballinger.

Kornai, J. (1980). *Economics of Shortage*. Amsterdam: North-Holland.

Kornai, J. (1984). Adjustments to Price and Quantity Signals in a Socialist Economy. In B. Csikós-Nagy, D. Hague, and G. Hall (Eds.), *The Economics of Relative Prices: Proceedings of a Conference Held by the International Economic Association in Athens, Greece* (pp. 60–77). London: Macmillan Press.

Kornai, J. (1986). Providing the Chinese Reformers with Some Hungarian Lessons (提供给中国改革者的匈牙利的一些经验教训). In China Economic System Reform Research Conference (Ed.), *Macroeconomic Management and Reform: Selected Speeches of the Macroeconomic Management Symposium* (pp. 61–94). Beijing: Economic Daily Press.

Kornai, J. (1990). *The Road to a Free Economy: Shifting from a Socialist System—The Example of Hungary*. New York: W.W. Norton.

Kornai, J. (1994). Transformational Recession: The Main Causes. *Journal of Comparative Economics, 19*, 39–63.

Kornai, J. (2006). *By Force of Thought: Irregular Memoirs of an Intellectual Journey*. Cambridge, MA: MIT Press.

Kornai, J. (2010). Wu Jinglian – Birthday Greetings 2010.1.5. Retrieved May 10, 2016, from http://www.kornai-janos.hu/Kornai%20WU%20Jinglian%20Birthday%20greetings%202010.III.3.pdf

Kosta, J. (1990). Zum Lebensweg von Ota Šik (Ota Šik's Path of Life). In H. G. Nutzinger and J. Kosta (Eds.), *Ota Šik. Kasseler Universitaetsreden Heft 8* (pp. 20–25). Kassel: Boxan Repro und Druck.

Kosta, J. (2004). *Never Give Up - A Life Between Fear and Hope (Nie Aufgeben – Ein Leben Zwischen Bangen und Hoffnung)* (2d ed.). Berlin: Philo and Philo Fine Arts.

Kotz, D. M., and F. Weir (1997). *Revolution from Above: The Demise of the Soviet System.* London: Routledge.

Kraus, R. A. (1980). *Cotton and Cotton Goods in China, 1918–1936.* New York: Garland Publishing.

Krock, A. (1946). Veto of the OPA Bill Major Political Event. *New York Times,* June 30.

Kroll, J. L. (1978). Toward a Study of the Economic Views of Sang Hung-Yang. *Early China, 4,* 11–18.

Kromphardt, W. (1947). Marktspaltung und Kernplanung in der Volkswirtschaft. *Dortmunder Schriften Für Sozialforschung, 3,* Hamburg.

Kulke, U. (2007). An Undiplomatic Diplomat and the Love of Liberty: An Interview with Erwin Wickert (Ein Undiplomatischer Diplomat und die Freiheitsliebe: Ein Interview mit Erwin Wickert). Retrieved May 20, 2017, from https://www.welt.de/politik/article800571/Ein-undiplomatischer-Diplomat-und-die-Freiheitsliebe.html

Kuznets, S. (1945). National Product in Wartime. In *Oxford Research Encyclopedia of African History.* New York: National Bureau of Economic Research. https://doi.org/10.1093/acrefore/9780190277734.013.42

Laguerodie, S., and F. Vergara (2008). The Theory of Price Controls: John Kenneth Galbraith's Contribution. *Review of Political Economy, 20*(4), 569–593.

Lai Xiaogang (2011). *A Springboard for Victory: Shandong Province and Chinese Communist Military and Financial Strength, 1937–1945.* Leiden: Brill.

Lam Lai Sing (2011). *The Romance of the Three Kingdoms and Mao's Global Order of Tripolarity.* Bern: Peter Lang.

Lange, O. (1936). On the Economic Theory of Socialism: Part One. *Review of Economic Studies, 4*(1), 53–71.

Lange, O. (1967). The Computer and the Market. In C. H. Feinstein (Ed.), *Socialism, Capitalism and Economic Growth* pp. 158–161). Cambridge: Cambridge University Press.

Lapwood, R., and N. Lapwood (1954). *Through the Chinese Revolution.* Letchworth: The Garden City Press.

Lardy, N. R. (1983). *Agriculture in China's Modern Economic Development. Foreign Affairs* (*Vol. 62*). Cambridge: Cambridge University Press.

Lardy, N. R. (1984). *Agricultural Prices in China.* World Bank Staff Working Paper No. 606. Washington, DC: The World Bank.

Lardy, N. (1988). Reconsidering China's Economic System (中国经济体制再论). *Comparative Economic and Social Systems, 2,* 17–52.

Lardy, N., and K. Lieberthal (1983). Introduction. In N. Lardy and K. Lieberthal (Eds.), *Chen Yun's Strategy for China's Development: A Non-Maoist Alternative* (pp. xi–xliii). Armonk, NY: M. E. Sharpe.

Lavoie, D. (1985). *National Economic Planning: What is Left?* Cambridge, MA: Ballinger Publishing Company.

Leon, D., and V. Shkolnikov (1998). Social Stress and the Russian Mortality Crisis. *Journal of the American Medical Association, 279*(10), 790–791.

Leung, J. K., and M. Y. M. Kau (1992). Editor's Introduction to On the Ten Major Relationships. In J. K. Leung and M. Y. M. Kau (Eds.), *The Writings of Mao Zedong,*

1949–1976, *Vol. II*, January *1956–December* 1957 (pp. 43–45). Armonk, NY: M. E. Sharpe.

Levy, D. M., and S. J. Peart (2008). Socialist Calculation Debate. *The New Palgrave Dictionary of Economics 1961*, 1074–1077.

Li Chaomin (2016). The Influence of Ancient Chinese Thought on the Ever-Normal Granary of Henry A. Wallace and the Agricultural Adjustment Act of the New Deal. In *The History of Ancient Chinese Economic Thought* (pp. 210–224). Abingdon: Routledge.

Li Feng (2013). *Early China: A Social and Cultural History*. Cambridge: Cambridge University Press.

Li Jingwei (1988). Deng Xiaoping Said During Meeting with Alfonsin: The Third World Is the Greatest Force for Peace (邓小平会见阿方辛时说：第三世界是最大的和平力量). *People's Daily*, May 16, 1.

Li Xiannian (1956). Speech by Comrade Li Hsien-Nien, Vice-Premier and Minister of Finance. In Eighth National Congress of the Communist Party of China, *Vol. II, Speeches* (pp. 206–224). Beijing: Foreign Language Press.

Li Xianglu (2016b). Remembering a Venerable Elder at the Forefront of Reform (回忆一位站在改革前沿的长者). *Yanhuang Chunqiu Magazine*, 2, 18–24.

Li Yining (1979). *Galbraith's Institutional Economics* (论加尔布雷思的制度经济学说). Beijing: Commercial Press.

Li Yining (1986). The Basic Line of Thought on China's Reform (改革的基本思路). *Beijing Daily*, May 19, 3.

Li Yining (1988). Comparing Two Schools of Reform Thought (两种改革思路的比较). In *Selected Works of Li Yining* (pp. 89–94). Xian: Xian People's Press.

Li Yining (1988a). Comparing Two Schools of Reform Thought (两种改革思路的比较). In *Selected Works of Li Yining* (pp. 89–94). Xian: Xian People's Press.

Li Yining (1988b). Should Price Reform or Ownership Reform be Prioritized? (价格改革为主还是所有制改革为主). *Science of Finance*, 2, 86–90.

Li Yining (1989). *Reflections on China's Economic Reform* (中国经济改革的思路). (Peng Xiaomeng, Ed.). Beijing: China Prospect Book Company.

Li Yining (1990). *Chinese Economy in Disequilibrium* (非均衡的中国经济). Beijing: Economic Daily Press.

Li Yining (2012). Li Yining: Biographical Note. In *Economic Reform and Development in China* (pp. vi–ii). Cambridge: Cambridge University Press.

Li Yining (2014). *Chinese Economy in Disequilibrium*. Berlin: Springer.

Lim, E. (2008). Preface II: The Opening of the Mind to the Outside World in China's Reform and Opening Process (序二：中国改革开放过程中的对外思想开放). In Wu Jinglian, Fan Gang, Liu He, Justin Yifu Lin, et al. (Eds.), *30 Years of Reform Through the Eyes of 50 Economists: Review and Analysis* (中国经济50人看三十年：回顾与分析) (pp. 43–51). Beijing: China Economics Press.

Lim, E. (2014). The Influence of Foreign Economists in the Early Stages of China's Reforms. In *The Oxford Companion to the Economics of China* (pp. 47–53). Oxford: Oxford University Press.

Lin, C. C. (1981). The Reinstatement of Economics in China Today. *The China Quarterly*, 85(3), 1–48. https://doi.org/10.1017/S0305741000028010

Lin Chen (1988). "Control the Money Supply, Reform Prices": Interview with Economist Wu Jinglian ("管住货币，改革价格"：访经济学家吴敬琏). *Besides Hope*, 29, 13–16.

Lin Chun (1977). On the Role of the Forces of Production in Historical Development (论生产力在历史发展中的作用). *Historical Research*, 5, 37–53.

Lin Man-houng (2006). *China Upside Down: Currency, Society, and Ideologies, 1808–1856*. Cambridge, MA: Harvard University Asia Center.

Lin Yifu (1992). Rural Reforms and Agricultural Growth in China. *The American Economic Review, 82*(1), 34–51.

Linder, W. (1990). Monetary Aspects of Recent Developments in Eastern Europe: A Summarized Assessment. *Economic Education Bulletin, XXX*(8), 14–27.

Ling Huanming (1988). Intellectual Response to China's Economic Reform. *Asian Survey, 28*(5), 541–554.

Ling Tseng, and Lei Han (1959). *The Circulation of Money in the People's Republic of China*. Moscow: Gosfinizdat.

Lipton, D., and J. Sachs (1990). Creating a Market Economy in Eastern Europe: The Case of Poland. *Brookings Papers on Economic Activity, 21*(1), 75–147.

Lipton, D., and J. D. Sachs (1992). Prospects for Russia' s Economic Reforms. *Brookings Papers on Economic Activity, 2*, 213–283.

Liu Guoguang, and Zhang Zhuoyuan (1985). Economic System Reform and Macroeconomic Management: Commentaries on the "International Conference on Macroeconomic Management" (经济体制改革与宏观经济管理："宏观经济管理国际讨论会"评述). *Economic Research, 12*, 3–19.

Liu Guoguang et al. (1987). Economic Reform and Macroeconomic Management: Commentaries on the International Conference on Macroeconomic Management. *Chinese Economic Studies, 20*(3), 3–45.

Liu Guoguang, and Zhao Renwei (1979). Relationship Between Planning and the Market Under Socialism (关于社会主义经济计划与市场的关系问题). *Economic Research* (经济研究), 7(4), 11–21.

Liu Guoguang, and Zhao Renwei (1982). Relationship Between Planning and the Market Under Socialism. In G. C. Wang (Ed.), *Economic Reform in the PRC: In Which China's Economists Make Known What Went Wrong, Why, and What Should be Done About It* (pp. 89–104). Boulder: Westview Press.

Liu Hong (2002). *Wu Jinglian — Scientific Critical Biographies of Contemporary Chinese Economists* (吴敬链 — 当代中国经济学家学术评传). Xi'an: Shaanxi Normal University Press.

Liu Hong (2009a). Dong Fureng: Preserve Integrity to Become Great (董辅礽：守身为大). Retrieved November 16, 2016, from http://news.whu.edu.cn/info/1005/24464.htm

Liu Hong (2009b). The Bashanlun Roundtrip (巴山论之行). *Economic Observer*, September 4.

Liu Hong (2010). *The Eighties: Glory and Dreams of Chinese Economic Scholars* (八〇年代:中国经济学人的光荣与梦想). Guilin: Guanxi Normal University Press.

Liu Suinian, and Wu Qungan (1986). *China's Socialist Economy: An Outline History (1949–1984)*. Beijing: Beijing Review.

Liu Wei (2011). Research on China's 1988 "Crashing through the Barrier of Price Reform" (1988年中国"价格闯关"研究). Central Party School.

Loeffler, B. (2002). *Social Market Economy and Administrative Practice: Federal Ministry for Economic Affairs Under Ludwig Erhard (Soziale Marktwirtschaft und Administrative Praxis Das Bundeswirtschaftsministerium Unter Ludwig Erhard)*. Wiesbaden: Franz Steiner Verlag.

Loewe, M. (1974). *Crisis and Conflict in Han China, 104 BC to AD 9*. London: George Allen and Unwin Ltd.

Loewe, M. (1985). Attempts at Economic Co-ordination During the Western Han Dynasty. In S. R. Schram (Ed.), *The Scope of State Power in China* (pp. 237–268). London: School of Oriental and African Studies.

Loewe, M. (2001). Review of Erling v. Mende, Bertram Schefold, and Hans Ulrich Vogel, Huan Kuan, Yantie lun: Vademecum zu dem Klassiker der Chinesischen Wirtschaftsdebatten. *Early China, 26*, 285–289.

Lou Jiwei (2011). *The 1985 Program Office – Transcription of Lou Jiwei's Tsinghua Lecture, 16-19 September, 2011* (1985年方案办 一 楼继伟清华讲课). Unpublished manuscript, Beijing.

Lou Jiwei (2017). Lou Jiwei Looks Back on 40 Years Since Entering Tsinghua: 2017 Tsinghua University School of Economic Management Graduation Ceremony Speech (楼继伟回首清华入学40年：清华大学经济管理学院2017毕业典礼演讲). Retrieved July 3, 2017, from http://www.sohu.com/a/153915867_641792

Lou Jiwei, and Zhou Xiaochuan (1984). On the Direction of Reform in the Price System and Related Modeling Methods (论我国价格体系改革方向及其有关的模型方法). *Economic Research, 10*, 13–20.

Lou Jiwei and Zhou Xiaochuan (1989). On the Direction of Reform in the Price System. *Chinese Economic Studies, 22*(3), 14–23.

Lowenstein, M. (2019). Return to the Cage: Monetary Policy in China's First Five-Year Plan. *Twentieth-Century China, 44*(1), 53–74.

Lu Hao (2002). *Li Yining - Scientific Critical Biographies of Contemporary Chinese Economists* (厉以宁 一 当代中国经济学家学术评传). Xi'an: Shaanxi Normal University Press.

Lu Mai, and Feng Minglian (2012). The Evolution of China's Reform and Development Process. In M. Wang (Ed.), *Thirty Years of China's Reform* (pp. 27–69). Oxon: Routledge.

Lu Nan and Li Mingzhe (1991). Use of Input-Output Techniques for Planning the Price Reform. In *Chinese Economic Planning and Input-Output Analysis* (pp. 81–92). Oxford: Oxford University Press.

Luo Guanzhong (1959). *Romance of the Three Kingdoms* (C. H. Brewitt-Taylor, Ed.). Adelaide: University of Adelaide.

Luo Xiaopeng (1987). "Turning Unified Procurement into Tax" Propaganda Outline (统购改税试点宣传提纲). In *Research on Grain Issues in China* (中国粮食问题研究) (pp. 229–243). Beijing: Economic Management Press.

Luo Xiaopeng (2008). Luo Xiaopeng: Commentary on the History of Price Reform (罗小朋：价格改革历史述评). Retrieved June 1, 2017, from http://luo-xiaopeng.blog.sohu.com/107129688.html

Luo Zhiru and Li Yining (1978). *The British Economy in the 20th Century: Research on the "British Disease"* (二十世纪的英国经济："英国病"研究). Beijing: People's Publishing House.

Macarini, J. P. (2000). A Política econômica da ditadura militar no limiar do "milagre" brasileiro: 1967/9. *Texto Para Discussão IE/UNICAMP, 99*.

Macfarquhar, R. (2009). Foreword. In Bao Pu, R. Chiang, and A. Ignatius (Eds.), *Prisoner of the State: The Secret Journal of Premier Zhao Ziyang* (pp. xvii–xxv). New York: Simon & Schuster.

Maddison, A. (2001). *The World Economy: A Millennial Perspective*. Paris: OECD.

Maddison, A. (2007). *Chinese Economic Performance in the Long Run, 960–2030 A.D.* (2d ed.) Paris: OECD.

Madra, Y. M., and F. Adaman (2010). Public Economics After Neoliberalism: A Theoretical-Historical Perspective. *The European Journal of the History of Economic Thought, 17*(4), 1079–1106, doi:10.1080/09672567.2010.482997

Mallory, W. H. (1926). *China: Land of Famine*. Worcester, MA: Commonwealth Press.

Mandel, E. (1995). *Trotsky as Alternative*. London; New York: Verso.

Mandeville, B. (1970). *The Fable of the Bees*. London: Penguin Books.

Mansfield, H. C. (1947). *Historical Reports on War Administration: A Short History of OPA.* Washington, DC: Office of Temporary Controls and Office of Price Administration.

Mao Zedong (1960 [1940]). *On New Democracy.* Beijing: Foreign Language Press.

Mao Zedong (1977). *A Critique of Soviet Economics.* New York: Monthly Review Press.

Mao Zedong (1986). Opening Speech at the First Plenary Session of the CPPCC, September 21, 1949. In M. Y. M. Kau and J. K. Leung (Eds.), *The Writings of Mao Zedong, 1949–1976, Vol. I,* September 1949–December (pp. 3–7). Armonk, NY: M. E. Sharpe.

Mao Zedong (1992). On the Ten Major Relationships. In J. K. Leung and M. Y. M. Kau (Eds.), *The Writings of Mao Zedong, 1949–1976, Vol. II,* January *1956–December* 1957 (pp. 43–66). Armonk, NY: M. E. Sharpe.

McGregor, R. (2006). Chinese Support of Foreign Investment Put to the Test. *Financial Times,* January 15, 2006. Retrieved from https://www.ft.com/content/7e31fcaa-85e7 -11da-bee0-0000779e2340

Medvedev, V. (1998). Price Reform—The Missing Link? Failure of Political Will. In M. Ellman and V. Kontorovich (Eds.), *The Destruction of the Soviet Economic System: An Insiders' History* (p. 158). New York: Routledge.

Mehrling, P. (1998). *The Money Interest and the Public Interest: American Monetary Thought, 1920–1970.* Cambridge, MA: Harvard University Press.

Meisner, M. (1977). The Maoist Legacy and Chinese Socialism. *Asian Survey, 44*(11), 1016–1027.

Meisner, M. J. (1999). *Mao's China and After* (3d ed.). New York: The Free Press.

Merklein, R. (1980). China is Currently a Great Laboratory (China Ist Derzeit ein Grosses Laboratorium). *Der Spiegel,* December 1, 167–187.

Middle-Aged and Young Economic Scientific Workers Conference (1985a). Report Nr. 1: Two Ways of Thinking About Price Reform (价格改革的两种思路). *Economic Research Reference Material,* 1252.

Middle-Aged and Young Economic Scientific Workers Conference (1985b). Report Nr. 2: Several Issues Interrelated with Price Reform (与价格改革相关的若干问题). *Economic Research Reference Material,* 1252.

Mihm, S. (2017). Milk Wars Curdled U.S.-Canada Relationship Long Ago. (April 29, 2017). Retrieved April 30, 2017, from https://www.bloomberg.com/view/articles/ 2017-04-29/milk-wars-curdled-u-s-canada-relationship-long-ago.

Milburn, O. (2007). The Book of the Young Master of Accountancy: An Ancient Chinese Economics Text. *Journal of the Economic and Social History of the Orient, 50*(1), 19–40.

Miller, C. (2016). *The Struggle to Save the Soviet Economy: Mikhail Gorbachev and the Collapse of the USSR.* Chapel Hill: The University of North Carolina Press.

Mills, D. Q. (1975). Some Lessons of Price Controls in 1971–1973. *The Bell Journal of Economics, 6*(1), 3–49.

Mises Institute (2005). Introduction – Inflation and Price Control by L. von Mises. Retrieved April 30, 2017, from https://mises.org/library/inflation-and-price-control.

Mitter, R. (2020). Shaped by Conflict: New Writing on China's Wartime Experience in the Early Twentieth Century. *Twentieth-Century China, 45*(1), 113–118.

Mont Pelerin Society (2019). Past Presidents. Retrieved October 10, 2019, from https:// www.montpelerin.org/past-presidents-2/

Murphy, M., M. Bobak, A. Nicholson, R. Rose, and M. Marmot (2006). The Widening Gap in Mortality by Educational Level in the Russian Federation, 1980–2001. *American Journal of Public Health, 96*(7), 1293–1299. https://doi.org/10.2105/AJPH .2004.056929

Musgrave, R. A. (2008). Hansen, Alvin (1887–1975). *The New Palgrave Dictionary of Economics*. Retrieved April 30, 2017, from http://www.dictionaryofeconomics.com/article?id=pde2008_H000014.

Myers, J. T. (1989). China: Modernization and "Unhealthy Tendencies". *Comparative Politics*, *21*(2), 193–213.

Myers, R. (1986). The Agrarian System. In J. Fairbank and A. Feuerwerker (Eds.), *The Cambridge History of China* (pp. 230–269). Cambridge: Cambridge University Press.

National Bureua of Economic Research (2012). US Business Cycle Expansion and Contraction. Retrieved April 30, 2017, from http://www.nber.org/cycles/US_Business_Cycle_Expansions_and_Contractions_20120423.pdf.

National Bureau of Statistics (2010). Compilation of sixty years' of statistics of the New China (新中国六十年统计资料汇编). Beijing: China Statistical Press.

Naughton, B. (1989). Inflation and Economic Reform in China. *Current History*, *September*, 269–291.

Naughton, B. (1991). Inflation in China: Patterns, Causes and Cures. In Joint Economic Committee Congress of the United States (Ed.), *China's Economic Dilemmas in the 1990s: The Problems of Reforms, Modernization, and Interdependence* (pp. 135–159). Armonk, NY: M. E. Sharpe.

Naughton, B. (1993). Deng Xiaoping: The Economist. *China Quarterly*, *135*, 491–514.

Naughton, B. (1995). *Growing out of the Plan: Chinese Economic Reform*, 1978–1993. Cambridge: Cambridge University Press.

Naughton, B. (2013). Editor's Introduction: Biographical Preface. In Barry Naughton (Ed.), *Wu Jinglian: Voice of Reform in China* (pp. 97–118). Cambridge, MA: MIT Press.

New York Times (1946). Letters to the Times: Price Control Recommended - Economists Favor Continuation of Act for Another Year. April 9, 23.

Nicholls, A. J. (2000). *Freedom with Responsibility: The Social Market Economy in Germany 1918–1963*. Oxford: Oxford University Press.

Nolan, P. (1988). *The Political Economy of Collective Farms: An Analysis of China's Post-Mao Rural Reforms*. Cambridge: Polity Press.

Nolan, P. (1993). The Causation and Prevention of Famines: A Critique of A. K. Sen. *Journal of Peasant Studies*, *21*(1), 1–28.

Nolan, P. (1995). *China's Rise, Russia's Fall: Politics, Economic and Planning in the Transition from Stalinism*. Basingstoke: Macmillan Press.

Nolan, P. (2004). *China at the Crossroads*. Cambridge: Polity Press.

Nolan, P., and Dong Fureng (Eds.) (1990). *The Chinese Economy and its Future: Achievements and Problems of Post-Mao Reform*. Cambridge: Polity in Association with Basil Blackwell.

Notzon, F. C., Y. M. Komarov, S. P. Ermakov, C. T. Sempos, J. S. Marks, and E. V. Sempos (1998). Causes of Declining Life Expectancy in Russia. *Journal of the American Medical Association*, *279*(10), 793–800.

Novokmet, F., T. Piketty, and G. Zucman (2017). From Soviets to Oligarchs: Inequality and Property in Russia 1905–2016. *NBER Working Papers*, 23712. Retrieved from http://www.nber.org/papers/w23712

Observatory of Economic Complexity (2018). Country Profile Russia. Retrieved April 1, 2018, from Observatory of Economic Complexity website: https://oec.world/en/profile/country/rus

Oi, J. C. (1986). Peasant Grain Marketing and State Procurement: China's Grain Contracting System. *The China Quarterly*, *106*(3), 272–290.

Oi, J. C. (1989). Market Reforms and Corruption in Rural China. *Studies in Comparative Communism*, *22*(2–3), 221–233.

Oi, J. C. (1989). *State and Peasants in Contemporary China: The Political Economy of Village Government*. Berkeley: University of California Press.

Oi, J. C. (1999). *Rural China Takes Off: Insitutional Foundations of Economic Reform* (pp. 19–34). Berkeley: University of California Press.

Ötsch, W. O., S. Pühringer, and K. Hirte (2018). *Netzwerke des Marktes: Ordoliberalismus als Politische Ökonomie*. Wiesbaden: Springer.

Pantsov, A. V., and S. I. Levine (2015). *Deng Xiaoping—A Revolutionary Life*. Oxford: Oxford University Press.

Popov, V. (2007). Shock Therapy Versus Gradualism Reconsidered: Lessons from Transition Economies after 15 Years of Reforms. *Comparative Economic Studies*, *49*(1), 1–31. https://doi.org/10.1057/palgrave.ces.8100182

Parker, R. (2005). J. K. Galbraith: *A 20th Century Life*. London: Old Street Publishing.

Peebles, G. (1991). *Money in the People's Republic of China: A Comparative Perspective*. Sydney: Allen & Unwin.

People's Daily (1949). Editorial, October 2, 1949.

People's Daily (1987). Let the Struggle Against Bourgeois Liberalization Penetrate Deeply (把反对资产阶级自由化的斗争引向深入). May 17, 1.

People's Daily (1988a). Deng Xiaoping Stressed at the Symposium "China and the World in the 21st Century" That Conditions Were Ready to Take on the Risk of Comprehensive Reform of Prices and Wages (邓小平会见"九十年代的中国与世界"会议代表时强调我们有条件冒全面改革物价工资风险), June 4, 1.

People's Daily (1988b). The Political Bureau of the CPC Central Committee Held the 10th Plenary Meeting and Approved the Preliminary Plan of Price and Wage Reform in Principle (中央政治局召开第十次全体会议 原则通过价格工资改革初步方案). August 19.

Pepper, S. (1986). The KMT-CCP Conflict 1945–1949. In J. Fairbank and A. Feuerwerker (Eds.), *The Cambridge History of China* (pp. 723–788). Cambridge: Cambridge University Press.

Pepper, S. (1999). *Civil War in China: The Political Struggle, 1945–1949*. Roman & Littlefield Publishers. https://www.amazon.com/Civil-War-China-Political-1945-1949/dp/0847691349

Perkins, D. H. (1964). Price Stability and Development in Mainland China (1951–1963). *Journal of Political Economy*, *72*(4), 360–375.

Perkins, D. H. (1966). *Market Control and Planning in Communist China*. Cambridge, MA: Harvard University Press.

Perry, E., and S. Heilmann (2011). Embracing Uncertainty: Guerrilla Policy Style and Adaptive Governance in China. In Elizabeth J. Perry and Sebastian Heilmann (Eds.), *Mao's Invisible Hand: The Political Foundations of Adaptive Governance in China* (pp. 1–29). Cambridge, MA: Harvard University Press.

Peterson Institute for International Economics (2017). Anders Åslund. Retrieved January 20, 2017, from https://piie.com/experts/former-research-staff/anders-aslund?author_id=455

Phillips-Fein, K. (2009). Business Conservatives and the Mont Pelerin Society. In P. Mirowksi and D. Plehwe (Eds.), *The Road from Mont Pelerin: The Making of the Neoliberal Thought Collective* (pp. 280–303). Cambridge, MA: Harvard University Press.

Pigou, A. C. (1944). Review: The Road to Serfdom by F. A. Hayek. *The Economic Journal*, *54*(214), 217–219.

Pines, Y. (2009). *Envisioning Eternal Empire: Chinese Political Thought of the Warring States Era*. Honolulu: University of Hawai'i Press.

Pines, Y. (2018). Legalism in Chinese Philosophy. In *Stanford Encyclopedia of Philosophy*. https://plato.stanford.edu/entries/chinese-legalism/

Polenske, K. R. (1991). Chinese Input-Output Research from a Western Perspective. In K. R. Polenske and X. Chen (Eds.), *Chinese Economic Planning and Input-Output Analysis* (pp. 1–26). Hong Kong: Oxford University Press.

Popov, V. (2000). Shock Therapy Versus Gradualism: The End of the Debate. *Comparative Economic Studies, XLII*(1), 1–57. https://doi.org/10.5539/ass.v4n2p17

Popov, V. (2007). Shock Therapy Versus Gradualism Reconsidered: Lessons from Transition Economies after 15 Years of Reforms. *Comparative Economic Studies, 49*(1), 1–31. https://doi.org/10.1057/palgrave.ces.8100182

Program Office (Office for Researching a Reform Programme of the State Council) (1986, April 25). *Basic Outline for Reform in the Next Two Years* (明后两年配套改革的基本思路). Unpublished document.

Reddaway, P., and D. Glinski (2001). *The Tragedy of Russia's Reforms: Market Bolshevism Against Democracy*. Washington, DC: United States Institute of Peace.

Research Department of Party Literature (1991). *Major Documents of the People's Republic of China—Selected Important Documents Since the Third Plenary Session of the Eleventh Central Committee of the Communist Party of China (December 1978 and November 1989)* (Central Committee of the Communist Party, Ed.). Beijing: Foreign Languages Press.

Research Group for an Overall Plan under the Economic System Reform Commission (1986). Design of an Overall Plan for Economist System Reform (经济体制改革总体规划构思). *Economic Research Reference Material*, 35.

Reynolds, B. (Ed.) (1987a). *Reform in China: Challenges and Choices – A Summary and Analysis of the CESRRI Survey Prepared by the Staff of the Chinese Economic System Reform Research Institute*. Armonk, NY: M. E. Sharpe.

Reynolds, B. (Ed.) (1988). *Chinese Economic Reform: How Far, How Fast?* Boston: Academic Press.

Reynolds, B. L. (1987b). Introduction to the English Edition. In B. L. Reynolds (Ed.), *Reform in China - Challenges and Choices: A Summary and Analysis of the CESRRI Survey Prepared by the Staff of the Chinese Economic System Reform Research Institute* (pp. xv–xvii). Armonk, NY: M. E. Sharpe.

Richter, I., and D. Montgomery (1994). *Labor's Struggles, 1945–1950: A Participant's View*. Cambridge: Cambridge University Press.

Richter, J. (2000). In Memoriam: Dr. Jiri Skolka. *Review of Income and Wealth, 46*(1), 129–130.

Rickett, W. A. (1993). Kuan tzu 管子. In M. Loewe (Ed.), *Early Chinese Texts: A Bibliographical Guide* (pp. 244–251). New Haven: Birdtrack Press.

Rickett, W. A. (1998). *Guanzi: Political, Economic and Philosophical Essays from Early China. Vol. II*. Princeton: Princeton University Press.

Riskin, C. (1969). Red China is No Monolith - Review: China's Economic System by A. Donnithorne. *Columbia Journal of World Business, 4*(1), 89–90.

Riskin, C. (1987). *China's Political Economy: The Quest for Development Since 1949*. Oxford: Oxford University Press.

Robbins, L. (1934). Restrictionism and Planning. In *The Great Depression* (pp. 125–159). New York: Books for Libraries Press.

Robbins, L. (1937). Foreword. In *The Economics of Inflation: A Study of Currency Depreciation in Post-War Germany* (pp. 5–6). Northampton: John Dickens & Co. Ltd. https://www.amazon.com/Economics-Inflation-Currency-Depreciation-Germany/dp/1406722413

Robbins, L. (1945). *An Essay on the Nature and Significance of Economic Science* (2d ed.). London: Macmillan and Co.

Robinson, J. (1969). *The Cultural Revolution in China* (J. Collier, Ed.). Harmondsworth: Penguin Books.

Rockoff, H. (1984). *Drastic Measures. A History of Wage and Price Controls in the United States.* Cambridge: Cambridge University Press.

Rodrik, D. (2010). Diagnostics before Prescription. *Journal of Economic Perspectives, 24*(3), 33–44. https://doi.org/10.1257/jep.24.3.33

Roland, G., and T. Verdier (1999). Transition and the Output Fall. *Economics of Transition, 7*(1), 1–28. https://doi.org/10.1111/1468-0351.00002

Ronan, C. A. (1978). *The Shorter Science and Civilisation in China 1: An Abridgement of Joseph Needham's Original Text.* Cambridge: Cambridge University Press.

Rong Jingben (1989). Preface. In Editorial Board of Comparative Social and Economic Systems (Ed.), *Corruption: Exchange of Money and Power* (腐败：货币与权力的交换) (pp. 1–5). Beijing: China Prospect Book Company.

Rong Jingben (2008). Memories of One Episode in 30 Years of Reform and Opening Up (忆改革开放三十年中的一段往事). *Teahouse for Economists, 37*, 45–49.

Rostow, W. W. (1954). *The Prospects for Communist China.* New York: The Technology Press of Massachusetts Institute of Technology and John Wiley & Sons, Inc.

Rowe, W. T. (2001). *Saving the World: Chen Hongmou and Elite Consciousness in Eighteenth-Century China.* Stanford: Stanford University Press.

Rowe, W. T. (2018). *Speaking of Profit: Bao Shichen and Reform in Nineteenth-Century China.* Cambridge, MA: Harvard University Asia Center.

Sachs, J. (1992). Building a Market Economy in Poland. *Scientific American*, March, 34–40.

Sachs, J. (1992a). Building a Market Economy in Poland. *Scientific American*, March, 20–26.

Sachs, J. (1992b). Privatization in Russia: Some Lessons from Eastern Europe. *The American Economic Review, 82*(2), 43–48.

Sachs, J. (1994a). *Poland's Jump to the Market Economy (Lionel Robbins Lecture, 3).* Cambridge, MA: MIT Press.

Sachs, J. (1994b). Russia's Struggle with Stabilization: Conceptual Issues and Evidence. *The World Bank Research Observer*, 57–80. https://doi.org/10.1093/wber/8.suppl_1.57

Sachs, J., and D. Lipton (1990). Poland's Economic Reform. *Foreign Affairs, 69*(3), 47–66.

Samuels, W. J. (2008). Taussig, Frank William (1859–1940). *The New Palgrave Dictionary of Economics.* Retrieved April 30, 2017, from http://www.dictionaryofeconomics.com/extract?id=pde2008_T000016.

Sandler, C. (1943). Out Under Fire: Galbraith, OPA's Price Chief, Quits in Midst of Maxon Feud. *Washington Post*, June 1, 1.

Sargent, T. J. (1982). The Ends of Four Big Inflations. In Robert E. Hall (Ed.), *Inflation: Causes and Effects* (pp. 41–98). Cambridge, MA: University of Chicago Press.

Schmalzer, S. (2016). *Red Revolution, Green Revolution: Scientific Farming in Socialist China.* Chicago: Chicago University Press.

Schram, S. R. (1988). China After the 13th Congress. *The China Quarterly, 114*, 177–197.

Schran, P. (1977). China's Price Stability: Its Meaning and Distributive Consequences. *Journal of Comparative Economics, 1*, 367–388.

Schwartz, B. I. (1964). *In Search of Wealth and Power : Yen Fu and the West.* Cambridge, MA: Harvard University Press.

Schumpeter, J. A. (1997). *Ten Great Economists: From Marx to Keynes.* London: Routledge.

Secretariat of the Meeting of Young Adult Economic Workers (2003). The Meeting Report of the Young Adult Economic Science Workers Academic Discussion Meeting. In C. H. Keyser (Ed.), *Professionalizing Research in Post-Mao China: The System Reform Institute and Policymaking* (pp. 157–158). Armonk, NY: M. E. Sharpe.

Secretariat of UNIDO (1984). An Input-Output Table for China 1975. *Industry and Development (United Nations Industrial Development Organization)*, 10, 47–59.

Selden, M. (Ed.) (1979). *The People's Republic of China: A Documentary History of Revolutionary Change*. New York: Monthly Review Press.

Shih, V. C. (2008). *Factions and Finance in China: Elite Conflict and Inflation*. Cambridge: Cambridge University Press.

Shirk, S. L. (1993). *Political Logic of Economic Reform in China*. Berkeley: University of California Press.

Šik, O. (1965). *The Czechoslovakian Economy on New Paths (Die Tschechoslowakische Wirtschaft auf Neuen Wegen)*. Prag: Orbis.

Šik, O. (1967a). *Plan and Market Under Socialism*. Prague: Prague, Academia, 1967.

Šik, O. (1967b). Socialist Market Relations and Planning. In C. H. Feinstein (Ed.), *Socialism, Capitalism and Economic Growth: Essays Presented to Maurice Dobb* (pp. 133–158). Cambridge: Cambridge University Press.

Šik, O. (1976). *Das Kommunistische Machtsystem*. Hamburg: Hoffmann und Campe Verlag.

Šik, O. (1981). *Communist Power System*. New York: Praeger Publishers.

Šik, O. (1982). Angst vor dem Machtverlust. *Wirtschaftswoche*, 35(5), 56–59.

Šik, O. (1988). *Prague's Spring Awakening: Memories (Prager Frühlingserwachen: Erinnerungen)*. Herford: Busse Seewald.

Simkin, C. G. F. (1978). Hyperinflation and Nationalist China. In A. R. Berstrom, A. J. L. Catt, M. H. Peston, and B. D. J. Silverstone (Eds.), *Stability and Inflation: A Volume of Essays to Honour the Memory of A. W. H. Phillips* (pp. 113–131). Chichester: John Wiley & Sons.

Sixth Plenary Session of the 11th Central Committee of the Communist Party (1986). Resolution on Certain Questions in the History of Our Party Since the Founding of the People's Republic adopted on June 27, 1981. In *China's Socialist Economy: An Outline History (1949–1984)* (pp. 578–636). Beijing: Beijing Review.

Skolka, J. (1984). Use of Input-Output Models in the Preparation of Price Reform in China. *Industry and Development (United Nations Industrial Development Organization)*, 10, 61–73.

Slobodian, Q. (2018). *Globalists: The End of Empire and the Birth of Neoliberalism*. Cambridge, MA: Harvard University Press.

Smith, A. (1999). *The Wealth of Nations*. London: Penguin Books.

Smith, P. (1993). State Power and Economic Activism During the New Policies, 1068–1085: The Tea and Horse Trade and the "Green Sprouts" Loan Policy. In R. P. Hymes and C. Schirokauer (Eds.), *Ordering the World: Approaches to State and Society in Sung Dynasty China* (pp. 76–127). Berkeley: University of California Press.

Solinger, D. J. (1984). *Chinese Business Under Socialism: The Politics of Domestic Commerce in Contemporary China*. Berkeley; Los Angeles: University of California Press.

Song Guoqing (1987). Rules and Regulations for Implementing "Turning Unified Procurement into Tax" in Ningjin County, Hebei Province (河北省宁晋县统购改税实施细则). In Gao Xiaomeng (Ed.), *Research on Grain Issues in China* (中国粮食问题研究) (pp. 46–55). Beijing: Economic Management Press.

Song Guoqing (1995). Interest Rate, Inflation Expectation and Savings Tendency: The Role of Expectations from the Perspective of Savings During Two High Inflation Periods (利率、通货膨胀预期与储蓄倾向—从两次高通胀期间的储蓄倾向看预期的作用). *Economic Research*, 7, 3–10.

Spengler, J. (1964). Ssu-Ma Ch'ien, Unsuccessful Exponent of Laissez Faire. *Southern Economic Journal, 30*(3), 223–243.

Stiglitz, J. E. (1994). *Whither Socialism? Wicksell Lectures.* Cambridge, MA: MIT Press.

Stiglitz, J. E. (1999). *Whither Reform? Ten Years of Transition.* Paper Prepared for the Annual World Bank Conference on Development Economics, Washington, DC, April 28–30.

Stiglitz, J. E. (2014). Transition to a Market Economy: Explaining the Successes and Failures. In S. Fan, R. Kanbur, S. Wei, and X. Zhang (Eds.), *The Oxford Companion to the Economics of China* (pp. 36–41). Oxford: Oxford University Press.

Stout, R. (1946). *The Silent Speaker.* New York: Viking Press.

Stuckler, D., L. King, and M. McKee (2009). Mass Privatisation and the Post-Communist Mortality Crisis: A Cross-National Analysis. *The Lancet, 373*(9661), 399–407. https://doi.org/10.1016/S0140-6736(09)60005-2

Su Shaozhi (1988). Response to Commentary, 15 January 1988. *Bulletin of Concerned Asian Scholars, 20*(1), 28–35.

Sun Faming (2011). *On the Gathering and Dispersing Tide: China's Rural Development Research Group* (潮聚潮散: 记中国农村发展问题研究组). Hong Kong: Strong Wind Press.

Sun Yan (1995). *The Chinese Reassessment of Socialism, 1976–1992.* Princeton: Princeton University Press. Retrieved from http://ezproxy.lib.cam.ac.uk:2048/login?url=http://dx.doi.org/10.1515/9781400821754

Sun Yefang (1978). Forcefully and Confidently Grasp the Concept of Socialist Profit (要理直气壮地抓社会主义利润). *Economic Research, 9,* 2–14.

Sun Yefang (1982). The Role of "Value." In K. K. Fung (Ed.), *Social Needs Versus Economic Efficiency in China: Sun Yefang's Critique of Socialist Economics* (pp. 36–81). Armonk, NY: M. E. Sharpe.

Swann, N. L. (1950). *Food and Money in Ancient China: The Earliest Economic History of China to A.D. 25 (Han Shu 24).* Princeton: Princeton University Press.

Taussig, F. W. (1919). Price-Fixing as Seen by a Price-Fixer. *Quarterly Journal of Economics, 33*(2), 205–241.

Teiwes, F. C. and W. Sun (2007). *The End of the Maoist Era: Chinese Politics During the Twilight of the Cultural Revolution, 1972–1976.* Armonk, NY: M. E. Sharpe.

Teiwes, F. C., and W. Sun (2011). China's New Economic Policy under Hua Guofeng: Party Consensus and Party Myths. *China Quarterly, 66,* 1–23.

Teiwes, F. C., and W. Sun (2013). China's Economic Reorientation after the Third Plenum: Conflict Surrounding "Chen Yun's" Readjustment Program, 1979–1980. *China Quarterly, 70,* 163–187.

Teiwes, F. C., and Warren Sun (2015). *Paradoxes of Post-Mao Rural Reform: Initial Steps Toward a New Chinese Countryside, 1976–1981* (W. Sun, Ed.). London: Routledge.

Tian Yuan and Chen Desun (1984). Thinking About the Reasoning on Price Reform (关于价格改革思路的思路). *Economic Daily,* September 29, 3.

Thorsten, M., and Y. Sugita (1999). Joseph Dodge and the Geometry of Power in US-Japan Relations. *Japanese Studies, 19*(3), 297–314.

Tobin, J. (1973). The Economy of China: A Tourist's View. *Challenge, 16*(1), 20–31.

Toporowski, J. (2007). Wlodzimierz Brus. *Royal Economics Society Newsletter, 139.*

Toporowski, J. (2018). *Michał Kalecki: An Intellectual Biography Volume II - By Intellect Alone, 1939–1970.* Cham: Palgrave Macmillan.

Tower, S. A. (1946). Quick Action Urged: New Stabilizer Tells Congress "Speculative Fever" Is Rampant. *New York Times,* February 19.

Trescott, P. B. (2007). *Jingji Xue: The History of the Introduction of Western Economic Ideas into China, 1850–1950.* Hong Kong: The Chinese University Press.

Trescott, P. B. (2012). How Keynesian Economics Came to China. *History of Political Economy*, *44*(2), 341–364.

Trotski, L. (1937). *The Revolution Betrayed: What Is the Soviet Union and Where Is It Going?* London: Faber.

Truman, H. S. (1945a). Radio Address to the American People on Wages and Prices in the Reconversion Period. (October 30, 1945b). Retrieved April 30, 2017, from http://www.presidency.ucsb.edu/ws/index.php?pid=12303

Truman, H. S. (1945b). Executive Order 9599. (August 18, 1945a). Retrieved April 30, 2017, from http://www.presidency.ucsb.edu/ws/index.php?pid=77920

Truman, H. S. (1946). Radio Address to the Nation on Price Controls. (June 29, 1946). Retrieved April 30, 2017, from http://www.presidency.ucsb.edu/ws/?pid=12438

Truman, H. S. (1955). *Memoirs of Harry S. Truman. Vol. I: Year of Decisions 1945*. London: Hodder and Stoughton.

Tsakok, I. (1979). Inflation Control in the People's Republic of China, 1949–1974. *World Development*, *7*(8–9), 865–875.

UNICEF. (2001). *A Decade of Transition*. Regional Monitoring Report, Vol. 8. Florence: UNICEF Innocenti Research Center.

US Department of State. (1949). *United States Relations with China – With Special Reference to the Period 1944–1949*. Washington, DC: Department of State Publications.

Vandermeersch, L. (1985). An Enquiry into the Chinese Conception of the Law. In S. R. Schram (Ed.), *The Scope of State Power in China* (pp. 3–27). London: School of Oriental and African Studies.

von Glahn, R. (2016). *The Economic History of China: From Antiquity to the Nineteenth Century*. Cambridge: Cambridge University Press.

von Mises, L. (1963). Economic Calculation in the Socialist Commonwealth. In Friedrich A. Hayek (Ed.), *Collectivist Economic Planning* (6th ed., pp. 87–130). London: Routledge & Kegan Paul.

von Mises, L. (1974a). Inflation and Price Control. In *Planning for Freedom and Twelve Other Essays and Addresses* (pp. 72–82). Illinois: Libertarian Press.

von Mises, L. (1974b). Middle-of-the-Road Policy Leads to Socialism. In *Planning for Freedom and Twelve Other Essays and Addresses* (pp. 18–35). Illinois: Libertarian Press.

van der Sprenkel, O. B. (1951). Part One. In O. B. van der Sprenkel, R. Guillain, and M. Lindsay (Eds.), *New China: Three Views*. London: Turnstile Press. https://www.amazon.com/Michael-Lindsay-Robert-Guillain-Sprenkel/dp/B0000CHRHO

van de Ven, H. (2003). *War and Nationalism in China, 1925–1945*. London: Routledge.

van de Ven, H. (2018). *China at War: Triumph and Tragedy in the Emergence of the New China*. Cambridge, MA: Harvard University Press.

Vogel, E. F. (2005). Chen Yun: His Life. *Journal of Contemporary China*, *14*(45), 741–759.

Vogel, E. F. (2011). *Deng Xiaoping and the Transformation of China*. Cambridge, MA; London: Belknap Press of Harvard University Press.

Wagner, D. B. (1997). *The Traditional Chinese Iron Industry and Its Modern Fate*. Richmond: Curzon.

Wagner, D. B. (2001). *The State and the Iron Industry in Han China*. Copenhagen: NIAS Publishing.

Wagner, D. B., and J. Needham (2008). *Science and Civilisation in China. Vol. 5. Chemistry and Chemical Technology. Party 11. Ferrous Metallurgy*. Cambridge: Cambridge University Press.

Walker, K. (1984). Chinese Agriculture During the Period of Readjustment, 1978–1983. *China Quarterly*, *100*, 783–812.

Wang Hui (2009). *The End of the Revolution: China and the Limits of Modernity*. London: Verso.

Wang Mengkui (2014). About the Author. In China Development Research Foundation (Ed.), *Chinese Economists on Economic Reform - Collected Works of Ma Hong* (pp. xii–xvi). Oxon: Routledge.

Wang Tong-eng (1980). Economic Policies and Price Stability in China. In *China Research Monograph, No. 16*. Berkeley: Institute of East Asian Studies, University of California, Center for Chinese Studies.

Wang Xiaolu (2019). *The Road of Reform 1978–2018* (改革之路：我们的四十年). Beijing: Social Science Documents Publisher.

Wang Xiaoqiang (1979). Critique of Agrarian Socialism (农业社会主义批判). *Unfinished Manuscripts* (未定稿), *49*.

Wang Xiaoqiang (1980). Critique of Agrarian Socialism (农业社会主义批判). *Issues in Agricultural Economics*, *2*, 9–20.

Wang Xiaoqiang (1989). Transcending the Logic of Private Ownership. *Chinese Economic Studies*, *23*(1), 43–56.

Wang Xiaoqiang (1998). *China's Price and Enterprise Reform*. Basingstoke: Macmillan.

Wang Xiaoqiang, and Ji Xiaoming (1985). Thoughts on the Model of Nonstock Enterprises (企业非股份化模式的思考). *Economic Daily*.

Wang Xiaoqiang, and Zhang Gang (1987). An Overview of the CESRRI Survey. In R. Bruce (Ed.), *Reform in China - Challenges and Choices: A Summary and Analysis of the CESRRI Survey Prepared by the Staff of the Chinese Economic System Reform Research Institute* (pp. xxv–xxxii). Armonk, NY: London: M. E. Sharpe.

Wang Xiaoqiang, and Ji Xiaoming (1988). Thoughts on the Model of Nonstock Enterprises. *Chinese Economic Studies*, *22*(2), 38–46.

War Records Section Bureau of the Budget (1946). *The United States at War: Development and Administration of the War Program by the Federal Government*. Washington, DC: United States Government Printing Office.

Weber, I. M. (2018). China and Neoliberalism: Moving Beyond the China Is/Is not Neoliberal Dichotomy. In D. Cahill, M. Cooper, and D. Primrose (Eds.), *SAGE Handbook of Neoliberalism* (pp. 219–233). London: SAGE.

Weber, I. M. (2019a). Unlikely Partners: Chinese Reformers, Western Economists, and the Making of Global China. Review of *Unlikely Partners: Chinese Reformers, Western Economists, and the Making of Global China*, by Julian Gewirtz. *The China Quarterly*, *237*, 257–259. https://doi.org/10.1017/s0305741019000080

Weber, I. M. (2019b). On the necessity of money in an exchange-constituted economy: the cases of Smith and Marx, *Cambridge Journal of Economics*, *43*(6), 1459–1483. https://doi.org/10.1093/cje/bez038

Weber, I. M. (2020a). Origins of China's Contested Relation with Neoliberalism: Economics, the World Bank, and Milton Friedman at the Dawn of Reform. *Global Perspectives*, *1*(1), 1–14. https://doi.org/10.1525/gp.2020.12271

Weber, I. M. (2020b). Das Westdeutsche und das Chinesische »Wirtschaftswunder«: Der Wettstreit um die Interpretation von Ludwig Erhards Wirtschaftspolitik in Chinas Preisreformdebatte der 1980er. *Jahrbuch für Historische Kommunismusforschung*, *2020*, 55–69.

Weber, I. M. (2021). The Ordoliberal Roots of Shock Therapy: Germany's "Economic Miracle" in China's 1980s Reform Debate. In: Slobodian, Q. and D. Plehwe (Eds.), *Market Prophets from the Margins: Neoliberals East and South*. Brooklyn: Zone Books (forthcoming). (Available as The New School for Social Research Department of Economics Working Paper, No. 03/2019.).

Weber, I. M. (2022). The (Im-)Possibility of Rational Socialism: Mises in China's Market Reform Debate. *Journal of the History of Ideas* (forthcoming).

Weber, I. M., and G. Semieniuk (2019). American Radical Economists in Mao's China: From Hopes to Disillusionment. *Research in the History of Economic Thought and Methodology*, *37*, 31–63.

Wemheuer, F. (2014). *Famine Politics in Maoist China and the Soviet Union*. New Haven: Yale University Press.

Wen Tiejun (2012). *Eight Crises: Lessons from China, 1949–2009* (八次危机：中国的真实经验，1949–2009). Beijing: People's Eastern Press Media Limited.

Will, P.-E. (1990). *Bureaucracy and Famine in Eighteenth Century China*. Stanford: Stanford University Press.

Will, P.-E., and R. Bin Wong (1991). *Nourish the People: The State Civilian Granary System in China, 1650–1850*. Michigan: University of Michigan Centre for Chinese Studies.

Witzel, M. (2002). Introduction. In Morgen Witzel (Ed.), *The Economic Principles of Confucius and His School, Vol. I* (pp. v–xv). Bristol: Thoemmes Press.

Wood, A. (1984). *Papers of Adrian Wood. World Bank Mission In China (February to April 1984) for 1985 Report*. Brighton: Private Papers.

Wood, A. (1985). *Papers of Adrian Wood. World Bank Visit to China to Discuss Draft 1985 Report (March 1985)*. Brighton: Private Papers.

Wood, A. (1989). Deceleration of Inflation with Acceleration of Price Reform: Vietnam's Remarkable Recent Experience. *Cambridge Journal of Economics*, *13*(4), 563–571. https://doi.org/10.1093/oxfordjournals.cje.a035112

Wood, A. (1990). Nominal Pause, but a Degree of Real Progress. Financial Times, Thursday, Oct. 4, p. 25.

World Bank (1983). *China: Socialist Economic Development, Vol. 1*. Washington, DC. Retrieved from http://www-wds.worldbank.org/external/default/WDSContentServer/WDSP/IB/2001/01/20/000178830_98101903340233/Rendered/PDF/multi_page.pdf.

World Bank (2019). GDP (Constant 2010 US$). Retrieved March 1, 2019, from https://data.worldbank.org/indicator/NY.GDP.MKTP.KD?locations=CN-RU-1W

World Bank (2019). Life Expectancy at Birth, Total (Years) - Russian Federation, China. Retrieved September 23, 2019, from https://data.worldbank.org/indicator/SP.DYN.LE00.IN?locations=RU-CN

Wu Jinglian (1984). Discussion. In B. Csikós-Nagy, D. Hague, and G. Hall (Eds.), *The Economics of Relative Prices: Proceedings of a Conference Held by the International Economic Association in Athens, Greece* (pp. 82–85). London: Macmillan Press.

Wu Jinglian (1985a). Once More On Preserving the Positive Economic Environment of Economic Reform (再论保持经济改革的良好经济环境). *Economic Research*, *5*, 3–12.

Wu Jinglian (1985b). Development Policy and Macroeconomic Control in the Early Stages of Economic Reform (经济改革初战阶段的发展方针和宏观控制问题). *People's Daily*, February 11.

Wu Jinglian (1988). Rent Seeking Theory and the Downsides of the Chinese Economy ("寻租"理论与我国经济中的某些消极现象). *Comparative Economic and Social Systems*, *5*, 1–2.

Wu Jinglian (1989). Our Worries and Proposals—Viewpoints of Several Economists (我们的忧思和建议：几位经济学者的意见). *Essential Reports, 9*.

Wu Jinglian (2005). *Understanding and Interpreting Chinese Economic Reform*. Mason, OH: Thomson South-Western.

Wu Jinglian (2013a). A Further Stage of Intellectual Biography. In B. Naughton (Ed.), *Wu Jinglian: Voice of Reform in China* (pp. 145–153). Cambridge, MA: MIT Press.

Wu Jinglian (2013b). The Divergence in Views and the Choice of Reform Strategy (1988). In B. Naughton (Ed.), *Wu Jinglian: Voice of Reform in China* (pp. 199–212). Cambridge, MA: MIT Press.

Wu Jinglian (2013c). *Voice of Reform in China* (B. Naughton, Ed.). Cambridge, MA: The MIT Press.

Wu Jinglian, and Fan Shitao (2012). China's Economic Reform: Processes, Issues and Prospects (1978–2012). In G. C. Chow and D. H. Perkins (Eds.), *Routledge Handbook of the Chinese Economy* (pp. 54–75). London: Routledge.

Wu Jinglian, and Ma Guochuan. (2016). *Whither China? Restarting the Reform Agenda*. Oxford: Oxford University Press.

Wu Jinglian, Rong Jingben, and Ma Wenguang (1982). Šik on the Socialist Economic Model (论社会主义经济模式 — 奥•锡克). In *Discussion of Socialist Economic System Reform: Transcription of W. Brus' and O. Šik's Lectures in China* (论社会主义经济体制改革：［波］弗•布鲁斯，[捷]奥•锡克，中国社会科学院经济研究所学资料室编) (pp. 45–115). Beijing: Law Press (unpublished manuscript).

Wu Jinglian, and Zhou Xiaochuan (1989). *The Integrated Design for China's Economic Reform* (中国经济改革的整体设计) (Peng Xiaomeng, Ed.). Beijing: China Prospect Book Company.

Wu Jinglian and B. L. Reynolds (1988). Choosing a Strategy for China's Economic Reform. *American Economic Review*, 78(2), 461–466.

Wu Jinglian, Zhou Xiaochuan, Li Jiange, Song Guoqing, and Liu Jirui (1988). Programme Outline for Medium-Term Economic System Reform: Wu Jinglian's Research Group (经济体制中期改革规划刚要: 吴敬琏课题组). In *Visions for China's Reform* (中国改革大思路) (pp. 197–240). Shengyang: Shengyang Press.

Wu Jinglian, Zhou Xiaochuan, Lou Jiwei, Li Jiange, Liu Liqun, and Shi Xiaomin (1988). A Comprehensive Vision to Carry Reform Forward. *Reform, 1*, 67–76.

Wu Yuan-Li (1956). *An Economic Survey of Communist China*. New York: Bookman Associates.

Wu Xiaogang, and D. J. Treiman (2004). The Household Registration System and Social Stratification in China: 1955–1996. *Demography, 41*(2), 363–370.

Xiao Qiu (1985). The "Dodge Plan" and the Transformation of Japan's Economic System ("道奇计划"和日本经济体制的转变). *Comparative Economic and Social Systems, 2*, 25–27.

Xu Bin (2019). Intragenerational Variations in Autobiographical Memory: China's "Sent-Down Youth" Generation. *Social Psychology Quarterly* (print forthcoming).

Xuan Zhao, and W. Drechsler (2018). Wang Anshi's economic reforms: proto-Keynesian economic policy in Song Dynasty China, *Cambridge Journal of Economics, 42*(5), 1239–1254. https://doi.org/10.1093/cje/bex087

Xue Muqiao (1960). *The Socialist Transformation of the National Economy in China*. Beijing: Foreign Languages Press.

Xue Muqiao (1979). *Economic Work in the Shandong Liberated Areas During the War of Anti-Japanese Resistance and Liberation* (抗日战争时期和解放战争时期山东解放区的经济工作). Beijing: People's Press (人民出版社).

Xue Muqiao (1981). *China's Socialist Economy*. Beijing: Foreign Language Press.

Xue Muqiao (1982a). Price Adjustment and Reform of the Price Control System. In K. K. Fung (Ed.), *Current Economic Problems in China* (pp. 63–79). Boulder: Westview Press.

Xue Muqiao (1982b). Thirty Years of Arduous Efforts to Create an Economy. In K. K. Fung (Ed.), *Current Economic Problems in China* (pp. 29–36). Boulder: Westview Press.

Xue Muqiao (1985). Several Problems Concerning Prices (关于物价的几个问题). *People's Daily*, January 28.

Xue Muqiao (1989). Several Problems Concerning Prices (Translation of Chinese Original, *People's Daily*, January 28, 1985). *Chinese Economic Studies*, 22(3), 24–33.

Xue Muqiao (1996). *Memoir of Xue Muqiao* (薛暮桥回忆录). Tianjin: Tianjin People's Press (天津人民出版社).

Xue Muqiao (2011). Advice on Seizing Opportunities to Adjust the Price System, June 20, 1984. In China Development Research Foundation (Ed.), *Chinese Economists on Economic Reform - Collected Works of Xue Muqiao* (pp. 108–110). London: Routledge.

Xue Muqiao (2011a). The Key to "Price Adjustment" with Regard to the Means of Production is to Control Capital Construction, June 1986. In China Development Research Foundation (Ed.), *Chinese Economists on Economic Reform - Collected Works of Xue Muqiao* (pp. 115–117). Oxon: Routledge.

Xue Muqiao (2011b). Strengthen Macro-Control via Economic Measures (Extract), September 1986. In China Development Research Foundation (Ed.), *Chinese Economists on Economic Reform - Collected Works of Xue Muqiao* (pp. 118–122). Oxon: Routledge.

Xue Muqiao (2011c). Introduction. In C. D. R. Foundation (Ed.), *Chinese Economists on Economic Reform - Collected Works of Xue Muqiao* (pp. 1–15). Oxon: Routledge.

Xue Muqiao, Liu Zhuofu, and Jili Liao (1982). Report on the Symposium on Soviet and Eastern European Economic System Reform (苏联、 东欧经济体制改革座谈会简报). Unpublished.

Yang Dali (1996). *Calamity and Reform in China: State, Rural Society, and Institutional Change Since the Great Leap Famine.* Stanford: Stanford University Press.

Yang Guansan, Yang Xiaodong, and Xuan Mingdong (1987). The Public Response to Price Reform. In B. L. Reynolds (Ed.), *Reform in China - Challenges and Choices: A Summary and Analysis of the CESRRI Survey Prepared by the Staff of the Chinese Economic System Reform Research Institute* (pp. 59–75). Armonk, NY: M. E. Sharpe.

Yang Jisheng (1998). *Deng Xiaoping's Era: A Record of China's Reform and Opening Up* (邓小平时代：中国改革开放纪实). Beijing: Central Translation and Compilation Press.

Yang Peixin (1980). On Some Contemporary Issues in Economic and Financial Research (关于当前经济金融研究的几个问题). *Guangdong Financial Research (Internal Publication of the Guangdong Financial Research Society)*, 26, 1–26.

Ye Shichang (2014). On Guanzi Qing Zhong. In L. Cheng, T. Peach, and F. Wang (Eds.), *The History of Ancient Chinese Economic Thought* (pp. 98–106). Abingdon: Routledge.

Young, A. N. (1965). *China's Wartime Finance and Inflation, 1937–1945.* Cambridge, MA: Harvard University Press.

Yu Xiafu and Feng Xiuju. (1988). During a Meeting with Mengistu Deng Xiaoping Said: The Situation Forces Us to Further Reform and Open Up (邓小平会见门格斯图时说：形势迫使我们进一步改革开放). *People's Daily*, June 23, 1.

Yun, O. (1998). Price Reform—The Missing Link? Passing the Buck. In M. Ellman and V. Kontorovich (Eds.), *The Destruction of the Soviet Economic System: An Insiders' History* (pp. 158–159). New York: Routledge.

Zanasi, M. (2020). Economic Thought in Modern China: Market and Consumption, c. 1500–1937. Cambridge: Cambridge University Press.

Zhang Musheng (2009). Interview with the Director of the Tax Magazine Publisher Zhang Musheng (杂志社记者专程采访了时任中国税务杂志社社长的张木生). *Southern Window,* June 30.

Zhang Shaojie (2008). Postscript (校后跋). In *Professionalizing Research in Post-Mao China: The System Reform Institute and Policymaking* (改革与政策制定——毛以后中国的专业化研究) (pp. 259–266). Hong Kong: Strong Wind Publisher.

Zhang Shuguang (2017). *The History of Chinese Economic Studies: 60 Years of the Institute of Economics, Vol. 2* (中国经济学风云史：经济研究所60年，上卷二). Singapore: World Scientific Publishing.

Zhang Weiying (1984a). Putting the Reform of the Price System at the Centre Provides Impetus for the Reform of the Whole Economic System (以价格体制的改革为中心，带动整个经济体制的改革). In E. G. State Council Technology Economics Research Centre (Ed.), *Expert Recommendations Vol. III (Internal Material)* (pp. 3–20). Internal Material – Expert Recommendation, III, June. State Council Technology Economics Research Centre.

Zhang Weiying (1984b). Price System Reform is the Central Link of Reform (价格体制改革是改革的中心环节). *Economic Daily*, September 29, 3.

Zhang Weiying (2015). *Logic of the Market: An Insider's View of Chinese Economic Reform.* Washington, DC: Cato Institute.

Zhao Jing (2014). Fu Guo Xue and the "Economics" of Ancient China. In Cheng Lin, Terry Peach, and Wang Fang (Ed.), *The History of Ancient Chinese Economic Thought* (pp. 66–81). Abingdon: Routledge.

Zhao Renwei (1980). Professor Brus on the Reform of the System of Economic Management (布鲁斯教授谈经济管理体制的改革). *Chinese Academy of Social Sciences Bulletin*, 2.

Zhao Renwei (1982). Brus on Socialist Economic System Reform (论社会主义经济体制的改革 — 弗 布鲁斯). In *Discussion of Socialist Economic System Reform: Transcription of W. Brus' and O. Šik's Lectures in China* (论社会主义经济体制改革：［波］弗•布鲁斯，[捷]奥•锡克，中国社会科学院经济研究所学资料室编) (pp. 1–44). Beijing: Law Press (unpublished manuscript).

Zhao Renwei (2007). Discussing a Letter from Sun Yefang. In *Income Distribution and Other Topics* (收入分配及其他) (pp. 368–376). Shanghai: Shanghai Far East Press.

Zhao Ziyang (1987). Advance Along the Road of Socialism with Chinese Characteristics. *Beijing Review*, 45, 9–15.

Zhao Ziyang (2009). *Prisoner of the State: The Secret Journal of Zhao Ziyang* (1st ed.). New York: Simon & Schuster.

Zhao Ziyang (2016a). A Tentative Plan for Economic System Reform in the Next Two Years, 11 March, 1986 (今后两年经济体制改革的设想). In *Collected Works of Zhao Ziyang (1980–1989): Vol. 3 (1985–1986)* (赵紫阳文集 *(1980–1989)*：第一卷 *(1985–1986))* (pp. 304–305). Hong Kong: Chinese University Press.

Zhao Ziyang (2016b). Dialog with Professor Linder of the University of Zurich in Switzerland (会见瑞士苏黎世大学林德教授的谈话). In Editorial Group of the Collected Works of Zhao Ziyang (Ed.), *Collected Works of Zhao Ziyang (1980–1989): Vol. 4 (1987–1989)* (赵紫阳文集 *(1980–1989):* 第三卷 *(1987–1989))* (pp. 476–483). Hong Kong: Chinese University Press.

Zhao Ziyang (2016c). Dialogue with Milton Friedman, September 19, 1988 (同弗里德曼的谈话，一九八八年九月十九日. In Editorial Group of the Collected Works of Zhao Ziyang (Ed.), *Collected Works of Zhao Ziyang (1980–1989): Vol. 4 (1987–1989)* (赵紫阳文集 *(1980–1989):* 第三卷 *(1987–1989))* (pp. 510–518). Hong Kong: Chinese University Press.

Zhao Ziyang (2016d). Discussion of a Plan for Price and Wage Reform at the Standing Committee of the Political Bureau of the CPC, May 16 and 19, 1988 (在中央政治局常委讨论物价和工资改革方案时的讲话，一九八八五月十六日，十九日). In Editorial Group of the Collected Works of Zhao Ziyang (Ed.), *Collected Works of Zhao Ziyang (1980–1989): Vol. 4 (1987–1989) (赵紫阳文集 (1980–1989): 第三卷 (1987–1989))* (pp. 438–441). Hong Kong: Chinese University Press.

Zhao Ziyang (2016e). Implement the Central "Decision" by Steadily Advancing Price Reform, 21 October 1984 (贯彻中央《决定》稳步推进价格改革). In *Collected Works of Zhao Ziyang (1980–1989): Vol. 2 (1983–1984)* (pp. 533–541). Hong Kong: Chinese University Press.

Zhao Ziyang (2016f). On the Economic Work in 1986, 8 January, 1986 (关于一九八六年的经济工作). In *Collected Works of Zhao Ziyang (1980–1989): Vol. 3 (1985–1986) (赵紫阳文集 (1980–1989)：第一卷 (1985–1986))* (pp. 247–251). Hong Kong: Chinese University Press.

Zhao Ziyang (2016g). On the Reform of the Urban Economic System and Issues in Current Industrial Production, 15 March, 1986 (关于城市经济体制改革和当前生产问题). In *Collected Works of Zhao Ziyang (1980–1989): Vol. 3 (1985–1986) (赵紫阳文集 (1980–1989)：第一卷 (1985–1986))* (pp. 306–317). Hong Kong: Chinese University Press.

Zhao Ziyang (2016h). Right Time to Adjust the Prices of Synthetic and Cotton Cloth, Change the Composition of the Population's Dressing Material, 5 October 1982 (适时调整化纤和棉织品价格改变居民衣料结构. In *Collected Works of Zhao Ziyang (1980–1989): Vol. 1 (1980–1982) (赵紫阳文集 (1980–1989)：第一卷 (1980–1982))* (p. 573). Hong Kong: Chinese University Press.

Zhao Ziyang (2016i). Speech to the Central Leadership Finance Group in Response to a Report on the Economic Situation, January 14, 1988 (在中央财经领导小组听取国家计委汇报经济形势的讲话，一九八八年一月十四日). In Editorial Group of the Collected Works of Zhao Ziyang (Ed.), *Collected Works of Zhao Ziyang (1980–1989): Vol. 4 (1987–1989) (赵紫阳文集 (1980–1989): 第三卷 (1987–1989))* (pp. 357–361). Hong Kong: Chinese University Press.

Zhao Ziyang (2016j). The Basic Stability of Prices Must Be Preserved (物价必须保持基本稳定), November 25, 1981. In *The Collected Works of Zhao Ziyang (1980–1989), Vol. I (1980–1982)* (pp. 335–338). Hong Kong: Chinese University Press.

Zhao Ziyang (2016k). The Question of the Coastal Development Strategy, January 1988 (沿海地区经济发展的战略问题). In Editorial Group of The Collected Works of Zhao Ziyang (Ed.), *Collected Works of Zhao Ziyang (1980–1989): Vol. 4 (1987–1989) (赵紫阳文集 (1980–1980: 第三卷 (1987–1989))* (pp. 341–355). Hong Kong: Chinese University Press.

Zhao Ziyang (2016l). The Relationship Between Handling Price Reform Well and Enlivening Enterprises, 14 October and 11 November, 1986 (处理好价格改革与搞活企业的关系). In *Collected Works of Zhao Ziyang (1980–1989)： Vol. 3 (1985–1986) (赵紫阳文集 (1985–1986)：第一卷 (1980–1982))* (pp. 460–462). Hong Kong: Chinese University Press.

Zhao Ziyang (2016m). Views on Comprehensive Economic System Reform and the Plan for Price Reform, 11–12 June, 1986 (对经济体制改革总体思路和价格改革方案的看法). In *Collected Works of Zhao Ziyang (1980–1989)： Vol. 3 (1985–1986) (赵紫阳文集 (1985–1986)：第三卷 (1980–1982))* (pp. 401–406). Hong Kong: Chinese University Press.

Zhao Ziyang (2016n). Work Report to the Second Plenary Session of the 13th CPC Central Committee (在中共十三届二中全会上的工作报告). In Editorial Group of the Collected Works of Zhao Ziyang (Ed.), *Collected Works of Zhao Ziyang (1980–1989): Vol. 4 (1987–1989)* (赵紫阳文集 *(1980–1989):* 第三卷 *(1987–1989))* (pp. 405–416). Hong Kong: Chinese University Press.

Zhao Ziyang, and E. Lim (2016). Conversation with the First World Bank Resident Representative in China, Edwin Lim, 21 June, 1986 (会见世界银行首任驻华代表林重庚时的谈话). In *Collected Works of Zhao Ziyang (1980–1989): Vol. 3 (1985–1986) (*赵紫阳文集 *(1985–1986)：*第一卷 *(1980–1982))* (pp. 415–420). Hong Kong: Chinese University Press.

Zheng Yongnian, and Huang Yanjie (2018). *Market in State: The Political Economy of Domination in China.* Cambridge: Cambridge University Press.

Zhou Xiaochuan (1992). The Theoretical and Psychological Obstacles to Market-Oriented Reform in China. In J. M. Kovacs and M. Tardos (Eds.), *Reform and Transformation in Eastern Europe Soviet-type Economics on the Threshold of Change* (pp. 178–190). London: Routledge.

Zhou Xiaochuan, Lou Jiwei, and Li Jiange (1984). Price Reform Must Not Increase the Fiscal Burden (价格改革无需增加财政负担). *Economic Daily,* September 29, 3.

Zhou Xiaochuan, and Zhu Li (1987). China's Banking System: Current Status, Perspective on Reform. *Journal of Comparative Economics, 11*(3), 399–409.

Zhu Jiaming (1985). On China's Present Economic Development Stage (论我国正经历的经济发展阶段). *Forum of Young Economists, 2*(April), 13–23.

Zhu Jiaming (1989). On the Current Stage of China's Economic Development - A Typical Development in a Nontypical Country. *Chinese Economic Studies, 23*(2), 8–21.

Zhu Jiaming (2009). *Collected Works of Zhu Jiaming, Volume 2, 1984–1989 (*朱嘉明文集, 第二卷, *1984–1989).* Unpublished Manuscript.

Zhu Jiaming (2013). *Crossroads of China's Reform* (中国改革的歧路). Taipei: Linking Books.

Zhu Jiamu, Fu Zhubian, and Liu Shukai (Eds.) (2000). *Chronicle of Chen Yun, 1905–1995, Vol. 1* (陈云年谱，1905–1995, 上). Beijing: Central Document Publishing House.

Zinser, L. (1991). The Performance of China's Economy. In C. of the US Joint Economic Committee (Ed.), *China's Economic Dilemmas in the 1990s: The Problems of Reforms, Modernization, and Interdependence* (pp. 102–118). Armonk, NY: M. E. Sharpe.

Zündorf, I. (2006a). *Der Preis der Marktwirtschaft: Staatliche Preispolitik und Lebensstandard in Westdeutschland 1948 bis 1963.* Munich: Franz Steiner Verlag.

Zündorf, I. (2006b). Staatliche Verbraucherpreispolitik und Soziale Marktwirtschaft in Westdeutschland 1948–1963. In Andre Steiner (Ed.), *Preispolitik und Lebensstandard: Nationalsozialismus, DDR und Bundesrepublik im Vergleich* (pp. 129–170). Cologne: Böhlau Verlag.

INDEX

1920 financial crisis 42
1944 Northwestern Financial
  Conference 76
1989 social movement 13, 225, 243,
  255, 256

activist economic policy 27, 30, 35, 36,
  38, 40n21, 42, 48, 207, 268
Adler, Solomon 72, 75
agricultural education institute 154, 272
Agricultural Institute, Chinese Academy
  of Social Sciences 157, 159
agricultural products 66, 92, 181n27, 211,
  234, 264, 269; output of 72, 85n2,
  86n15, 91, 93, 95, 112n5, 112n10, 138,
  163, 165, 288; prices of 9, 50–52, 92,
  95, 96, 100, 108–109, 113n14, 113n18,
  138, 141, 142, 153, 165, 235, 241, 242,
  280; production of 77, 79, 99, 121, 124,
  125, 156, 158, 162, 242, 255
agricultural reform 18, 79, 91, 100, 108,
  124–126, 138, 144, 153, 155–165, 174,
  183, 196, 234–235, 237, 241–242, 267,
  271, 272, 274–275, 280–283, 286,
  288, 289
Agricultural Research Office, State
  Council 286
agriculture 27, 28, 32, 35, 73, 79, 89,
  93–95, 103, 107, 110, 111–112n1, 119,
  139, 153, 154, 158, 163, 164, 178, 196,
  267, 275, 284; collective 95, 111, 272;
  economics of 48; interest groups in 50;
  machines used in 61; productivity of

20–21, 33, 106, 108; reform of 18, 126,
  144, 153, 157, 161, 164, 167, 174, 234,
  237, 241, 271, 272, 283; subsistence 32,
  33, 38; taxes on 75; traditionalists of
  30, 39n7; as a type of economy 82, 83,
  91, 156, 183; as a type of society 24
Alfonsin, Raul 247
Allende, Salvador 247
American Economic Association 57,
  147n15, 222–223n18
Anhui province 156, 160, 161, 167, 170,
  285
An Zhiwen 167, 194, 203, 218, 220, 271
army: People's Liberation 147n18; Red
  Army 104, 155; supplying 21, 30,
  75, 81
artisans 34
Åslund, Anders 127
asset management responsibility system
  206, 219, 277
austerity 4, 5; in Brazil 245; in China 78,
  185, 188–190, 192, 209, 225, 240, 243,
  245, 247, 251, 252, 256, 261, 280; in
  Japan 222n10; in Wang Anshi 34; see
  also macroeconomic stabilization

Bai Meiqing 134, 201
Bai Nanfeng 17, 157, 159, 172,
  271–272, 285
Bai Nansheng 157, 172, 271
Bajt, Aleksander 194, 199
balanced standard 30, 32
Balcerowicz, Leszek 60

banking 73, 77, 195, 212, 231, 251;
central 74, 85n3, 194, 212, 230, 231;
government-run 83
bankruptcy 42, 81, 199, 214, 217, 265;
government 29–30
Bao Tong 201, 214, 224n38, 243, 272
Baran, Paul A. 180n6
Baruch, Bernard 50, 57; *see also* Baruch
Plan
Baruch Plan 50; *see also* Baruch, Bernard
Bashan Conference 193, *194*, 196–200,
205, 207, 222n16, 223n25, 271,
274–276, 279–281, 284, 287
Beijing City Price Bureau 215; *see also*
Ma Kai
Beijing Institute of Automation 167, 280
Beijing Young Economists Association 289
beipiao 77–80
Benn, Tony 65
"big bang": in China 1, 13, 66, 126, 127,
130, 133, 135, 140, 145, 174, 179, 184–
185, 192, 201, 204, 205–207, 213–214,
218–220, 225–226, 233, 234, 247, 250,
253, 255, 261, 264–265, 268–269; in
post-war USA 42, 44; in post-war West
Germany 5, 12, 130; in Russia 2–3,
6, 7, 66; theory 4, 6, 7–8, 126, 184;
Vietnam 14n7; *see also* shock therapy
black market 52, 54, 82, 95, 97, 140,
143, 175
Bockman, Johanna 187, 269n1
Bodde, Derk 86n16
"bolshevism" 46
bonds 74, 82, 255
boom–bust cycle 49, 59–60, 64
bottlenecks 47, 57, 210, 235, 255, 266
bourgeoisie: Chinese 69, 79
Bowles, Chester 52, 68n17
Brazil 221n5, 243–245, 260
Bresciani-Turroni, C. 69
Bretton Woods 85n3; institutions of 4; *see
also* World Bank
Brown, Prentiss 52
Brus, Włodzimierz 127, 131, 135–137,
137, 147nn16–17, 149n33, 149n37, 186,
188, 189, 191, 193, 200, 203, 216, 280,
286; at the Bashan conference 205;
lectures in China 128–129; on market
socialism 149n19; at the Moganshan
conference 143–146, 201; on prices
132–33, 140–141, 143, 167, 195–196,
262; as proponent of Stalinism 132
bulk buying 81
bullionism 78, 85n9
Bundesbank 194

bureaucracy 19, 20, 29, 35, 36, 74, 75,
82, 105, 118, 121, 132, 176, 187, 232,
236, 264
bureaucrats 18, 19, 36, 75, 118, 121,
125, 130, 157, 187, 189, 224n38, 232;
entrepreneurial 35; merchant 18, 32,
42; price-fixing 43
Bureau of Industry and Commerce 76
Bureau of Labor Statistics living cost
index 52
Bureau of Purchase of Daily Necessities
for Resale at Equitable Prices 75
Burns, Arthur 57

Cairncross, Alec 12, 222n16, 276; at the
Bashan conference 193–195, 196, 197,
200, 222n16, 223n25; on price controls
59–60, 207, 223n21, 268
capital flight 73
capitalism 105, 116, 117, 127, 132, 148n23,
158, 161, 162, 228, 268; American 55;
global 1, 2, 3, 10, 236, 238, 239, 267,
269; monopoly 207; neoliberal xii, 10
"capitalist roaders" 116, 155, 273
capitalists 46, 72, 75, 81; financial 75
ceiling prices 49, 51, 52, 57, 63, 64,
79; *see also* General Maximum Price
Regulation
Central Committee, CPC 107, 117,
119, 147n18, 162, 176, 252, 253, 272,
274–275, 279, 282, 288, 289
Central Finance and Economics Leading
Group 135, 282
Central Intelligence Agency 69
central planning 61–64, 66, 68n19, 129,
186, 198, 200; agencies 102, 103, 107
Central Planning Commission 159
Central Working Conference 118–119
Chamberlin, Edward 57
Chen Boda 180n7, 288; *see also* Chen
Xiao
Chen Daisun 207, 278
Cheng Zhiping 180n19, 182–183, 203,
234, 242, 254, 273
Chen Hansheng 77
Chen Huan-Chang 40n13
Chen Lantong 181n25
Chen Xiao 180n7, 288
Chen Xiwen 157
Chen Yizi 11, 152, 224n35, 224n38, 257,
272–273, 276, 278, 281, 285–286;
delegation to Latin America 226, 244,
247; delegation to West Germany
250–251; investigation in Hungary and
Yugoslavia 216, 253; at the Moganshan

Youth Conference *172*, 174–175; purge of 154; rural studies 154–155, 157–160, 161; at the System Reform Institute 167, 170, 188, 202, 210, 215

Chen Yun 89, 93, 94, 106, 107, 112n6, 114n34, 131, 155, 159, 230, 240, 248, 249, 252, 254, 273–274, 279, 282; as architect of reform 84, 111, 166, 227, 229; criticism of Zhao Ziyang 239, 241; and economic warfare 76, 77, 155; on price stabilization 70, 79–80, 97–98, 125–126; at the Wuxi conference 117–119

Chiang, Kai-Shek 73, 80, 156

Chicago 54, 283, 284

"Chicago boys" 247

China Banking Regulatory Commission 189, 276

China Economic System Reform Research Association 222n17, 275, 279

China Economic System Reform Research Institute *see* System Reform Institute

China International Trust Investment Corporation 243, 289

China's Socialist Economy (Xue Muqiao) 85n10, 120, 121, 287

Chinese Academy of Social Sciences (CASS) 94, 104, 105, 115, 132, 152, 159, 160, 171, 258, 273–277, 280, 282–285, 289; Economic Research Institute 115, 181n25, 221n7, 223n28; Institute of Industrial Economics 132, 146; Milton Friedman at 130, 148n23; Technical Economics Department 166

Chinese Civil War 38, 71, 80, 84, 107, 138, 152, 156, 263, 273, 274, 279, 280

Chinese Government Salt Revenue Administration 37

The Chinese Inflation, 1937–1949 (Chou Shun-Hsin) 70

Chinese People's Political Consultative Conference 80, 147n18, 160

Chinese Rural Development Issues Research Group *see* Rural Development Group

Chinese War of Liberation 80; *see also* revolution: communist, China

Chou, Shun-Hsin 70

Chow, Gregory 181n30

class: commercial and financial capital 75; landlord 70; private merchant 21, 25, 26

classical economics 45

coal 83, 85n13, 86nn14–15, 99, 102, 125, 138, 139, *170*, 172, 178, 219, 235, 254, 266, 269; *see also* energy

Cold War xii, 1, 59, 112n11, 187

collectivism 111, 119, 163

Columbia University 73, 278

Comintern (Third International) 77

command economy 5, 66, 98, 102, 111, 261, 266, 267–268; Vietnam 14n7

commerce 12, 21, 29, 31, 33, 35, 72, 76, 93, 113n24, 122, 152, 242, 255, 264; state 12, 18, 19, 35, 36, 91, 123, 124, 139, 150n45, 176, 242, 273

commodity classification 99, 134

"Common Program" 80

communism 1, 6, 141, 147n19, 186, 253; in China 12, 38, 69–72, 75–81, 83–84, 84n1, 85n2, 85n13, 90–92, 98, 107, 113n14, 115, 121, 131, 148n23, 149n37, 156, 159, 168, 177, 187, 229, 260

Communist Party, China 155, 162, 180n7, 240, 252, 268, 271–274, 276, 279, 280, 282, 283, 288; Shandong Provincial Committee 78; *see also* communism

Communist University of the Toilers of the East (Moscow) 283

Communist Youth League 154–156, 272

comparative civilization study 17, 272

Comparative Economic and Social Systems (journal) 189, 190

competition 61–63, 66, 142, 168, 213, 214; free 62, 63, 117, 203, 218, 232, 238, 264; imperfect 55; interstate 21; perfect 55, 132, 195, 208, 214, 252; state 20

Confucianism 31

Confucius 31; followers of 62

Congress: American 49, 51, 52, 57, 58, 61

conservatives: in Britain 59; *versus* reformers in Chinese reform 9, 184

consumer goods 5, 57, 73, 114n34, 123, 134, 143, 165, 181n24, 196, 205, 217, 235, 242, 252, 253; essential 81, 102, 120; nonessential 8, 35, 97–98, 102, 122, 123, 131, 266

consumer price index (CPI): China *8*, 202, 230, *231*, 234, 242, 253; Russia *7*

consumption 47, 48, 96, 211–212, 241, 245; demand 56, 64, 81, 96, 97; goods 45, 46, 51, 54, 59, 60–61, 73, 75, 80, 81, 98, 99, 110, 122, 123, 190; income for 29; luxury 134; prices 51, 141; rural 90, 94; supply for 45, 46, 54; taxation of 67n3; urban 92, 96, 98, 104, 234–235

co-operatives 79, 80
corruption 13, 32, 75, 140, 190, 210, 227, 230, 232, 236, 239, 255, 256, 258, 258n4, 261, 264, 267
cost-plus pricing 99–101, 103, 110; *see also* price types
Cowles Commission for Research in Economics 53
crisis 107, 111, 140, 165, 172, 187, 190–191, 255, 256, 257, 264; 1997 Asian financial 3; 2008 global xi; balance of payment 244; capitalist 148n23; collective farming 154; deficit 34; fiscal 70, 74; foreign account 105; Han dynasty 29; industrial 73; of planned economy 171, 277, 284; procurement 92; of socialist command economies 66; Song dynasty 34, 35
crowding out 54
Cultural Revolution 13, 103, 109, 113n13, 114n29, 116, 121, 147–148n21, 152–155, 157, 166, 179n6, 207, 259, 271–276, 278, 280–286, 288; economics during 115, 119, 149n29; reversal of 105–106, 158
currency 3, 21, 30, 69, 70, 72, 76–79, 81, 83, 85n6, 85n8, 90, 107, 163, 195, 199, 212, 287; German reform of 1948 5, 14n5, 60, 130, 188, 222n10, 251, 264; reform 5, 73
currency manipulation 79
Czechoslovakia 131, 133, 134–135, 149n30; Economic Research Institute 135, 136, 148n24

Day, Alexander F. 113n26
debt: government 46, 73, 238, 245; speculator 81
decentralization 136, 177, 187
"Decision on the Economic System Reform" 184
deficit 71; budget 5, 125; crisis 34; fiscal 30, 80, 109, 139, 143, 235; foreign 60, 241; treasury 29
deflation 25, 82, 256
deindustrialization, Russia 2, 268
Delfim Netto, Antônio 244–245
demand 23, 45, 47, 55, 56, 60, 64, 83, 92, 98, 123, 124, 168, 198, 209, 211, 212, 217, 220, 242; aggregate 47, 48, 55, 96, 190, 201, 233, 234, 235, 241; consumer 59, 81, 96, 97; effective 40n14, 45, 48, 141, 143; excess 5, 46, 56, 57, 80, 186, 195, 208, 231, 240, 262, 266; inelastic

28, 58, 190; pressure 49, 55, 73; shock resulting from 23; state 24–25, 27; *see also* supply and demand
Democratic Party 52
Deng Liqun 89, 117–118, 135, 155, 159, 160, 272–275, 278
Deng Pufang 276
Deng Yingtao 155, 157, 272, 273, 281
Deng Xiaoping 1, 84, 95, 104–111, 114n33, 116, 120, 155, 157, 162, 170, 228, 230, 241, 244, 252, 253, 273–274, 276, 281, 282, 288; 1992 Southern Tour 268; in the Civil War 160; on economic work 109, 115, 118; market reforms of 38, 105, 119, 156, 202, 227; proposal for big bang 13, 225, 226, 242, 247, 248–250, 255, 262; on socialist market economy 117; on student protests 229; suppression of 1989 social movement 257; visit to Japan 188
deregulation 12, 175, 176, 182, 219, 221–222n7, 252
Development Research Centre, State Council 173, 187, 278, 284
"Directives on Investigation and Research" (Xue Muqiao) 78
division of labor 6, 20
Dobb, Maurice 43, 148n24
Dodge, Joseph 188, 189, 222n10
Dodge Line, 1948 14n5, 188–189; *see also* Dodge, Joseph
Dong Biwu 180n7
Dong Fureng 11, 114n34, 128, 149n31, 193, 274, 277, 279
"dual society" 97
dual-track system *see* price system, dual-track in China; price system, multi-tiered
Duke Huan 20, 27
Duke Wen 24
Dunstan, Helen 35, 41
Du Runsheng 153, 160, 163, 223n28, 237, *237*, 274–275, 281, 286

Eastern Europe 14n3, 60, 116, 126, 129, 132, 137, 140, 151n52, 174, 178, 187, 189, 190, 196, 219, 250, 264, 272; émigré economists 13, 119, 127, 129, 135–137, 140–142, 145, 149n33, 150n38, 151n57, 154, 185, 189, 196, 200, 201, 203, 207, 215, 217, 249, 260, 262, 276, 286, 287
The Economic Daily 181n28

economic governance 3, 18, 19, 37, 38, 68n15, 70–71, 74, 84, 115–116, 200
Economic Problems of Socialism in the USSR (Stalin) 127
Economic Research Office, State Planning Commission 146n7
economics (discipline) 12, 17, 18, 36, 38, 65, 66, 77, 138, 161, 187, 188, 191, 209; development 2; Eastern European reform 154; introduction in China 18, 207; mainstream 11, 181n30, 185, 189, 222n9, 252, 262; Malthusian 73; mathematical 178, 186; micro- 163, 173–174; reinstatement of in China 13, 115–116, 118, 128–130, 145, 181n29, 268; as a science 43–44, 53, 152; socialist 120, 269n1; welfare 232; *see also* neoclassical economics
Economics of Shortage (Kornai) 143, 186, 188
economic sovereignty 3, 14n5
economic warfare 12, 38, 70, 71, 75–77, 79, 81, 94, 113n14, 152, 274, 279, 280, 287
Economic Work in the Shandong Liberated Areas during the War of Anti-Japanese Resistance and Liberation (Xue Muqiao) 71
economism 106, 115
The Economy of the USSR (1990) 4, 5
egalitarianism 108–111, 119
Emminger, Otmar 194–197, 200
Emperor: Wendi 29–30, 32; Wudi 29–31; Zhao 31; *see also* Jiaqing Emperor
Engels, Friedrich 128, 158
Engels, Wolfram 130
energy 66, 72, 102, 125, 134, 174, 220, 235, 266; price of 173, 201, 204, 205, 217, 219; shortage of 139, 236, 252, 261; supply elasticity of 217, 266
enterprise reform 199, 206, 214, 221, 223n20, 235, 238, 241, 281, 283, 284, 286; Sichuan province 123, 126, 201
"equable marketing" 30, 32, 75, 81
equilibrium 23, 43, 46, 101, 127, 143, 148–149n28, 167, 172, 198, 262, 265; disequilibrium 55, 56, 206, 208, 252; prices at 43, 167, 184, 185, 214, 218, 263; theory, Walrasian 206, 208–209
Erhard, Ludwig 5, 60, 219, 222n10; "miracle" 12, 60, 67n13, 130–131, 147n20, 148n22, 188, 195, 200, 203, 208, 219–220, 222n8, 251, 264, 265, 273
European Bank for Reconstruction and Development 5

expenditure 45, 126, 199, 242, 256; consumer 54; government 54, 102; military 80, 82, 112n11
experimentalism 7, 13, 48, 268; *see also* experimentation
experimentation 13, 36, 76, 113n26, 181n31, 241, 267; as reform approach 10, 71, 84, 122, 145, 154, 188, 190, 211, 261, 266; *see also* experimentalism
Eyferth, Jacob 91, 113n20

fabi 76–79
Fable of the Bees (Mandeville) 40n13
famine 17, 26, 36, 89–90, 95, 98, 107, 112n9, 113n24, 150n4, 154, 156, 283; prevention 26, 27, 29, 33, 36, 37; relief 36, 37, 155
Fang Lizhi 236
Fan Li 39n9
Fan Shitao 11
fascism 61, 147n37; German 69
Feng Lanrui 158, 228
Feng Mingliang 11
Fewsmith, Joseph 146n8, 180n12, 208
fiat money 35, 90
Financial and Economic Commission: Central Committee 70, 279; State Council 279
Financial and Economic Committee, National People's Congress 274
Fisher, Irving 50, 57
Five Year Plans 112n11; Seventh 200
fixed capital 133, 148n27
Fock, Jenő 253–254
foreign direct investment 106, 238, 244
foreign exchange 72, 107, 114n32, 167
"four gentlemen of reform" 104, 277, 284, 286, 289
Four Modernizations 257
"free disposal of surplus" 123–124
Friedman, Milton 67n10, 68n21, 174, 181n30, 208, 286; as advocate of "big bang" 60, 195, 219, 220; on price control 63, 64–65, 66, 180n17; visit to China 13, 127, 130, 143, 148nn22–23, 188, 253, *254*, 258n13
fuel 43, 75, *170*; supply prices 69, 177
Fuhrmann, Uwe 60
Fukuyama, Francis 1
full employment 45–47, 67n4

Galbraith, John Kenneth 33, 64–65, 67n7, 68n20, 179n6, 207, 208; attacks on 52–53; on monopolies 62; on price control

12, 44, 55–56, 60, 67n10, 68n21, 73, 267; visit to China 222–223n18; on the war economy 47–51, 64, 66; *see also* institutionalist economics; price-fixers

Galbraith's Institutional Economics (Li Yining) 207

Gale, Esson M. 28, 31, 37, 40n23

Gao Liang *172*, 175, 277

Gao Shangquan 193, 194, 202–203, 215, 218, 275

Gao Yang 163

Gao Xiaomeng 163

General Lockhart 74

General Maximum Price Regulation 50–52; *see also* ceiling prices

German Council of Economic Experts 219

Germany xi–xii, 49, 60, 222n10; West 12, 60, 136, 219, 250–251, 268, 273, 286

Gewirtz, Julian 10, 14n8, 147–150n40, 197, 222n16, 240, 274n2, 274nn6–7, 274n10

Giersch, Herbert 185, 222n16, 251

globalization 259, 268

"golden age of reform" 13, 217

Gong Yu 40n21

Gorbachev, Mikhail 6, 257

government spending 45, 230; countercyclical 26, 27, 33, 39n10, 40n13

gradualism 6, 10, 12, 145, 187, 197, 204, 264–268; experimental 84, 145, 188, 190; planned 145, 146; *see also* marketization, from the margins

grain 17, 24–30, 34–37, 39n9, 40n13, 72, 74, 75, 77, 78, 80–83, 91–94, 97, 99, 101, 103, 104, 108–109, 114n35, 119, 125, 126, 150n44, 156, 163–165, 183–184, 234, 241, 269; as a determinant of prices 24, 25; merchants 83; output 85n2, 90, 92, 93, 104, 112nn9–10, 159–160, 164; private hoarding of 36, 72; seasonal price fluctuations of 25, 26; system for provision of 78, 79, 92, 96, 183, 211, 234; tax 75, 81

granaries 36–38, 41n27, 70; Ever Normal 35, 36, 37, 50, 75, 164, 183; public 25, 30, 35, 36, 50, 93

Granick, David 136, *137*

Great Depression 45, 48–49, 59, 60; *see also* 1920 financial crisis

Great Famine 17, 89–90, 95, 98, 107, 112n9, 113n24, 154–156, 283; *see also* famine

Great Leap Forward 17, 90, 93–94, 97, 107, 112–114n34, 138, 155, 254, 274, 279, 280, 287

Green Sprout Loans 34, 35, 97

gross domestic product 2, 244, 259; China 2, *2*, *8*, 14n7, 89–90, 253; per capita 90; Russia 2, *2*, 7; Vietnam 14n7

gross national product: of the United States 54, *54*, 56

Guangzhou 37

Guan Zhong 20, 27

Guanzi 17–21, 28–32, 34–35, 37, 39n7, 39n11, 40n15, 70, 78, 79, 82, 98, 120, 138, 139, 164, 175, 177, 254, 266; historical context of 21; "light-heavy" principles of 18–19, 21–25, 39n2, 39n10; methods to stabilize the grain price of 24–27; salt and iron monopoly suggested in 18–19, 27

"guerrilla policy style" 39n2, 70

guerrilla warfare 76, 84

Guo Chongyi 160

Guo Shuqing 189, 191, 194, 195, 197, 203, 222n15, 223n25, 233, 255, 275–276

Gu Zhun 174, 286

Hahn, Frank 65–66, 262

Halpern, Nina 10

Han dynasty 29, 40n16, 249; fiscal administration 30

handicrafts (in peasant households) 20

Hansen, Alvin 47–48, 57, 67nn2–3; *see also* institutionalism

Han Shu 24, 34, 39n12

Harris, Seymour 53, 67n7

Harvard University 2, 47, 48, 53, 85, 185, 207, 275, 278, 281, 290

Hayek, Friedrich 44–45, 61–64, 66, 66n1, 68n19, 69, 161, 172, 187, 197, 261, 263, 270n2, 289

Hebei province 163, 180n15, 278

He Jiacheng *172*, 175, 206, 223n28, 277, 281

Henderson, Leon 48–50, 52, 67n7, 73

He Weiling 11, 154, 160, 215, 243, 276

Hicks, John 185

historical materialism 109, 116, 158

Hitler, Adolf 69

hoarding 23, 36, 39n12, 56, 72, 81, 126, 242, 253

Hong Kong 154, 167, 202, 237, 246, 281, 286; peasants fleeing to 105

Honig, Emily 153, 179n5

household contracting *see* household responsibility system
household registration system 97, 111–112n3, 150n49
household responsibility system (Household Production Contracting Responsibility System) 94, 152, 155–156, 160–165, 179nn12–13, 211, 273, 275, 285, 288
Hsu, Robert C. 10
Hua Guofeng 105–108, 111, 124, 156, 228
Huang Jiangnan 171, *172*, 277, 284, 286
Huan Kuan 29, 31–32, 34, 40n20, 40n23
Hua Sheng 11, *172*, 174, 176, 206, 219, 223n20, 223n28, 238–239, 276–277, 281
huilong 97, 101
Hungary 85n1, 129, 136, 142, 185, 197–198, 202, 204, 209, 215–217, 219, 220, 249, 250, 260, 273, 275–277, 281, 286
Huo Guang 31, 34, 40n20
Hu Qiaomu 104, 109, 116, 288
Hu Yaobang 84, 117, 155, 157–158, 160, 162, 165, 229, 272, 282
hyperinflation 14n7, 69, 221n5, 243, 246; Chinese 12, 70, 71–72, 75–76, 80–83, 84–85n1, 110, 148n23, 187, 225, 227, 230, 246, 253, 263; German 84–85n1; Russian 84–85n1, 269; *see also* inflation

idealism 32, 38, 203, 261, 264
imperialism 36, 244; anti-imperialism 207
imperial system: Chinese 17, 32, 34, 38, 70, 92, 121
imports 72, 74, 94, 105–107, 114n32, 139, 178, 238, 241, 244
income *3*, 55, 113n16, 163, 195, 234, 244, 252; consumption 29, 46; government 28, 37, 71, 74–75, 79, 165, 167; individual 56, 60, 73, 102, 109; real 2, 58–59, 91, 202, 242, 245, 249; rural 96, 97, 139, 150n50, 183
industrial: depression 72; growth 139, 184; production *53*, 72, 85n2, 244, 255
industrial goods 48, 53, 61, 75, 83, 95, 112, 138, 168, 181n27, 182, 252; as inputs 99, 138, 184, 190; prices of 108, 134, 165, 190
industrialization 262; big push 106, 111, Chinese 7, 10, 14n7, 90–96, 98, 99, 101–103, 110–111, 112n9, 113n14, 153, 183, 218, 227, 234, 243–244, 266, 267, 273, 282; Latin American 243, 245,

259; rural 93–94; Soviet 113, 131, 180n6, 260; Vietnam 14n7
Industrial Revolution 6
industrial structure 55, 73, 83, 86n15, 90, 139, 165, 182
industry 5, 29, 31, 34, 73, 95, 102, 108, 111, 112n11, 133, 139, 150n46, 156, 217, 235, 254; bosses of 49; heavy 91, 93, 94, 96, 106, 107, 110, 111, 128, 147n13; light 93, 94, 107, 122, 180n22, 211, 212, 238; rural 235; system 101
inequality 2, 5, 13, 14n3, 26, 27, 32–33, 39n12, 97, 244
inelasticity: of demand 28, 58, 186, 195, 217; of supply 48, 195, 217
inflation 5, 46–48, 63–64, 65, 67n11, 130–131, 133, 141–144, 148n22–23, 258n12; in Brazil 245; in China 6, 13, 30, 69–73, 75, 80, 82–84, 86n17, 90, 96, 97, 113n24, 125–126, 138, 139, 173, 183, 188, 192, 195, 198, 199, 204, 205, 206, 211, 212, 214, 217, 218, 220, 222n9, 225, 226–227, 230–231, *231*, 233–235, 238–243, 245–249, 252, 253, 255–256, 258n13, 262, 265–266, 269, 271, 280; cost-push 125, 130, 195, 220, 235, 238, in Germany 61; price-wage spiral 42, 46, 49, 73, 212, 217–218, 235; in Russia 6, 90; in the United States 50, *51*, 52, 53, 55–60; wage–push 42, 49; *see also* hyperinflation; stability
input-output 49, 128, 133–135, 148–149n28, 149n29, 167, 172
Institute of Economics, CASS 117, 128–129, 131, 193, 274, 277, 279, 283, 284, 286
Institute of Economics, Hungarian Academy of Science 215
Institute of International Economics 222n16
Institute of Marxism-Leninism, CASS 276
institutionalism 12, 13, 47, 232: *see also* Cairncross, Alec; Galbraith, John Kenneth; Hansen, Alvin
International Development Association 121
International Economic Association 185
International Monetary Fund 5
investment 29, 72, 90, 94–96, 102, 106, 108, 110, 112n11, 113n16, 124, 126–128, 132, 129, 142, 143, 168, *170*, 190, 199, 202, 204, 205, 212–213, 217, 234, 235, 238, 244, 245, 255, 262, 278; disinvestment 73
invisible hand 6, 65–66, 117, 262; *see also* Smith, Adam

iron 19, 29, 37, 40–41n22, 99, 114n32, 170; monopoly 27, 30–31, 33, 34, 37, 40nn17–18, 55, 264; necessity of 28; pig 86n15, 138; revolution 21, 33

Japan 14n5, 114n29, 114n32, 188–189, 190, 222n10, 233, 237, 272; invasion of China 71, 72, 77, 79, 85n1, 279; surrender of 56
Jedermann Programm 61
Jiang Yue 172, 175, 277
Jiaqing Emperor 77
Jin dynasty 249
Journal of Economic Literature 196

Kalecki, Michael 58, 60, 67n11, 127
Kang Sheng 104
Kantorovich, Leonid 185
Karl, Rebecca 85n7, 206
Kende, Péter 136–137, 137, 140, 142, 149n35, 149n37, 150n38
Keynes, John Maynard 39n1, 39n10, 40n13, 44–48, 50, 54, 55, 61–62, 67nn2–3, 71, 96, 179n6
Keynesianism 47, 48, 129, 148n23, 194, 212
Keyser, C. H. 10, 179n3
Khachaturov, V. R. 186
Kiel Institute for the World Economy 251
King, F. H. H. 37
Klein, Naomi 187
Knight, Frank 57
Kohl, Helmut 60
Korean War 63, 82, 86n17, 112n11
Kornai, Janos 143, 185–189, 191, 194, 196–201, 204, 205, 212, 214–217, 223n22, 249–252, 262
Kosta, Jiří 136, 137, 149nn36–37, 191
Krueger, Anne 232
Kung, H. H. 74
Kuomintang 37, 70–77, 79, 80, 83, 85n3, 90, 126, 287
Kuznets, Simon 57, 67n7

laissez-faire 36, 46; *see also* neoclassical economics
Lange, Oskar R. 66–67n1, 127–129, 145, 167, 172, 206, 207
Latin America 226, 243–247, 259, 260, 289; *see also* Brazil
law of value 95, 101, 110, 116, 120–121, 127, 128, 134, 147n9, 176, 223n26, 243, 283, 287
Lenin, Vladimir 116, 158, 180n6; *see also* Marxism

Lerner, Abba 57
Liao Jili 134, 136, 137, 140, 150n40, 193, 279
liberalism 1
liberalization: bourgeois 229, 274; economic 1, 4, 166, 188, 197, 260; trade 4, 184; *see also* price liberalization
Li Jiange 172, 173, 215, 233, 277–278, 280
Li Keqiang 279
Li Kui 24, 39n7, 39n9
Lim, Edwin 11, 136, 137, 140, 144, 149n30, 172, 193, 196, 200, 205, 222n16, 223n25, 223n27
Li Mingzhe 181n27
Lin, Cyril 128, 222n16, 223n25
Lin Biao 155
Lin Chun 157–159
Linder, Wilhelm 220, 252, 258n11
Li Peng 147n11, 229, 239–241, 252–254
Lipton, David 4–6, 127
list prices 81–83, 85n12
literati 18, 31–34, 38, 42
Liu Bocheng 156
Liu Guoguang 94, 114n34, 117, 131, 136, 144, 149n31, 194, 203, 221n7, 243, 250, 257, 279–280
Liu Jirui 189, 191, 275
Liu Shaoqi 155, 273
Liu Zhuofu 136–138, 142–143, 150nn40–41, 280
Li Xianglu 115, 152, 162, 167, 176, 243, 278
Li Xiannian 112n6, 119, 240, 254
Li Yining 206–209, 219, 220, 223n31, 235, 251, 258n10, 272, 278–279
Li Yu 78
loans 102, 114n28, 212; foreign 37, 72, 80, 121; seasonal 35, 39n9
Loewe, Michael 31
London School of Economics 158
longue durée 11
Lou Jiwei 166, 191, 194, 203, 215, 233, 239, 255–256, 277, 280–281
Lu Liling 174
Lu Mai 11, 171, 215, 281
Lu Nan 181n27
Luo Xiaopeng 154, 155, 159, 163, 164, 171, 172, 175, 194, 200, 223n20, 223n28, 238, 277, 281–282
Luo Zhiru 207, 278
Lushan conference 73

macroeconomic stabilization 90, 129, 132, 142, 173, 184, 185, 188, 193, 195, 199–202, 204, 211, 212, 222n9, 233,

240, 243, 251, 255, 258n6, 261, 264; *see also* austerity; stability
Ma Guochuan 11
Ma Hong 132, 134, 135, 146n7, 168, 180n21, 194, 203, 218, 282
Malthus, Thomas 40n13, 73
Ma Kai *172*, 215
Mandate of Heaven 70, 75
Mandeville, Bernard 40n13
Maoism 9, 91, 103, 106, 109, 110, 111n1, 116, 117, 147–148n21, 179n6; continuous revolution in 13, 259–260; development model of 13
Maoist period xi, 13, 90, 91, 94–99, 101, 104, 106, 110–112n3, 119, 127, 138, 141, 153, 156, 183, 207, 267, 280, 286
Mao Yushi 181n30
Mao Zedong 84, 105–106, 112n10, 156–158, 179n6, 228, 250, 282; death of 90, 111, 154; on development 93, 108, 112n11, 116, 146n2; on economic warfare 75; proclamation of the PRC 80; on revolution 227
market creation 7, 11–13, 18, 19, 37, 71, 76, 145, 175, 239, 263; modes of 2, 11, 66; *see also* marketization
market economy 4–7, 12, 67n1, 117, 130, 190, 210, 234, 251, 262, 265, 269; free 61; social 61, 251; socialist 117, 268–269, 275, 282; transition to 5, 6, 12, 191, 201, 206, 209, 218, 238–239, 247, 253, 268
market integration 30, 68n20, 70–72, 74, 75, 80, 81, 113n14, 176, 182, 236–238, 267
marketization 1, 2, 7, 10, 12, 13, 71, 135, 147, 182, 184, 191, 200, 210, 213, 225, 226, 229, 230, 232, 236, 239, 248, 249, 260, 268, 269; from the margins 1, 7, 13, 184, 194, 198–199, 221, 227, 238, 252; *see also* gradualism; market creation
market socialism 66–67n1, 127–129, 131, 132, 145, 147n16, 147n19, 207, 262; *see also* Socialist Calculation Debate
Marx, Karl 100, 113n27, 146n9, 148n27, 158, 172
Marxism 77, 95, 100, 120, 128, 155, 158, 179–80n6, 181n30, 189, 191, 262, 283
Material Allocation Bureau 182
material balance system 102, 128, 178
May Fourth Movement 206–208
Ma Yinchu 73
means of production 28–30, 99, 122, 124, 125, 147n13, 163, 205, 230

mechanization 36, 94, 106, 108, 162
Memorial to the Throne in Ten Thousand Characters 34–35
Middle East 244
military expansionism: in the Han dynasty 29
Mises Institute 63
Mitchell, Wesley 52, 57
modernization: China 36, 105, 107, 156, 227, 236; Latin America 243
Moganshan Youth Conference 165, 171, *172*, 191, 203, 206, 223n28, 272, 277, 278, 280, 281, 284–286, 289
Moganshan World Bank Conference 135–138, 144, 146, 172, 175, 190, 193, 196, 264, 274, 279, 280, 287
monetarism 138, 185, 188, 231, 233, 245, 262; *see also* Milton Friedman
monetary policy 4, 5, 43, 83, 97, 188, 192, 194, 195, 212, 230, 231, 233, 235, 243, 252, 255, 262, 283
monetary system 78, 84
money 17, 30, 33, 35, 39n10, 40n21, 45, 76, 77, 96, 97, 113n14, 126, 147, 195, 245, 251, 253, 255; quantity of 25, 63–64, 71–73, 75, 130, 139, 188, 212, 230–231, 233, 235, 240–241, 253; value of 12, 24–26, 56, 70, 73, 78–79, 81–83, 85n9, 98, 252; velocity of 71, 73; *see also* hyperinflation; inflation; prices
moneylenders 35
money supply 25, 26, 212, 230, 231, 233, 240, 241, 253; *see also* macroeconomic stabilization; money
monopolies 23, 30, 33, 34, 35, 62, 132, 133, 173, 174, 204, 207–209, 214, 265, 267; natural 33, 62; state 19, 35, 74–75, 81, 92, 97, 111, 132, 139; *see also* iron; salt
Monopoly Capital (Baran and Sweezy) 180n6
Montias, Michael 185, 287
Mont Pelerin Society 61, 185, 251, 289
morality 18, 26, 32, 36, 38, 70, 264
Moscow National Institute of Economics 274

National Association of Manufacturers (US) 61, 67n11, 68n17
National Bureau of Statistics 279, 280, 283, 287
National Council for Social Security Fund 167, 281

National Economic System Reform
Commission *see* System Reform
Commission
Nationalists *see* Kuomintang
National Symposium on Theories of
Pricing 189
natural disasters 27, 33; *see also* famine
natural resources 22, 28, 33, 35, 39n12,
137; *see also* raw materials
Needham, Joseph 34, 40nn15–17, 40n21
Neiser, Hans 57
neoclassical economics 4, 10, 12, 13, 23,
80, 128, 150n41, 165, 167, 181n30, 185,
189–190, 207, 232, 262, 268, 269n1; *see
also laissez-faire*
neoliberalism xii, 1, 3, 4, 10, 13, 61, 130,
185, 187, 188, 195–198, 232, 251, 259,
260, 264; in China 13, 203, 232, 247,
258n13, 268, 269n1; role of state in 3
New China 69, 274
New Deal 48–50; *see also* Roosevelt,
Franklin Delano
New Policies (Wang Anshi) 34
New York City 73
New York Times 57, 68n17
Nixon, Richard 63, 105, 127, 155,
222–23n18
Nolan, Peter 11, 112nn10 – 11, 153, 180n8
North Korea 250
Northwestern University 173, 289
Northwestern Revolutionary Base
Area 76

Office of Price Administration (OPA)
48–52, 55–58, 61, 67n5, 67n11,
68n17, 73
Okita, Saburo 188–189
one-child policy 73
On New Democracy (Mao Zedong) 179n6
"On the Ten Major Relationships" (Mao
Zedong) 93, 107, 108, 112n11
opium addiction 77
Opium War: first 37
Organization for Economic Cooperation
and Development 5
output 53, 64, 143; agricultural 72,
90–94, 104, 111, 112n5, 138, 163–165,
183; China 6, 73, 81, 85n2, 86n15,
112nn9–10, 139, 140, 144, 150n46, 213,
230, 234, 236, 288; global 2; Russia 6
oversupply 47, 124, 139, 168, 173; *see also*
surpluses
Oxford University 127–129, 137, 185,
223n25, 276, 277, 289

package reform 13, 119, 145, 146, 189,
198, 200–205, 207–215, 217–220, 226,
231, 233, 234, 236, 239, 240, 243, 246,
248, 250–253, 258, 258n6, 261–263,
271, 272, 275, 277, 280, 287; *see also*
shock therapy
Pearl Harbor: attack on 78
Peking University xi, 154, 163, 173,
206–207, 220, 272, 273, 276, 278,
282–285, 288, 289
Peng Xiaomeng 222n13, 223n31
People's Bank of China 83, 86n16, 102,
103, 148n23, 166, 231
People's Republic of China (PRC) 80,
81, 84, 89–92, 96, 111, 122, 257, 262,
274, 279
People's University of China 149n29, 216
petroleum *170*; China Petroleum
Company 87n13; exports 99, 106–107;
Petroleum Group 106–108
planned economy 4, 5, 43, 93, 101, 105,
117, 171, 174, 176, 186, 198, 210–211,
217, 221n1, 229, 258n10, 260, 262, 269,
270n2, 277, 279, 284, 287
Poland 5, 43, 190–191, 195, 249; German
invasion of 48; inflation in 85n1
Policy Research Office, Central
Secretariat 117, 271, 273, 275, 278,
282, 289
Politburo 241, 248, 252
Politburo Standing Committee 107,
162, 249
political economy 7, 17, 19, 20, 29, 31–32,
41n26, 77, 91, 127, 153, 163, 191, 263,
282, 283, 287, 288; New Political
Economy 113n14
Political Research Office 104, 155, 273
political system 6, 20, 127, 129, 135, 141,
142, 152, 196, 253
"politics in command" 105
Polish Communist Party 191
Polish Price Commission 136
population 22, 32, 104, 113; rural 77, 90,
92–93, 95, 96, 104, 111, 112n3, 266;
urban 75, 92, 93, 96, 109, 230
poverty 6, 32, 36, 89, 104, 105, 144, 165,
209, 228, 244, 282; rural 90, 91, 157,
271
pragmatism 12, 32, 36, 38, 53, 55, 65,
107, 116, 156, 174, 230, 247, 264,
266–268
precious metals 78
price/s: consumer 50, 242, 253, 265;
determination 4, 7, *8*, *9*, 95, 98, 99,

101, 124–125, 134, 219, 263, 266;
floating 124–125, 139, 175; fluctuations
26, 111, 120, 124, 126, 134, 139,
150n45, 164, 172, 178; free market
55, 125, 132–134, 192; index 52, *82*,
86n17, *231*; level 5, 6, 24–26, 31, 46,
50, 52, 60, 70, 76, 80, 82–83, 119,
131, 138, 141, 143, 182, 192, 195, 199,
212, 217, 220, 235, 240, 241, 242, 262;
master (Western Zhou) 21; mechanism
4, 6, 62, 66, 127, 187, 195, 208;
negotiated 113n23, 123, 125, 138–139;
relative 4, 5, 70, 83, 95, 100, 102, 138,
153, 166, 185, 186, 217, 241, 251, 265;
procurement 96, 110, 112n13, 113n26,
124, 138, 141, 159, 163–164, 168, 183,
234–235, 240; scissors 95–96, 113n14;
state-planned 124, 134, 235; structure
68n19, 110, 119, 122, 126, 129, 133,
203, 265; wholesale 49, 50, 82, 84n1,
86n17, 100
Price Control Act 57–58; *see also* price
controls
price controls: in China 10, 30, 69,
73–74, 76, 83, 92, 98, 111, 121, 130,
143, 176, 189, 195, 209, 214, 232, 242,
253, 255, 256, 265, 266; in Germany
219; as a means to finance war 38, 46;
in Russia 6; theory of 42, 47, 55–56,
63, 64, 66, 67n10, 130, 261, 262;
in the United Kingdom 59–60; in
the United States 43, 44, 46, 48–50,
53–54, 57–62, 65, 68n20, 207, 268;
see also Price Control Act; price
stabilization
price-fixers 42–44, 49, 52, 55, 56, 123,
188; *see also* Galbraith, John Kenneth;
Taussig, Frank William
price-fixing *see* price controls
Price-Fixing Committee 43, 50
price liberalization 38, 132, 184; in China
168, 173, 189, 192, 195, 196, 198, 199,
204, 208–211, 216–217, 219–221, 225,
232–234, 240, 242–243, 247, 249, 251–
253, 261, 263, 265, 269, 271, 273, 275,
276, 278, 281, 283; in Czechoslovakia
131, 134; in Eastern Europe 264; in
Hungary 142; in Poland 190; post-
World War II 43; in Russia 6, 8; theory
of 4, 5; in the United States 44; in
Vietnam 14n7; in West Germany 60,
130, 131, 268; in Yugoslavia 133, 204;
see also wholesale price liberalization
Price Reform Group 170

Price Research Centre 135, 136, 172, 173,
282, 284, 287
Price Research Institute 181n27
price stabilization 5, 38, 44–45, 62, 70;
in ancient and imperial China 17–20,
25–26, 31–32, 34, 35–37, 39n9, 75; in
modern China 12, 13, 70–71, 73–76,
80, 82–84, 85n13, 86n17, 90–91, 94,
96, 97–98, 107, 118, 121, 124–125, 138,
139, 155, 164–165, 175–178, 192, 195,
198–200, 204, 234, 240–242, 254–255,
280, 287; in the United States 48–50,
52, 53, 56, 67n5; *see also* price controls
price system 65, 132, 141, 181n27,
190, 192, 197; dual-track in China
7, 8, 10, 61, 71, 120, 144, 152, 154,
165, 177–178, 180n17, 181n31, 182,
183–185, 187–188, 190, 192, 196, 201,
205, 209–211, 213, 214, 221, 221n1,
225, 227, 231–232, 234, 235, 238,
241, 248, 252, 255, 260–263, 273,
277, 281, 289; Maoist period 13, 91,
95, 98, 101, 111, 116, 119, 121, 122,
144, 267; multi-tiered 11, 61, 71, 120,
123, 140–141, 144, 145, 152, 154, 163,
164, 165, 173–178, 180n17, 181n31,
182–185, 188, 190, 192, 196, 198,
201, 205, 209–211, 213, 214, 221,
221n1, 225, 227, 231, 232, 234, 235,
238–239, 241, 248, 252, 260–261,
263–269, 273, 277, 281, 289; reform
177, 178; Soviet 140; in the United
States 51
price types 99, 100, 125, 138; *see also* cost-
plus pricing
price–wage spiral *see* inflation
Princeton University 74, 181n30, 276
private capital formation 54
privatization 4; in China 34–35, 184,
194, 198, 234, 238, 239; in the United
Kingdom 4
production goods *9*, 47, 217, 220
profiteering 32, 36, 150n45, 190, 232,
235–236
profit rate 54, 59, 133, 138–139, 148n27,
168, *169*, *170*, 180n24, 181n26, 192,
204
profits 8, 17, 60, 72, 73, 79, 99–100,
102–103, 109–110, 114n28, 122, 123,
125, 128, 132, 133, 177, 211–213, 255,
283; corporate 46, 52, 54, 59, 139,
148nn27–28, 150n47; as a motive 24,
26, 29, 217, 232; state 26, 28, 30, 32,
33, 35, 74

Program Evaluation and Review
Technique (PERT) 191
Program Office, State Council 200,
202–205, 214, 215, 218–219,
223nn24–25, 233, 249, 251–252,
263, 271, 273, 275, 276, 278, 281,
284, 287
propaganda 31, 45, 274, 288
psychology 179n4; public 46
purchasing power 45–47, 50, 54, 57, 59,
67n4, 75, 82, 98

Qin dynasty 20, 29
Qing dynasty 35–36, 41nn26–27
Qiu Shufang 189, 191, 275
quantity theory of money 39n10

rationalism 48
rationing 46–48, 54–56, 59, 73, 98, 99,
145, 166, 180n20
raw materials 29, 48, 57, 58, 69, 98, 100,
102, 125, 134, 142, 167, 168, 173–177,
181n23, 182, 192, 196, 201, 205, 211,
213, 214, 217–219, 223, 235, 236, 238,
241, 244, 261, 266; see also energy
Reagan, Ronald 65
recession 64; in post-socialist countries 6;
in the United States 59
"reform and opening up" 1, 17, 247,
275, 276
reindustrialization 7, 218, 266, 273;
see also industrialization
renminbi (RMB) 81, 83, 98
rent-seeking 232, 239; theory 232–233
reorganization 48; industrial 48; post-war
economic 56
Republic of China 36, 153, 207
retail products 8
Research Office, Central Secretariat 135
Research Office, State Council 158, 278,
280
Research Office, State Economic
Commission 282
revolution 1, 89, 116, 227; 1911, China 37,
154; communist, China 12, 76, 77, 80,
84, 90, 91, 98, 159; green 90, 111n1;
Russian 43
The Revolution Betrayed see Trotsky, Leon
Rex, Stout 67n11
Ricardo, David 40n13
Rickett, W. A. 22, 39n6
rioting 74, 252
The Road to a Free Economy (Kornai) 197
The Road to Serfdom (Hayek) 62

Robbins, Lionel 43–44, 66n1, 69–70,
263, 270n2
Robinson, Joan 179n6
Rodrik, Dani 2
Rong Jingben 148n26, 189, 221n7, 232
Roosevelt, Franklin Delano 52;
administration 48; see also New Deal
Rubin, I. I. 146n9
rural development 93
Rural Development Group 152, 159–165,
167, 171, 180n12, 183, 223n20, 223n28,
271, 272, 274–276, 278, 281, 283, 285
Rural Development Research Centre,
State Council 163, 215, 223n28
rural economy 35, 77, 94–95, 97, 111,
258n4
Rural Policy Research Office 275, 289
Russia 1–2, 4, 6, 14n3, 14n6, 60, 127, 140,
232, 253, 268, 269; split with China
112n11

Sachs, Jeffrey 4–6, 60, 127, 195, 197
salt 28, 70, 71, 83, 99; monopoly 18,
27–31, 33, 34, 37, 74–75, 77, 78, 81,
83, 86n14, 264; production 28, 29, 30,
40n14, 40n16, 79
Salt and Iron Debate 17–18, 29–35,
37–40n21, 42, 55, 62, 70, 74, 75, 79,
264, 267
"salt channel" 79
Samuelson, Paul 57, 179n6, 263
Sang, Hongyang 30–32, 34, 40n15,
40nn19–20, 45, 53, 55, 62, 74, 81,
121, 267
Sargent, Thomas 80
saving 5, 29, 46, 48, 55, 56, 59, 82,
258n12; compulsory 46, 47, 67n4;
personal 54, 56, 64, 82, 86n16, 113n16,
252; rate of 253; voluntary 45–46
scarcity 22–23, 45, 93, 101, 125, 209, 283;
economics of 54
Schumpeter, Joseph 43
sectoral profit rates 169
self-interest 24, 264
semicolonialism 77, 84
semifeudalism 77, 84
Shandong province 37, 77–80, 85n8, 156,
162, 189, 276, 283, 287, 289
Shanghai 84n1, 94, 114n32, 132, 136, 144,
237, 275, 279
"shock doctrine" (in neoliberalism) 187,
195, 234, 236
shock therapy xii, 1–3, 6–11, 13, 44, 84,
119, 145, 184, 185, 198–199, 201, 202,

218, 221, 226, 232–234, 247, 250, 257, 258n11, 260–262, 263–265, 268; critique of 68n22, 187, 252; debates over 12, 206; effects of 14n4, 14n6; logic of 4–6, 13; in Russia 2, 253; in Vietnam 14n7; *see also* package reform

shortages 5, 17, 47, 57, 59, 60, 74, 78, 143, 166, 176, 186, 190, 217, 235, 236, 238; capital 244; energy 139; grain 36, 72, 183; labor 72

Sichuan province 123, 126, 156, 201, 202; Price Bureau 122, 124, 147

Šik, Ota 127, 131–136, 148nn24–28, 149n30, 149n33, 149n37, 167, 185, 186, 188, 189, 191, 203, 204, 216, 279, 280, 286

Sima Guang 34–35

Simons, Henry 57

Sino-Japanese War 71

Skolka, Jiri 135

Smith, Adam 6, 117, 148n23; *see also* invisible hand

Smith, Paul J. 35

socialism 43, 63, 66–67n1, 100, 109, 114n29; state 5, 114n29, 117, 120, 127, 129, 131, 132, 137, 142, 143, 147n19, 148n23, 157, 158, 161, 162, 179n6, 186–187, 227–229, 262, 268–269, 275, 283, 288; transition from 12, 42, 44; transition to 116

Socialist Calculation Debate 43–44, 63, 65, 127, 128, 263

socialist internationalism 105; *see also* Third Worldism

socialist reform 219; in Poland 43

social justice 47

social welfare 93

Song Guoqing 163, 183, 221, 234, 244, 282–283

Soros, George 215, *216*, 224n38, 243, 272, 276, 278

Southeast Ministry of Industry 156

South Korea 237

Soviet Economic Association 186

Soviet Union 66, 90, 91, 97, 114n29, 129, 132, 153, 250, 279; breakdown of 65

speculation 37, 72–75, 81, 83, 97, 150n45

Spring and Autumn Annals 39n4

Spring and Autumn period 19–21

Sraffa, Piero 67n12

stability 10, 26, 122, 125, 131, 138, 142, 174, 178, 204, 206, 209, 218, 221, 239, 240, 242, 252; economic 3, 24, 30, 57, 129, 131, 138, 252; price 17, 26, 35, 36,

52, 53, 56, 59, 60, 70, 74, 83, 90, 122, 126, 130, 141, 143, 145, 241, 243, 245, 255; social and political 60, 96, 131, 134, 141, 247, 249, 253, 265; under Mao 90, 91, 96, 98, 101, 102, 110

Stalin, Joseph 92, 127, 158, 180n6

Stalinism 5, 91, 106, 114n34, 127, 131, 149n37, 180n6, 180n8, 274, 279

state: as a facilitator of trade 21, 35–36, 83–84, 85n13, 86n14, 91, 123–125, 139, 184, 242, 267; imperial Chinese 20–22; as a participant in the market 7, 12, 25–28, 32, 36, 37, 70, 81, 83, 97, 98, 99, 109, 111, 123–126, 139, 150nn44–45, 157, 163, 164–165, 168, 172, 177, 183, 269; relationship with the market 3, 7, 11–12, 18, 19, 21, 29, 30, 33, 35, 37, 38, 42, 55, 61, 62, 68n18, 75, 83, 93, 101, 113n24, 120–121, 129, 132, 134, 138, 172, 174–176, 189–190, 198, 229, 231, 232, 234, 236, 252, 255, 264, 266, 287; revenue 22, 26, 28–30, 82, 139, 151

State Agricultural Commission 160

state allocation system 59, 61, 99, 102, 103, 139, 163, 175–176, 178, 182, 190, 204, 263

State Commission for Restructuring the Economic System 191, 275

"statecraft" (*jingshi*) 18, 20, 66, 70, 80

state-owned enterprises 4, 80, 100–103, 113n26, 114n28, 124, 150n47, 168, *170*, 175, 199, 204, 214, 234, 236, 265, 266, 283

State Planning Commission 122, 125, 140, 146n7, 147n11, 149n29, 149n34, 271, 273, 276, 278, 279, 288

State Price Bureau 117, 122, 125, 126, 135, 138, 143, 147n11, 149n34, 165, 180n19, 182, 273

State Price Regulation Commission 138, 280

state trading agencies 70, 76, 81, 83–86n14, 97, 178

statistics 22, 118, 153, 159

steel 47, 55, 58, 64, 86n15, 94, 96, 99, 112n9, 114n32, 127, 128, 139, 178, 182, 190, 201, 205, 219, 220, 235, 252, 266, 269; *see also* raw materials

Stiglitz, Joseph 1

stocks 79, 81, 93, 101, 168, 178; public 36, 50; speculation on 73, 75

strikes 59, 60, 61, 67n12, 73, 131, 242, 249; hunger 257

Strumiński, Juliusz 136, *137*, 137, 140–142, 145, 151n52
"A Study of the Peasant Question in China" 158; *see also* Zhang Musheng
subsidies 74, 103, 109, 110, 125, 138, 150n44, 159, 174, 180n20, 189, 192, 204, 218, 234–235, 241, 242; wage 142
Sun Faming 11
Sun Yefang 96, 128–130, 147n21, 153, 163, 274, 279, 283, 286, 287, 288; imprisonment 116; on the law of value 116, 121; on market socialism 147n16
supply and demand 19, 35, 57, 60, 80, 82–83, 120, 132, 196, 206, 264; as a mechanism of price determination 22, 43, 101, 117
surplus value 100, 113n27
surpluses 7, 17, 25, 26, 50, 91, 92, 95, 99, 120, 121, 123–125, 138, 164, 183, 234, 266
Su Shaozhi 116, 158, 228
Sweezy, Alan 57
Sweezy, Paul 57, 179n6
System Reform Commission 140, 149n34, 167, 172, 180n23, 202, 219, 233, 248, 272, 276, 279
System Reform Institute 159, 167, 170, 175, 184, 188, 194, 200, 202, 206, 209–213, 215, *216*, 216, 221, 235, 236, 239, 243–245, 250, 251, 257, 271, 273, 276, 278, 281, 283, 285, 289

Tang Zongkun 105, 115, 116, 146n5, 166, 181n25, 284
Tardos, Márton 215
Taussig, Frank William 43–44; *see also* price-fixers
taxation 23, 26–28, 32, 45, 46, 47, 48, 55, 67n3, 96, 164, 281; direct 26; evasion of 74
technocratic governance 36, 263
Thatcher, Margaret 4, 65, 187
Third Worldism 105; *see also* socialist internationalism
Tiananmen Square 13, 89, 107, 224n38, 256–257, 268, 273, 274, 290; massacre on 226, 256; protestors 257, 290
Tian Jiyun 202, 205, 218
Tian Yuan *172*, 172, 194, 203, 284
Tobin, James 194–196, 199, 212, 222n16, 222–223n18
totalitarianism 49, 62, 69
trade 4, 37, 76, 78, 79, 97, 184; domestic 85n13; foreign 47, 72, 85n13,

99, 114n30, 140, 175, 201, 204; interregional 40n23; long-distance 21, 40n18, 77; salt 70, 75, 77, 78, 79, 83; state 84, 92, 109
transportation 30, 72–74, 81, 142, 150n44, 190
Tsinghua University 166, 167, 203, 279, 280, 288
Trotsky, Leon 113n14, 158, 179n6
Truman, Harry S. 42, 56–59
Twelfth Party Congress, CPC 166; Third Plenary Session 109, 156

unemployment 5, 42, 65n 148n23; frictional 55
unified grain procurement system 183
unified purchase system 92, 97, 99, 180nn14–15, 211, 234, 281
Union of Radical Political Economics 127
United Kingdom 4, 12, 47, 54, 59–60, 187, 193, 223n21, 268
United Nations Department of Economic Affairs 58
United Nations Development Program 223n25
United Nations Industrial Development Organization 149n29
urban reform 144, 166
urban–rural divide 91–93, 153
US State Department 74, 85n3

van der Sprenkel, Otto 82
Vietnam 105; 1989 price liberalization 14n7
Vietnam War 63
von Glahn, Richard 29–30
von Mises, Ludwig 61, 63, 64, 66, 66n1, 270n2

wage bill 97, 102, 139, 150nn47–48, 235
wage controls 44, 50–52, 57, 58, 65, 66, 82, 96, 113n19, 130, 142, 202, 213, 249
wage fund 45, 46, 67n4, 96
wage increases 5, 42, 45, 50, 58, 72, 195, 211–212, 217–218, 265
Wagner, D. B. 34, 37, 40n15, 40n16, 40n18, 40n21
Wallace, Henry A. 50
Wall Street 50
Wan Li 149n34, 152, 156, 162, 165, 229
Wang Anshi 34–35, 121
Wang Gengjin 159, 160
Wang Qishan 157, 171, *172*, 175, 215, 247, 277, 281, 284–286, 289
Wang Xiaolu 11, 157, 171, *172*, 285

Wang Xiaoqiang 11, 159, 188, 206, 237, *237*, 238, 272, 273, 278, 283, 285; delegation to West Germany 250–251; on enterprise reform 221; experiences as a sent-down youth 157, 158–159; on price reform 173, 211, 213; in the Rural Development Group 160, 162; at the System Reform Institute 167, 170, 202, 210; trip to Hungary and Yugoslavia 215, *216*, 223, 224n34

war economy 12, 45, 48, 55–56, 67n10, 110, 143, 189, 268

War Industries Board 50

warlord period in China 37

War of Resistance and Liberation (China) 76; *see also* Chinese Civil War

Warring States period 19–21, 40n14, 40n16, 42

Washington consensus 4

Washington Post 52

wealth 5, 17, 20, 23, 24, 27, 32, 33, 35–36, 47

Wemheuer, Felix 36, 112n4

Wendi *see* Emperor

Weng Yongxi 104–105, 157, 171, 246, 277, 284, 286, 289

Western Zhou Period 20, 21, 26, 32

wholesale price liberalization 5, 13, 134, 191, 225, 227, 232, 235, 236, 245, 248, 251, 268, 273, 275, 276, 278, 279, 280, 281, 286, 287; West Germany 12; *see also* shock therapy

Will, Pierre-Étienne 41n27

Wilson, Woodrow 50

wine monopoly 30, 33, 34

Wood, Adrian 104, 121, *137*, 147n11, 180n21, 181n28, 222n16, 256

World Bank 5, 13, 90, 104, 113n16, 119, 121–125, 127, 135–139, 145–147n11, 150n38, 165, 172, 178, 181n25, 185, 186, 190, 191, 193, 196, 200, 203, 205, 222nn16–17, 223n20, 256, 260, 264, 274–276, 279–282, 284, 286, 287; *see also* Bretton Woods, institutions

World War I 42–44, 46, 47, 50, 53, 56, 85n1

World War II 38, 44, 45, 49, 50, 53–56, 64–67, 67nn8–9, 70, 73, 83, 130, 188, 223n21, 267

Wudi *see* Emperor

Wu Jinglian 11, 130, 132, 134, 148n26, 189, 208, 210, 215, 222n16, 223n24, 223n31, 226, 246–247, 253, *254*, 277,

286–287; at the Bashan conference 194, 199; on corruption 232; at the Economics Research Institute 135–136, 221n7; at the Moganshan conference 144; on price reform 185–186, 187, 188, 191, 195, 200, 205, 231, 233, 239, 243, 248, 250, 258n6; at the System Reform Institute 203

Wuxi conference 116–117, 146n5, 284

Xue Muqiao 82, 112n10, 141, 146nn7–10, 150nn46–48, 150, 151nn50–51, 222n16, 279, 280, 282, 283, 287, 288; as architect of reform 84; at the Bashan conference 194; on economic warfare 71, 78–79, 85n8, 153; on the law of value 120–121, 128, 146n9; at the Moganshan conference *137*, 139–140, 150n40, 165; on price reform 90–91, 110, 120–121, 134–135, 136, 138–139, 205, 243, 246, 257–258; "reeducation by labor" 116; rural studies 77–78

Xu Lu 181n25

Xu Qingfu 85n9

Yale University 185, 187, 287

Yang Xiaokai 181n30

Yao Yilin 149n34, 218, 240, 241, 249, 252, 254

Yeltsin, Boris 6

Young, Arthur N. 74, 85

Yugoslavia 129, 131, 133, 199, 202, 204, 209, 215–217, 219–220, 249, 250, 260, 265, 273, 275–277, 281, 286, 288

Yu Guangyuan 146n7, 283, 287, 288

Zhang Gang *172*, 223n34, 277

Zhang Jinfu 176, 203

Zhang Musheng 157, 161, 180n7, 288–289

Zhang Shaojie *172*, 175, 277

Zhang Weiying *172*, 173, 181n30, 206, 223n28, 283, 289

Zhang Xuejun 238, 277, 281

Zhao Renwei 104, 117, 126, 129, 130, 149n31, 189, 194, 197, 222n16, 279

Zhao Ziyang 13, 115, 140, 149n34, 172, 176, 226, 229, *237*, 252, *254*, 271–273, 275, 277, 278, 284, 285–286; accusations against 224n38, 258; on agricultural reform 164, 210; on coastal development 237–238, 241, 244; creation of the System Reform Institute 170; during the 1989 social movement 256–257, 268; on economic reform 134, 177, 188, 201, 221, 223n23, 225, 227, 229–230, 234, 236–237, 240–241; experience during the Civil War 152–153; as General Secretary 240; meeting with Milton Friedman 253; meeting with Western economists 193–194; as premier 162; on price reform 126, 131, 165–168, 177, 183, 191, 201–203, 205, 210, 213–214, 218–221, 226, 235, 239–243, 245–246, 248–249, 257; on the primary stage of socialism 227–228;

reforms in Sichuan 126; tour of Guangdong 237
Zhejiang Academy of Social Sciences 170
Zhou Enlai 104, 112n10, 180n7, 240, 287, 288
Zhou Qiren 157, 171, *172*, 206, 223n28
Zhou Xiaochuan 166, 203, 215, 231, 233, 239, 253–255, *254*, 257, 277, 280
Zhou Xincheng 216
Zhu Jiaming 11, 157, 170, *172*, 222n9, 226, 243, 245–247, 277, 284, 286, 289–290
Zhu Rongji 166, 203, 231, 274, 281, 287

Printed in the United States
by Baker & Taylor Publisher Services